JESUS
ON THE
MOUNTAIN

A Study in Matthean Theology

Terence L. Donaldson

Journal for the Study of the New Testament
Supplement Series 8

Copyright © 1985 JSOT Press

Published by
JSOT Press
Department of Biblical Studies
The University of Sheffield
Sheffield S10 2TN
England

Printed in Great Britain
by Redwood Burn Ltd.,
Trowbridge, Wiltshire.

British Library Cataloguing in Publication Data

Donaldson. Terence L.
    Jesus on the mountain: a study in Matthean theology.
    —(Journal for the study of the New Testament
    supplement series, ISSN 0143-5108; 8)
    1. Mountains in the Bible   2.Bible. N.T.
    I. Title   II. Series
    261.5'5   BS257.5

    ISBN 0-905774-74-4
    ISBN 0-905774-75-2 Pbk

CONTENTS

PREFACE

This monograph is a slightly revised version of a doctoral dissertation presented to the Toronto School of Theology in December 1981. It represents the fruition of an idea that began to germinate in earlier stages of my theological training. While doing research for a Master's thesis on *Heilsgeschichte* in the Gospel of Matthew, I realized the salvation-historical significance of the mountain-top pericope with which the Gospel concludes (28.16-20) at about the same time as I became aware of the prominence within Jewish eschatological expectation of sacred mountain phenomena—particularly with respect to Zion, the 'holy mountain of Yahweh'. Preliminary investigation convinced me that the apparent similarities between these two patterns of thought were substantial enough to warrant further study. The results of such a study, set out in the pages to follow, will, I hope, demonstrate that the idea of an eschatological mountain motif in the Gospel of Matthew is not a case of a 'mountain hanging by a hair'—as the Rabbis described arguments with slender scriptural support—but that sacred mountain conceptions in Second-Temple Judaism provide a vantage point from which Matthew's oft-observed fondness for mountain settings can be seen in new and clearer perspective.

One does not bring a program of doctoral studies to a successful conclusion without assistance of various kinds and from people too numerous to mention here. I would be ungrateful, however, if I did not acknowledge with thanks my indebtedness to several people in particular. First of all, to my family, for encouragement and practical support, and particularly to my parents, who taught me early to read the Bible and to respond to its message. To Professors Larry W. Hurtado, George T. Montague, John C. Hurd and Heinz O. Guenther, in whose classes my interest in Synoptic studies was aroused and my critical perceptiveness sharpened. To the Social Sciences and Humanities Research Council of Canada, for a Doctoral Fellowship that allowed me to pursue my studies relatively undistracted by financial anxieties. To Dr R.T. France, until recently Warden of Tyndale House, Cambridge, who helped to facilitate a three-month period of research at Cambridge University. To Professors Schuyler

Brown, Ben F. Meyer and E.G. Clark, for valuable aid at several points during my research. To Lorna Hassell, librarian at Wycliffe College, and her assistants Katie Woelfle and (more recently) Gayle Ford, not only for efficient and cheerful library service but also for many small kindnesses that made the library a congenial place in which to work. To Dr Richard N. Longenecker, my thesis supervisor, for his enthusiastic support of this project from its earliest stages, for perceptive and thorough editorial advice that made possible a clearer and more concise presentation that would otherwise have been the case, and, above all, for the model that he supplies for all his students of rigorous scholarship combined with warm personal concern. And especially to my wife, Lois, whose enthusiasm, creativity and support have made this period of study not a time of sacrifice but a shared venture.

LIST OF ABBREVIATIONS

(i) *Primary Sources*

Acts Pil.	Acts of Pilate
Adam and Eve	Life of Adam and Eve
Apoc Abr	Apocalypse of Abraham
Apoc. Pet.	*Apocalypse of Peter*
Ass Mos	Assumption of Moses
1–2 Bar	1–2 Baruch
Clement	
Prot.	*Address to the Greeks*
Paed.	*The Tutor*
Str.	*Miscellanies*
Cyprian	
Ep.	*Epistles*
Test.	*Testimonies*
Demosthenes	
Or.	*Orations*
Desc. Chr.	*Descent of Christ into Hell*
Ep. Arist.	Epistle of Aristeas
Epiphanius	
Pan	*Panarion*
Eusebius	
H.E.	*Ecclesiastical History*
Irenaeus	
Ag. Her.	*Against Heresies*
JB	Jerusalem Bible
Josephus	
Ant.	*Jewish Antiquities*
War	*The Jewish War*
Jub	Jubilees
Justin Martyr	
1 Apol.	*First Apology*
Dial.	*Dialogue with Trypho*
Lactantius	
Inst.	*Divine Institutes*
Life Dan.	Life of the Prophets: Daniel
Life Jer.	Life of the Prophets: Jeremiah

LXX	Septuagint
1–2–4 Macc	1–2–4 Maccabees
MT	Masoretic Text
Nag Hammadi	
ApocryJn	II,1 *Apocryphon of John*
GEgypt	III,2 *Gospel of the Egyptians*
SJC	III,4 *Sophia of Jesus Christ*
ApocPaul	V,2 *Apocalypse of Paul*
1ApocJas	V,3 *First Apocalypse of James*
PetPhil	VIII,2 *Letter of Peter to Philip*
PS	*Pistis Sophia*
NEB	New English Bible
NIV	New International Version
Origen	
Cels.	*Against Celsus*
Princ.	*On First Principles*
Comm. Jn	*Commentary on John*
Oxy. Pap.	Oxyrhynchus Papyri
Philo	
Dec.	*On the Decalogue*
Ebr.	*On Drunkenness*
Leg.	*Allegorical Interpretation*
Mig.	*On the Migration of Abraham*
Mos.	*On the Life of Moses*
Q. Ex.	*Questions on Exodus*
Q. Gen.	*Questions on Genesis*
Ps Sol	Psalms of Solomon
Quest. Barth.	Questions of Bartholomew
Qumran	
CDC	Damascus Rule
1QapGen	Genesis Apocryphon
1QM	War Scroll
1QpHab	Pesher on Habakkuk
1QS	Community Rule
1QSa	Rule of the Congregation
1QSb	Blessings
4Q163pIsa[c]	Pesher on Isaiah
4Q164pIsa[b]	Pesher on Isaiah
4QDibHam	Words of the Heavenly Lights
4QFlor	Florilegium
4QShirShab	Song of the Sabbath Sacrifice
11QJNar	Aramaic text on the New Jerusalem
11QPsZion	Apostrophe to Zion
11QTemple	Temple Scroll

Rabbinic texts

Ber.	Berakoth
Dem.	Demai
Shab.	Shabbath
Pesaḥ.	Pesaḥim
Sukk.	Sukkoth
Roš. Haš.	Rosh ha-Shana
Taʿan.	Taʿanith
Ḥag.	Ḥagiga
Giṭ.	Giṭṭin
Soṭ.	Soṭa
Ḳid.	Ḳiddushin
B. Bat.	Baba Bathra
Sanh.	Sanhedrin
Zebaḥ.	Zebaḥim
Men.	Menaḥoth
Ḥul.	Ḥullin
Aboth R. Nat.	Aboth de Rabbi Nathan
Kuth.	Kuthim

Gen R. (etc.)	Genesis Rabbah
Mek.	Mekilta
Midr. Ps	Midrash on the Psalms
Pesiḳ. R.	Pesiḳta Rabbati
Pesiḳ. R. Kah.	Pesiḳta de Rab Kahana
Pirke R. El.	Pirke de Rabbi Eliezer
Sifre Dt	Sifre Deuteronomy
RSV	Revised Standard Version
Sib Or	Sibylline Oracles
Sir	Sirach
T. 12 Patr.	Testaments of the Twelve Patriarchs
T. Levi	Testament of Levi
T. Zeb.	Testament of Zebulun
T. Naph.	Testament of Naphtali
T. Ash.	Testament of Asher
T. Ben.	Testament of Benjamin
Tertullian	
Marc.	*Against Marcion*
Jud.	*Against the Jews*
Tg.	Targum
Frag. Tg.	Fragment Targum
Tg. Neoph.	Targum Neophyti
Tg. Ps.-J.	Targum Pseudo-Jonathan
Tob	Tobit

Wisd	Wisdom of Solomon
Xenophon	
Anab.	*Anabasis*

(ii) *Secondary Literature*

AnBib	Analecta Biblica
ANQ	*Andover Newton Quarterly*
APOT	*Apocrypha and Pseudepigrapha of the Old Testament.* 2 vols. Edited by R.H. Charles. Oxford: Clarendon Press, 1913.
AssSeign	*Assemblées du Seigneur*
ASTI	*Annual of the Swedish Theological Institute*
ATR	*Anglican Theological Review*
ATRSup	Supplement to the *Anglican Theological Review*
BA	*Biblical Archaeologist*
Bauer–Arndt– Gingrich	*A Greek-English Lexicon of the New Testament.* Translated and adapted from W. Bauer's *Griechisch-Deutsches Wörterbuch* by W.F. Arndt and F.W. Gingrich. 2nd edn. Chicago: University of Chicago Press, 1979.
Bib	*Biblica*
BibLeb	*Bibel und Leben*
BibTod	*Bible Today*
BJRL	*Bulletin of the John Rylands Library*
BLE	*Bulletin de littérature ecclésiastique*
BR	*Biblical Research*
Brown–Driver– Briggs	*A Hebrew and English Lexicon of the Old Testament.* Edited by F. Brown, S.R. Driver and C.A. Briggs. Oxford: Clarendon Press, 1907.
BTB	*Biblical Theology Bulletin*
BZ	*Biblische Zeitschrift*
BZAW	Beihefte zur *ZAW*
CahJos	*Cahiers de Joséphologie*
CBQ	*Catholic Biblical Quarterly*
CBQMS	CBQ Monograph Series
CQR	*Church Quarterly Review*
CTM	*Concordia Theological Monthly*
DJD, V	*Discoveries in the Judean Desert. V: Qumrân Cave 4.* Edited by J.M. Allegro. Oxford: Clarendon Press, 1968.
ErJb	*Eranos Jahrbuch*
EstBib	*Estudios bíblicos*
EThL	*Ephemerides theologicae lovanienses*

EvQ	*Evangelical Quarterly*
EvTh	*Evangelische Theologie*
Exp	*Expositor*
ExpT	*Expository Times*
FRLANT	Forschungen zur Religion und Literatur des Alten und Neuen Testaments
HNT	Handbuch zum Neuen Testament
HSM	Harvard Semitic Monographs
HTKNT	Herders theologischer Kommentar zum Neuen Testament
HUCA	*Hebrew Union College Annual*
ICC	International Critical Commentary
IDB	*Interpreter's Dictionary of the Bible.* Edited by G.A. Buttrick *et al.* 4 vols. New York / Nashville: Abingdon Press, 1962.
IDBSup	Supplement to *IDB.* Edited by K. Crim *et al.* Nashville: Abingdon Press, 1976.
IEJ	*Israel Exploration Journal*
Int	*Interpretation*
ITQ	*Irish Theological Quarterly*
JAAR	*Journal of the Americal Academy of Religion*
JBL	*Journal of Biblical Literature*
JES	*Journal of Ecumenical Studies*
JETS	*Journal of the Evangelical Theological Society*
JQR	*Jewish Quarterly Review*
JR	*Journal of Religion*
JSNT	*Journal for the Study of the New Testament*
JTS	*Journal of Theological Studies*
Liddell–Scott	*A Greek-English Lexicon.* Compiled by H.G. Liddell and R. Scott. 9th edn. Revised by H.S. Jones. 2 vols. Oxford: Clarendon Press, 1940.
LumVie	*Lumière et Vie*
LuthQ	*Lutheran Quarterly*
MeyerK	H.A.W. Meyer, Kritisch-exegetischer Kommentar über das Neue Testament
NIGTC	New International Greek Testament Commentary
NovT	*Novum Testamentum*
NTApoc	E. Hennecke, *New Testament Apocrypha.* 2 vols. Edited by W. Schneemelcher. Translated by R. McL. Wilson. London: Lutterworth Press, 1963, 1965.
NTD	Das Neue Testament Deutsch
NTS	*New Testament Studies*
OJRS	*Ohio Journal of Religious Studies*
PRS	*Perspectives in Religious Studies*

QLP	*Questions liturgiques et paroissiales*
RB	*Revue biblique*
RechBib	Recherches bibliques
RevQ	*Revue de Qumran*
RSR	*Revue des sciences religieuses*
RHPR	*Revue d'histoire et de philosophie religieuses*
RThPh	*Revue de théologie et de philosophie*
RThR	*Reformed Theological Review*
SBLDS	Society of Biblical Literature Dissertation Series
SBLMS	Society of Biblical Literature Monograph Series
SBS	Stuttgarter Bibelstudien
SBT	Studies in Biblical Theology
SJT	*Scottish Journal of Theology*
SNTSMS	Society for New Testament Studies Monograph Series
StEv	*Studia Evangelica*
StTh	*Studia Theologica*
StudNeot	Studia neotestamentica
TDNT	*Theological Dictionary of the New Testament*. 10 vols. Edited by G. Kittel and G. Friedrich. Translated by G.W. Bromiley. Grand Rapids: Eerdmans, 1964–76.
TDOT	*Theological Dictionary of the Old Testament*. Edited by G.J. Botterweck and H. Ringgren. Translated by J.T. Willis and D.E. Green. Grand Rapids: Eerdmans, 1974–.
Theol	*Theology*
THKNT	Theologischer Handkommentar zum Neuen Testament
TLZ	*Theologische Literaturzeitung*
TPQ	*Theologisch-Praktische Quartalschrift*
TZ	*Theologische Zeitschrift*
UF	*Ugaritische Forschungen*
VT	*Vetus Testamentum*
VTSup	Supplement to *VT*
ZAW	*Zeitschrift für die alttestamentliche Wissenschaft*
ZKT	*Zeitschrift für katholische Theologie*
ZNW	*Zeitschrift für die neutestamentliche Wissenschaft*
ZTK	*Zeitschrift für Theologie und Kirche*

PART I
SETTING DIRECTIONS

Chapter 1

THE PROBLEM AND THE TASK

1. *Jesus on the Mountain: A Deliberate Matthean Motif*

It has often been noted that mountains frequently appear in the First Gospel as sites for events in the life and ministry of Jesus.[1] A preliminary analysis of the ὄρος data in Matthew and the other Synoptics provides reasons for believing that this is no mere accident, but rather a deliberate and intentional feature of the Matthean redaction. This is suggested in the first instance by the use of ὄρος in Matthew itself. Though some of the eleven instances in which ὄρος appears in the framework of Matthew's narrative[2] are passing references which do not appear to have engaged the attention of the evangelist,[3] or subsequent references to settings which have already been mentioned,[4] there are six important passages in Matthew where a mountain serves as the setting for a significant event in the ministry of Jesus: the third temptation (4.8); the Sermon on the Mount (5.1; 8.1); the healing and feeding of the multitude (15.29); the Transfiguration (17.1, 9); the Olivet Discourse (24.3); and the Great Commission (28.16). Not only does this list include some of the most prominent events in the gospel story, but important theological and christological themes swirl around this whole chain of Matthean mountains.

The importance of the mountain setting for Matthew is evidenced not only by the theological themes with which it is associated, but also by the fact that these mountain scenes occur at important junctures in the Matthean narrative. Of greatest significance in this regard is the appearance of τὸ ὄρος as the setting for Matthew's closing pericope (28.16-20), a passage which is increasingly being recognized as providing the key and climax to the whole Gospel.[5] To this important incidence of ὄρος one can add the appearance of a mountain setting at the conclusion of Jesus' preparation for ministry

(4.8), at the beginning (5.1) and end (15.29) of his ministry with the Galilean crowds, and at the points where Jerusalem and the cross begin to loom over the narrative (17.1) and where Jesus gives his final teaching before his passion (24.3). When these structurally significant occurrences of ὄρος are taken together, the likelihood emerges that even though Matthew's mountain terminology is not uniform[6] (a phenomenon for which we shall have to account), the setting nevertheless serves as one of the devices by which Matthew structured his narrative and moved it forward.

The importance of the mountain setting for Matthew as suggested by such 'vertical' considerations is further borne out by a 'horizontal' comparison of Matthew with the other Synoptics. While Jesus appears in mountain settings in Mark and Luke,[7] there are several indications that, in contrast to these Gospels, the Matthean situation is the result of conscious redactional activity rather than just the random inclusion of traditional elements. The first thing to note is the uniqueness of most of the Matthean scenes. Though Matthew has evidently depended on Mark for the mountain settings of the Transfiguration Narrative and the Olivet Discourse, in the case of the other four passages listed above, the mountain setting is unique to Matthew.[8] And in three of these passages (4.23–5.1; 15.29-31; 28.16-20), the ὄρος reference is part of an extended Matthean summary statement which displays many of the evangelist's special concerns.

Also to be considered is the pattern of Matthew's selection of ὄρος references from the tradition. The three most characteristically Matthean mountain scenes (4.23–5.1; 15.29-31; 28.16-20) present a generally positive picture of the person of Jesus and of his ministry with the disciples and crowds. Opposition and unbelief are generally foreign to Matthew's presentation of 'Jesus on the mountain'. Of the eight Markan appearances of Jesus on or near a mountain, Matthew has taken over or adapted seven which are consistent with this picture,[9] but, significantly, has omitted the one which is not, *viz.* the mountain-top encounter with demons and pigs.[10] Furthermore, though there is no reason to believe that Matthew had access to the tradition underlying Lk 4.28-30, this account of the attempt to kill Jesus by throwing him down from a mountain serves to throw into relief the positive nature of the Matthean mountain scenes.

Finally, the kind of evidence from vertical analysis that suggests a redactional pattern for Matthew is completely lacking in Mark and

Luke. Both Gospels contain mountain scenes which display widely differing characteristics and which cannot be easily described under a single heading;[11] in neither of them is there evidence of a redactional or structural role for the ὄρος setting such as can be found in Matthew;[12] and both of them seem interested in developing other geographical patterns.[13] The presence of mountain settings in Mark and Luke, therefore, enhances rather than diminishes the possibility that ὄρος functions in Matthew as a deliberate redactional motif.

Thus, though we need to carry out a full study of Matthew's mountain scenes before we can declare with certainty that there is indeed a *Bergmotiv* in the Gospel, the preliminary indications are that such a study would be fruitful. This being the case, a series of questions about the possible redactional significance of this chain of mountain scenes presents itself. Looking first at the mountain scenes in isolation: Are there common features in the role played by the mountain settings in each of these passages? Can these mountain scenes be characterized under a single heading or seen as examples of a common form? We have already noted the 'positive' nature of these scenes, but it is possible to be more precise? Then, considering the setting of these mountain scenes in the Gospel itself: Does ὄρος play a literary role in Matthew's development of his Gospel? Is there a structural pattern to be discerned in the mountain passages and the themes with which they deal? Further, looking at the mountain scenes in the context of the first century religious and cultural milieu: Does the mountain in Matthew draw on any recognizable pattern of religious mountain symbolism? Is there, for example, any OT typology at work? Did the evangelist intend that the mountain setting function not only as a literary device but also as a theological symbol, evoking already existing forms of sacred mountain theology? Finally, assuming that answers can be found to all these questions: What light does the mountain motif shed on the wider redactional questions of Matthew's theological purposes and the life setting in which these purposes find their place? It is within the framework provided by these questions that the following study will be carried out.

2. *Matthew's Mountain Motif in Current Discussion*

As has been noted, Matthew's interest in mountain locales has not escaped scholarly attention. Though there has been no full-scale study,[14] questions raised by the ὄρος data have been recognized and some preliminary dicussion has been carried on. Much of this discussion is either wide of the mark or superficial; still, several authors have provided insights which may serve as the basis for further study.

The most frequently encountered comments on Matthew's ὄρος motif have to do with the first set of questions enumerated above, i.e. with the matter of the common characteristics which these mountain scenes display and which the mountain setting serves to bring into focus. For most scholars who make comments of this kind, the mountain in Matthew is to be seen as a place of revelation. In fact, such a view is encountered so often[15] that many commentators simply repeat it without elaboration as if it were a self-evident truth.

This approach, however, must be judged as unsatisfactory, not only because of repeated failures to spell it out in detail and to search for supporting parallels in the OT or current Jewish religious thought,[16] but also because it is an inadequate and even misleading characterization of Matthew's mountain scenes. Mt 15.29-31, which as one of the uniquely Matthean mountain passages should figure largely in any assessment of the motif, cannot be described as revelatory at all. Nor does the idea of revelation appear in any determinative way in the third temptation. Revelatory features are present in the other four main passages, but to describe these as simply scenes of revelation is to relegate more important and characteristic elements—e.g. the emphasis on the authority of Jesus (Mt 7.28f.; 28.18b), the gathering of the crowds for messianic ministry (4.23–5.1), the community mandate aspect of 28.16-20—to the shadows.

Just as unsatisfactory is the description of mountains in Matthew as places of solitude and nearness of God.[17] While this may be true to a certain extent for Luke, the presence of the crowds on the mountain in Mt 5.1 and 15.29—a feature which distinguishes Matthew's mountain scenes sharply from those of the other Synoptics—makes this a totally inadequate description for Matthew. Wellhausen was right when he observed that mountains in Matthew are places of activity not solitude.[18]

A real advance, however, has been made by several scholars who point to recurring christological and ecclesiological themes which appear in Matthew's mountain passages. Schmauch, for example, drawing attention to the absence of opposition and to the emphasis on the relationship between Jesus and those who have gathered around him on the mountain, sees the mountain motif as having to do with the creation of an eschatological community bound to a teacher.[19] While his focus on teaching as the characteristic feature of the mountain events is wide of the mark,[20] his idea that the mountain is the place where the eschatological community is gathered and constituted—a theme also suggested by Strecker[21]—surely deserves further consideration. Also to be taken into account is the suggestion, made in varying ways by Livio,[22] Ryan,[23] Daniel and Kingsbury,[24] that mountains function as places of christological manifestation.

Several scholars have moved beyond merely finding common elements in Matthew's mountain scenes to an attempt to discover the literary role of the motif in the structure of the Gospel as a whole. Frieling's thesis of a seven-fold chiastic structure is not borne out by the evidence.[25] More insightful, however, is the suggestion made by Schmauch and worked out in a more systematic way by Lange that each of Matthew's mountain scenes is linked in one way or another to the final one in the sequence.[26] Though questions can be raised about Lange's selection of mountain passages,[27] the recognition that Mt 28.16-20 serves as a summary and climax for many of Matthew's key themes means that the possibility of this passage functioning in a similar way for his mountain motif as well is worth investigating in greater detail than has been the case to this point.

The area in which current investigation of Matthew's mountain motif is weakest is that represented by the third set of questions above, i.e. the possibility that ὄρος functions in Matthew as a theological symbol which introduces into the text, by means of typology or of allusion to contemporary sacred mountain traditions, its own independent meaning. Several scholars, including Lange, assume without any real attempt at justification that no mountain typology is present in Matthew at all.[28] But though the opposite *a priori* assumption is also to be avoided, Matthew's undeniable interest in OT themes (evidenced both by direct citation and by allusion[29]), suggests that such a conclusion cannot be reached apart from a thorough investigation of the alternative. Yet even where the possibility of an OT background is taken seriously, the absence of any systematic consideration of religious mountain symbolism in the OT and contemporary Jewish thought means that such assessments of this possibility as have been made must be judged as speculative and premature. Though a fair amount of work has been done on sacred mountain conceptions in the OT,[30] corresponding features within Second-Temple Judaism have been largely ignored,[31] and no thorough attempt has been made to see the ὄρος data of the Gospels against the background which these two bodies of literature provide.

The most common suggestions for the background against which Matthew's mountain scenes are to be viewed have to do with Mount Sinai. As we have seen, Sinai occasionally figures in the characterization of these Matthean settings as 'mountains of revelation'. More frequently it is argued that Matthew's mountain scenes are part of a developed New Sinai/New Moses typology.[32] Though such a view is not implausible, two weighty considerations stand in the way of its full and immediate acceptance. The first has to do with the absence of any study of religiously significant mountains and sacred mountain symbolism in the milieu in which Matthew was written. The assumption seems to be made by many that if a first-century reader familiar with biblical tradition encountered an obviously symbolic mountain in a piece of literature, then Sinai would immediately spring to his mind as the only possible background against which such symbolism could be seen. But was Sinai so prominent in contemporary thinking, particularly in view of the continuing significance within Judaism of Zion? Perhaps it was, but this would need to be demonstrated on the basis of a study of the relevant literature.

The second objection has to do with the Gospel of Matthew itself. Though Moses allusions are indeed present in the Gospel, study has shown that wherever Moses typology is present it is not allowed to stand on its own but is gathered up into larger christological patterns.[33] Even if Sinai typology is present in Matthew's mountain motif, might not the situation here be the same?

Zion has also been suggested as a relevant background for the mountain motif in Matthew—particularly by Schmauch, who points to its place in prophetic literature as a locus of eschatological fulfilment.[34] In view of (1) Zion's prominence in the OT as God's 'holy mountain', (2) the continuing importance of Jerusalem for Second-Temple Judaism, and (3) Matthew's evident concern to define his community's existence over against that of Judaism, further investigation of this possibility seems eminently worthwhile.

Thus a thorough study of Matthew's use of the mountain setting in his presentation of the ministry of Jesus appears to be justified. A preliminary survey of the data suggests that it is a deliberate Matthean motif which is potentially important for the redactional investigation of the First Gospel, not only for the theological themes which it brings into focus but also for the possible theological freight which it might carry in and of itself. Though the importance of the motif has not gone unrecognized, it has not been thoroughly investigated, and much of the study that has been done has been superficial or misdirected. Some solid contributions have been made, most notably Schmauch's suggestive comments on the background of the motif and its place in Matthean theology and Lange's literary analysis. But Schmauch's work is sketchy and little attuned to the concerns of redaction criticism, and the insights of Lange into the redactional significance of the motif have been short-circuited by his refusal to consider the possibility of an OT background. The most glaring lacuna is the absence of any systematic study of religiously significant mountains and sacred mountain symbolism in Second-Temple Judaism, especially in view of the eschatological significance of the mountain setting which quickly becomes apparent from a study of the relevant literature. In the light of all these considerations, a full-scale study of the mountain scenes in Matthew is not only defensible, but also has the potential of providing further insight into the Matthean redaction.

3. *The Meaning of* τὸ ὄρος *in the Gospels*

Before proposing such a study, however, one further preliminary matter needs to be addressed. This concerns the meaning of the articular but unspecified τὸ ὄρος, found frequently in the Gospels— especially in the phrase εἰς τὸ ὄρος.[35] Foerster has argued on the basis of Hebrew, Greek and Aramaic evidence that ὄρος can refer not only to 'a (single) mountain', but also to a more broadly defined geographical area such as a 'mountain range', 'desert', or 'field', with the result that εἰς τὸ ὄρος should be rendered 'into the hill country'.[36] On the basis of such a translation he maintains that the Gospel occurrences of εἰς τὸ ὄρος (those of Matthew included) are purely geographical references with no possible literary significance or typological overtone. And though the same conclusions are not always drawn, this translation is also proposed by Dalman, Black, and others.[37]

Foerster's conclusions have to be judged in the light of his evident desire to exclude any 'mythological' element from biblical mountains. Yet it must be granted that this is a possible meaning for τὸ ὄρος, especially in a milieu where Semitic influence was at work. Evidence for a broader meaning for τὸ ὄρος in classical or purely Hellenistic usage is limited.[38] But in Hellenistic Jewish usage, the fact that both הר and טור can mean 'hill country' as well as 'mountain'[39] has had its effect on the semantic range of ὄρος. In the LXX, הר is rendered principally by ὄρος, the adjective ὀρεινός ('of the mountains or hill country'), or its substantive ὀρεινή ('mountainous region, hill country').[40] All of the 22 occurrences of ὀρεινός/ὀρεινή for הר are in instances where the meaning 'hill country' is demanded by the context. But there is not a clear semantic difference to be made between ὀρεινός and ὄρος, for τὸ ὄρος is often used as well to render this more general meaning of הר.[41] Thus there is some LXX evidence that the semantic range of ὄρος is as broad as that of הר. A similar situation is found in 1 Maccabees, where τὸ ὄρος means 'mountainous country' in probably four places,[42] and in Josephus, where perhaps six such references can be cited.[43]

But although 'to the hills' is a possible rendering of εἰς τὸ ὄρος in the Gospels, several factors combine to make it unlikely. First of all, even in Hellenistic Jewish usage, 'the mountain' is by far the more common and natural sense of τὸ ὄρος. Since the Greek writer had at his disposal the less ambiguous terms ὀρεινός and ὀρεινή (as well as ὄρη), ὄρος came to be used in the sense of 'hill country' much less frequently than was the case with הר.[44] Wherever τὸ ὄρος is used in this way, the meaning is clearly demanded by the context.

Further, in Gospel usage not only is there no single instance of τὸ ὄρος where the translation 'hill country' is contextually required, there are positive indications that this translation is to be excluded. When Synoptic writers want to refer to 'the mountains' or 'hill country', they do so in other ways. Though Luke is the only NT writer to use the term ὀρεινή (Lk 1.39, 65), the plural ὄρη is used frequently—by Matthew no less than the others—to convey this generalized meaning (Mk 5.5; Mk 13.14 // Mt 24.16 // Lk 21.21; Mt 18.12; cf. Heb 11.38; Rev 6.15, 16). Moreover, there are instances in the Synoptics where a prepositional phrase with τὸ ὄρος is unambiguously used with references to a specific single mountain. The Markan *Vorlage* to Lk 9.28 refers to 'a high mountain' (εἰς ὄρος ὑψηλόν; Mk 9.2); Luke has replaced this with εἰς τὸ ὄρος προσεὔχασθαι, thus using the phrase under discussion to refer to the single 'high mountain' of Mark. Also in Mk 9.9 // Mt 17.9 // Lk 9.37, ἐκ (ἀπὸ) τοῦ ὄρους refers to the individual mountain of the Transfiguration. The use of εἰς τὸ ὄρος in Mt 28.16 also most probably refers to a single mountain appointed as a rendezvous.[45]

Finally, even if it could be demonstrated that in pre-Matthean Synoptic usage εἰς τὸ ὄρος meant 'into the hills', this would by no means prove that Matthew, with his evident interest in mountain settings, used the phrase in the same way.[46]

Thus, although 'to the hills' is a possible translation of εἰς τὸ ὄρος, it is highly unlikely in the Synoptics,[47] where this meaning is usually conveyed by the plural εἰς τὰ ὄρη, is nowhere contextually required, and, in fact, is excluded in at least some of its occurrences.

Nevertheless, since there is apparently no parallel to the articular τὸ ὄρος used without any contextual indication as to the particular mountain which is in view, the phrase remains striking and demands some explanation. Though other suggestions have been made,[48] it is probably to be seen as a highly stylized term which grew out of a common belief that the mountain setting was typically associated with Jesus and was characteristic of his ministry. Just as it might be said of a student that he spent the day 'in the library' (though in fact he might have been at any one of several libraries), or of a fisherman that he went 'to the lake' (when there was no one specific lake in which he did all his fishing), so it was said of Jesus that he went εἰς τὸ ὄρος. '*The* mountain' is an indication of the setting which, it was believed, Jesus characteristically chose for his ministry. Though we do not intend to raise the *Sitz im Leben Jesu* question in this redactional study, it is likely that this usage represents a preference for mountain locales in the ministry of Jesus himself.[49]

4. *The Proposed Study*

The purpose of this study, therefore, is to carry out a thorough redaction-critical investigation of the mountain motif in the First Gospel, taking into consideration the significance of mountains as religious sites and theological symbols in the religious-cultural milieu in which the Gospel took shape. Our attention will be focussed on those passages in which a mountain functions as the setting for an event in the life and ministry of Jesus. This is not to ignore the fact that ὄρος also appears five times in sayings material (5.14; 17.20;

18.12; 21.21; 24.16); but these non-framework uses of the term are
for the most part just taken over by the evangelist from his sources[50]
and—with one important exception[51]—do not have any real bearing
on Matthew's redaction or theology. Of the framework occurrences
of ὄρος, there can be no question that our study will have to include
the ὄρος ὑψηλὸν (λίαν) of the Temptation and Transfiguration
Narratives (Mt 4.8; 17.1), as well as the εἰς τὸ ὄρος setting of the
Sermon (5.1), the gathering of the ὄχλοι (15.19), and the Great
Commission (28.16). Jesus is also found εἰς τὸ ὄρος in Mt 14.23. But
this mountain is not the setting for an extended event in the ministry
of Jesus, and the reference is just taken over from Mark with no
apparent redactional interest. Thus we will not devote a separate
chapter to this passage, though it will come into the discussion of Mt
15.29[52] and we will return to consider its place in the pattern which
emerges from our study of the more extended Matthean mountain
scenes.[53] The Mount of Olives also appears in framework material,
especially as a setting for the Eschatological Discourse (24.3). This
mountain is different from the others in that it is a specified
geographical locale; for this reason Lange omits it.[54] Nevertheless, it
falls into our general category of 'mountain settings in Jesus'
ministry', and we will discover that there are reasons for its inclusion
in the overall Matthean pattern.[55] Our study, then, will focus on the
Matthean mountain settings in 4.8; 5.1 // 8.1; (14.23); 15.29; 17.1 //
9; 24.3; and 28.16.

In our study of the mountain setting in these passages, we will be
inquiring into its function as a purely *literary motif*, i.e. as a term
which does not necessarily carry any theological significance in and
of itself, but which is used as a literary device by which the author
organizes his Gospel and developes some of its themes. We will then
ask further whether the literary motif functions as well as a *theological
symbol*, i.e. as a term which points in some way to external conceptions
or categories which are *ipso facto* imported into the text. In order to
speak with any confidence in this area, it will be necessary to carry
out a study of sacred mountains and religious mountain symbolism
in the OT and the Second-Temple period. On the basis of such a
literary and theological analysis we hope to be in a position to assess
the extent to which the mountain scenes exemplify a common
underlying pattern or schema. At the far end of our study we will be
concerned to see what light may be shed by our investigations on the
wider questions of Matthean theology and of the life setting in which
this theology was forged.

Chapter 2

METHODOLOGICAL CONSIDERATIONS

Our study of Matthew's mountain motif will be comprised of two
major components: (i) an investigation of the function and meaning
of the mountain as a religiously significant site or symbol in the
milieu in which the Gospel was written; and (ii) a redaction-critical
study of the mountain scenes in Matthew with a view to discovering
the literary and theological role played by ὄρος in the Gospel. Before
proceeding with the study, however, there is methodological groundwork to be laid in each of these areas.

1. *Investigation of Background*

We have assumed to this point that if ὄρος in Matthew carries any
extra-Matthean religious significance—i.e. if it functions as a
theological symbol, as we have defined this term—then in order to
understand this significance it will be necessary to set Matthew's
mountain theme against the background of Second-Temple Judaism.
This assumption will require some elaboration, justification, and, at
certain points, qualification.

In the first place, though the use of mountains as religiously
significant sites and symbols is an almost universal and timeless
phenomenon,[1] there is little to be gained from any comprehensive
survey, even if it were possible within the limits of this study. Such
an enterprise would, for the most part, yield only analogical (as
opposed to genealogical) parallels which could not possibly have
influenced the Matthean usage. Though an awareness of comparative
religions investigation into sacred mountain phenomena alerts us to
features in the material under consideration which might otherwise
go unnoticed, our primary attention must be given to those streams
of religious tradition which may reasonably have influenced early
Christianity in general and Matthew in particular.

Second, it is assumed here that the church for which Matthew was written was Jewish-Christian in orientation and so dependent for its world of ideas largely on the traditions of Second-Temple Judaism. In view of the fact, however, that the *Sitz im Leben* of Matthew's Gospel is a matter of some dispute, such an assumption requires further examination and justification.

The problem of the life-setting of Matthew arises from the presence in the Gospel of two tendencies that exist somewhat in tension. On the one hand, the Gospel exhibits a number of character- istics which appear to reflect a Jewish-Christian milieu: the emphasis on OT fulfilment, particularly in the formula quotations;[2] the concern for the abiding validity of the law (5.17-20; 23.1-3; cf. 7.21- 23); the particularism of the mission of Jesus and his disciples (10.5f.; 15.24); and numerous cases where Jewish practices are unexplained (Mt 15.2; cf. Mk 7.2-4), rabbinic discussion are reflected (Mt 19.3), and the like.[3] On the other hand, a certain distance—even alienation— from Judaism and things Jewish is seen in the universalistic interest in the Gentile mission (4.15; 10.18; 12.21; 13.38; 24.14; 28.19f.), the harsh polemic against the Jewish leaders (e.g. ch. 23), statements such as '*their* synagogues' (4.23), '*their* scribes' (7.29), and a number of 'replacement pericopes' (8.5-13; 20.1-16; 21.28-32, 33-45; 22.1-14).

Matthew has traditionally been seen as a Jewish-Christian Gospel.[4] As this traditional position has been worked out within the framework supplied by redaction-critical concerns, it is argued that the Gospel was written for a Greek-speaking but largely Jewish-Christian church which was in the process of consolidating its own life and self- understanding in a context in which, as a result of increasing Pharisaic opposition, it was being pushed in a greater or lesser degree to the margins of Jewish life.[5] This church was open to the Gentile mission, but valued its Jewish heritage and wanted to give a greater place in Christian practice to a re-interpreted Torah, in order to counter the antinomianism which it feared was endemic in that mission.[6] If Matthew wrote in and for such a church, then it can be safely assumed that both he and his readers were thoroughly conversant not only with the OT but also with developed exegetical traditions of Second-Temple Judaism.

In the past three decades, however, there has been a growing group of scholars who take the second tendency outlined above as evidence of a 'Gentile bias',[7] and as determinative for the life-setting of the Gospel. For these scholars, Matthew's church is a church in transition;

it originated as a Jewish-Christian community, but by the time of the writing of the Gospel it had become largely Gentile. Though the evangelist included Jewish-Christian material that had been handed down in his church—either out of a respect for tradition,[8] or in a conscious attempt to describe a Jewish stage of *Heilsgeschichte* which had been superseded[9]—when the Gospel is seen from the perspective of its last redactional layer it takes the shape of a Gentile-Christian manifesto celebrating the fact that the kingdom of God, once the domain of Jews only, has now passed to Gentiles.[10] If the First Gospel arose in such a setting, then, although it cannot be denied that the evangelist had an interest in the OT, it would no longer be likely that the literature of Second-Temple Judaism could be of much help in ascertaining the way in which the OT was read and understood by the evangelist and his readers.

We cannot enter here into a thorough study of Matthew's *Sitz im Leben*. It is our considered opinion, however, that the 'Gentile bias' reading of Matthew is ill-founded.[11] The attempt to assign all Jewish-sounding material to the tradition appears to be a case of special pleading, especially in view of the presence of such tendencies in unmistakably redactional material (e.g. Mt 24.20)[12] and of the open-endedness of the Jewish mission in Matthean perspective (ch. 10, esp. v. 23).[13] The pervasiveness of this material throughout the Gospel gives it a face-value Jewish-Christian orientation that is difficult to ignore. To think that Matthew expected to make a Gentile-Christian statement by composing a Gospel which exhibits opposite characteristics to such an extent is virtually to abandon the redaction-critical assumption of the theological and literary competence of the evangelists. And to think that he expected his readers to recognize the purely *heilsgeschichtliche* value of such material is to assume a level of subtlety and sophistication in his readers that is difficult to envisage.

But not only is a Gentile-Christian *Sitz im Leben* difficult in view of the Jewish-Christian material, it is by no means required by the anti-Judaistic element in the Gospel. The assumption seems to be that opposition to Pharisaic Judaism implies *ipso facto* a Gentile-Christian standpoint.[14] Such an assumption, however, does not take into account the diversity and party-spirit that characterized first-century Judaism and which disappeared only with the triumph of Pharisaism over competing Jewish groups. Both Matthean tendencies can be more satisfyingly explained by seeing Matthew's church as part of one of these groups.

We must return to the *Sitz im Leben* question at the end of our study, asking what refinements should be made in light of our investigations. Here we need only state that our initial position most closely resembles that of Hummel:[15] Matthew's Gospel was written in the period after the war but before the *Birkath ha-Minim* declaration was fully in force, for a Hellenistic Jewish-Christian community which, while open to a properly-conceived Gentile mission even as it held on to its Jewish heritage, was being forced to re-examine its own identity as the Pharisees of Jamnia carried out their reconstruction of a more narrowly defined Judaism.

So we will carry out our investigation on the assumption that Matthew wrote for a church which was not only familiar with the OT, but also was conversant with the way in which the OT was read and interpreted in contemporary Judaism. This does not necessarily imply that Matthew has taken over any mountain symbolism from this milieu; whatever symbolic or typological elements are present in Matthew's mountain motif will have to be established by exegesis. But exegesis is itself dependent in turn on an understanding of the milieu in which a text was written; and if the mountain in Matthew functions as a theological symbol, then it is within the life and literature of Second-Temple Judaism that the 'semantic range' of this symbol is to be established.

Now this does not mean that our investigation can ignore other mountain conceptions that were abroad in the Mediterranean world. Not even in Palestine did Judaism exist in a vacuum; as Hengel has demonstrated, it was influenced early and deeply by the categories and thought forms of Hellenism.[16] But given the milieu in which Matthew was written, such Hellenistic elements as are present in the Gospel (even at the subconscious level) were mediated via Judaism. Thus, while we must note the influence of Hellenism on the development of sacred mountain conceptions in Judaism—and though the mountain settings in Gnostic literature will demand special attention—we will look only briefly at Hellenism in and of itself.

Our investigation of the traditions and thought forms which may have influenced Matthew in his emphasis on mountain settings, then, will focus on the OT and the literature of Second-Temple Judaism. With respect to the OT, our primary interest will lie not in the developmental history which stands behind the text, but in the final shape of the text in its first-century setting. The most relevant historical-critical question that can be asked is not: How did the various theological strands and literary units which make up the OT come to be? but: How was the OT read and understood by Jewish and Christian communities in the first century AD? In that these communities stood at the end of a continuous religious history and a process of development that had their roots in ancient Israel, we cannot remain unaware of history-of-religions and history-of-traditions perspectives, with their interest in the historical development of a given religious tradition or theological idea in the period for which the OT supplies evidence. Insights derived from such studies will be incorporated into our OT discussion at pertinent points. But for brevity's sake, our primary interest will be in (i) the literary-theological function of sacred mountains and mountain symbolism in the OT in its final form, and (ii) the function of this aspect of the OT in the religious and exegetical life of first-century Judaism.[17]

With respect to the literature of Second-Temple Judaism, we will be interested not only in what this material can tell us about the way in which OT mountain theology was understood and applied in this period, but also in its innovations and developing traditions which may have influenced the milieu in which the Gospel of Matthew was written. The term 'Second-Temple Judaism' is one of convenience and not meant to imply that our interest is limited to material produced before AD 70. Later Rabbinic, Targumic, and Samaritan writings are also relevant to our study, both because they often contain earlier material and because even though written later they often display the flowering of tendencies whose roots are deep within an earlier period. In addition to this material, of course, we will be investigating apocryphal and pseudepigraphal works, the literature from Qumran, the LXX, and the writings of Philo and Josephus. Critical assumptions concerning this material will be indicated at relevant points in the study.

Our goal in this background study is not to come to any specific conclusions about the Matthean mountain motif, even assuming that the ὄρος functions symbolically in the Gospel. Rather it is to map out the range of religious meaning associated with the mountain site/ symbol in those traditions with which Matthew and his community probably were familiar. Conclusions about Matthew will have to await the study of the Matthean mountain passages themselves.

2. *Redaction Criticism*

The primary analytical tool to be used in our investigation of
Matthew's mountain scenes is that which has come to be know as
Redaction Criticism. This discipline assumes that the evangelists
were authors and theologians in their own right, who, living in the
midst of concrete and (at least potentially) identifiable church
situations, shaped the Gospel traditions as they received them in
order to address particular issues and needs which were present in
those church situations. In this approach the Gospels are seen not as
shapeless collections of units of tradition, but as carefully-crafted
theological statements; the evangelists, by the same token, are not
merely tradents but competent exegetes; the community not only
transmits the Gospel tradition, but provides the setting in which and
for which the tradition is shaped and interpreted.

Reduced to its simplest terms, the redaction-critical task is two-
fold: first, to uncover and examine the varous theological and
practical motives which governed the evangelist in his work; and
second, to use the results of this study to illuminate the setting in
which this work was done. The first aspect of the task proceeds both
in a 'horizontal' way (comparing the Gospel with its sources in order
to discover significant patterns in the way in which the evangelist has
altered, deleted, rearranged, or recast the material as he received it)
and in a 'vertical' way (looking at the overall composition of the
Gospel to discover its themes and the structures on which it is
built).[18]

The second aspect of the task is characterized by a built-in
circularity. Bultmann's description of the circular procedure that the
form critic must follow holds for the redaction critic as well (for
'forms' read 'theological concerns of the evangelist'):

> It is essential to realize that form-criticism is fundamentally
> indistinguishable from all historical work in this, that it has to
> move in a circle. The forms of the literary tradition must be used to
> establish the influences operating in the life of the community, and
> the life of the community must be used to render the forms
> themselves intelligible.[19]

It is impossible (as this study has already demonstrated) to begin a
redactional-critical investigation of one of the Gospels without
making some initial assumptions about the setting in which it was
produced. But the redaction-critical process is not complete until

these initial assumptions are re-examined—and consequently confirmed, refined, or revised—in the light of what is discovered about the theological and practical concerns that motivated the evangelist.

Redaction Criticism is not an independent process, but must be carried out in conjunction with the disciplines of Source and Form Criticism, especially in the area of horizontal analysis. With respect to Source Criticism, the separation between tradition and redaction on which redaction-critical analysis depends is in turn dependent on the ability to identify the sources which an evangelist had at his disposal. In company with most redaction critics we will assume that, in addition to his special material, Matthew's primary sources were Mark and Q. Yet we cannot remain oblivious to the fact that the two-source solution to the Synoptic problem is currently being vigorously called into question.[20] Arguments by Butler, Farmer and others for the priority of Matthew have failed to convince many outside their own circles, but they have created enough of a situation of doubt that the redaction critic cannot depend on the results of horizontal analysis alone. Vertical analysis—viz. the understanding of Matthew in terms of Matthew—takes on increased importance in the current climate as an independent means of testing the results of horizontal analysis.[21]

Nor can Redaction Criticism be carried out in isolation from Form Criticism, though the precise nature of the relationship between these two disciplines is a matter of some dispute and confusion. There are some who take the position that Redaction Criticism is just a logical extension of the assumptions of Form Criticism, and that it necessarily builds on the form critic's results.[22] But in view of the redaction-critical emphasis on the individuality and creativity of the evangelist, and of the fact that the only real prerequisite to the redaction-critical task is the ability to separate tradition and redaction, the situation is rather that Redaction Criticism offers a corrective to excessive form-critical emphases on the anonymous sociological factor in the formation of the Gospels, and that the two enterprises are semi-independent.

Attention must be drawn, however, to the qualifications inherent in the terms 'corrective' and 'semi'. Redaction Criticism does not represent a rejection of the assumptions of Form Criticism, for both disciplines grow out of the same fundamental insight that the literary material of the Gospel tradition was created in the context of living Christian communities, and that it was preserved because it met the needs and served the purposes of those communities. Nor are they totally independent disciplines. Each walks the same path up to the point of the separation of tradition from redaction, and each—even though they move in different directions from this point—is enhanced in a secondary way by an awareness of the results of the other. Redaction-critical analysis—particularly in the case of material for which we have no independent source access (Mk, M, L)—aids the form-critical procedure by helping to determine more accurately the tradition with which it has to work. In its turn, the form-critical determination of the meaning of a pericope within its original setting will greatly assist in a fuller understanding of the re-interpretation which is given to the pericope by the evangelist. Since Redaction Criticism and Form Criticism are subsidiary aspects of the larger study of the history of the Synoptic tradition, the redaction critic must needs do his work in conversation with the form critic.[23]

This admittedly sketchy picture of redaction-critical methodology[24] will perhaps come into sharper focus as we turn to the specific redactional problem of Matthew's mountain motif and outline the stages through which our investigation will move.

(a) The first step in the study of a particular mountain setting will be to examine its place and significance in pre-Matthean tradition. Using source and form analysis we will attempt to work backwards to the form of the narrative in which the mountain setting first appears, analysing its form and function in this narrative (using such aspects of our background study as may be relevant), and then noting any changes in other subsequent but pre-Matthean stages, if such exist. Since we are dealing with six important, difficult, and often-discussed passages, this stage of the study must be reported in compressed form. Nevertheless, Matthew's redactional handling of the tradition cannot really be understood without some understanding of its earlier form and significance. It should be noted that our primary interest is in the history of the narratives as literary forms, rather than in the history of the events which they relate; thus, questions of authenticity and of the *Sitz im Leben Jesu* are peripheral to our concern.

(b) With this pre-Matthean analysis completed, we shall then turn to a consideration of the literary and theological significance of the mountain setting in its Matthean context, using horizontal analysis and again drawing on elements from our background study where relevant.

(c) The results of this horizontal analysis will then be treated and refined by considering via vertical analysis the place and significance of the passage with its mountain setting in the overall composition of the Gospel.

(d) After all six passages have been treated in this way, we will then assess the overall redactional significance of the mountain motif, drawing conclusions concerning its literary function and theological meaning.

(e) Since this single motif is no more than a small 'archaeological trench' in the large 'tell' of Matthean theology, an attempt will be made to place this particular motif within the larger theological patterns of the Gospel.

(f) Finally, we will return to the question of the life-setting which is presupposed by such a theological statement as our study reveals.

PART II
SACRED MOUNTAINS AND MOUNTAIN SYMBOLISM
IN ISRAEL'S EXPERIENCE

Chapter 3

IN HISTORY-OF-RELIGIONS PERSPECTIVE

Sacred mountains and mountain symbolism were common features in the landscape of Israel's religious life from earliest times up to the end of the Second-Temple period and beyond. Given the context in which the religion of Israel developed, this is not surprising. At the simplest level, these features reflect the mountainous nature of the land of Palestine, whose topography is dominated by two extended ridges of mountains, one on either side of the Jordan Valley. From the beginning, Israel's existence was closely identified with this hill country (cf. Dt 11.11; 1 Ki 20.23).

But a more significant aspect of the context in which Israel's mountain theology developed is the fact that throughout its history Israel lived in contact with other cultures—Mesopotamian, Canaanite, Babylonian, Persian, Hellenistic—in which sacred mountain phenomena were also present to a greater or lesser extent.[1] *Religionsgeschichtliche* study of sacred mountains and related patterns of thought aids the understanding of Israel's mountain theology as it has identified areas of borrowing, provided a context in which Israel's distinctives can be more clearly seen, and defined categories within which the Jewish phenomena can be examined.

In the discussion of the mountain traditions of Israel, three such categories have frequently come into play. One of these is that of the *Weltberg*, a concept which has generally been associated with Mesopotamian and Babylonian cosmology.[2] In this construct, the earth is seen as a dome-shaped mountain rising out of the cosmic sea, with heaven at its peak and the underworld at its base. Some have suggested that in such passages as Is 2.2, where tiny Mount Zion is depicted as the highest of all mountains, OT thought was influenced by such cosmology (i.e. because of its site at the top and centre of the dome, Jerusalem is of necessity the high spot of the earth).[3] Such an approach, however, has been largely abandoned, principally because of doubts as to the relevance of the concept even in Mesopotamia,[4] the virtual absence of OT material in which such concepts are explicitly reflected, and the much greater fruitfulness of Canaanite parallels in the Ugaritic material.[5]

Another category which has also had a lengthy history and is of more relevance to Jewish thought is that of the *Weltnabel*, i.e. the idea that a mountain centre or other sacred place is the centre or 'navel' of the earth. This conception was widespread in the ancient world,[6] and prominent in Greek mythology, especially in connection with Delphi.[7] In later Judaism, and particularly in Rabbinic tradition, this idea was fully incorporated into the developing traditions relating to Mount Zion.[8] Its influence on OT thought has been argued by Wensinck, and more recently by Childs and Terrien,[9] who see it as a concept borrowed from the Canaanites.

Yet the OT material suggesting such an influence is scanty, and its relevance to the *Weltnabel* concept open to question.[10] Moreover, a Canaanite source for the Omphalos idea in the OT is doubtful, since it does not appear to have been a prominent feature of Canaanite cosmology.[11] Admittedly, the possibility that Ezekiel may have been influenced by such a concept cannot be ruled out.[12] Yet one cannot help but conclude that although *Weltnabel* ideas were prevalent in later Judaism, their importance for the development of OT mountain theology has been exaggerated.

A third important category is that of the 'cosmic mountain', i.e. a mountain which plays a role in the origin or structure of the cosmos. This mountain conception takes several forms; in fact, the *Weltnabel* idea can be seen as one form of cosmic centre. This category also includes the idea of the mountain as the *axis mundi*, i.e. with its roots in the underworld and its peak in the heavens, it is the place at which heaven, earth, and the underworld are linked together. A further cosmic idea, closely related to the *axis mundi* concept, is that the mountain, with its peak in the heavens, is the home of the gods.[13]

It will become evident in our more detailed study that many aspects of the Sinai and Zion theology of the OT can be generally described in cosmic terms.[14] Moreover, this category will be especially significant in our investigation of apocalyptic literature with its heightened interest in cosmic elements. A more specific *religions-geschichtliche* application of cosmic mountain conceptions has been attempted in the case of the OT material with respect to Canaanite parallels, particularly those that have become known to us through the Ugaritic discoveries at Ras Shamra. The relevance of Canaanite parallels has long been recognized,[15] and the presence in the OT of material borrowed from Canaanite sources widely acknowledged.[16] The most thorough work in this area has been done by Clifford, who, on the basis of a careful comparison of texts, comes to the conclusion that Sinai is best understood in terms of traditions associated with the mountain of El, and Zion with those connected with Baal's Mount Zaphon.[17]

Clifford's study makes two important contributions. First, it provides a firm historical context for OT mountain theology. We now see more clearly how widespread sacred mountain thinking was in the ancient Near East, and so can appreciate that sacred mountains in Israel's experience were not unparalleled or unexpected features, but parts of a wider pattern of religion. Israel's theology developed in a religious milieu in which mountains played an important role, and so it is not surprising that Israel developed a mountain theology of its own.[18] Second, Clifford's work emphasizes the importance of the contributions of comparative studies in the interpretation of formerly obscure passages, such as Ps 48.2 ('Zaphon/the far north') and Is 14.13 ('the mount of assembly in the remotest part of Zaphon').

Yet at the same time Clifford's study brings the limitations of the *religionsgeschichtliche* approach into sharp focus. Comparative study of a given religious tradition which does not also give due consideration to the meaning and function of the tradition in its own context and on its own terms will produce skewed results. Clifford's tendency to allow the Canaanite context to dictate the framework for his analysis of the OT data demonstrates at least three limitations of this approach.[19]

In the first place, *Religionsgeschichte* by its very nature tends to place an inflated value on parallels and similarities, which often results in a failure to take sufficient account of differences and distinctives. Clifford's study of OT mountain theology has missed completely, for example, the unique and important role played by the people of Israel at both Sinai and Zion.[20] People were not, of course, absent from the sacred mountains of the Canaanites; indeed, these mountains functioned primarily as places of worship. Yet in the myths of El and Baal, within which the sacredness of the mountains was conceived, the people do not appear. The physical presence of people at a mountain sanctuary was a consequence of the sacredness of the mountain, but such sacredness was determined by conceptions in which the category 'the people' played no part. In the OT, however, Sinai and Zion are sacred because there Yahweh bound his people to himself in covenant relationship and there (at least, on Zion) covenant promises will be fulfilled in the eschatological future.[21] The sacredness of both Sinai and Zion stems from the fact that on these mountains the relationship between Yahweh and his people was constituted, is maintained, and will be consummated.

Second, to demonstrate that one religion has been influenced by another in a specific element does not necessarily fully account for the presence of that element in its new religious setting. Clifford operates on the assumption that to demonstrate a Canaanite parallel to an OT concept is to account for its rise. Now it is true that the sacred mountain theology of the OT arose in a context where related Canaanite conceptions were already at work. Yet, as we will see in the case of both Sinai and Zion, the decisive and creative factor was not the already-present cosmic idea, but certain dramatic historical events which were interpreted by Israel as acts of Yahweh in their midst and on their behalf.[22] No matter how much dry tinder lay about, these historical events provided the necessary spark. To attempt to account for OT mountain theology apart from these historical experiences on which the faith of Israel rested is to miss the heart of the matter.

Third, even where an incident of borrowing or external influence has been identified, it cannot be assumed that the borrowed element functions in the same way in its new setting. Allowances must be made for the fact that religious traditions are demonstrably capable of assimilating foreign elements by reinterpreting them and working them into their own characteristic patterns of thought. Though OT depictions of Sinai and Zion have been influenced by cosmic Canaanite conceptions, the nature of Yahweh's presence on these mountains stands in marked contrast to the Canaanite situation. In the cosmic mountain theology of Canaan (and elsewhere), mountains, because of their height, were thought to penetrate the heavens and thus to become places where the deity might be encountered. In the OT, however, where little emphasis is placed on height,[23] Yahweh's presence on the mountain is due not to any feature intrinsic to the mountain itself, but to his own elective will. Pains are taken to show that Yahweh *comes* to Sinai and that he *chooses* Zion as his abode, rejecting other mountains which might appear to have been more likely choices.[24] Though cosmic overtones are to be found in OT mountain theology, there is never a suggestion that Yahweh's presence on the mountain is due to any pre-existing cosmic features; rather, mountains become sacred because of Yahweh's presence.

Thus in the more detailed study of the mountain phenomena of the OT and Second-Temple Judaism to follow, our central concern will be to come to an understanding of Israel's sacred mountain traditions as seen 'from within', taking fully into account the distinctive features of Israel's history and theology. In the process the results and categories of history-of-religions study will be taken into account, but in such a way that Israel's own witness to its experience will not be muted.

Chapter 4

IN THE OLD TESTAMENT

1. *Mountains of Secondary Importance*

Sinai and Zion are the most significant mountain sites and symbols in the OT, and as such will be the focus of our attention in this chapter. Yet they are only part of a much broader OT phenomenon.[1] Other mountains appear frequently[2] and in a variety of ways in the OT text. Mountains are often encountered, for example, as purely literary symbols. This is true both for specified individual mountains[3] and for the generalized plural הרים (often used in parallel with גבעות).[4] Though some cosmic elements are present in this symbolism,[5] an emphasis on height, which was common in Canaanite thought, does not appear.[6] In fact, height is seen in the OT as a characteristic of sites for the worship of Baal,[7] or as a symbol of human pride (e.g. Is 2.12-17).

Individual mountains are also encountered in OT narrative sections as settings for a number of significant events: the coming to rest of Noah's ark (the mountains of Ararat; Gen 8.4); Abraham's binding of Isaac (a mountain in the land of Moriah; Gen 22.2); the deaths of Aaron (Mount Hor; Num 20.22-29; Dt 32.50) and Moses (Mount Nebo/Pisgah; Dt 3.27; 32.48-52; 34.1-7). Taking the text as it stands, however, these mountains appear as little more than geographical details. Any theological significance that may have been present in the history of these traditions has been sharply attenuated.

There are also traces in the OT of mountains other than Sinai and Zion that functioned as sacred and cultic sites within Israel. The hill-country setting of the important cultic centre at Bethel[8] receives occasional notice in the text.[9] Also, the northern city of Shechem, near Mount Gerizim, was a place of worship long before the time of the Samaritans.[10] Gerizim, with its twin, Mount Ebal, was remembered as the site of a covenant-renewal ceremony (Dt 11.29; 27.1-13;

Josh 8.33), and in the divided-kingdom period it continued as the northern counterpart to Zion (Am 6.1). Another locally sacred mountain is referred to in the 'Blessing of Moses' (Dt 33.18f.) in connection with the tribes of Zebulon and Issachar. Though unnamed, it has been suggested that the mountain here is Carmel[11] or Tabor.[12]

Mount Carmel appears as well as the site of a local religious centre in the time of Elijah and Elisha. In the account of the contest with the prophets of Baal, it is said that Elijah repaired (ירפא) the altar of Yahweh that had been thrown down (1 Ki 18.30). His successor Elisha also seems to have made Mount Carmel the centre of his prophesying activity (2 Ki 2.25; 4.25).

Yet in the OT as a whole, the religious significance of these mountains is quite muted. There was not room in the religious life or literary traditions of Israel for many sacred mountains; in comparison with Sinai and Zion, all others pale into insignificance.

2. *Sinai/Horeb: The Mountain Of The Law*

The mountain setting is prominent in the accounts of the giving of the law. הר occurs in Exodus, Leviticus, Numbers and Deuteronomy more than sixty times in this connection. In addition to instances where הר appears in juxtaposition with סיני or חורב, it is used to designate the site of the giving of the law in other ways: it appears by itself forty-eight times; four times we encounter 'the mountain of God' (הר האלהים; Ex 3.1; 4.27; 18.5; 24.13); 'the mountain of Yahweh' (הר יהוה) appears once (Num 10.33).

The most characteristic designations for the mountain of the law, however, are 'Sinai' and 'Horeb'. Though סיני also appears in the 'March in the South' hymns[13] and in references to the 'Wilderness of Sinai',[14] it is most prominent in Exodus, Leviticus and Numbers as the site of the giving of the law, usually (fifteen of seventeen times) as הר סיני.

Apart from the 'March in the South' hymn of Dt 33.2, the name Sinai does not appear in Deuteronomy or in the Deuteronomic history. The Deuteronomic name for the mountain of the law is Horeb, a term also found twice in Exodus. In the first of these Exodus references, Horeb is designated as 'the mountain of God' (Ex 3.1). The other Exodus reference is the only OT occurrence of the term הר חורב (Ex 33.6); though Horeb in Deuteronomic usage is

clearly a mountain site, this specific term does not appear. Horeb
does not seem to be as clearly defined a geographical concept as
Mount Sinai, for some events which apparently took place some
distance from the site of the giving of the law were said to have taken
place at Horeb (e.g. Ex 17.6). Yet Horeb is not just 'an indefinite
location which has gathered certain traditions of wandering to itself',
as Clifford describes it.[15] Although Sinai and Horeb are never
directly equated, the Exodus accounts of the burning bush (on
Horeb) and the giving of the law (on Sinai) are woven together
almost seamlessly by means of Ex 3.12.

If we look at the literary and theological significance of the
mountain of the law in the OT as a whole, a somewhat conflicting
picture emerges. On the one hand, Sinai and Horeb play a sharply
limited and circumscribed role in the OT. Unlike Zion traditions,
which arose out of ongoing political and religious institutions, the
Sinai material relates only to a single event in the past and to a
mountain which was not a continuing sacred site within Israel. In
contrast to the prominence of this mountain in the Pentateuch, one is
struck by its almost complete absence from the rest of the OT.

Horeb appears in Deuteronomic history in a remembrance of the
Mosaic covenant (1 Ki 8.9; cf. 2 Chron 5.10) and in the account of
Elijah (1 Ki 19.8)—an account whose intention appears to be the
presentation of Elijah as the 'prophet like Moses'.[16] Elsewhere it
appears only in Ps 106.19 and Mal 4.4. References to Sinai are even
more scarce. Apart from the 'March in the South' hymns of Dt 33.2,
Judg 5.5 and Ps 68.8, the only extra-Pentateuchal reference to Sinai
is in the late recitation of salvation history in Neh 9.13. So, unlike
Zion theology—which, as we will see, continued to grow and develop
throughout the OT period—Sinai traditions remained static. Except
for the Elijah account, the Sinai motif did not fuel any ongoing
religious events or traditions within Israel. The law, of course,
continued to have a central place in the religious life of the nation.
But the fact of the present possession of the law seems to have made
it unnecessary to relive the event of the giving of the law in the same
way that, say, the Exodus event continued to be remembered and
relived.

On the other hand, the relative scarcity of Sinai theology outside
the Pentateuch by no means minimizes its importance. The pivotal
place of the Pentateuch in the OT cannot be underestimated, and the
Pentateuch is dominated by the Sinai event. This domination is

evident not only in the sheer bulk of the Sinai account,[17] but also, as Cohn points out, in the fact that it provides the focus for the whole narrative of the Exodus and the wandering period.[18] The Exodus leads up to it (cf. Ex 3.12) and it points ahead to the extrance into the land. Moreover, the Sinai event is the basic presupposition for the rest of the OT, for it was at Sinai that Yahweh bound Israel to himself as his people. Despite its circumscribed place in the OT, Mount Sinai with its associated events was absolutely foundational to Israel's theological self-understanding and forms one of the summits of OT salvation history.

Two theologically significant features of the Sinai accounts are of particular relevance for our present investigation. First, the encounter between God and his people on the mountain was in the form of a theophany. In a scene described in terms of storm imagery,[19] Yahweh comes in cloud and fire to Mount Sinai to meet with Moses. The contrast with the cosmic mountain theology of the Canaanites is evident. There is no hint in the narrative of the idea that the mountain, because of its height, was in the divine domain. Moses meets with Yahweh on the top of Sinai not because its top was in heaven but because Yahweh comes (Ex 19.9) or descends (Ex 19.18; 34.5) to the mountain. God's presence is in no way tied to the mountain by any quality pertaining to the mountain itself. Rather, Yahweh comes to the mountain in his freedom,[20] and it becomes sacred because of his presence (Ex 19.10-15).

The second point to note is that the event on the mountain is not just a theophany, but a theophany which is part of a larger covenant-making ceremony. The Sinai event is not just a revelation of God or even of his will. Rather, it is an event in which Yahweh binds his people to himself in covenantal relationship. The text speaks not of any one-sided coming to the mountain. Both Yahweh and Israel come to Sinai, there solemnly to ratify the covenant.

It is clear from the account that the mountain locale is not just a casual geographical reference, but a central part of the story. The mountain site is announced beforehand as the goal of the Exodus (Ex 3.12). In the Deuteronomic retelling of the events, the reader is constantly reminded of the mountain. In both prospect and retrospect, then, the mountain setting is decidedly in view. Moreover, in the Sinai narrative itself, the mountain is kept in the foreground by dint of sheer repetition. As the place chosen by Yahweh, the mountain is the means by which the covenantal relationship becomes localized in

space and time. Its significance in the Pentateuchal accounts cannot
be overestimated.

Moving on from the question of the literary and theological
importance of the mountain setting in the accounts of the giving of
the law, we turn to the development of the Sinai/Horeb material. In
the critical discussion of the history of the Sinai narratives, there is
scholarly consensus on two points: first, that behind the accounts lies
a historical event of foundational significance for Israel as a people;[21]
second, that the literary accounts have their *Sitz im Leben* in the
ongoing cultic life of Israel, perhaps in covenant renewal ceremonies
(e.g. Dt 31.10-13).[22] The major area of divergence among scholars
has to do with the question of the relationship between the Exodus
and Sinai accounts. Noth and von Rad argue forcefully that the two
traditions were originally independent, becoming connected only at a
later stage—Noth on the basis of his multi-tribe/multi-tradition
theory of Israelite origin,[23] von Rad on the basis of his observation
that Sinai is absent from the early Israelite 'creeds' or recitations of
Heilsgeschichte (Dt 26.5-9; Josh 24.2-13; Ps 105; 136).[24] This
separation of Exodus and Sinai, however, has been vigorously
challenged by Mendenhall, who points to the similarity between the
Sinai covenant and Hittite suzerainty treaties.[25] In his analysis,
what von Rad defines as a creed is just the historical preamble to the
covenant itself. Mendenhall's approach has been developed further
by Beyerlin,[26] and the connection between Sinai and Exodus is
argued on other grounds by Weiser[27] and Nicholson.[28]

Unresolved questions about the developmental history of the Sinai
accounts, however, do not have nay fundamental bearing on our
investigation into the place of Sinaitic mountain theology in the life
of Israel. In the first place, this development was complete at an early
date: the fact that the Davidic covenant is never incorporated into
the history of the Sinai covenant points to a pre-monarchy crystallization of the Sinai material.[29] Moreover, as already observed, the
Sinai motif was restricted to the accounts of tribal confederacies in
the pre-conquest period.[30] As a relatively static tradition, it did not
spill over into the ongoing religious life and literature of Israel in the
post-Davidic period, probably because of the rising importance of
Mount Zion.[31]

The importance of the Sinai narratives for our survey of mountain
theology in the OT is this: Although the significance of Sinai as a
sacred mountain was encased within the past, Sinai still loomed large

on Israel's spiritual horizon. As the place where Yahweh bound Israel
to himself in covenantal relationship and gave it the law, Sinai played
a foundational role as the mountain associated with Israel's constitution as a people.

3. *Mount Zion*

The other important sacred mountain in the OT is Mount Zion, the
site of the temple at the heart of Jerusalem.[32] Though tiny even by
Palestinian standards, this mountain is at the centre of some of the
most lofty theological conceptions and elevated religious language in
the whole of the OT. Mount Zion and Mount Sinai stand as the two
historical-theological pivots on which all OT *Heilsgeschichte* turns.

ציון is one element in a larger cluster of related terms which refer to
the site of the temple, to the temple itself, or to the city as a whole.
This terminology is quite fluid, as can be seen, for example, in Mic
3.12–4.2, where the terms 'the mountain of the house', 'the mountain
of the house of the Lord', 'the mountain of the Lord', 'Zion', and
'Jerusalem' are used synonymously within the space of three verses.
הר is prominent in this cluster, appearing more than sixty times in
this way in the OT. The most frequent constructions with הר are
הר ציון and הר קדשי (הר קדשו and הר קדשך, הר קדשי including) הר הקדש, which
account for about forty of the occurrences. In addition, we find הר בית־
יהוה (2 Chron 33.15; Mic 4.1; Is 2.2), הר יהוה (Ps 24.3; Is 2.3; 30.29;
Mic 4.2; Zech 8.3), הר הבית (Mic 3.12; Jer 26.18), הר מרום ישראל
(Ezek 17.23; 20.40; 34.14[33]), הר נחלתך (Ex 15.17),[34] and הר with
some other qualifying expression (Ps 68.16; 78.54; Is 25.6, 10; Ezek
43.12). ציון also appears without הר about 160 times. And when we
add in the 750 or so occurrences of Jerusalem, together with other
assorted terms, we end up with as many as two thousand OT
references to the Jerusalem–Zion theme.[35]

As far as the distribution of these terms in the OT is concerned, the
major concentration is in the Psalms and the prophetic literature,
particularly Isaiah. Neither ציון nor (with the exception of Ex 15.17)
הר used with reference to Zion occurs in the Pentateuch.[36] In view of
what has already been said about the date of the Sinai traditions, this
should not surprise us. What is surprising, however, is the virtual
absence of הר or ציון in the historical books. הר ציון occurs once in
Isaiah's oracle of 2 Ki 19.31, and בהר בית־יהוה in 2 Chron 33.15. ציון by
itself is found a total of only six times. Thus it appears that this

sacred mountain concept found its *Sitz im Leben* not in the more restrained milieu of the Deuteronomic historians, but in the political and cultic circles of Jerusalem (where Zion was celebrated as a present ideal) and in the prophetic movements which grew up around them (where the centre of concern was the restoration of Zion in the future).

(i) *Mount Zion as a Present Religious and Political Reality*
The most fundamental feature of OT Zion theology is the concept of election: Mount Zion has been chosen by Yahweh as the place of his abode. All other themes dealing with the importance of Zion as a political and religious centre find their basis in this fundamental concept.[37] The Davidic covenant, for example, is seen by the psalmist as one consequence of the prior election of Mount Zion:

> The Lord swore to David a sure oath
> from which he will not turn back;
> 'One of the sons of your body
> I will set on your throne.
> If your sons keep my covenant
> and my testimonies which I shall teach them,
> their sons also for ever shall sit upon your throne.'
> For [כִּי] the Lord has chosen Zion;
> he has desired it for his habitation (Ps 132.11-13).

A similar theme is found in Ps 78, generally regarded as early, where the choosing of Mount Zion appears at the end of the psalmist's recitation of salvation history as the underlying reality of the Davidic covenant (vv. 67-71).

Because the covenant with David was seen to rest on the election of Zion, rather than vice versa, the election of Zion could be treated on its own, without reference to David. This is the case in Ps 68.15f., where the northern mountains of Bashan are rebuked for their envy of 'the mount which God desired for his abode'.[38] The theme of the election of Zion is also related to the wider covenantal concept of the possession of the land. In the recitations of *Heilsgeschichte* in Ex 15.1-18 and Ps 78, the possession of the mountain which God chose for his abode is seen as the goal of the Exodus and conquest; so the election of the mountain and the covenantal provision of life in the land are seen as closely connected.[39]

Although Sinai and Zion motifs are generally separate and distinct, there is some evidence that Israel was conscious that the doctrine of the election of Zion involved a shift from Sinai as the centre of God's dealings with his people. This shift is probably present in Ps 68, a psalm which is, admittedly, difficult to interpret. The earlier part of the psalm mentions Sinai in connection with the wilderness experience (v. 8); the temple in Jerusalem appears in v. 29. The transition between the two mountain sites is found in vv. 15-18, where the election of Zion is treated. The key verse is 17b; literally: 'Adonai with them, Sinai in the holy place'. Though the exact translation is a matter of some uncertainty, the majority of commentators and translators recognize here some some of transition from Sinai to Zion.[40] A similar transfer probably lies behind the application in Is 24.23 and 29.6-8 of 'Man of War' imagery to Zion, imagery which was formerly associated with Sinai.[41]

Arising from this basic idea that Zion is God's chosen place are a number of themes relating to the dual political-religious role which Jerusalem played within Israel. Though it is somewhat artificial to distinguish between the political and the religious within Israel, we will look first at those themes which deal with Zion in terms of throne, kingship and sovereignty, and then at those which deal with Zion as a centre of worship.

One theme found in those psalms designated Royal Psalms[42] is that Zion is the place of the enthronement of the king. Of particular interest for our purposes is Ps 2.6, where Yahweh declares: 'I have set my king on Zion, my holy mountain'. In two other psalms, though הר is not used explicitly, Zion appears as the place of the king's mighty sceptre (Ps 110.2) and the place which God has chosen for the throne of David and his line (Ps 132.11-18). Particularly emphasized in each of these passages is the king's sovereignty over the nations of the earth.

Yet despite the importance of Davidic theology, for Israel it was Yahweh who was ultimately king. The Davidic king was but the anointed means by which Yahweh's kingship became actualized; Yahweh's kingship, in fact, is often declared without reference to an earthly king (e.g. Ps 47). As this theme was developed, Mount Zion became the site of Yahweh's throne and the centre of his rule. This is clearly the case in Ps 48, a psalm which draws heavily on Canaanite imagery to praise 'the holy mountain, the city of the great king'.[43] Similar ideas without the use of הר are found in Ps 99.1-5, 146.10, Jer 8.19, and elsewhere. In some passages—probably to preserve the idea of divine transcendence—a distinction is made between Zion and

Yahweh's heavenly throne; in Ps 99.5 and 132.7, for example, Zion is seen as the earthly footstool of Yahweh's heavenly throne.[44]

Since Zion is the centre of Yahweh's rule of the world, then it is to be expected that it would be a particularly secure stronghold. And so there is, in fact, a marked emphasis in Zion theology on the inviolability of Zion.[45] Taunts are raised against earthly kings for their futile attempts to assault Zion—attempts which lead inevitably to disaster. Especially important in this regard are Psalms 2, 46, 48 and 76. Because mountains were natural sites for strongholds, it is not surprising that הר is found in two of these psalms (Ps 2, 48). In a related reference, Mount Zion is seen as eternal and immovable (Ps 125.1).

But it was in its cultic role as the centre of worship that Zion influenced the people of Israel most directly and extensively. Here, in the belief that the holy mountain was the centre of God's presence with his people and of the people's response of praise and worship, we find the heart of Zion theology. The idea of election is basic here too: Mount Zion is the place which Yahweh has chosen for his sanctuary. In Ps 78.67-71, for example, a passage which has already caught our attention, the psalmist rejoices over the election of הר ציון; and then, before moving on to speak of the election of David, he describes the building of the sanctuary.

The extent to which ideas of cult and worship permeated Zion theology can be seen in the pervasive use of הר הקדש as a synonym for Jerusalem/Zion. The psalmist calls the people to 'worship at his holy mountain' (Ps 99.9), and concerns are expressed that those who worship there be holy too (Ps 15.1; 24.3). Even the nations are invited to participate in praise and worship at Zion (Ps 102.21f.), and a post-exilic psalmist sees the restoration of Zion particularly in terms of a restoration of worship (Ps 51.18f.).

More, however, than just the site of a temple, Mount Zion is the place of Yahweh's abode, the actualization of his promise to be present with his people. Or, perhaps it could be said that Jerusalem was the place of worship because Yahweh had made it his abode. Although there was occasionally some sensitivity to the need to preserve God's transcendence,[46] there often appears in the Psalms the bold assertion that Yahweh dwells in Zion (Ps 9.11; 43.3; 68.16; 74.2; 76.2). Frequently הר is used in this connection: 'thy holy hill and thy dwelling' (Ps 43.3); 'the mount which God desired for his abode, yea, where the Lord will dwell for ever' (Ps 68.16; cf. 74.2).

Since the holy mountain of Yahweh is the localization of his presence with his people, it is not surprising that Zion is seen as the source of salvation (Ps 14.7; 20.2; 53.6) and blessing (Ps 128.5; 133.3; 134.3). In Ps 46.4, Zion is described in cosmic terms as the source of the mythical river which brings fertility to the earth. The fertility which in the OT is often ascribed to mountains in general[47] is here attributed in an ultimate way to Zion. Clements's summary of Israel's theology of the temple is also applicable to Zion as God's holy mountain:

> The entire ideology of the Jerusalem temple centred in the belief that, as his chosen dwelling place, Yahweh's presence was to be found in it, and that from there he revealed his will and poured out his blessing upon his people.[48]

The sheer mass of material dealing with Zion and the extent to which much of the theology of the OT has been expressed in terms of Zion concepts is even more striking when one realizes that Jerusalem came into Israel's history at a relatively late date.[49] When we turn from the literary-theological question to that of the history of the tradition, the question to be answered is this: What accounts for the rise and success of this tradition, and how did the material develop? Rarely does one encounter the view that Zion theology was largely an exilic and post-exilic phenomenon.[50] The mere fact of belief in Zion's inviolability is sufficient in itself to indicate a pre-exilic origin. Yet within this broad consensus, scholarly discussion of the origin of Zion theology centres on two factors: (i) Canaanite influence from pre-Davidic Jerusalem, and (ii) the impact of David's choice of Jerusalem as a religious-political centre.

The Jebusite theory, which emphasizes the first of these factors, finds the origins of Zion theology in Canaanite worship already present in Jerusalem when David captured it.[51] Jebusite inhabitants of Jerusalem worshipped El-Elyon, a manifestation of El, a god with whom was associated a sacred mountain.[52] Proponents of this view make the not implausible assumption that the fortified stronghold which David captured (2 Sam 5.6-10) was already considered a sacred place. Some even suggest that the priest Zadok, who mysteriously appeared at this time, was a Jebusite priest.[53]

Now there is no doubt that Canaanite concepts have been taken up into the OT, both in connection with Zion (e.g. Ps 48) and in other contexts (e.g. Is 14.12-14). And it is quite possible that the pre-

Davidic status of Mount Zion was a factor in its choice as the site for the ark. But whether such external considerations played foundational roles in the origin and development of Zion theology is open to serious question.[54] As Clifford demonstrates,[55] the more obvious parallels to Zion are with Zaphon, the mountain home of Baal, and not with the mountain of El. In addition, even if borrowing did take place, sacred mountain concepts functioned quite differently in Israel, acting as vehicles for Israel's distinctive ideas of election and covenant. Though Canaanite parallels can explain some of the features of Zion theology, it is doubtful that they can account for its rise or its success in later OT thought.

More obvious reasons for the origin and development of Israel's Zion theology are David's choice of Jerusalem as his political centre, and the subsequent installation of the ark in Jerusalem—first in the 'city of David' (2 Sam 6.1-19) and later in Solomon's temple (1 Ki 8.1-6)[56]—which made the city the religious centre as well.[57] Noth has cogently argued that of these two factors, the latter was more significant.[58] Kingship was a recent innovation in Israel and its glories were short-lived. Moreover, much of the material of Zion theology functions independently of the monarchy. The ark, on the other hand, was already a focus of worship for the tribal confederacy, and so was a greater unifying factor than the monarchy. Thus, as Noth argues, Mount Zion was first considered sacred because of the presence of the ark and, subsequently, of the temple. Later, under the influence to a certain extent of Canaanite ideas, but more particularly because of mountain ideas already present in Israel's thinking,[59] Zion came to be seen as sacred in its own right, the holy mountain of Yahweh.

The *Sitz im Leben* of the developing Zion material, therefore, is probably to be found in the ceremonies and festivals in which the religious and political aspects of Israel's national life were celebrated and maintained. And while it may be necessary to reserve judgment on some scholarly reconstructions of specific life settings, there can be no doubt that it was in the court and cult that Zion theology developed and was elaborated.[60]

The Royal Psalms, for example, clearly arose in court settings,[61] produced perhaps for ceremonies celebrating the coronation of new kings. Some scholars argue that these psalms, together with others relating to the enthronement of Yahweh (Ps 47; 93; 96–99), find their home in an annual re-enactment of the enthronement, a ceremony which took place at the Feast of Tabernacles or at a New Year's festival.[62] This thesis, however, though possible, is seriously weakened by the absence of solid OT evidence, which forces it to rely to an inordinate extent on parallels drawn from other cultures in the ancient Near East.

Nevertheless, the ceremonies and rituals of temple worship afforded numerous contexts in which kingship could be celebrated and the glories of Zion proclaimed and praised. Of special interest in this connection are the pilgrimages to Jerusalem for sacred festivals. The 'Songs of Ascent' (Ps 120–134), many of which are pre-exilic, were in all likelihood produced for use by Jewish pilgrims.[63] Thus, as with Sinai material, Zion theology must be seen as the combination of a historical event and ongoing cultic observances.

We can conclude, therefore, that although Mount Zion came onto Israel's spiritual horizon relatively late, it quickly became the dominant feature of the landscape. Mount Sinai was almost forgotten as Mount Zion gathered to itself many of the threads of Israel's religious tradition. Here on his holy mountain Yahweh is present with his people; here his king rules; here stands his sanctuary. If Sinai was the mountain of Israel's constitution, Zion, the holy mountain of God, became the living centre of Israel's political and religious existence— the site and sign of God's continuing presence with his people.

(ii) *Zion Theology in Eschatological Perspective*

One measure of the power and importance of Zion as a theological symbol is the extent to which it was able to be used as a vehicle for religious hopes and ideals in a variety of changing circumstances and outlooks. When we turn to the prophetic corpus, we find ourselves in the midst of a completely different attitude towards court and cult than is present in the Zion theology of the Psalms. The prophets perceived themselves as messengers of Yahweh in a situation where Yahweh's people had broken the covenant by repeated disregard for its demands, and where the old order as a consequence must needs be called into question. It was not necessary to convince the nation of the corruption of the monarchy; its failure was plain for all to see. The harsh word that the prophets (especially Isaiah, Micah and Jeremiah) spoke to the nation was that, because covenantal obligations had been disregarded, the presence of the temple and the observance of its rituals were of no benefit in ensuring that covenantal blessings would continue. To a nation celebrating the inviolability of Zion, the prophets announced the unthinkable: Yahweh himself would destroy it.

But this did not mean that Zion theology was to be discarded. The prophets also held out a vision of a renewed and restored Zion—a vision which gathered up many of the aspects of present Zion theology and projected them into the future. The ideal Zion of the psalmists became the eschatological Zion of the prophets.

In the prophetic literature, a number of recurring themes cluster around the idea of the eschatological restoration of Zion. In fact, these themes appear so frequently and in such similar combinations[64] that it is evident that we are dealing with a traditional pattern of eschatological expectation, though it is just as clear that the pattern was by no means fixed or static. Von Rad has accurately characterized this pattern as 'a rich and living cycle of concepts', 'a fluid tradition which the prophets could actualize in quite different ways'.[65] Yet the unifying centre for this cycle of concepts is constant: the eschatological restoration of Zion, the holy mountain of God, as the centre of a renewed Israel and the seat of Yahweh's world-wide kingdom.

a. The Gathering of Scattered Israel

The most common theme in this *mélange*, one that could almost be said to be indispensable,[66] is the idea that when Zion is restored Yahweh will gather his scattered people into renewed fellowship on his holy mountain. This idea is the major thrust of Jer 31.1-25, a passage which forms part of Jeremiah's 'Book of Consolation'. Although parts of this chapter deal specifically with promises of blessing to the northern tribes (vv. 2-6, 15-22) and perhaps date from an earlier part of Jeremiah's career,[67] in their present form they have been incorporated into a vision of a post-exilic gathering of the whole scattered nation. Of particular interest are vv. 7-14, where the prophet describes the gathering of the scattered remnant 'from the north country' and 'from the farthest parts of the earth'. They move in a vast procession which includes the blind, the lame and the distressed, and they are comforted and strengthened by Yahweh himself (vv. 8b-9). Their destination is the 'height (מרום) of Zion' (v. 12a), where they will experience a life of plenty and joy (vv. 12b-14).

A similar picture, though with differing emphases, is found in Ezekiel—a prophet with a recurring interest in the re-establishment of a renewed Israel on a purified holy mountain. Levenson demonstrates how Ezekiel's vision of the city-temple on the mountain described in chs. 40–48 is the culmination of a motif that has been carefully developed in earlier chapters.[68] One of these preparatory passages is Ezek 20.33-44, which views the return from exile as a second Exodus. Here God promises to 'gather you out of the countries where you are scattered, with a mighty hand and an outstretched arm, and with wrath poured out' (v. 34). As the phrase 'with wrath poured out' suggests, the gathering is first for judgment (vv. 33-39). But then the gathered and purified people will serve Yahweh 'on my holy mountain, the mountain height of Israel' (v. 40).

Though the theme of the eschatological gathering of the nation to Zion is found frequently in all parts of Isaiah, nowhere is it as explicitly stated as in Is 35. The chapter appears as a sequel to the bleak picture of the destruction of Edom in ch. 34. But whereas in Is 34 the Lord comes in judgment to reduce the land of Edom to desolation, in Is 35 he comes in redemption turning the wasteland into a garden. The purpose of this blossoming of the desert is disclosed only in the last verse: God is preparing a highway on which those who have been redeemed as a result of the judgment of the nations will 'come to Zion with singing, with everlasting joy upon their heads' (v. 10; cf. Is 51.11). Every provision is made for the pilgrim on his way to Zion: water is provided in the desert (vv. 6b-7); protection is afforded from dangerous beasts (v. 9); divine strength is offered (vv. 3f.), even to the point of miraculous healing (vv. 5-6a). Elsewhere in Isaiah we find the exiles summoned by trumpet from Assyria and Egypt 'to worship at the holy mountain in Jerusalem' (Is 27.13), or carried there as an offering by the nations (Is 60.4; 66.20). In these passages from Isaiah, as in similar passages from Jeremiah and Ezekiel, the restoration of Zion is the signal for, and partially consists of, the return of the scattered nation to Yahweh's holy mountain.

b. The Pilgrimage of the Nations
A closely related (and probably earlier) concept is that the nations would also participate in an eschatological pilgrimage to Zion. There is, of course, some ambiguity with respect to the relationship of the nations to Zion in the final period. Sometimes the prophets looked for the defeat of the nations at Zion in a final battle (Is 29.8; Joel 3.9-21; Mic 4.11-13) and the establishment of Zion as the centre of God's rule over the nations (Is 24.23)—ideas which may well be eschatolo-

gical counterparts to the theme of the inviolability of Zion.[69] When
this expectation is expressed in terms of the eschatological procession
to Zion, the nations are depicted as coming to Zion in a subservient
role, bringing tribute to Jerusalem, carrying the exiles back home,
serving Israel and doing obeisance to her king.[70]

But alongside this view of the final destiny of the nations there is a
more positive presentation of the eschatological procession of the
nations to Zion in which they come to worship Yahweh and to share
in the eschatological blessings. Indeed, it is in this prophetic conception
that the recurring OT theme of Israel as Yahweh's witness to the
nations reaches its high water mark.

The archetypical passage for such an idea is Is 2.2f. // Mic 4.1f.,
where the eschatological prominence of Zion is a sign to the nations
to seek the God of Zion:

> It shall come to pass in the latter days
> that the mountain of the house of the Lord (הר בית־יהוה)
> shall be established as the highest of the mountains,
> and shall be raised above the hills;
> and all nations shall flow to it,
> and many peoples shall come and say:
> 'Come, let us go up to the mountain of the Lord,
> to the house of the God of Jacob;
> that he may teach us his ways
> and that we may walk in his paths'.
> For out of Zion shall go forth the law,
> and the word of the Lord from Jerusalem.

This note is sounded elsewhere as well. Yahweh will bring foreigners
to his 'holy mountain' to worship at the world sanctuary (Is 56.6-8).
The nations will participate in a banquet on 'this mountain' (Is 25.6-
10a), i.e. Mount Zion,[71] in celebration of the enthronement of
Yahweh (cf. Is 24.23). The members of foreign nations will beg the
returning exiles to be allowed to accompany them to Jerusalem, for
they 'have heard that God is with (them)' (Zech 8.20-23). In these
passages, the eschatological mountain is the hope of the Gentiles;
they will participate in the final gathering on the mountain, and their
salvation will be a by-product of its restoration.[72]

c. Eschatological Blessings
One feature of this final gathering on the mountain of God is that
Israel and the nations will participate alike in a variety of eschatolo-

gical blessings. We have already noticed the expectation of a banquet for the nations, 'a feast of fat things' at which Israel's shame will be finally removed (Is 25.6-10a). This banquet is one element in a wider prophetic expectation of a coming age when Yahweh will feed his people in plenty. And while this expectation is often expressed in general terms referring to a renewed fruitfulness of the earth and the prosperity of Israel,[73] Zion, the holy mountain, also plays an important role. There the once-scattered flock will find abundant pasture:

> They shall come and sing aloud on the height of Zion,
> and they shall be radiant over the goodness of the Lord,
> over the grain, the wine, and the oil,
> and over the young of the flock and the herd;
> and their life shall be like a watered garden,
> and they shall languish no more (Jer 31.12; cf. Ezek 34.26f.).

Cosmic imagery enters this picture as well, as Zion is seen as a new Eden, the source of the river of life which produces food in abundance (Ezek 47.1, 6b-12; cf. 28.12-16).[74]

Material abundance is not the only blessing to be found on the mountain; here physical disabilities and even death will be abolished. The blind and the lame are on several occasions mentioned as participants in the pilgrimage to Zion (Is 35.5-6a; Jer 31.8; Mic 4.6f.). Not only will the physically afflicted be made into a remnant and a strong nation on Zion (Mic 4.6f.), they will be healed as well:

> Then the eyes of the blind shall be opened,
> and the ears of the deaf unstopped;
> then shall the lame man leap like a hart,
> and the tongue of the dumb sing for joy (Is 35.5-6a).

And in the final banquet on the mountain, even death will disappear (Is 25.8).

d. New Law / New Giving of the Law

Eschatological Zion is also to be the scene of a new giving of the law—even the giving of a new law. We have noted already that there was some consciousness within Israel of a transfer of God's presence from Sinai to Zion.[75] Such a transfer also appears in the Zion eschatology of the prophets; on occasion Zion takes over the functions of Sinai, not only succeeding it but even replacing it.

In Is 2.2f. Zion is depicted as a 'new Sinai': the nations will come to the renewed mountain to learn God's ways, for 'out of Zion shall go forth the Torah' (v. 3).[76] In view here is not necessarily a new Torah, but a new revalation of the Torah that will be universal in scope.

The law also comes into view in Jeremiah's vision of the return to the holy mountain in ch. 31. Here we have not a new law—not even a new giving of the law—but a new capacity in the hearts of the people to keep the law. As von Rad notes, this hope that the law would be written on the hearts of the people was the most profound aspect of Jeremiah's vision of the future.[77]

Ezekiel, however, actually does have new commandments in view. As Levenson observes, Ezekiel stands on the mountain as a new Moses, receiving a visionary blueprint of the new temple just as Moses once received plans for the tabernacle, and relaying elaborate instructions for service in the temple and for life in the land.[78]

Thus, just as the final redemption is often pictured as a new Exodus, so eschatological Zion, the goal of this Exodus, stands in these passages as a new Sinai. In the future Zion will be the place where the law is heard.

e. Enthronement

An important feature of Zion as a present reality is the attention given to it as the home of the king, the site of the enthronement of Yahweh or of his king. So it is not surprising that when attention shifted from the present to the future, the restored holy mountain was also seen as a place of enthronement. The enthronement of the Davidic Messiah is especially in view in Ezekiel. In Ezek 17.22-24 he is depicted as a young twig planted 'on the mountain height of Israel'; in 34.23-31 as the Shepherd-Prince who will tend the flock as it grazes on Mount Zion.

Alternatively, Yahweh himself is to be enthroned on Zion in the last days. In Zech 14.8-11, Yahweh in Jerusalem is 'king over all the earth'. With respect to Isaiah, mention has already been made of the enthronement of Yahweh 'on Mount Zion and in Jerusalem' in 24.23. A similar expectation is found in Is 52.7. In Ezekiel, the enthronement of Yahweh stands alongside that of David, appearing in 20.33, 40; 43.7 and (expressed in a pastoral metaphor) 34.11-16. Of the latter passage Levenson comments:

> Thus, the elaborate metaphor of the shepherd in ch. 34 describes what in a regal context critics call the enthronement of YHWH. His taking command of the flock is the pastoral equivalent of his better-known assumption of kingship in the enthronement Psalms.[79]

The enthronement of Yahweh also stands alongside that of the Davidic Messiah in Mic 4.6f. and 5.2-4, verses which are part of the larger passage 4.1–5.9 dealing with the eschatological gathering of the scattered remnant to the restored mountain of God in Zion. In 4.6f., it is Yahweh himself who will reign over the gathered nation:

> and the lame I will make the remnant;
> and those who were cast off a strong nation;
> and the Lord will reign over them in Mount Zion
> from this time forth and for evermore.

Mic 5.2-4 deals with the ruler (מושל) of Israel who will come forth from Bethlehem.

Thus, although Zion theology and messianism often run on parallel tracks in the OT,[80] they converge in this point: the vision of eschatological Zion as the mountain of enthronement.

f. Pastoral Imagery

A final item in our discussion has to do not with one element of Zion eschatology which stands alongside the others, but with a range of imagery which was commonly used to depict the scattering of the exiles and their future gathering to Zion—one in which virtually all of these other subsidiary motifs come to expression. This imagery, common in the rest of the OT, is drawn from the pastoral realm: Yahweh or his king is the Shepherd and Israel is the sheep of his flock. The eschatological development of this metaphor is found in Isaiah, Jeremiah, Ezekiel and Zechariah.

As the metaphor expresses it, Israel's leaders have been worthless shepherds (Jer 23.1f.; 25.34-38; Ezek 34.1-4) with the result that the sheep have been scattered over the mountains (Jer 23.2; 50.6; Ezek 34.5f.; Zech 10.2). But God will punish the shepherds (Jer 23.2; 25.34-36; Ezek 34.7-10; Zech 10.3) and will gather the scattered flock (Is 40.11; Jer 23.3; 31.10; Ezek 34.10-16), setting up as their shepherd a Davidic King (Jer 23.5f.; Ezek 34.23f.). The fold to which the sheep are gathered is the 'height of Zion' (Jer 31.10), 'the mountain height of Israel' (Ezek 34.14),[81] and there God promises to feed them abundantly:

> I will make them and the places round my hill (גבעתי) a blessing;
> and I will send down the showers in their season; they shall be showers of blessing. And the trees shall yield their fruit, and the earth shall yield its increase, and they shall be secure in their land (Ezek 34.26f.; cf. Jer 31.12-14).

The feeding of the flock is the pastoral equivalent of the banquet on the mountain.

So it appears evident that a wide variety of eschatological themes and expectations have clustered in rich and living patterns around the vision of a restored mountain of God. Before turning to the traditio-historical discussion, we conclude this section by observing that the term הר and the concept of the 'holy mountain' receives heavy emphasis in these patterns.[82] The mountain is the highest of all mountains; it is the locale for the eschatological banquet; it is the exalted site of the new temple in Ezekiel's vision. Even the frequent prophetic theme that the mountains and valleys would be levelled on that day (e.g. Is 40.3f.) is brought into service in this motif: only Jerusalem will remain aloft (Zech 14.10). A rough indication of the importance of הר can be gained from a survey of the passages dealing with Zion eschatology listed above.[83] Of the fifty or so designations for Jerusalem in these passages (e.g. Zion, house, city, etc.), fully twenty involve the term הר, the largest single category. Thus the holy mountain of Yahweh is one of the most prominent features in OT eschatology.

Since many elements of traditional Zion theology have reappeared in different guises in the Zion eschatology of the prophets (e.g. the inviolability of Zion; Zion as the source of blessing; as the site of the throne; as the centre of Yahweh's dealings with the nations), it is clear that this eschatological vision did not arise in a vacuum. Undoubtedly it was deeply rooted in the Zion theology of court and cult.[84]

Its initial formulation was in all likelihood by Isaiah himself. The origin of Is 2.2-4 is a much-discussed question, one which is exacerbated by the presence of the same material in Mic 4.1-4. But though unanimity has not been reached, a strong case can be made for the Isaianic authorship of the passage.[85] The argument as proposed by von Rad and elaborated by Wildberger has two points. First, the theme of Is 2.2-4 is consistent with the rest of Isaiah; in fact, the prophet's overriding concern is with Zion as first judged and then restored. Second, much of Is 2.2-4 can be paralleled in traditional Zion theology. If these arguments stand, the first expression of Zion eschatology was Isaiah's creative reinterpretation in eschatological perspective of such traditional aspects of Israel's religion as annual pilgrimages to Jerusalem and the belief that the nations were under the sovereignty of Yahweh. In this reinterpretation, annual pilgrimages to Jerusalem served as the model for the future pilgrimage of the nations to a restored and glorious Zion.

There is some evidence in Jeremiah that the division of the kingdom into Israel and Judah provided fuel for the continuation of Zion eschatology from its Isaianic beginnings.[86] But it was the destruction of the temple in 587 BC and the scattering of the people far from Zion which were most influential in the development of this theme and its rise to pre-eminence in Jewish eschatology. Thereafter, though royal messianism was optional for Jewish eschatology, the restoration of Zion was not. The hope for the gathering of the nation from exile, as developed in Jeremiah, Ezekiel and Isaiah 40–66, was, along with the law, a major factor in preventing the disintegration of Judaism during the exile and beyond.[87]

The post-exilic period witnessed a further development. The return from exile was, from all accounts, a disillusioning experience. It was not a glorious pilgrimage to the exalted mountain of God, but an arduous existence around a shabby temple. The prophets of this period, however, proclaimed that the vision had not failed, but had only been deferred. It would be the return to Zion of Yahweh, not of the people, that would trigger the eschatological events.[88]

This shift of focus to the indefinite future provided the basis for a development which came to full expression in later apocalyptic literature. Here, disillusionment with the inglorious return from exile became disillusionment with history itself as a vehicle of salvation; the Zion ideal came to be seen as no longer realizable in this world. A human temple would no longer suffice. Expectations began to turn to a divinely-made temple—even to a ready-made heavenly temple descending to earth.[89]

Nevertheless, up to the end of the OT period, Mount Zion occupied centre-stage in the prophetic vision of the future. The holy mountain of Yahweh was the site where eschatological events would be focussed. The vision of an eschatological mountain of God gathered up into itself features inherent in earlier mountain symbolism —not only of Zion theology, but also of Sinai. The eschatological mountain stands in the OT not as one mountain motif among others, but as the culmination of the sacred mountain ideas of ancient Israel. It draws together various strands of thought and weaves them into a vivid tapestry of eschatological hope. At the centre of this tapestry stands Mount Zion, the mountain of Israel's consummation.

4. *Summary*

Although the sacred mountains of the OT have some features in common with cosmic mountains of other cultures, and though their portrayals have been influenced at certain points by Canaanite mythology, they cannot really be classified as cosmic mountains. The essential features of Sinai and Zion theology—the importance of historical events, divine election, the role of the people—are unique to Israel. The sacredness of OT mountains rests on historical events in which Yahweh in his freedom came to bind Israel to himself as his people. As physical localizations of the relationship between Yahweh and his people, the sacred mountains of the OT can most accurately be described as covenant mountains.

Looking at the OT in literary and theological perspective, the two 'covenant mountains' of Sinai and Zion have an absolutely central role to play in the theological self-understanding of Israel. They are the two theological-geographical pivot points on which all of OT *Heilsgeschichte* turns. In particular, Mount Zion is given great significance as an eschatological site. In fact, the idea of the eschatological restoration of Zion is a magnet which has attracted other eschatological themes to itself, resulting in a traditional yet fluid pattern which forms one of the most prominent and persistent strands in OT eschatological expectation. And in all of this, the concept 'mountain' and the term הר are to the fore.

Looking at the OT from a *Traditionsgeschichte* perspective, while Sinai theology became fixed and static, Zion theology continued to develop in response to changing situations throughout the OT period. In particular, Zion eschatology, which rests on Zion theology and picks up some Sinai overtones, was still a lively and developing tradition at the beginning of the Second-Temple period.

Chapter 5

IN SECOND-TEMPLE JUDAISM

1. *Mount Zion*

(i) *As a Present Religious and Political Reality*

In the tumultuous period from 200 BC to AD 100, when external forces on several occasions threatened the annihilation of Judaism and internal tensions seemed ready to bring about its disintegration, it was the Zion ideal which, along with the Torah, provided the ideology that enabled Judaism to survive. Of course, there were differences between the Zion ideal as developed in the OT and that of Second-Temple Judaism. After Zerubbabel, the Davidic ideal receded into the background, as Jewish society in this period was constituted in several different political configurations: a vassal city-state with the High Priest as *de facto* political leader; an independent nation ruled by the Hasmonaean priest-kings; a subject nation under direct or mediated foreign rule. Attempts to square such varying political situations with traditional Zion theology produced a variety of attitudes towards the present temple, its cult, and those who maintained it. The Hasmonaeans and their supporters gloried in the restored and purified temple,[1] and their praise was matched by the Diaspora writer of the Letter of Aristeas (83f.). At the same time, however, there was a strain of disillusionment with the present temple[2] which developed to such an extent in the Qumran community that they separated themselves entirely from the Hasmonaean 'Wicked Priest' and his defiled temple.[3] In addition, this period also saw several types of new traditions attached to the Zion ideal,[4] two of which we will be examining in more detail in what follows.

Yet the Zion ideal as it came to expression in the OT (particularly the Psalms) continued to be the starting point for a theology of Zion and the temple within Second-Temple Judaism. The building of the temple by Solomon, for example, was seen as one of the great events of the OT (1 Enoch 89.50; Wisd 9.8). Likewise, the election of Zion received particular emphasis (e.g. 4 Ezra 5.25). The basic OT theme that Zion was chosen by Yahweh as his dwelling place received explicit expression—for example, in an apparently pre-sectarian hymn found at Qumran which exhibits clear echoes of Ps 78.67-72:

> Thy dwelling place . . . a resting place in Jeru[salem the city which] thou hast [chosen] from all the earth that thy [name] might remain there for ever (4QDibHam 4.1-3).

The election of Zion was also a frequent Rabbinic theme,[5] though with care taken to preserve the transcendence of God.[6] The persistence of OT Zion theology in this period is perhaps best typified by the 'Apostrophe to Zion' (11QPsZion), a psalm studded with OT Zion motifs, with roots especially in Is 54, 60–62 and 66.[7]

A full study of the development of Zion/Jerusalem/temple theology in the Second-Temple period would take us far beyond the limits of our study.[8] The main issue to be dealt with here has to do with the place of the mountain as a sacred site and symbol in the Zion theology of the period. To what extent was *mountain* imagery an aspect of Zion theology that was emphasized for its own sake?

Looking at the question first from the point of view of terminology, we need note that expressions with ὄρος, הר or טור continued to form a prominent part of the wider collection of terminological equivalents for 'Zion'. In the Apocrypha and Pseudepigrapha we encounter 'Mount Zion' (Jub 1.28; 4.26; 8.19; 18.13; 2 Bar 13.1; 1 Macc 5.54; etc.), 'the mountain of the house' (1 Macc 4.46), 'the mountain of the temple' (1 Macc 16.20), 'the mountain of our fathers' (4 Macc 4.20), and 'the (thy) holy mountain' (Wisd 9.8; 1 Enoch 26.2). Qumran had a range of terms as well: 'the holy mountain',[9] 'the mountain of the height of Israel',[10] and (probably) 'his holy mountain',[11] and 'the mountain of Yahweh'.[12] Of the Targumic terms for Zion, we note in particular the frequent טור בית מקרשא (e.g. Tg. Ps.-J. Ex 15.13; Tg. Ps.-J. Dt 33.19; Tg. Jer 26.18; 31.12). In Rabbinic literature הר בית became by Tannaitic times a fixed technical term for the Temple Mount—though it should be noted that unlike the other terms listed here, this referred not to the whole Jerusalem/Zion/temple complex, but to one constituent part which, though sacred, was by no means the holiest or most important part of the whole.[13] Nevertheless, as we will see, the mountain aspect of Zion theology was important for the Rabbis.

The importance of mountain symbolism in thinking about Zion in this period is seen not only in the terminology, but also in the frequently encountered tendency to emphasize the mountain nature of Zion. Indeed, in some of the cosmic and apocalyptic developments considered below, the mountain motif overshadowed all other features. But even within more traditional treatments of the Zion theme, the mountain motif often stepped to the fore. In the recitation of *Heilsgeschichte* in Enoch's 'Dream Vision' (1 Enoch 89–90), though 'mountain' does not explicitly occur (the result no doubt of the symbolic literary style of the passage), the height and loftiness of the 'tower . . . built . . . for the Lord of the sheep' (i.e. the temple) receives particular stress (1 Enoch 89.50). A similar emphasis on the height of the temple site is found in a passage from the Letter of Aristeas in which the term does appear:

> When we arrived in the land of the Jews we saw the city situated in the middle of the whole of Judea on the top of a mountain of considerable altitude (ἐπ' ὄρους ὑψηλὴν ἔχοντος τὴν ἀνάστασιν). On the summit the temple had been built in all its splendour . . . (Ep. Arist. 83f.).

Important also is the attention paid by the Rabbis to the fact that the sanctuary could be called a 'mountain' (e.g. Sifre Dt 71[b] (§28); Pesaḥ 88a; Midr. Ps 81.2).

The readiness of 'the mountain' to intrude into discussions of Zion can be most clearly seen in a number of passages in the LXX and the Targums dealing with Zion or Jerusalem, where ὄρος or טור appear with no corresponding הר in the MT. LXX Is 63.18, for example, reads ἵνα μικρὸν κληρονομήσωμεν τοῦ ὄρους τοῦ ἁγίου σου for the MT למצער ירשו עם קדשך. In its reconstruction of this difficult Hebrew sentence[14] the LXX has substituted τὸ ὄρος τὸ ἁγίον σου for קדשך. Similarly, LXX Ps 77(78).54 has εἰς ὄρος ἁγιάσματος αὐτοῦ for גבול קדשו, and Is 65.9 reads the singular κληρονομήσει τὸ ὄρος τὸ ἁγίον μου for יורש הרי. Terms involving ὄρος evidently became standard for the temple complex and were freely substituted for less familiar terms.

A similar situation is found in the Targums. Tg Jer 31.12, for example, reads בטור בית מקדשא for the MT במרום ציון. Similarly Tg. Ps.-J. Ex 15.13 has the same term טור בית מוקדשך for the MT נוה קדשך. Here again, a mountain term has become standard and has replaced other terms, even one containing 'Zion' itself. The Targumist introduced טור in order to make explicit the implicit reference to Zion in Is 5.1 as well. Here the parable of Israel as a disappointing vineyard virtually disappears[15] with the 'vineyard on a very fruitful hill' (כרם בקרן בן־שמן) becoming 'an inheritance on a lofty mountain' (אחסנא טור רם).[16] Although these Targumic examples may come from a later period, LXX parallels indicate that we have here something of a long-standing tendency.[17]

From such scattered examples it can be seen that the idea of the sacred mountain continued to be an essential element in Zion traditions. Zion theology in general led naturally to mountain symbolism and mountain terminology in particular. The two concepts were linked in such a way that the one suggested the other.

The prominence of the mountain in the Zion theology of this period can also be seen from the fact that the linkage often moved in the opposite direction as well. The appearance of הר in the MT often called forth a theological Zion interpretation in Targumic and Midrashic material. This was not really remarkable in the case of such verses as Ps 78.54, Ex 15.17 or Ezek 20.40, all of which were interpreted with explicit reference to the sanctuary.[18] In these cases the Zion interpretation was in keeping with implicit contextual references to Zion. But there are other instances where Zion interpretations were attached to decidedly non-Zion passages solely on the strength of the appearance of הר. A prime example of this phenomenon concerns the sacred mountain of Zebulon and Issachar in Dt 33.18f. Although a mountain in the northern territory of Issachar and Zebulon could not possibly be equated with Zion,[19] for the Targumist the conjunction in the MT of הר and יזבחו זבחי־צדק overrode all other considerations: the mountain of sacrifice in Dt 33.19 was obviously to be identified with the site of the temple (טוור בית מקרשא), an interpretation found in both Pseudo-Jonathan and the Fragment Targum.

The most striking example of the phenomenon where הר triggers a Zion interpretation is the interpretation of 'Lebanon' as symbolic of Jerusalem or the temple. This interpretation is frequent in the Targums[20] and Rabbinic literature,[21] and can be dated as early as R. Joḥanan b. Zakkai (c. AD 70).[22] Further, as Vermes points out, there is evidence for the Lebanon-temple linkage at Qumran (1QpHab 12.3f.) and in Sirach (24.10-13; 50.8f., 12),[23] which indicates that the tradition arose early in the period under discussion.

At first glance, the equation appears strange and arbitrary. Closer study of the data, however, indicates that the point of departure for the tradition was Dt 3.25,[24] a verse which is the most frequent prooftext for the equation.[25] The first step in the growth of the tradition seems to have been the interpretation of ההר הטוב הזה in this verse as a reference to the mountain of the sanctuary, in a manner similar to the Targumic interpretation of Dt 33.19 discussed above. This interpretation appears explicitly in the Targums, where Moses' request to see 'that good mountain and Lebanon' is interpreted as a request to see the site of the temple.[26] Once this interpretation of 'that good mountain' was made, it was a short step to equate 'Lebanon' with ההר הטוב הזה and hence with the temple mountain—a step made explicitly in Pseudo-Jonathan. So mountain imagery was important enough within Second-Temple Judaism that the mere appearance of הר in the Hebrew text was often all the catalyst necessary to evoke the whole complex of Zion theology, even if the temple was not at all in view in the passage.

In our discussion thus far of the place of the mountain symbol within the Zion theology of the Second-Temple period, we have limited our attention to material which falls within the general contours of the OT pattern. Zion theology, however, continued to develop and to incorporate new elements during our period. And in two of the most important of these developments, the mountain played a central role. In fact, it was the mountain setting that provided the link by which such new elements were joined to Zion theology.

The first of these developments was the tendency to retroject Mount Zion back into the early history of Israel—viz. to link many of the important figures and events of Genesis with the mountain of the sanctuary. This tendency has roots in the latest strata of the OT itself, and is found in full flower in Rabbinic and Targumic material. As we will have occasion to observe later, this Zion tradition was taken over virtually intact by Samaritanism, where it was applied to Mount Gerizim, and by Jewish Christianity, where it was applied to Golgotha.[27]

The oldest and most durable element of this phenomenon was the linking of the mountain in the land of Moriah on which Abraham bound Isaac (Gen 22.2) with the mountain of the temple. The earliest trace of such a link is found in the OT itself. 2 Chron 3.1 identifies the site of Solomon's temple with Mount Moriah, though without any mention of Abraham. The link with Abraham was made explicit, however, in the exegesis of Gen 22 throughout our period. In Jub

18.13, the site of the *Akedah* is explicitly stated to be Mount Zion. Josephus presents this link as an established tradition: 'that mount on which King David [*sic*] afterwards erected the temple' (*Ant.* 1.226). The tradition is absent in Philo and has not been found in Qumran, though in 1QapGen 19.8 Abraham is said to have visited מורא קדישא (i.e. Zion[28]) on his journey from Bethel to Egypt. In the Targums and Rabbinic literature, however, the tradition is widespread. It appears in the Fragment Targum, in Neophyti, in Pseudo-Jonathan, and in numerous Rabbinic references.[29] The Moriah–Zion connection, in fact, can be said to be a fixed datum of Jewish biblical exegesis.

This connection is part of a larger tradition in which all of the other important early biblical figures were brought into relationship with the mountain of the temple in a similar manner. The full-blown tradition can be seen most conveniently in Targum Pseudo-Jonathan and Pirke de R. Eliezer.[30] Here the retrojection of Mount Zion into the biblical account went back as far as Adam himself, for it was on this mountain that the creation of Adam took place. Targum Pseudo-Jonathan reports that Adam was created on the 'mountain of worship' (מוור פולחנא)—Mount Moriah—out of dust gathered from the temple site and from the four corners of the world.[31] It was on this mountain as well that Adam dwelt after he had been expelled from Eden:

> And the Lord God removed him from the Garden of Eden; and he
> went and dwelt on Mount Moriah (בטור מוריה), to cultivate the
> ground from which he had been created (Tg. Ps.-J. Gen 3.23).

Pirke R. El. 20 explains that Mount Moriah was near the gate of Eden. And it was nearby, in the Cave of Machpelah, that he was buried (Pirke R. El. 20).

Noah, the next major figure in the Genesis story, was associated with this mountain as well. The mountain where Noah dwelt after the ark had come to rest is implicitly equated in this tradition with the mountain of Adam's creation, for Noah's altar is said to have been built by Adam,[32] later rebuilt by Abraham (Tg. Ps.-J. Gen 22.9; cf. Aboth R. Nat. 1.7 [17b] and then discovered by David (Pesiḳ. R. 43.2).

Isaac and Jacob were also associated with this site. Mount Moriah was, of course, the place where Isaac was bound and displayed his devotion. It was also his place of prayer on other occasions, for we read that he returned to 'the mountain of worship, the place where his father had bound him', in order to pray concerning Rebekah's barrenness (Tg. Ps.-J. Gen 25.21; Pirke R. El. 32). Jacob's dream of Bethel is also said to have taken place on the temple site (Tg. Ps.-J. Gen 28.11, 17, 22; cf. Midr. Ps. 91.7; Gen R. 69.7). In fact, the stone used by Jacob as a pillow was made from the altar on which Isaac had been bound (Pirke R. El. 35).

Though it is somewhat separate from the main body of this tradition, there is some evidence of a similar link between Mount Moriah and Mount Sinai. Tg. Neoph. Ex 4.27 describes Mount Horeb as 'the mountain of the sanctuary of the Lord', though this may be a textual error.[33] A more certain identification of Sinai and Zion is found in Midr. Ps 68.9:

> Whence did Sinai come? R. Jose taught: Out of Mount Moriah; out of the place where our father Isaac had been bound as a sacrifice, Sinai plucked itself out as a priest's portion is plucked out of the bread. For the Holy One, blessed be He, said: Since their father Isaac was bound upon this place, it is fitting that his children receive Torah upon it.

Although this is a rather isolated example[34] and one which stands apart from the more common Rabbinic tendency to allow Sinai to overshadow Zion,[35] it is the ultimate example of this long-standing tendency within Judaism to orient all sacred history around only one holy mountain, viz. Mount Zion/Moriah.

The fully developed form of this tradition is found only in later Jewish material.[36] While this does not necessarily preclude an earlier date for the tradition itself, such a dating can be made with confidence only where the tradition can be identified in earlier literature.[37] There is some evidence, however, that elements which went into the final form of this tradition were simmering in the Second-Temple period.

With respect to Adam, there are some hints in earlier materials that his burial place was connected with the site of the sanctuary.[38] Jub 4.29 says that Adam's sons buried him 'in the land of his creation'. Although there is nothing explicit here, the phrase is strikingly similar to that in Tg. Ps.-J. Gen 3.23: 'the ground from which he had been created', a phrase which served as the exegetical hook for the Moriah traditions. And in the Life of Adam and Eve, which is probably a first century AD work,[39] Adam asks to be buried 'towards the sunrising in the field of yonder dwelling' (Adam and Eve

45). Early connections between the Garden of Eden and the mountain of the sanctuary appear not only in Jub 4.25 (though here with reference to Enoch, not Adam),[40] but even as early as Ezek 28.12-14.

In the case of Noah, again in Jubilees we find an emphasis on the mountain. In contrast to Gen 8.20, Jub 6.1 states that Noah constructed his altar 'on that mountain', i.e. the mountain where the ark came to rest. In both Jubilees (7.1-16) and Josephus (*Ant.* 1.109), Noah and his sons are said to have settled on the mountain and lived there for some time.[41] While this mountain is not identified with Moriah or Zion, the conjunction of altar and mountain hints at the presence of an early stage of the later tradition.

Similar hints are to be found in the Jubilees account of Jacob's dream at Bethel (chs. 27–32). The Genesis narrative is followed fairly closely in Jub 27.19-27, except for the addition in v. 19 that Bethel was in a mountain location (cf. 1QapGen 21.7: 'the mountain of Bethel'). Later it is denied that the site of Jacob's dream was to be the site of the temple, for when Jacob purposed to build at Bethel 'that place, and . . . to sanctify it and make it holy for ever', God said: 'Do not build this place and do not make it an eternal sanctuary . . . for this is not the place' (Jub 32.16, 22). Nevertheless, even this denial is evidence that connections between Jacob's Bethel and the mount of the sanctuary were being made in some circles as early as the second century BC. So, although the tradition in which all of Israel's history becomes oriented around Mount Zion continued to develop after the fall of the second temple, the tradition was deeply rooted in the Second-Temple period. This was especially true for Abraham and Mount Moriah, the oldest element in this tradition and without a doubt the seed from which the rest developed. But, as we have seen, elements of the tradition associated with Adam, Noah and Jacob were germinating in the second century BC as well.

In discussing the religious and theological significance of Sinai and Zion in the OT, we suggested that they are best categorized as 'covenant mountains'—mountains whose religious significance stems from the role that they play in salvation history, in the establishment and maintenance of the covenant relationship between Yahweh and his people.[42] In the tradition presently under discussion, Zion's role as *the* covenant mountain *par excellence* was expanded as earlier covenants with Adam, Noah and the patriarchs (and perhaps even with Moses) were brought into relationship with this mountain. Zion became the origin, as well as the goal, of Israel's *Heilsgeschichte*. Just as the prophets projected the Zion ideal into the future, seeing it as the place of the consummation of salvation history, these traditions retrojected Zion into the past, seeing it as the centre of salvation history from earliest times.

Our special interest here is in the role of Mount Zion *qua* mountain. It is important to note that these earlier events have been incorporated into Zion *Heilsgeschichte* by means of the sacred mountain idea, either by identifying biblical mountains with Mount Zion (e.g. Moriah, Ararat) or by reading mountains into the biblical account and then making the Zion identification (e.g. Adam and Mount Moriah, Jacob at 'Luz on the mountains'). In the cases of the Noah and Jacob traditions in particular, it is clearly evident that the role of the mountains was introduced prior to and independent of any Zion connection.[43] So it can be said that in Second-Temple Judaism the mountain *qua* mountain was considered a place where salvation-historical events should occur, and it was by means of the mountain nature of Zion that earlier events in Israel's history were gathered around Zion.

The second important development in Zion theology which has a bearing on our mountain investigation is the great interest shown during this period in Zion as a cosmic centre. In the formation and development of OT Zion theology, as we have seen, some influence of the cosmic mountain ideas of the ancient Near East can be detected, though these are marginal and far from the centre of OT thought.[44] In the period under discussion, however, when Hellenism with its syncretistic religious tendencies flowed like a tide over the Mediterranean world, cosmic ideas[45] flooded into the religious thought of Judaism and were taken up into its Zion theology.[46]

To begin with, the Omphalos myth, whose influence on OT thought appears to have been minimal,[47] was, by the beginning of the period under discussion, an explicit part of Zion theology. The earliest evidence of this is the use of ὀμφαλός to render טבור in a description of Jerusalem in LXX Ezek 38.12 (cf. LXX Judg 9.37). Josephus also reports that ὀμφαλός was commonly applied to Jerusalem; his decidedly non-mythological explanation of this term (i.e. the centre of Judea) does not conceal its cosmic origins.[48] Likewise, the cosmic navel idea is to the fore in early apocalyptic literature. In Jubilees, Shem's inheritance is described as 'the middle of the earth', and Mount Zion, which falls in Shem's territory, is 'the centre of the navel of the earth' (Jub 8.12, 19). And Enoch, on one of his cosmic journeys, travels to 'the middle of the earth'—which from the description can only be Jerusalem[49]—where he sees 'a holy mountain' (1 Enoch 26).

It is important to note that in these early connections of Zion theology with the Omphalos myth, the mountain aspect of Zion is prominent. In Jub 8.19, not only is the navel said to be Mount Zion, but this mountain, along with Mount Sinai and the Garden of Eden, have been 'holy places facing each other' since the time of creation.[50] In 1 Enoch 26 as well it is 'a holy mountain' that is found at the centre of the earth. These references suggest that the mountain aspect of Zion served as the vehicle by which navel mythology came to be firmly attached to Jewish thought about the temple.

In Rabbinic tradition, where the Omphalos myth is frequently encountered in midrashic speculation about the temple, the mountain setting receded into the background as other aspects—e.g., the foundation stone of the temple[51] or the Sanhedrin[52]—were seen as the navel of the earth. The mountain link was not forgotten: the site of the creation of Adam, for example, identified as Mount Moriah, is described as 'a clean place on the navel of the earth'.[53] But generally speaking, the link between 'navel' and 'mountain', which was to the fore in apocalyptic literature, received less attention from the Rabbis.

In the Rabbinic ascription of the Omphalos myth to Zion, the idea of 'centre' is present. Jerusalem and/or the temple are regularly referred to as the centre or bosom of the earth,[54] and this idea is linked with the navel concept: the Sanhedrin, for example, is called 'navel' because it meets in Jerusalem, the centre of the earth.[55] The emphasis in Rabbinic tradition, however, falls on other aspects of the myth,[56] particularly as these are associated with the *Shetiyyah* (or foundation) stone of the temple. This stone, on which the ark was supposed to have rested (Cant R. 3.10 §4; Pesiḳ. R. Kah. 26.4), and which in one strand of tradition is identified with Jacob's stone (Pirke R. El. 35; Midr. Ps 91.7), is seen as playing an important part in the structure and creation of the world. It is the stone which supports not only the temple, but the whole world as well;[57] from it the world was created, just as (it was assumed) the formation of an embryo moved outwards from the navel.[58] Further, the tradition that Zion or Jerusalem was the foundation or starting point of creation is common without reference to the Omphalos myth.[59]

Cosmic influence is also apparent in the emphasis on the height of Zion. The temple is said to be higher than all of Eretz Israel, which in turn is higher than the rest of the world.[60] Thus the land of Israel was not affected by the flood,[61] so that the dove was able to find an olive branch on the Mount of Olives to bring to Noah.[62] The tradition that the temple is the source of light for the world[63] is probably another result of the influence of cosmic ideas.

Also of importance here is the cosmic notion of the *axis mundi*— i.e. of Zion as the sacred site which links heaven, earth and the underworld. In the Second-Temple period, the *axis mundi* appears in connection with mountains other than Zion that are seen as sites of revelation or points of entrance into the heavenly realm.[64] In Rabbinic literature, however, *axis mundi* ideas are explicitly associated with the temple site. Again, the mountain aspect of Zion is not prominent. It may well be, as in the case of the navel idea, that the mountain aspect of Zion was the vehicle by which the *axis mundi* concept came into Jewish thought. But if this was the case, the vehicle was largely discarded by the time the Rabbinic tradition crystallized.

The most graphic expression of the link between the temple and the heavenly sphere appears in Pesiḳ. R. 40.6, a Tannaitic passage concerning the land of Moriah:

> the land which, if it were an arrow, would shoot up through the heavens directly to the heavenly altar.[65]

Elsewhere the role of the temple site as the 'gate of heaven' is prominent,[66] and the temple or its altar is said to be 'directly opposite' the throne of glory or the heavenly holy of holies.[67]

The temple site is also clearly associated with the waters of the deep and the underworld. The pits under the altar into which the libations flowed were from Tannaitic times said to lead to the abyss (Sukk. 49a), though there was a disagreement as to whether the pits were dug by David or were there from creation (Sukk. 49a, 53a). The *Shetiyyah* stone appears in this tradition as that which holds back the waters of the abyss from flooding the earth.[68] From this material it can be seen that although the mountain link here is not as clear as in the case of the Omphalos myth, the cosmic mountain idea of the *axis mundi* has also become attached to Zion.

Another element of cosmic mythology incorporated into the Zion theology of the period was the growing belief that a heavenly Jerusalem and temple lay behind the corresponding earthly realities.[69] Motivation for this growing belief—which was incorporated into

Jewish eschatology as the notion of a heavenly Jerusalem descending to earth in the last day[70]—is to be found in the widespread disillusionment with the earthly temple which was a feature of the Second-Temple period.[71] Nowhere, however, do we find the idea of a heavenly *Urbild* for the sacred mountain itself.[72] It appears that ideas of Zion as a cosmic mountain and of the temple as a replica of the heavenly sanctuary were parallel developments that were not brought into a relationship with each other. Nevertheless, though the mountain was not always prominent in the cosmic elaborations of the Zion traditions, there can be little doubt that Zion's *mountain* nature served as an important bridge by which cosmic ideas were incorporated into the Zion theology of the Second-Temple period.

In Jewish thinking about Zion as a present reality during this period, then, the mountain continued to be an important feature—one which often formed the nucleus around which other motifs came to expression. Mountain themes and terminology were often introduced into the interpretation of biblical passages dealing with Zion, and the appearance of הר was on occasion sufficient in itself to draw the text in which it stood into a Zion orbit. In addition, the mountain aspect of Zion was the catalyst for two major developments in the Zion theology of the period: (1) Mount Zion/Moriah as the centre of salvation history from the time of creation, and (2) Zion as a cosmic centre.

(ii) *In Eschatological Perspective*
In discussing the place of Zion in OT prophetic literature, we observed that one of the most pervasive and durable elements of eschatological hope was the expectation of a gathering of the scattered nation to a restored and purified holy mountain of God. This expectation was the hub around which a number of subsidiary themes evolved: e.g. the pilgrimage of the nations to Zion; the enthronement of Yahweh or his anointed; the eschatological banquet; the renewal of Torah.[73] Throughout the Second-Temple period and beyond, this OT expectation continued to be a living tradition—a state of affairs which is not surprising when one considers factors in this period (e.g. a growing Diaspora during the Persian and Ptolemaic eras, the Seleucid desecration of the temple, and eventually the Roman destruction of the temple and scattering of the nation) which would provide fertile soil indeed for such hope. Despite changes in Jewish eschatology during this period (e.g. a growing belief in

resurrection, the sharp contrast sometimes drawn between This Age and the Age to Come, the incorporation of cosmic elements)[74] Zion eschatology provided one of the unshakable pillars on which Judaism rested during this troubled time.[75]

Throughout the literature of this period we find numerous reiterations of traditional Zion eschatology. Tob 14.5-7, for example, is representative of a number of extended passages which, though in a variety of literary styles, repeat the OT hope for the restoration of Zion and the gathering of the scattered nation:

> And afterward they will return, all of them, from their captivity, and build up Jerusalem with honour, and the house of God shall be builded in her, even as the prophets of Israel spake concerning her. And all the nations which are in the whole earth, all shall turn and fear God truly, and all shall leave their idols, who err after their false error. And they shall bless the everlasting God in righteousness. All the children of Israel that are delivered in those days, remembering God in truth, shall be gathered together and come to Jerusalem and shall dwell for ever in the land of Abraham with security, and it shall be given over to them; and they that love God in truth shall rejoice, and they that do sin and unrighteousness shall cease from all the earth.[76]

These passages contain the expectation of a rebuilt, glorious temple and of a future central role for Jerusalem.[77] The gathering of the scattered exiles is another important theme in these passages—a theme which also frequently appears elsewhere,[78] especially in the Targums where the gathering of the exiles is repeatedly inserted into the text.[79] The petition that God should return the exiles and restore Jerusalem is a common feature of prayer and liturgy as well.[80]

The eschatological pilgrimage of the Gentiles to Jerusalem is also often depicted in the literature of Second-Temple Judaism. They come to Zion to bring gifts to the Messiah[81] and to escort Israelites back to their homeland.[82] In some references to the eschatological procession, the Gentiles are viewed in favourable terms and are depicted as sharing in the Messianic blessing;[83] elsewhere this procession is seen in more negative terms: the nations come for judgment and servitude.[84] Though generalizations do not always hold true, it does seem fair to say that a more positive attitude towards Gentiles is to be found in the Diaspora literature (Tobit, the LXX, Sib Or III), while a more negative outlook is found in Palestinian literature (Ps Sol; 2 Bar; Jub; 1 Enoch is the rare exception).[85] It is not correct, however, to characterize the difference between these negative and positive outlooks as a case of particularism versus universalism. Even in literature that looks for the eschatological salvation of the Gentiles, the universal perspective arises out of and is seen as a consequence of the particularistic hope of the restoration of Jerusalem and the return of the exiles to the land. Jewish universalism is paradoxical: only by means of an emphasis on the particularity of Jerusalem and Zion does the possibility of Gentile salvation arise.

As for other elements of Zion eschatology, the literature of this period contains occasional references to the enthronement theme,[86] the renewal of Torah,[87] and Zion as the location of the messianic banquet for the righteous.[88]

As in the Zion eschatology of the OT, the mountain aspect of Zion continued to be an important part of eschatological expectation in this period. The passages to be discussed fall into two groups. The first is a collection of purely terminological references, where interest in the mountain as an eschatological site is limited to the use of the mountain term itself. In a second group of passages, the mountain *qua* mountain plays a more prominent role in the literary expression of the eschatological hope. We will deal with these two groups of passages in turn.

In the former category, there are, first of all, a half dozen LXX and Targumic references in which ὄρος or טור, used of eschatological Zion, is present in a manner not found in the original. In LXX Is 63.18, as we have seen,[89] the LXX renders the obscure Hebrew of the MT as ἵνα μικρὸν κληρονομήσωμεν τοῦ ὄρους τοῦ ἁγίου σου, which has the effect of turning a historical statement into an eschatological one. Similar transformations of historical passages dealing with (Mount) Zion are found in Tg. Is 31.4, where Mount Zion is described as the place where 'the kingdom of the Lord of hosts comes to dwell', and Tg. Is 16.1 where the statement

They have sent lambs to the ruler of the land,
from Sela, by way of the desert,
to the mount of the daughter of Zion (MT)

is interpreted in terms of the eschatological pilgrimage of the nations to Mount Zion with gifts for the Messiah:

They shall bring tribute to the Messiah of Israel, who has prevailed over him who was as a wilderness, to the mount of the congregation of Zion (טור כנשתא דציון).

In addition, LXX Is 65.9 and Tg. Ezek 37.22 replace the plural 'mountains' in eschatological passages with the specific term 'holy mountain', and LXX Ezek 34.26 has τοῦ ὄρους μου for the MT גבעתי as the place of eschatological gathering for the flock of God.

In Rabbinic literature, there are scattered references to the role of Mount Moriah/Zion in the time of eschatological fulfilment.[90] Generally speaking, however, these passages are to be seen as the result of biblical mountains becoming caught in the exegetical net of Rabbinic *middoth*, rather than as evidence for any sustained Rabbinic interest in the eschatological mountain *per se*. In this material, in fact, interest in Zion eschatology is sharply attenuated as the focus rests more and more on Zion as a cosmic centre.

Of more significance is 4Q171 3.8-13, a section of the Qumran commentary on Ps 37 which expresses the expectation that the Qumran community would one day 'possess the mountain of the height of Israel' (cf. Ezek 17.23; 20.40), while the present occupants of Zion would be 'cut off and destroyed for ever'. This passage represents only one strand in the community's belief about Jerusalem and the temple; such diversity provides evidence of the struggle which the sect underwent as it attempted to adjust its inherited Zion theology and eschatology to its central conviction of the absolute corruption and ruin of contemporary Jerusalem. We find, for example, a collection of references in which the community itself is seen as a replacement for the Jerusalem temple:[91] atoning for sin by means of prayer and holiness,[92] the community is described as בית קודש (sanctuary), as קודש קודשים (holy of holies),[93] and, in one much-discussed reference, perhaps as מקדש אדם.[94] At the same time, there are several unmistakable references to the appearance of a heavenly, divinely-constructed temple.[95] In addition, we have in the Temple scroll a lengthy description of an ideal temple, which has been interpreted either as an interim man-made sanctuary for the period until Yahweh builds the eschatological temple,[96] or as the eschatological temple itself.[97] Though the nature of the relationship among these various elements is not easy to determine,[98] it is apparent that interest in 'community-as-temple' did not crowd out more traditional Jerusalem- and temple-centred eschatology—which, as in 4Q171 3.8-13, could even be expressed in traditional mountain terms.[99]

Finally, we cite the account in 1 Maccabees of the evacuation of the Jews in Gilead of Galilee by Judas, and their procession to Jerusalem (1 Macc 5.23, 45-54). Though historically this procession was necessitated by the fact that the Maccabeans were not yet strong enough to offer protection to Jews in Galilee, the author of 1 Maccabees narrates the event in such a way that clear echoes can be detected of OT passages dealing with the expected final gathering to Zion:

> And Judas gathered together those that lagged behind and encouraged the people all the way through until he came to the land of Judah. And they went up to Mount Zion (εἰς ὄρος Σιων) with gladness and joy, and offered whole burnt offerings, because not so much as one of them was slain until they returned in peace (1 Macc 5.53f.).

As Goldstein observes, 'our author's echoes here of prophecies of Isaiah are so audacious that he must be hinting that he saw their fulfilment in Judas' victories'.[100] While not overlooking the fact that 1 Maccabees in Greek is a translation from the Hebrew original, Goldstein sees similarities with the LXX of Isaiah in ἐπισυνάγων (v. 53; cf. LXX Is 52.12) and εὐφροσύνη (v. 54; cf. LXX Is 35.10; 51.11; 52.9). If he is correct (and there are other examples of such 'realized eschatology' in the early Hasmonaean period[101]), then this passage provides us with another use of ὄρος Σιων in an eschatological context.

The 'realized eschatology' of the Hasmonaeans provides the basis for the first example in our second category of eschatological mountain references. This example has to do with the curious note in Josephus that Simon, or one of his successors, went to considerable trouble to level the mountain (ὄρος) near the temple on which the Jerusalem citadel had stood.[102] Though Josephus explains this action from a military-strategic point of view, the inclusion of statements that the action was taken 'in order that the Temple might be higher' and 'in order that it [i.e. the citadel mountain] might not block the view of the Temple' indicates a more fundamental interest in the height and visibility of the temple itself—which may well have been related to the common expectations of Zion eschatology. Given the belief in Hasmonaean circles that they were seeing the dawn of the eschatological age, it is probable that this action of insuring that no ὄρος stood higher than that of the temple was meant as a fulfilment of such passages as Is 2.2f.[103]

In contrast to such a woodenly literalistic interpretation of the OT hope, other passages from the Second-Temple period which fall into this category are extravagantly symbolic. In Jewish apocalyptic literature—with its interest in cosmic speculation, its periodizing and calendrical concerns, its penchant for elaborate symbolism, and its radical two-age eschatology—the mountain of Zion appears as a striking apocalyptic symbol and traditional Zion eschatology is reworked with heavily cosmic overtones. This blending of cosmic and eschatalogical themes is one of the distinctives of apocalyptic. In Rabbinic literature, by contrast, similar cosmic and eschatological motifs are treated independently and run along parallel tracks.

The first of these apocalyptic reworkings of Zion eschatology is found in Jubilees. Though the author of Jubilees believed that an eschatological beginning had been made in the events of the Maccabean-Hasmonaean era,[104] he still looked forward to the final coming of the New Age when 'the sanctuary of the Lord shall be made in Jerusalem on Mount Zion' and God himself becomes 'King on Mount Zion for all eternity' (Jub 1.27f.).[105] Expanding on this traditional piece of Zion eschatology, the author goes on to see this mountain as a cosmic mountain, one of the four 'holy places' which God has placed on the earth:

> For the Lord has four places on the earth, the Garden of Eden, and the Mount of the East, and this mountain on which thou art this day, Mount Sinai, and Mount Zion (which) will be sanctified in the new creation for the sanctification of the earth; through it will the earth be sanctified from all (its) guilt and uncleanness throughout the generations of the world (Jub 4.26).

Of these four cosmic centres, only Mount Zion has eschatological significance; it will be the source of sanctification in the new creation. Since for the author of Jubilees it is God himself who will build the sanctuary (Jub 1.17), we encounter here the coalescence of the twin apocalyptic themes of (1) the heavenly origin of the eschatological city/temple, and (2) Zion as a cosmic mountain.[106]

In 2 Bar 36.1–40.4, Mount Zion comes into view in the interpretation of an apocalyptic vision in which the overthrow of the nations and the restoration of Israel is depicted by means of the symbols of a vine, a fountain, a forest and mountains. At the end of the vision, only one cedar is left before the (messianic) vine and fountain. It is identified as the 'last leader of that time' who

> will be bound, and they will take him up to Mount Zion, and My Messiah will convict him of all his impieties, and will gather and set before him all the works of his hosts. And afterwards he will put him to death and protect the rest of My people which shall be

found in the place which I have chosen. And his principate will
stand forever, until the world of corruption is at an end, and then
the times aforesaid are fulfilled (2 Bar 40.1-3).

The appearance here of Mount Zion—which does not appear in the
vision itself and is not equated with any of the elements of the
vision[107]—is striking. Mount Zion has been introduced into the
interpretation in an almost matter-of-fact way, as the place where the
leader of the Gentile nations will be destroyed, where the people of
God will be established and where the Messianic Age will be
inaugurated.

The most elaborate development of Zion eschatology is to be
found in Ezra's vision and its interpretation in 4 Ezra 13.1-53, a
passage in which the mountain aspect of Zion is the centre of
attention and is explicitly linked with messianic expectation. In the
passage the nations of the earth, depicted as a 'multitude of men',
gather to do battle with the messianic 'Man':

there was gathered together from the four winds of heaven an
innumerable multitude of men to make war against the Man that
came out of the sea. And I beheld, and lo! he cut out for himself a
great mountain and flew up upon it. But I sought to see the region
or place from whence the mountain had been cut out; and I could
not (vv. 5-7).

After the battle with the multitude on this mountain, the author
continues:

I beheld the same Man come down from the mountain and call
unto him another multitude which was peaceable. Then drew nigh
unto him the faces of many men, some of which were glad, some
sorrowful; while some were in bonds, some brought others who
should be offered (vv. 12f.).

The description of the messianic mountain as 'cut out' in a manner
not apparent to Ezra must be seen as a clear allusion to the stone 'cut
out by no human hand' which grows to be a great mountain in the
vision in Dan 2.34f.,[108] even though in Daniel the mountain is a
symbol for the kingdom while here it is the site of messianic
activity.[109] In addition, the terms 'Man' (vv. 3, 5, etc.), 'Son' (v. 52),
and the phrases 'as it were the form of a man' and 'this man flew with
the clouds of heaven' (v. 3) appear to have been heavily influenced by
the apocalyptic vision in Dan 7.[110]

In the interpretation, however, the mountain where all this

messianic activity takes place is explicitly stated to be Mount Zion,[111] and the mysterious origin of the mountain is interpreted in terms of the common expectation of the heavenly origin of eschatological Zion:

> It shall be, when all the nations hear his voice, every man shall leave his own land and the warfare which they have one against another; and an innumerable multitude shall be gathered together as thou didst see, desiring to come and fight against him. But he shall stand upon the summit of Mount Sion. And Sion shall come and shall be made manifest to all men prepared and builded, even as thou didst see the mountain cut out without hands. But he, my Son, shall reprove the nations . . . (vv. 33-37).

Even if the vision arose independently of this interpretation, as Stone contends,[112] the interpretation is by no means inappropriate, for traditional elements of Zion eschatology are present in the vision itself: the defeat of the nations; the gathering of a 'peaceable multitude' to the mountain (identified as the ten lost tribes; v. 40); the pilgrimage of the nations carrying Israelites back to the land (v. 13). The interpretation just reinforces this imagery with its picture of Mount Zion as the universally visible place of judgment and fulfilment.

Thus in Ezra's vision and its interpretation the mountain has been singled out from other elements of the Zion complex and has become the means by which traditional Zion eschatology has been united with features from Dan 2 and 7—with both then being incorporated into an apocalyptic vision of the coming of the End in which the mountain is the central symbol. While not wanting to pre-judge our study of Matthew, it is instructive to note that this vision in 4 Ezra—which must be seen as the high water mark of eschatological mountain interest—was composed at about the same time as the First Gospel.

To sum up our survey of Zion eschatology, then, we can say that in 4 Ezra 13 we see in a most striking manner what has been observed as a general tendency throughout Second-Temple Judaism: (1) Zion eschatology as developed in the OT continued to be a central element in Jewish hope for the future; and (2) the mountain aspect of Zion continued to be an important part of this eschatological hope—to such an extent in Ezra's vision that eschatological significance appears to be attached to the mountain first of all *qua* mountain, and only secondarily as Mount Zion.

2. *Other Mountains*

Interest during this period in 'the mountain' as a site and symbol of religious, theological and particularly eschatological significance was not limited to Mount Zion. An investigation of references in the literature of the period to other mountains—actual or literary, named or unnamed—produces an almost chaotic and disorderly collection of exegetical traditions, literary constructions and historical situations which are linked only by a common interest in the mountain symbol or setting. The existence of this lively interest tends to confirm the observation made several times during our investigation of Zion traditions in the Second-Temple period that it was the mountain aspect of Zion which often served as focus and catalyst for the developing tradition. Zion theology, then, was one part of a wider religious pattern in Judaism. It both rested on and contributed to the tendency to view הההר/טורא/τὸ ὄρος as religiously significant and theologically suggestive terms.

(i) *Mountains in Biblical Narratives*
One indication of the general interest in mountains in this period is the tendency to insert mountains into the reformulation of biblical narratives. We have already seen one aspect of this in our discussion of the retrojection of Zion into biblical *Heilsgeschichte*.[113] But even prior to and independent of this development in Zion theology, mountains are frequently encountered in exegetical and midrashic treatments of OT texts where none appear in the MT.

The greatest concentration of such references is found in Jubilees, though the tendency is present in Josephus, in Qumran literature and in Rabbinic traditions as well. Examples of this tendency include the following: mountains are mentioned in the Jubilees account of creation (Jub 2.7); Enoch is said to have offered sacrifices 'on the mountain' in Eden (Jub 4.25); Noah's ark came to rest on Mount Lûbar, where he proceeded to build an altar, plant a vineyard and dwell with his sons (Jub 6.1; 7.1, 16f.; 1QapGen 12.13; Jos. *Ant.* 1.109), and where eventually he was buried (Jub 10.15); the portions allotted to Noah's sons contain a number of specific mountains (Jub 8.21-26); Isaac dwelt in the mountains (Jub 29.19; cf. 36.19f.); Bethel, where Abraham built an altar and Jacob encountered God, is called 'the mountain of Bethel' (1QapGen 21.7) and 'Luz on the mountains' (Jub 27.19); the Cave of Machpelah, where the patriarchs were buried, is located 'in the mountain' (Jub 46.9f.); Miriam is said to have died on a mountain (*Ant.* 4.78; Soṭ. 13b).

Many of these mountain traditions were later incorporated into the 'retrojection of Zion' tendency found in its most complete form in Targum Pseudo-Jonathan and Pirke de R. Eliezer. Such incorporation was possible, however, only because mountain settings were previously introduced into the narrative tradition. Interest in 'the mountain' for its own sake as a religiously significant site came first.

(ii) *Cosmic Mountains*

Another aspect of the interest in mountains during this period is the increasing frequency of cosmic mountains, especially in Jewish apocalyptic literature. In contrast to the cosmic elaboration of Zion theology, the Omphalos myth is not prominent here. Rather, mountains are seen as places of significance in the cosmic order of things and especially as points of entrance into the heavenly realm.

The greatest concentration of this tendency is in 1 Enoch, particularly in the 'Dream Visions' (1 Enoch 17–36)—passages describing Enoch's two journeys through the cosmically significant sites of the earth and the underworld. Mountains appear to form the most significant feature of the author's geo-cosmology. In the short span of chs. 17–26, Enoch sees twelve separate mountains or groups of mountains—including the 'mountains of the darkness of winter' (17.7), the seven burning mountains which serve as the place of imprisonment for the stars and the hosts of heaven (18.13-16), the 'great and high mountain' with its four repositories for the souls of the dead (22.1-4), and the 'holy mountain' at 'the centre of the earth' (i.e. Jerusalem).[114]

On three occasions Enoch encounters a mountain whose summit reaches into heaven (17.2; 18.6-8; 24.2–25.7). In the latter two references, the mountain is at the centre of a group of seven mountains and is said to be 'like the throne of God'. Of particular interest is the third reference:

> this high mountain, which thou hast seen, whose summit is like the throne of God, is His throne, where the Holy Great One, the Lord of Glory, the Eternal King, will sit, when He shall come down to visit the earth with goodness (1 Enoch 25:3),

The passage goes on to describe the fragrant tree near the throne which will be transplanted to the holy place (i.e. the temple) at the time of the End for the enjoyment of the faithful. This passage is a fine example of the way in which cosmic and eschatological motifs were combined in apocalyptic thought. The mountain with its peak

in heaven is at the same time and for that reason the place at which
God will initiate the events of the End. It is instructive to note that
although Zion eschatology is present in the passage (25.5f.), the
cosmic-eschatological mountain is clearly to be distinguished from
Zion, for the fragrant tree is to be transplanted from this mountain to
the temple site (25.5). The idea of the mountain as a site of
eschatological activity is here independent of Mount Zion. Eschatological significance can be the property of 'the mountain', not just of
Zion.

In several other apocalyptic references to cosmic mountains as
points of entry into heaven, the emphasis falls on the mountain as a
place of revelation, i.e. as the starting point for a revelation of the
mysteries of the heavenly sphere. Levi's vision of the seven heavens
can be taken as typical of this genre:

> Then there fell upon me a sleep, and I beheld a high mountain and
> I was upon it. And behold, the heavens were opened, and an angel
> of God said to me, Levi, enter. And I entered from the first heaven,
> and I saw . . . (T. Levi 2.5-7).

In Apoc Abr 18f., Abraham also views the throne of God and the
firmaments of heaven from a mountain vantage point.

Thus the incorporation of cosmic mountain symbolism into
apocalyptic literature produced both the characteristic fusion of
cosmic and eschatological mountain ideas and the concept of the
mountain as a place of revelation.

(iii) *Mount Sinai*

There is some evidence that Sinai was also viewed during this period
as a cosmic mountain, i.e. as the contact point between heaven and
earth where the Torah came to earth.[115] Because of the presence of
this cosmic influence, it may be the case that the Sinai tradition has
in turn helped to shape the development of the apocalyptic mountain
of revelation concept. But Sinai also appears to have been the
prototype during this period for another kind of mountain of
revelation—viz. a mountain on which revelations of the divine will or
of future events are bestowed. The lengthiest and most deliberate
examples in which Sinai functions in such a way are Jubilees and
11QTemple. Each of these works presents itself as a revelation
committed to Moses on Sinai,[116] and each contains a mixture of the
divine will for the present and the divine plan for the future. Also to
be noted in this connection is Apoc Abr 21–23 where, as Abraham

views heaven from the vantage point of Mount Horeb, God outlines for him the course of history from the fall until the punishment of the heathen and the ingathering of Israel.

Similar revelations are entrusted to other biblical figures on other mountains. Naphtali, for example, receives a vision on the Mount of Olives in which the future captivity of Israel is revealed (T. Naph. 5.1-8). Baruch is summoned to stand upon Mount Zion to receive a revelation of the events of the End (2 Bar 13.1). And on Mount Nebo everything that will take place in Israel until the coming of the End is revealed to Moses.[117] It is probable that the common underlying schema here of the mountain as a place of revelation was constructed on the pattern of Sinai, with Ezekiel's mountain of revelation (cf. Ezek 40.2) having some influence as well.

One other point to note about Mount Sinai is the increased emphasis that it received in Rabbinic tradition,[118] even to the point of displacing Zion.[119] In view of the Rabbinic emphasis on the Torah, such a development is not surprising.

(iv) *Miscellaneous Eschatological Mountains*

In addition to the cosmic-eschatological mountain of 1 Enoch 25.3, there are several other traditions in which eschatological events are expected to take place on mountains other than Zion. One of these has to do with the belief that at the time of the destruction of the first temple, a number of temple fixtures—including the ark—were hidden away to be miraculously revealed in the last days.[120] Though there was no consistent tradition as to the identity of the person who hid the vessels[121] or to the location of the hiding place,[122] in three passages a mountain plays a central part.

First, in 2 Macc 2.1-9, there is the tradition that Jeremiah took the tabernacle and ark 'away to the mountain which Moses had ascended to view the inheritance of God'. There he hid these things, saying:

> Unknown shall the spot be until God gather the people together
> and mercy come; then indeed shall the Lord disclose these things,
> and the glory of the Lord shall be seen . . . (2 Macc 2.7f.).

Here Mount Nebo is the place where God will gather his people and where eschatological fulfilment will take place.

The second pertinent passage is in the first century AD work, Lives of the Prophets.[123] Here there is another reference to Jeremiah's hiding of the ark, this time 'in a rock' (ἐν πέτρᾳ) between the two mountains on which Moses and Aaron were buried. In the last days, however,

> the ark will ... come forth from the rock and will be placed on Mount Sinai, and all the saints will be assembled to it there, awaiting the Lord and fleeing from the enemy wishing to destroy them (Life Jer. 11f.).

In this passage it is Sinai that plays the part of the eschatological mountain of gathering and of the revelation of the temple vessels.

A similar tradition is found in Samaritanism, though here of course with respect to the vessels not of the Solomonic temple but of the tabernacle. Josephus gives the following account of a would-be Samaritan Messiah:

> The Samaritan nation too was not exempt from disturbance. For a man who made light of mendacity and in all his designs catered to the mob, rallied them, bidding them to go in a body with him to Mount Gerizim, which in their belief is the most sacred of mountains. He assured them that on their arrival he would show them the sacred vessels which were buried there where Moses had deposited them (*Ant.* 18.85).

Despite Josephus's anti-eschatological bias, we can clearly see the Samaritan equivalent of the mountain-top revelation of the sacred vessels which was also present in Judaism.

There are two things to note about the function of the mountain as an eschatological site in these passages. First, though the role played by the mountain in each narrative is virtually identical, the mountains themselves are distinct. It appears that the eschatological significance of each of these mountains arose not from anything connected with the individual mountain itself, but from the general category 'mountain'. Mountains as mountains were viewed as sites full of eschatological potential. Secondly and more specifically, eschatological elements usually associated with Mount Zion appear to have floated free of their Zion moorings to become reattached to other religiously significant mountains. In the first two examples, the eschatological gathering of the scattered people is expected to take place not at Zion but at Mount Nebo (2 Macc 2.7) or Mount Sinai (Life Jer. 11f.); συνάγω—virtually a technical term for the eschatological gathering— appears in both passages. Though no specific Zion element appears in the Samaritan example cited from Josephus, we will have occasion to observe later the extent to which Mount Gerizim took over the functions and traditions of Zion.[124]

In addition to these examples in which some connections with Zion eschatology are evident, there are also independent eschatological traditions associated with other mountains. Mention has already been made of the stone in Daniel's vision which grew to be a great mountain filling the earth, and thereby symbolizing the final establishment of the world-wide kingdom of God (Dan 2.35, 44f.). Further, in Life Dan. 21, two mountains provide the portents for the final judgment and return of the exiles to Israel. Eschatological events are also associated with the Mount of Olives. Such an association, of course, is already present in Zech 14.4. But in the literature under review there are two further blocks of material to be mentioned. In Rabbinic literature we find the tradition that the resurrection was expected to take place on the Mount of Olives. This tradition, which is found in Pesiḳ. R.31.10 and Tg. Cant 8.5 and which has also influenced the artistic depiction of Ezek 37 in the Dura-Europos synagogue,[125] appears to be the product of the combination of Zech 14.4, which speaks of the Messiah splitting open the Mount of Olives, and the idea—such as is found in 1 Enoch 22.1-4—that the souls of the dead were stored in hollow places in a great mountain.[126]

Admittedly, this Rabbinc tradition cannot be dated early with any confidence. Yet there is evidence from the first century AD that eschatological activity was directly associated with the Mount of Olives. Josephus relates the account of a messianic pretender who led a band of enthusiasts from the desert to the Mount of Olives, from which he proposed to make his way into Jerusalem (*War* 2.261-263; *Ant.* 20.169-172). While in the former account no particular significance is attached to the mountain itself, in the parallel passage in *Antiquities* the Mount of Olives becomes the centre of the story and the place where eschatological signs were to be demonstrated. In this account, Josephus says that the prophet

> advised the common people to go out with him to the mountain called (the Mount of) Olives, which lies opposite the city at a distance of five furlongs. For he asserted that he wished to demonstrate from there (ἐκεῖθεν) that at his command the walls of Jerusalem would fall down through which he promised to provide them an entrance to the city.

The Mount of Olives appears in this account as more than an incidental geographical detail; the mountain seems to have been consciously chosen as the site of this promised eschatological demonstration.

No particular pattern emerges from these scattered references. But perhaps this lack of pattern is the point: in separate traditions and in a variety of ways the mountain repeatedly appears in this literature as the place where eschatological and messianic events are to occur.

(v) *The Mountain of the King*

There is a further set of Rabbinic passages—many of which can be dated to the Tannaitic period—which should be mentioned here: those that refer to the 'Mountain of the King' (הר המלך/טור מלכא).[127] Despite the highly suggestive nature of the term, for the most part it was used in a purely geographic sense, referring to an extended area within Palestine that included the hill country of Judah (Men. 87a) and extended into Galilee (Lam R. 2.2 §4). The casual way in which the term is used in these passages suggests that by Tannaitic times it was well established.

The origin of the expression, however, is shrouded in obscurity. Since there are no messianic overtones in these passages,[128] it is likely that the term was used originally with reference to an actual historical king. Büchler suggests Hyrcanus, Alexander, Herod or Agrippa. But Herod's reign was too unpopular and Agrippa's too short to account for the emergence during either of their reigns of such a term. A Hasmonaean origin is more likely[129]—though against this stands the complete absence of the term in earlier literature. So the question of origin has to remain open.

Despite the prosaic and purely geographical use of the term in most of the references, it is hard to believe that such a term could have arisen without reference to the OT idea of the king enthroned on the holy mountain of God (e.g. Ps 2.6). On the basis of Mek. Amal. 2.41-45, where the 'Mountain of the King' is linked with the temple mount on the basis of Dt 3.25, and Tg. Judg 4.5, where Deborah is said to have sat and judged on טור מלכא, it may be conjectured that the term originally referred to the king in Jerusalem and was later extended to cover the whole territory over which he ruled. Just as the term Zion could be extended to refer to the whole land, so terms referring to the temple mountain were often extended in a similar manner.[130] Perhaps something similar has happened in the case of the 'Mountain of the King'. Many questions remain, but these references provide some evidence for the continuation of the belief that טור/הר was the place of enthronement.[131]

(vi) *Mount Gerizim*

The final collection of material to be considered here is that set of traditions associated with Mount Gerizim, the holy mountain of the Samaritans. As a result of renewed interest in Samaritan studies in recent years,[132] it has been increasingly realized that the emergence of Samaritanism as a distinct entity separate from Judaism was a long and gradual process which did not reach completion until well after AD 70.[133] In the Second-Temple period the Samaritans were a sect within the wider limits of Judaism—a group with a distinct self-understanding, yet one which continued to be in contact with and hence open to influence from the religious circles centred on Jerusalem.[134] In fact, it was during the period from the third century BC to the beginning of the Christian era that the crystallization of distinctive Samaritan doctrines was in the process of taking place,[135] and in this formative period Samaritanism drew heavily on the theology and traditions of Judaism.[136] That is particularly true with respect to Samaritan theology concerning Mount Gerizim, for the influence of developed Jewish traditions about Mount Zion is apparent at every turn. In the extant Samaritan literature,[137] whole blocks of traditions have been detached from Zion and transplanted to Gerizim.

The fundamental Samaritan belief about Gerizim was that it is the one place of worship chosen by God for his people. The prayer for the Sabbath morning service speaks of

> the chosen place, Mount Gerizim, the house of God, towards Luz, the Mount of Thine inheritance and of Thy presence, the place which Thou hast made thy dwelling, Yahweh, the sanctuary, Yahweh, which Thy hand hath fashioned.[138]

The election of Gerizim is one of five items in the Samaritan creed,[139] and has been enshrined in the unique tenth commandment of the Samaritan decalogue[140] by means of the insertion of Dt 11.29 and 27.2-7 into the Ex 20 account—the one important difference being that the altar is commanded to be set upon Mount Gerizim rather than Mount Ebal. The eternal election of Mount Gerizim is indicated elsewhere in the Samaritan Pentateuch by means of the shift from the imperfect of בחר as is found in Dt 12:14 (MT) to the perfect.

In later Samaritan tradition, in addition to the cosmic idea that Mount Gerizim was not submerged by the flood (*Memar Marqah* 3.4; Gen R. 32.10; Dt R. 3.6), there is the same retrojection of Mount

Gerizim into patriarchal history as we found earlier in the case of
Mount Zion. In the *Memar* we read that Adam was created on
Mount Gerizim (2.10); that Noah sacrificed there (3.4); that Abraham
and Jacob built altars there (Bethel and Gerizim are equated; 2.10);
that the offering of Isaac took place there (2.10); that Moses longed to
see this 'goodly mountain'—i.e. as mentioned in Dt 3.25 (2.10).
Themes which, as we have seen, arose during a long period of
development within Judaism, were simply transferred from Mount
Zion to Mount Gerizim.[141] The 'detachability' of these Zion
traditions is also seen in the fact that they were taken over by later
Jewish Christian tradition and applied to Golgotha.[142]

The Samaritans also expected that Mount Gerizim would be the
focus of eschatological events. We have already noted the passage in
Josephus dealing with a would-be Samaritan Messiah and his
promise to reveal the vessels of the tabernacle on Mount Gerizim.[143]
That this was not just an isolated incident is evident from later
Samaritan expectations concerning the messianic *Taheb* who would
restore worship on Mount Gerizim:

> Happy is the *Taheb* and happy are his disciples who are like him,
> and happy is the world when he, who brings his peace with him,
> comes and reveals the divine favour and purifies Mount Gerizim,
> the house of God, and removes trouble from Israel, when God
> gives him great victory, overcoming therewith the whole world.[144]

Such an eschatological note, however, is not strongly sounded in
later Samaritan literature. With respect to the *Defter*, Brown speaks
of 'a certain hopelessness . . . as far as concerns their natural rejuvena-
tion', which stands in marked contrast, for example, to the tone of the
Eighteen Benedictions of Jewish liturgy.[145] The fervour of the
eschatological hope centred on Mount Gerizim evidently cooled
considerably in the years following AD 70; its high point seems to
have coincided with the peak of Jewish interest in the mountain as an
eschatological site.

So, while some of our description of Gerizim theology depends on
later sources, the earlier evidence is sufficient to demonstrate that in
Samaritanism we can see another indication of the trends which we
have observed throughout this section, namely, (1) the widespread
interest in mountains as sites for religious and (especially) eschatological activity, and (2) the extent to which most of these traditions

were free-floating—capable of becoming attached to various sacred mountains.

3. *Mountain Concepts in Hellenism*

Our study to this point has been confined to Jewish materials. This limitation of focus has come about not only out of a desire to keep the study within manageable limits, but also because it is here that the significant comparative materials are to be found. Even if one were to assume—with Strecker, Walker, *et al.*—a radical Gentile orientation of the final redaction of Matthew, one would find that the possible parallels in purely Hellenistic literature to Matthew's mountain conceptions are not extensive, and that what parallels there are have already been absorbed into Second-Temple Judaism.

The most immediate indication of this can be seen in the fact that there is a general decrease of interest in religiously significant mountains and mountain symbolism when one moves into the more Hellenistic of the Jewish literature. This is true of the Sibylline Oracles and, with the exception of his statement that Mount Sinai was the dwelling place of God,[146] of Josephus as well. It is especially true of Philo. Mountains, in fact, often fall out of Philo's rehearsal of OT narratives.[147] Few traces of traditional Zion theology are to be found in his writings,[148] and he frequently passes up opportunities to give symbolic interpretations of mountains where they do occur in Scripture.[149] Where mountain symbolism is developed by Philo, it is usually restricted to allegorical treatments of the higher path which the mind travels to God.[150]

Mountains were important in classical Greek religion. Every high mountain with its peak in the clouds was thought to be the dwelling place of Zeus,[151] and Mount Olympus in particular was seen as the gathering place of the gods. The Omphalos myth was also present, especially at Delphi.[152] Both of these mountain concepts, however, were aspects of a widespread cosmic mountain mythology which was not confined to Greece and had thoroughly permeated Judaism in the Second-Temple period.[153]

In the cults and mysteries of the Hellenistic world, mountain symbolism did not play a significant role. Although locally sacred mountains were on occasion fused with Greek religion in a syncretistic way,[154] from what can be known of the mystery religions themselves it appears that mountains did not have a central place in these cults or their soteriological dramas.[155]

Mountains, however, do appear with some frequency in Gnostic literature—both that which has been preserved in Christian sources and that recently discovered in the Nag Hammadi library. Given the radical dualism of the Gnostics and their disenchantment with the physical world, it is not surprising that mountains play little part in the Gnostic systems of thought themselves, as these have been summarized, for example, by Irenaeus (*Ag. Her.* 1). As places where the secret knowledge of these Gnostic myths was revealed, however, mountains are frequently encountered. Many of these mountain revelations are in the form of resurrection appearances of Jesus to his disciples on the Mount of Olives: Peter and the other disciples gather on this mountain where they see a great light and hear an extended Gnostic discourse;[156] John also receives special instructions from the Lord on the Mount of Olives;[157] the twelve disciples in company with seven women receive a revelation of the origin of the universe while on a mountain which, though in Galilee, is called the Mount of Olives.[158] The Mount of Olives, however, is not the only mountain of revelation; Mary,[159] James,[160] and John[161] are recipients of heavenly revelations on other unnamed mountains, and Paul is taken on a journey through the heavens from a mountain-top in Jericho.[162]

It is apparent that in these mountain references we do not encounter anything new. These mountain passages do not represent a radically new Gnostic formulation, but are rather to be seen as examples of the apocalyptic mountain of revelation in Christian and Gnostic dress. In fact, not only are both of the apocalyptic forms (the mountain as a point of entry into the heavens, and as a place where divine knowledge is communicated) present here, but they are present in conjunction with such other apocalyptic motifs as the cave on the mountain[163] and the mountain as the hiding place for things to be revealed in the end times.[164] And in the Christianized form in which we encounter them here, these mountains of revelation are not restricted to Gnostic literature but are found in more mainstream Christian sources as well.[165]

Now in our attempts to determine the function of τὸ ὄρος in the mountain passages of the First Gospel, these Gnostic and Christian parallels will be important at several points for comparative purposes. But as far as background material is concerned, the study of this later Gnostic literature reveals no trace of a peculiarly Gnostic type of religiously significant mountain which might have been in existence— assuming the existence of pre-Christian form of Gnosticism—when the Gospel tradition was taking shape. The Gnostic mountain of revelation is rooted in Jewish and Jewish Christian apocalyptic. Hellenism, then, does not provide any parallels to Matthew's mountain scenes that are not already present in Hellenized Judaism.

4. *Summary and Conclusions*

Our investigation of the mountain symbolism and theology that was present in Second-Temple Judaism cannot be allowed to pre-judge questions which have been raised about the mountain passages in the First Gospel. Nevertheless, we can draw the following summarizing conclusions about this aspect of the milieu in which the Gospel of Matthew was probably written:

(a) First, speaking in general terms, there was a common and widespread interest in the mountain as a symbol or site of religious and theological significance. The mountain feature of Zion was frequently emphasized for its own sake, and served as the catalyst or hook for several significant developments in Zion theology during this period—viz. Zion as a cosmic centre, and as the focal point of *Heilsgeschichte*. Indeed, the mere presence of הר in a biblical text was on occasion sufficient warrant to interpret the passage in accordance with Zion theology. Furthermore, the mountain continued to be a key element in Zion eschatology, not least in apocalyptic literature where cosmic and eschatological elements became fused in a new way. Interest in the religious significance of mountains was not restricted to Zion, for we have been able to point to a whole array of texts which bristle with theologically significant references to mountains—actual or symbolic, named or unnamed. So, in view of such a widespread interest in the mountain as a religious site and theological symbol, it is not very likely that the readers for whom Matthew was written would have taken the highly stylized and structurally prominent mountain settings of the First Gospel as merely casual geographical references.

(b) Of the two important OT mountains, Zion figures much more prominently than Sinai in the literary and religious imagination of the period. As in the OT itself, the continuing existence of the Jerusalem temple provided a wellspring for the Zion tradition that was not present for Sinai. So it was just not the case that a first-century reader, encountering a religiously significant mountain, would naturally and immediately think of Sinai.

(c) More specifically, we have been able to identify four types of religiously significant mountains in this period—at least two of which (the first and last in the following list) are uniquely Jewish:

1. *Covenant Mountain.* The sacred mountains of the OT are best viewed as covenant mountains, i.e. sacred sites at which the covenant relationship between Yahweh and his people was established and maintained. The most striking manifestation of this mountain category in the Second-Temple period was the tendency within Judaism (and later within Samaritanism and Jewish Christianity) to read the sacred mountain into the biblical text as the site for every significant event in *Heilsgeschichte*, even back to the creation of Adam himself.

2. *Cosmic Mountain.* With Hellenistic influence in Palestine providing a bridge for foreign ideas, there was an influx of cosmic concepts into Jewish thinking about Mount Zion and about mountains in general. Zion was seen as both Omphalos and *axis mundi*, and Zion along with other mountains became points of entry into the heavenly sphere. In Jewish apocalypticism there was a fusion of cosmic and eschatological elements—elements which in later Rabbinic thought were treated separately.

3. *Mountain of Revelation.* Particularly in Jewish apocalypticism, mountains often appear as places where revelations are bestowed. Revelational mountains were generally of two kinds: in one—which probably developed under the influence of the Sinai narratives—the revelation is in the form of divinely-given information, often concerning the events leading up to the End; in the other—which is more characteristically cosmic—the mountain provides a point of entry into the heavenly sphere, where the secrets of heaven and earth are revealed.

4. *Eschatological Mountain.* In this period, with its heightened interest in eschatology generally, there was also a focus on mountains as sites for eschatological events. The roots for such an interest are found in OT Zion eschatology, and there are many passages which focus on Mount Zion as an eschatological site. But other mountains functioned in this way as well: the mountain of the Messiah in 4 Ezra 13; the cosmic mountain of 1 Enoch 24–25; the various mountains associated with the revelation of the temple vessels; Mount Gerizim; the Mount of Olives which was the site of one attempted messianic gathering and was to be the place of the resurrection; Mount Sinai where Moses and Aaron were expected to gather the faithful. In all of these traditions the mountain *qua* mountain is treated as a site that

carries with it the potential and promise of eschatological activity. As such, the eschatological mountain is a special form of covenant mountain: it is the mountain where covenant promises are consummated.

(d) With respect to the eschatological mountain traditions, we have seen that in Rabbinic and Samaritan traditions after the end of the first century AD, eschatological interest in sacred mountains was sharply attenuated—with interest thereafter shifting to the mountain as a cosmic or salvation-historical centre. In other words, the First Gospel was written at a time when interest in mountains as eschatological and messianic sites had reached its high water mark.

(e) Finally, we noted on several occasions the extent to which traditions most frequently associated with Zion could float and become attached to other mountains. This was true on a large scale with respect to Mount Gerizim (and later Golgotha), and a similar phenomenon appears in a less thoroughgoing way in the case of several other mountains.

PART III
MOUNTAIN SETTINGS IN MATTHEAN REDACTION

Chapter 6

THE MOUNTAIN OF TEMPTATION

1. *The Mountain Setting in Pre-Matthean Tradition*

The first mountain scene in the Gospel of Matthew is found in the Temptation Narrative (4.8-10). Here, in the third temptation, the devil takes Jesus εἰς ὄρος ὑψηλὸν λίαν, where he offers him world sovereignty on the condition that Jesus worship him.

The same temptation account is found in Lk 4.5-8, though with two significant differences: the mountain setting is absent,[1] and the second and third temptations are in inverse order. There are, therefore, several questions about the history of the tradition that will have to be faced before dealing with the scene in its Matthean context. With respect to the temptation account in Q, it will be necessary to ask (1) whether a mountain setting was original to Q, and (2) which of the evangelists has preserved the original order. Then—particularly if it becomes apparent that Matthew took over a mountain setting found originally in Q—we will have to inquire as to the significance of this setting for the interpretation of the narrative in its original form and *Sitz im Leben*.

Analysis of the Synoptic temptation narratives reveals that behind Mt 4.1-11 and Lk 4.1-13 lie two sources: Mk 1.12f., which influenced the wording of the introductory and concluding framework in both Matthew and Luke, and a Q passage, which contained the triple temptation dialogue.[2] The Q account of the temptation appears to have stood as part of a section which included the preaching of John the Baptist (Mt 3.7-12 // Lk 3.7-9, 15-18) and probably the baptism of Jesus (Mt 3.13-17 // Lk 3.21f.).[3]

Our first source-critical question has to do with the origin of the mountain setting of Matthew's third temptation: Is it a Matthean insertion, or did the evangelist find it in his Q source? Most scholars believe that Matthew took εἰς ὄρος ὑψηλόν[4] from Q;[5] only rarely does one encounter the opposite opinion.[6] The fact that specific settings (desert,[7] temple) are given for the other two temptations, points in the former direction, for it leads one to expect that a setting for the third temptation would be specified as well. Moreover, Luke's version of this temptation shows signs of extensive editorial revision.[8] In particular, the verb ἀνάγω, which appears in Lk 4.5 in place of the mountain reference, is a characteristically Lukan word,[9] and the omission of a mountain setting along with the addition of ἐν στιγμῇ χρόνου can be seen as the result of Luke's desire to clarify the purely visionary nature of this temptation.[10] Thus both the form of the narrative and certain features characteristic of Luke's redactional style favour the view that the mountain reference was originally part of the Q account.

What about the original order of the three temptations in the Q scene? By far the greatest number of commentators believe that Matthew rather than Luke has preserved the original order.[11] The cumulative effect of the following four arguments has often been taken as decisive for the originality of the Matthean order.

The first of these arguments has to do with the form of the individual temptations. Dibelius,[12] Lagrange,[13] and others[14] note that the mountain temptation is formally distinct from the others, which suggests that the other two belong together as a pair. The desert and temple temptations are constructed on the basis of imperatives (εἰπέ, βάλε) predicated on the statement εἰ υἱὸς εἶ τοῦ θεοῦ. The mountain temptation, by contrast, lacks both an imperative and the υἱός statement, and is characterized by a more direct role on the part of the tempter.

A second argument relates to the sequence of the three temptations which, many feel, moves to a more logical climax in the Matthean order: in the final temptation in Matthew, Jesus is offered not private release from hunger, nor deliverance from personal harm, but world sovereignty.[15] This argument has been spelled out most fully by Gaechter[16] and Schulz,[17] who suggest that the Matthean sequence moves in an ascending order as to the audacity of the temptations (private miracle, presuming on God's protection, worshipping the devil), as to geographical height (desert, temple wall, high mountain), and as to the size of the audience (no one, temple crowd, whole world). Gaechter adds that these sequences seem not to be artfully contrived, but must have been part of the essential nature of the story.

Dupont,[18] followed by others,[19] proposes a third argument based on the order of the quotations from Deuteronomy. Although as found in Matthew the quotations are in inverted sequence (Dt 8.3; 6.16; 6.13), Dupont suggests that they correspond to the order of the events in Exodus—the provision of manna in the wilderness (Ex 16), the testing at Massah (Ex 17), and the worship of the golden calf (Ex 32).[20]

Given such persuasive arguments for the originality of the Matthean order, one wonders why Luke would have wanted to tamper with it at all. In fact, it was precisely the apparent inexplicability of such a Lukan restructuring of the narrative that led several earlier scholars to the conclusion that Matthew's more satisfying climactic structure must have been a rearrangement of the original order as preserved by Luke.[21] Such a negative argument, however, dissolved when Conzelmann demonstrated that the Lukan order—in which the temptations culminate in Jerusalem—corresponds to the geographical structure of Luke's Gospel in which Jesus moves relentlessly towards Jerusalem for his final struggle with Satan.[22] Though this geographical argument did not originate with Conzelmann,[23] he incorporated it into such a thorough and convincing analysis of Luke's theology that it is now generally accepted—and this is the fourth argument—that Luke had evident theological and structural reasons for altering the order.

These are weighty arguments. On re-examination, however, they are not as decisive as has generally been assumed.[24] Let us look again at each in turn.

Although there are undeniable similarities between the desert and temple temptations, the presence of a long OT quotation by Satan in the second suggests that the formal correspondence between the two is by no means complete. Such an observation does not necessarily favour the other order, but it does raise doubts as to whether the first two temptations in Matthew's order are bound together as closely as has been thought.

Further, it is by no means certain that a first-century Jewish reader would see the mountain temptation as the climax of the piece. Not only is the sequence 'desert–mountain–temple' a more natural geographical progression in a Palestinian setting,[25] but the temple—as the focal point of Jewish life—would be seen as the most important of the three settings. In addition, while world sovereignty had been achieved on a purely human level before, in the temple temptation

explicit *divine* aid was in view. Schürmann argues that the temptations reach a high point with the temple scene in that, whereas in
the two temptations the negative elements of distrust and apostasy
are readily apparent, in the temple temptation the appeal is to
something that has the appearance of the good—viz. trust in God for
protection.[26] And in the scriptural citation by Satan, and Jesus'
categorical response, 'You shall not put the Lord your God to the
test', it is possible to see the final approach and the final refusal.

As for the third argument, based on the order of events in Exodus,
the uncertainty of Dupont's assertion that Dt 6.13 refers to the
worship of the golden calf[27] weakens the force of this argument
considerably.

Finally, while it is true that Luke's Gospel ends in Jerusalem, and
that this would provide a theological motivation for changing the
order, it is just as true that Matthew's Gospel ends on a mountain
(28.16-20) and it is clear that Matthew intended a correspondence to
be seen between the final temptation and the closing scene of the
Gospel, for which the mountain setting is one of the links.[28] This
does not, of course, necessitate the conclusion that it was Matthew
who changed the original order, but it does mean that Matthew had
just as much theological motivation to do so as did Luke.

None of these observations, however, can be taken as a demonstration of the priority of the Lukan order; the evidence in favour of
the Matthean order is not to be lightly set aside. And in view of the
arguments outlined above, it would be foolhardy to build any thesis
solely on the assumption that Matthew changed the order. All we
have attempted to show here is that the possibility is by no means to
be ruled out. We will return later to the question with a further factor
favouring the Lukan order after we have looked at the significance of
the mountain temptation in its Q setting.

In the form-critical examination of the Temptation Narrative, it is
generally agreed that the closest formal parallels are to be found in
disputations over the interpretation of Scripture in Haggadic
midrash.[29] As for the relationship between the Mark and Q accounts,
similarities between the two (temptation by the devil, desert locale,
forty days) make it not at all likely that they were originally two
independent accounts.[30] Yet it is also difficult to see any direct
relationship between them, such as that Q is an expansion of Mark or
Mark a summary of Q.[31] It seems more likely that Mark is a
summary of, and Q a later form of, a single temptation story which
was rooted in Dt 8.2-5.[32]

The question of the purpose of the Temptation Narrative—particularly as this question bears on the nature of the temptations themselves—is one of the most vexed questions in the discussion of the passage. A common approach has been to interpret the temptations as appeals to Jesus to conform his ministry to the pattern of current Jewish messianic expectation, that is, to provide miraculous manna in the wilderness, to give a showy display of his divine authorization, to seek to achieve world sovereignty by political means. The purpose of the narrative, in this view, was to defend the messiahship of Jesus against Jewish accusations that he did not qualify as Messiah.[33] Such a position, however, was challenged by Bultmann, who denied that the temptations were messianic at all.[34] He argued that the idea of a messianic programme is not present, especially in the first two temptations (e.g. it is the hunger of Jesus and not of the crowds on which the first temptation turns!), and that for the early Church miracles were always signs of Jesus' messiahship, and not hindrances to it. So, Bultmann insisted, the temptations are to be seen as paradigmatic rather than messianic: Jesus provides an example for any pious man who wishes to obey God. The purpose of the narrative in his view is to defend Jesus against the Hellenistic charge that he was a magician. And though Bultmann later allowed a messianic element to be seen in the narrative,[35] his earlier position has influenced many.[36]

There are, however, incontrovertible messianic overtones throughout the narrative—e.g. the messianic notion of world sovereignty in the third temptation, which at least by the time of the Q version was bound together with the other two;[37] the almost certain reference to the messianically understood Ps 2 in the υἱὸς τοῦ θεοῦ statement;[38] and the significance of each of the sites in current eschatological expectation.[39] This means that a messianic significance for these temptations can be ruled out only by ignoring important interpretative indicators in the text.

A way forward in the interpretation of the Temptation Narrative has been demonstrated by a number of scholars who have shown that the key to the passage can be found in the conjunction of the Son statements with the Deuteronomy quotations, i.e. in a pattern of Sonship that is given definition in terms of ideal Israel.[40] The temptation is certainly not that Jesus should doubt the *fact* of his Sonship.[41] Nor is its central thrust that Jesus should adopt another pattern of messiahship, even though current Jewish messianic expectations stand in the background of Satan's appeals. Rather, the heart of the temptation is to be found in an attempt to induce Jesus to be unfaithful to a pattern of Sonship conceived in terms of the relationship between ideal Israel and the divine Father. It is a temptation away from Sonship, rather than towards any specific pattern of messianism.[42] Jesus was called to live out in his own experience the Sonship that was to have characterized Israel— a relationship with God which involves dependence on him for the provision of needs, trust in his presence without the need for demonstration, and acceptance of sovereignty only on his terms. Jewish messianism is present as the context in which this testing of the Son takes place, but it does not occupy centre stage.

Although the Temptation Narrative must have assumed its present form in the context of the Church's debate with the Synagogue, its original purpose was probably not a polemic against Jewish messianism[43] or Zealotism.[44] It would have been quite possible to refute Jewish conceptions or the Zealot call to armed resistance without presenting Jesus as Israel personified, God's true Son who like Israel was tested in the wilderness but unlike Israel stayed faithful to his calling. Such a view of the Messiah as a corporate personality who sums up in himself all that Israel was called to be—together with the view of *Heilsgeschichte* that it implies—is a profound piece of theological work. It is therefore preferable to view the triple temptation narrative as a theological construction which, while taking shape in the context of the Church's debate with and separation from the Synagogue in a pre-AD 70 situation, nevertheless was formed for the benefit of the Church, to deal in a creative way with the theological questions raised by that debate—such questions as: Why did Jesus' messiahship differ from common expectation? How did a Church that was being forced out of the Synagogue stand in continuity with the OT people of God? Who can claim to be true Israel?

Given such an interpretation of the Temptation Narrative—that popular messianism was the background against which Jesus' Sonship was put to the test—the question remains: What specific role was played by the mountain setting in the Q narrative? Though scholarship has not dealt with this question in any detail, several possibilities have been suggested.

The most common suggestion has to do with several passages in which a religious figure ascends a mountain to view the land, either the land of Israel or the whole world. The most prominent of these figures is Moses, who in Num 27.12-14, Dt 3.23-28, 32.48-52 and 34.1-4 is commanded by God to ascend Mount Nebo to the top of Pisgah so that he can see the land of promise which, because of the sin of the people at Meribah, he was not allowed to enter. This mountain experience of Moses did not go unnoticed in later exegesis; most significantly it provided the model for a similar experience in 2 Bar 76.1-4 where Baruch, before his assumption to heaven, was commanded to ascend to the top of 'that mountain' after forty days, whence he would see passing before him the territory of the whole earth.[45] Abraham was also invited by God to view the land that would be given to his descendants—though the fact that this was done from a mountain was implicit rather than explicit, in both the Genesis account (Gen 13.14-18) and in a later commentary on this passage (1QapGen 21.8-14).[46]

Echoes of these traditions—especially those having to do with Moses[47]—are no doubt present in the mountain temptation.[48] The features of ascent, viewing the land, and promise of possession, which are common to these traditions (with the exception of 2 Bar 76.1-4, where the element of possession is lacking), are all present in the mountain temptation. And as Dupont and Hill have observed, there are also verbal similarities between LXX Dt 34.1-4 and Mt 4.8f., though these do not extend beyond the common elements just mentioned.[49]

The parallel, however, is by no means complete. In these OT passages it is God, not Satan, who does the showing of the land. And though there is some evidence that in the Second-Temple period Satan tended to replace God in accounts of testing,[50] the idea of testing or tempting is not found in these passages. Furthermore, though Moses was barred from entering the land because Israel had failed to be the 'obedient Son' at Meribah, there is little similarity between the situations of Moses on Mount Nebo and Jesus on the Mountain of Temptation.

So, though the Moses/Nebo parallel has had some influence on the external details of the scene of temptation, it does not have any bearing on the content of the temptation. Because of the influence of Deuteronomy on the Temptation Narrative—both in its quotations and in the setting of the first temptation—commentators have been drawn to Moses/Deuteronomy parallels for the mountain temptation. But the presence of the temple as the site of the other temptation is an indication that we need not be bound to a Deuteronomy background here. Thus we are justified to look further for relevant parallels.

Kelly has noted several passages in Jewish literature where testing experiences and mountain settings are brought together.[51] The most striking of these is Apoc Abr 12-13, a midrash on Gen 15 with some elements from Gen 22 and 1 Ki 19.7f. (c. AD 100). In this passage, Abraham travels forty days and forty nights, fasting on the way, to Mount Horeb, where he is to offer a sacrifice in the presence of the angels. While he waits on the mountain, Azazel approaches and attempts to induce him to flee from the mountain of God. The presence of Azazel in this passage may be explained on the basis of the cosmic nature of the mountain: the mountain reaches into the heavenly realm, which thus brings Abraham into contact with Satan as well as the angels. Satan's presence on the Mountain of Temptation, however, does not really reflect such cosmic ideas, for he is active in the desert and the temple as well.

Kelly also cites two rabbinic parallels in which it might be argued that the elements of testing and mountain are brought together. In Sanh. 89b, a late tradition, Satan attempts to turn Abraham aside from his sacrifice of Isaac by means of three arguments based on scriptural quotations. In Dt R. 11.5, a Tannaitic tradition, the Angel of Death enters into a scriptural debate with Moses to convince him that the time of his death has arrived. Yet, since neither Mount Moriah nor Mount Nebo is mentioned in these passages, the parallels are helpful only for the overall disputational form of the Temptation Narrative, and not for an understanding of the mountain setting itself.

Though the presence of Satan does not necessarily indicate that the mountain setting owes something to cosmic mountain mythology, the emphasis on height in Mt 4.8 probably does. The high mountain from the vantage point of which the whole world can be viewed bears some resemblance to the cosmic mountain of apocalyptic literature— i.e. the mountain which is the centre and high point of the earth.[52]

None of these suggestions, however, comes close to the real significance of the Mountain of Temptation. In a perceptive article, Rengstorf argues that this mountain should be seen against the background of Mount Zion, especially with reference to Ps 2.6-8.[53] While Ps 2.7 is undoubtedly the source of the phrase εἰ υἰὸς εἶ τοῦ θεοῦ in the desert and temple temptations,[54] the absence of this phrase from the mountain temptation has caused some to look elsewhere for the background to Satan's offer here.[55] However, since in Ps 2.7f. the declaration 'You are my Son' is followed immediately by the promise of world sovereignty, it is scarcely to be doubted that the devil's promise of world sovereignty in Mt 4.8f. // Lk 4.5-7 arises from Ps 2.6-8 as well:[56] since you are the Son of God—Satan in effect is saying—world sovereignty is yours for the asking; ask of me and I will give it. Indeed the two passages are bound together by the important word δώσω. If this connection between Ps 2.6-8 and the mountain temptation is valid, then the Mountain of Temptation must be seen against the background of God's 'holy mountain' (v. 6), the place of the enthronement of the Son—and thus, because of the messianic interpretation of Ps 2, against a background of eschatological Zion, the place where the world-throne would be established.[57]

As corroborative evidence, we can point to several features pertaining to the Zion symbol of Second-Temple Judaism. As already noted,[58] it was widely expected that eschatological Zion would be a lofty site (e.g. Is 2.2), a mountain high enough that the eschatological pilgrimage of exiles and Gentiles could be clearly seen (1 Bar 4.36f.; 5.1-9; Ps Sol 11.1-3). Also, the term 'high mountain', which appears frequently in apocalyptic literature, is often used in connection with Zion as the cosmic-eschatological mountain of the final consummation.[59] So, although Mosaic and cosmic overtones are present, the dominant feature in the background to the mountain setting of the third temptation is Mount Zion.

Yet this is not all that can be said about the mountain setting of the third temptation. To this point we have followed most commentators in attempting to explain the mountain setting in terms of elements drawn solely from the mountain temptation itself (viz. ascent, viewing, possession, wilderness quotations from Dt, etc.). Scholarly study of the Temptation Narrative as a whole, however, has generally recognized that the three temptations are not to be seen as three isolated units, but must be interpreted together, with their corresponding elements brought into relationship with each other. Jesus' responses, for example, are to be understood, not individually in the context of their respective temptation scenes, but together, as a unified expression of a view of Sonship that incorporates a recapitulation of the Israel wilderness ideal. Similarly, the approaches of the devil belong together, probably as representing a combination of Ps 2 with current messianic expectations. In view of this, is it not likely that the settings as well are to be taken as part of a unified pattern?

With the exception of the wilderness setting, the settings of the three temptations have seldom been brought to the centre of the discussion. In fact, the wilderness setting of the first temptation, together with the quotations from Deuteronomy, have led to the result that the temple and mountain settings are obscured behind an interpretation based on the whole Moses–Deuteronomy–wilderness-Israel cluster of ideas. But when attention is focussed on the settings as important parts of the narrative, one becomes aware of a tension. For, though quotations from Deuteronomy are found in each temptation, only one temptation is located in the wilderness; the temple and mountain cannot really be fully brought into connection with this complex of ideas.[60] The question then is this: Is there a pattern to be found in the settings which will resolve this tension?

It is our contention that there is. Each of the three settings—wilderness, temple, mountain—was a place where eschatological events were expected to occur.[61] The existence of the Qumran community in the wilderness highlights a common belief in the Second-Temple period that the eschatological age of fulfilment would be accompanied by a return of the circumstances that characterized Israel's earliest experience in the wilderness.[62] As for the temple, we have already noted the place that it occupied, along with Jerusalem and Zion, in Jewish eschatological expectation.[63] In addition to material discussed above, further evidence that messianic signs were expected to be performed at the temple can be mentioned.[64] Pesik̦. R. 36.2, which contains the statement that the Messiah will proclaim Israel's redemption from the roof of the temple, is perhaps too late to be directly relevant here. In the writings of Josephus, however, there are several accounts of would-be Messiahs attempting to gain followings by promising to display 'signs of deliverance' in the temple.[65] As for the mountain, we have taken pains to demonstrate that mountain settings and symbols appear in a variety of traditions across the whole spectrum of Judaism in eschatological connections.[66]

None of this, of course, argues against the importance of Sonship as the key to the passage. These settings help to create a background of Jewish messianic expectation against which the devil's attempts to deflect Jesus from the path of Sonship take place. This does not mean that the Temptation Narrative should be interpreted as a complete rejection of Jewish messianic expectation. The point of the passage is rather that it is only by the humble obedience of the Son to the Father that fulfilment will take place. Because the desert, temple and mountain were the three main places at which eschatological fulfilment was expected, they were entirely appropriate settings for the testing of the Son and his vocation.

This analysis provides grounds for further speculation about the original order of this series of settings. There are a few scraps of evidence that may indicate that the sequence 'desert–mountain–temple' played a part in current eschatological expectation.[67] In Ezekiel, the prophet describes the departure of the glory of Yahweh as a process that took place in stages, ending at 'the mountain which is on the east side of the city' (i.e. the Mount of Olives; Ezek 11.23; cf. 10.4, 18). In his later vision on Mount Zion, Ezekiel watches the glory of the Lord return to the temple by the same route (43.2). This process fascinated the Rabbis, who expanded it to a series of ten steps: from the ark cover to the cherubim, to the threshold, to the court, altar, roof, wall, town, mountain, and finally to the wilderness; then, after waiting six months in the wilderness for Israel to repent, the divine presence returned to heaven.[68]

There is not much to build on here; the tradition is late[69] and deals with the departure of the glory of Yahweh, rather than its return. Nevertheless, we do have here the sequence of temple (even the temple roof!)–mountain–desert. And the tradition is explicitly based on Ezekiel, where the return is expected to retrace the path of the departure.

Moreover, there is some first-century evidence of eschatological deliverence moving along the path: 'desert–mountain–temple'. Josephus recounts the story of an Egyptian false prophet who gathered a band of followers in the desert, led them to the Mount of Olives, and there promised to lead them in a miraculous manner into the city and temple.[70] And from Josephus's description, it is apparent that these geographical settings played an important part in the event. In addition, the Gospel of Mark follows the same pattern: from the wilderness (1.12f.), to the Mount of Olives (11.1), and from there into the city and temple (11.11).

These may well be fragile threads with which to weave an argument. As indicated above, the evidence favouring the originality of the Matthean order is not to be lightly set aside, and no redactional argument can be built solely on the thesis that Matthew altered the order. Moreover, the prominence of Zion symbolism in the mountain temptation weighs against—even if it is not entirely incompatible with—a sequence depending so heavily on Mount of Olives traditions.

The main point insisted on here is that the geographical references play an important role in the narrative by acting as eschatologically significant settings for the three temptations. Nevertheless, it is at least possible that the settings of the Temptation Narrative were originally structured in Q to follow the eschatological sequence 'desert–mountain–temple'.

2. The Mountain Setting in Matthew's Redaction

We are now in a position to consider the importance of the mountain setting in Matthew's account of the Temptation. We shall look first at his handling of the Temptation Narrative as a whole, and then concentrate on the mountain itself.

The alterations that Matthew makes in his sources as he composes his Temptation Narrative are few:

(a)   the addition of καὶ νύκτας τεσσεράκοντα in v. 2;
(b)   the completion of the OT quotation by the addition of ἀλλ' ἐπὶ παντὶ ῥήματι ἐκπορευομένῳ διὰ στόματος θεοῦ in v. 4;[71]
(c)   the insertion of ὕπαγε, σατανᾶ in v. 10;[72]
(d)   the possible inversion of order in the last two temptations.[73]

While these horizontal changes are not extensive, they take on significance when seen in the vertical context of Matthew's Gospel as a whole.

It has been frequently noted that the addition of καὶ νύκτας τεσσεράκοντα in v. 2 makes an explicit connection between the fasting of Jesus and similar periods of fasting experienced by Elijah on his way to Horeb (1 Ki 19.8) and Moses on Sinai (Ex 24.18; 34.28; Dt 9.8, 18).[74] Although Gerhardsson sees 'forty days and forty nights' as only a traditional phrase drawn from the vocabulary of fasting which makes no reference at all to Moses (he sees only Israel typology at work here),[75] the presence of Moses typology here is made certain by the fact that Mosaic parallels appear elsewhere in the Gospel—particularly in Matthew's Infancy Narrative.[76] Just as Moses was miraculously delivered from the slaughter of Jewish infants, so was Jesus.[77] And just as Moses was forced to spend time in exile from his people, so was Jesus. In fact, Matthew signals his interest in Moses clearly in 2.20, where he speaks of Jesus' return to Palestine in a sentence drawn almost *verbatim* from the account of Moses' return from exile in Ex 4.19.[78]

But Moses typology does not dominate the introductory section of Matthew's Gospel. Davies and Kingsbury demonstrate that although

Moses typology is present, it is a secondary theme that has been caught up into the larger pattern of Son-christology.[79] When Jesus returns from Egypt, the parallel is drawn not with Moses[80] but with God's 'Son' Israel (Mt 2.15). In the Temptation Narrative, though Mosaic overtones are present in the period of fasting and the mountain viewing of the land, the dominant theme of the passage is, as we have see, the Sonship of Jesus who, unlike the first Son Israel, remains in a relationship of humble obedience to the Father. It is here that the explanation of Matthew's extension of the OT quotation in v. 4 is to be found: by the addition of the phrase, 'but by every word which proceeds from the mouth of God', Matthew changes Jesus' reply from a negative statement that food is not of ultimate significance for the Son of God to the positive one that humble obedience to the word of God is.[81] The climax of the whole introductory section of Matthew's Gospel (1.1–4.16) is found in the baptismal voice from heaven where Jesus receives his messianic calling as God's Son, and in the subsequent temptation where the nature of this relationship to the Father is explored and tested.

Yet 3.13–4.11 is not just the climax of the introductory section. In his development of Son-christology in this passage, Matthew states a theme which resonates throughout his Gospel. Several scholars have drawn attention to the undoubted interest that Matthew displays throughout his Gospel—especially in the Passion Narrative and in material related to it—in Jesus as the 'Son' or the 'Son of God'.[82] In 16.16, Peter confesses Jesus as 'the Christ, the Son of the living God' (cf. Mk 8.29: 'the Christ'), but then goes on to play the role of Satan in attempting to deflect him from the path of suffering which Sonship demands. In 26.53, Jesus refuses to appeal to his Father (τὸν πατέρα μου) for angelic deliverance from the imminent passion. After confessing his Sonship before the High Priest (26.63f.), the mocking crowds challenge Jesus to prove his Sonship by asking for divine deliverance and coming down from the cross (27.40, 43). Since each of these uses of 'Son of God' is redactional, it is evident that Matthew's prime concern in the Passion Narrative was to show that the path of Sonship into which Jesus was called at baptism led inevitably to the cross.[83] Despite attempts at every turn to deflect him from that path of humble obedience to the Father, Jesus remains faithful to his calling even unto death.

The important role that the Temptation Narrative plays in preparing for the passion can thus be seen. The temptations both foreshadow the passion, in that they recur until they reach a peak at Golgotha, and lead to the passion, in that the path of true Sonship confirmed during the temptation led inevitably to the cross. This is not just literary speculation; by means of several deft redactional touches, Matthew makes this very clear. First of all, as already noted, Matthew inserts ὕπαγε, σατανᾶ into Jesus' final rebuff of Satan's advances. This is echoed in 16.23, where the phrase ὕπαγε ὀπίσω μου, σατανᾶ—taken from Mark (8.33)—appears in Jesus' rejection of the diabolical suggestion made by Peter.[84] Since in 16.13-28 the confession of Jesus as 'Son of God' invokes the shadow of the cross, the insertion of ὕπαγε, σατανᾶ in 4.10 serves to link the issue of Sonship as raised at the Temptation with the path to the cross foreseen by Jesus in 16.21-28. Further, in his redaction of Mark's description of the mocking of the crowds, to Mark's κατάβ[ηθι] ἀπὸ τοῦ σταυροῦ Matthew adds εἰ υἱὸς εἶ τοῦ θεοῦ (27.40). The crowds' challenge to Jesus to prove his Sonship by avoiding the path of suffering is presented in exactly the same terms as Satan's temptations.[85] Likewise, in Jesus' rejection of a miraculous angelic deliverance from the cross (26.53), we seem to have an echo of the temptation in the temple to call on God for angelic deliverance.[86]

Thus Matthew's point is clear: in the Temptation Jesus began to move along a path of humble obedience to the Father which, if continued, would lead inexorably to the cross. Yet this is only half of what Matthew wants to say about Jesus as Son of God. For Matthew, the path of Sonship does not end with crucifixion but goes on to vindication. The glory rejected by the obedient Son at the beginning of the Gospel is fully bestowed at the end.

Hints of this coming vindication are found in the various 'Son of God' confessions which appear throughout the Gospel. Even before the resurrection, the demons (8.29), the disciples (14.33), Peter (16.16), and finally—in the only one of these occurrences not attributable to Matthew's redaction—the centurion (27.54) all recognize Jesus as Son of God. The vindication of the Son is also foreshadowed in the heavenly declaration: 'This is my beloved Son, in whom I am well pleased'—heard not only at the Baptism (3.17), but also at the Transfiguration (17.5), which functions in the Gospel as a proleptic vindication. Furthermore, Senior argues persuasively that Matthew's purpose in including the account of the resurrection of the 'holy ones' as a preamble to the centurion's confession (27.51-53) was to announce the divine vindication of the obedient Son:

death humbly accepted has brought the dawn of the age of resurrection.[87]

But the full declaration of the vindication of the Son appears only at the end of the Gospel, when the resurrected Jesus declares: 'All authority in heaven and on earth has been given to me' (28.18). Although we must leave until later a discussion of the christology of 28.16-20,[88] it is important here to note Kingsbury's observation that the only christological title used in this passage is 'Son' (v. 19).[89] Vindication of the Son is one of the many Matthean themes that come to full and final expression in this closing pericope.

A study of the Temptation Narrative reveals that it is closely linked in Matthew's thinking with this vindication theme as well. In the Baptism account, which sets the stage for the Temptation, Matthew has changed the words spoken from heaven from Mark's σὺ εἶ ὁ υἱός μου to οὗτός ἐστιν ὁ υἱός μου. The significance of this change is not primarily that it turns this into a public statement, but that it points forward to the Transfiguration, where the declaration of Jesus' Sonship is made in exactly the same words (17.5). The Baptism both sets the stage for the theme of the obedient suffering of the Son and points ahead to vindication. Another link between the Temptation and the Transfiguration is forged by the mountain setting of the two events. On the ὄρος ὑψηλὸν λίαν of 4.8, Jesus rejects a path to world sovereignty that would involve apostasy and chooses instead the humble path of obedience leading to the cross; on the ὄρος ὑψηλόν of 17.1, a proleptic vindication of this choice takes place as divine pleasure is reaffirmed ('with whom I am well pleased') and the authority of Jesus is declared ('listen to him'). While the ὄρος references are drawn from Matthew's sources, the link between the two passages in the intention of the evangelist is scarcely to be doubted.[90]

The ultimate statement of vindication, however, is reserved for the mountain scene with which Matthew closes his Gospel (28.16-20). And again, there are clear links to be seen between the third temptation and this closing passage. Many scholars have noted the deliberate thematic parallels between these two passages.[91] As Lange expresses it, the theological tensions raised in the third temptation are resolved in the final scene.[92] In the third temptation, world sovereignty is rejected by Jesus when offered on Satan's terms, even though sovereignty over the nations was promised to the Son (Ps 2.6-8); in the closing mountain scene, full authority over the whole world is bestowed as divine vindication of the path of Sonship which Jesus followed.

Links between these two passages, however, are not restricted to general thematic parallels; explicit verbal links are present as well.[93] One such is the use of the verb προσκυνέω (4.9, 10; 28.17). In 4.9, 10 Jesus refuses to worship Satan, for such is not his due. In 28.17 the disciples worship Jesus, since, as the one who bears universal authority, this is entirely his due. This link is supported by the fact that, though the verb in 4.9, 10 is drawn from Q, it is a characteristic-ally Matthean term. Of the thirteen Matthean occurrences (cf. 2 for Mk, 3 for Lk), six are in material unique to Matthew and five are additions to the Matthean *Vorlage*. Of particular interest is 14.33, where, in striking contrast to Mark, the disciples 'worshipped him, saying "You are the Son of God"'. For Matthew, worship is to be directed not to Satan but to Jesus, the obedient Son of God.

Another link is the use of δίδωμι in 4.8 and 28.18. Although the former use of the term depends on Q and the latter is conditioned to a certain extent by the OT background, on a vertical reading of the Gospel a link is to be seen: the giving of all authority to the Son results from his obedience to the Father and not his worship of Satan. The passages are further linked together by πᾶς, found in 4.9 and repeatedly in 28.18-20, and probably by the title 'Son', which underlies the Temptation Narrative and appears in 28.19.

The term ἐξουσία, appearing prominently in 28.18 and found also in Luke's account of the Temptation (Lk 4.6) would be embarrassing to our thesis if it could be shown that it appeared in Q. For if Matthew really wanted to link these passages together, what better means of doing so than by preserving the key term ἐξουσία? In all probability, however, the term is Lukan.[94] Although ἐξουσία is an important Matthean term, its importance in the First Gospel depends on the context of its usage (e.g. Mt 7.29; 9.8; 28.18), not its frequency. It appears more frequently in Luke (16 times; cf. 10 each for Mt and Mk), especially in the sense of secular authority over the earthly realm[95]—which is essentially the sense in which it is used here. So taking into account the evident Lukan paraphrase throughout this Temptation account, it is not likely that Matthew passed over a Q use of ἐξουσία.

In view of these links between the mountain temptation and the closing pericope—not only in parallel themes but also in several key linguistic details—it is reasonable to conclude that Matthew also intended to link these passages by means of a mountain setting.[96] On the Mountain of Temptation, the devil's offer of world sovereignty was rejected and the course was set that would lead to the cross; on the Mountain of Commissioning, world sovereignty was bestowed and the path of obedient Sonship vindicated. Almost seventy-five years ago Allen observed:

> By inserting the mountain [in 4.8], the editor may have intended to draw a contrast between the mountain upon which Christ refused messianic power with that other mountain (28.16) upon which at a later period He told disciples that all power was given to Him in heaven and upon earth.[97]

While we may want to revise his views of the origin of the term ὄρος, his stress on the deliberate nature of the contrast is entirely accurate. Schmauch and Frieling have spoken of the existence of a 'bow' (*Bogen*) between the Mountain of Temptation and the Mountain of Commissioning, under whose arch the main themes of Matthew's Gospel find their place.[98] Without wanting to minimize the importance of other mountains for Matthew, this is a fair description of the place occupied by the Mountain of Temptation in the structure and theology of the First Gospel.

Structurally, the mountain temptation at the end of Temptation Narrative corresponds to the mountain at the end of the Gospel. The action of the Gospel moves from the wilderness where baptism and temptation take place, on to the holy city where Jesus rejects the help of angels and goes humbly to the cross, and finally to the mountain in Galilee where world sovereignty is bestowed. We suggested some evidence for the position that the Temptation Narrative in Q was structured according to an eschatological-geographical sequence: wilderness–mountain–temple. If this was so, then Matthew broke the sequence so that he could end his Temptation Narrative as he ends his Gospel—on *der Berg der Herrschaft*. Yet even if Matthew's sequence was taken directly from Q, it still remains true that Matthew intended the climax of his Gospel to be foreshadowed in the climax of the Temptation Narrative.

We have argued that the theological significance of the mountain setting in the original narrative was that—along with desert and temple—it functioned as an eschatological site. Specifically, this mountain calls to mind the holy mountain of God in Ps 2.6, on which the Son is enthroned and receives world sovereignty. The third temptation, consequently, raises questions concerning salvation history and eschatological fulfilment, for it creates a tension between the obedience of the Son and the promised mountain enthronement of the Son. In Matthew's redaction, however, this mountain points ahead to the mountain at the end of the Gospel, where the fulfilment of salvation history is announced and where the turning point of the ages is fully begun.[99] The tension created in the opening mountain scene is released only in the final one. So the Mountain of Temptation sets the stage for Matthew's treatment of *Heilsgeschichte*.

But a more important theological issue that comes to focus on the Mountain of Temptation is that of christology—or, rather than speaking in terms of comparative importance, perhaps it could be said that Matthew's salvation history is grounded in christology. The Baptism and Temptation serve to introduce the concept that Sonship must be characterized by humble obedience leading to the cross. And this Matthean theme is taken up into another: that the path of obedient Sonship receives divine vindication, proleptically on the Mountain of Transfiguration and finally on the Mountain of Commissioning. As part of the Temptation Narrative, the mountain setting helps to define the path of true Sonship; as a link with the later mountains of Transfiguration and Commissioning, it foreshadows the vindication of the Son. Although the connection between 'Son' and 'mountain' is not as all-embracing as Kingsbury argues,[100] 'Son' is the chief christological term used in these mountain passages.

One other christological note should be at least mentioned here, for it is relevant to our discussion of several of the other mountain passages where the notion of the gathering of the eschatological people of God is to the fore. The 'Son' of the Baptism and Temptation accounts is defined against the background of Israel. He is thus a corporate rather than a solitary figure, a representative of God's people. So, while ecclesiology is featured more prominently in several of Matthew's other mountain scenes, the christological foundation of Matthean ecclesiology is laid in this first mountain appearance of Jesus.

Chapter 7

THE MOUNTAIN OF TEACHING

1. *The Mountain Pericope*

The second mountain in the Matthean chain appears as the setting for the so-called Sermon on the Mount (5.1–8.1), the first great discourse of the Gospel. Matthew keeps this setting before the reader by mentioning τὸ ὄρος both at the beginning (5.1) and end (8.1) of the Sermon.

Our task in this chapter will be to investigate the significance of this mountain setting in Matthew's redaction. This will be done by studying not only the content of the Sermon itself, but also the literary framework or narrative context in which it is placed. In fact, in what follows, our interest will be largely taken up with this contextual framework. Despite a growing awareness that the Sermon on the Mount must be studied in light of its context, its narrative framework in the First Gospel has generally received short shrift.[1]

It is clear that the concluding section of this framework consists of 7.28–8.1; 7.28a is Matthew's usual indication of the end of a discourse (cf. 11.1; 13.53; 19.1; 26.1), and 8.1 forms a link with the narrative to follow. The precise extent of the introductory section, however, is more difficult to determine. In studies of the Sermon where notice is taken of the framework, it is usually assumed that the introduction begins with 5.1. Even though the mention of οἱ ὄχλοι in 5.1 links this verse with the gathering of 'the crowds' in 4.25, it is often argued that Jesus' ascent up the mountain was for Matthew a retreat from the crowds, with the result that a sharp break is to be seen between 4.25 and 5.1.[2] This approach, however, fails to take into account 7.28–8.1, for there οἱ ὄχλοι are explicitly mentioned as forming part of the audience for the Sermon.[3] This being so, the ascent up the mountain in 5:1 cannot be taken as a separation of Jesus from the crowds. Consequently, the connection between 5.1

and 4.25 provided by the reference to οἱ ὄχλοι must be given its full weight. Thus the introduction to the Sermon goes back at least to 4:25. Yet since 4.25 is the conclusion of a summary statement that begins at 4.23, the immediate introduction to the Sermon must be seen as consisting of 4.23–5.1.[4]

This is confirmed by the repetition of most of 4.23 in the summary of 9.35. This *inclusio* demarcates a section which deals with Jesus' messianic ministry among the crowds, both in word (chs. 5–7) and in deed (chs. 8–9).[5] So 4.23 marks the beginning of the introduction of Jesus' public messianic activity, of which his teaching is given pride of place by the evangelist.

This does not mean that the Sermon is to be isolated from what precedes 4.23. The reference to Jesus' ministry in Galilee in 4.23 cannot be read apart from the Galilee formula quotation in 4.12-16. And, as Kingsbury observes, 4:17 also plays a structural role in marking the beginning of a new section.[6] The various devices by which Matthew structured his Gospel serve not to divide the material into isolated segments, but to bind the whole tightly together. Thus, though our attention will be focussed primarily on 4.23–5.1 and 7.28–8.1, we cannot afford to ignore the wider context. Nor can we undertake such a study without first considering the place and significance of the mountain setting in Matthew's sources.

2. *The Mountain Setting in Pre-Matthean Tradition*

The question of the place of τὸ ὄρος in Matthew's sources for the Sermon on the Mount can only be properly addressed in the context of a broader analysis of the source question as it relates to the setting of Matthew's Sermon. So it is necessary to note that once Matthew picks up the thread of Mark's narrative with the ministry of John the Baptist (Mk 1.2-8 // Mt 3.1-12), he follows Mark (though not without certain additions of his own) through the accounts of the Baptism (Mk 1.9-11 // Mt 3.13-17), the Temptation (Mk 1.12f. // Mt 4.1-11), the beginning of the Galilean ministry (Mk 1.14f. // Mt 4.12-17), and the call of the first disciples (Mk 1.16-20 // Mt 4.18-22). The next pericope in Mark (1:21-28) deals with Jesus' ministry in the Capernaum synagogue—his teaching, the astonishment of the crowds, and an encounter with a demon-possessed man. Although this pericope was omitted by Matthew, the statement in Mk 1.22 concerning the amazement of Jesus' hearers at the authoritative nature of his teaching appears as the conclusion to Matthew's Sermon (7.28f.) with the Markan wording virtually intact.[7] Thus, Matthew has apparently taken advantage of this first mention in Mark of διδαχή in order to insert his own extended example of the teaching of Jesus.[8]

To introduce this teaching section, Matthew constructed 4.23–5.1. This passage, however, is not a free Matthean composition, for extensive echoes of the phraseology of Mark's summary statements are to be found throughout.[9] The influence of Mk 1.39 on 4.23 is clearly apparent; note particularly the underlined words: καὶ ἦλθεν κηρύσσων εἰς τὰς συναγωγὰς αὐτῶν εἰς ὅλην τὴν Γαλιλαίαν (Mk 1.39). In addition, καὶ περιῆγεν and διδάσκων are found in the summary statement of Mk 6.6b. 4.24a appears to have been modelled on Mk 1.28 (καὶ ἐξῆλθεν ἡ ἀκοὴ αὐτοῦ εὐθὺς πανταχοῦ εἰς ὅλην τὴν περίχωρον τῆς Γαλιλαίας), and v. 24b is strongly reminiscent of Mk 1.32, 34 (ἔφερον πρὸς αὐτὸν πάντας τοὺς κακῶς ἔχοντας καὶ τοὺς δαιμονιζομένους... καὶ ἐθεράπευσεν πολλοὺς κακῶς ἔχοντας ποικίλαις νόσοις). Finally, 4.25 evidently depends on the account of the gathering of the crowds in Mk 3.7b-8 (καὶ πολὺ πλῆθος ἀπὸ τῆς Γαλιλαίας ἠκολούθησεν· καὶ ἀπὸ τῆς Ἰουδαίας καὶ ἀπὸ Ἱεροσολύμων καὶ ἀπὸ τῆς Ἰδουμαίας καὶ πέραν τοῦ Ἰορδάνου καὶ περὶ Τύρον καὶ Σιδῶνα, πλῆθος πολύ, ἀκούοντες ὅσα ἐποίει ἦλθον πρὸς αὐτόν).

Matthew's work here was not a clumsy scissors-and-paste dependence on Mark. He combined phraseology inspired by Mark's summaries with some distinctive statements of his own, and wove them all together into a unique summary statement with its own special role to play. Nevertheless, the influence of Mark is unmistakable—a fact that has a direct bearing on the question of Matthew's mountain setting. The crux of the question is Matthew's dependence on Mk 3.7b-8 in 4.25. The account of the gathering of the crowds in Mk 3.7-9 is immediately followed by the statement that in order to escape the crush of the multitude, Jesus ἀναβαίνει εἰς τὸ ὄρος (Mk 3.13a), where he proceeded to summon his disciples and to appoint the Twelve. Given the dependence of Matthew's account of the gathering of οἱ ὄχλοι in 4.25 on Mk 3.7b-8, and the similarity of language between 5.1 and Mk 3.13a (cf. Mt 5.1—ἀνέβη εἰς τὸ ὄρος), it is apparent that Matthew's mountain setting here has been drawn from Mark. The context, however, has been altered: in Mark, the mountain is a place of retreat from the crowds where Jesus calls his disciples and appoints the Twelve; in Matthew, where the appointment of the Twelve is postponed until their commissioning in ch. 10 (cf. Mk 6.7-13), it becomes the setting for an extended discourse to the disciples in the presence of the gathered crowds.

Source analysis, however, cannot stop here, for Luke also has a Sermon (Lk 6.20–7.1), which occurs 'on a level place' (ἐπὶ τόπου πεδινοῦ) and which was no doubt drawn from the same Q source as that in Matthew. Before raising the question of the geographical setting of the Sermon in Q, it is necessary to consider a more subtle feature of the comparison between these two Sermons, the fact that the setting of the Sermon in Luke also appears to have been brought into relationship with Mk 3.7ff.

Luke places his account of the Sermon at a later point in the Markan outline than does Matthew. For once Luke picks up the Markan narrative with the account of John the Baptist (Mk 1.2-8 // Lk 3.1-6), he follows it with minimal interruption in sequence[10] down to the account of the healing of the man with the withered hand (Mk 3.1-6 // Lk 6.6-11). At this point, however, he has inverted the order of the next two pericopae in Mark, recounting first the mountain-top choosing and commissioning of the Twelve (Lk 6.12-16; cf. Mk 3.13-19) and then, after Jesus descended 'to a level place', the gathering of the multitude for healing (Lk 6.17-20; cf. Mk 3.7-12). It is in the hearing of this crowd (cf. Lk 7.1) that Jesus addressed the Sermon to his disciples.

Thus it appears that both Matthew and Luke have brought their accounts of the Sermon into relationship with Mk 3.7-19, though in different ways. In both Matthew and Luke the crowds who gather to Jesus in Mk 3.7-12 become part of the audience for the Sermon, though Matthew accomplishes this by reserving the subsequent account of the choosing of the Twelve for a later time (Mt 10.1-4) while Luke makes this possible by inverting the two Markan pericopae. Both Matthew and Luke bring the Sermon into relationship with the mountain of Mk 3.13a, Matthew by adopting it as the site of the Sermon and Luke by having the Sermon take place as soon as Jesus had descended from it.

Such a coincidence between Matthew and Luke is striking— especially so on a two-source hypothesis, which assumes the independence of these two Gospels. Although sufficient attention has not been paid to this coincidence,[11] it calls for an explanation— particularly since no statement about the setting of the Sermon in Q can be made without an understanding of this phenomenon.

The possibility that we are dealing here with a pure coincidence can be dismissed out of hand. Nor do we make the solution any easier by calling the two-source theory into question.[12] On either an Augustinian or Griesbach hypothesis, the relationship between these passages is every bit as awkward as the one considered here. Nor does Vaganay's suggestion—that the Synoptic Gospels depended on an Ur-Gospel which contained a mountain Sermon (omitted by Mark at 3.13)[13]—offer any advantage over such a solution as we propose: that the introduction to the Sermon in Q contained something that led both Matthew and Luke to associate their Sermons with Mk 3.7-19. That the Sermon should have had an introduction in Q is not unreasonable, particularly in view of the fact that the Sermon seems to have stood in Q as part of an extended section.[14]

Some two-source theorists believe that this coincidence between the two evangelists can be explained by assuming that the Sermon appeared in Q with a mountain setting.[15] Yet though such a view is attractive because of its simplicity, one wonders whether the bare mention of a mountain in Q would have led both evangelists to the same passage in Mark. Moreover, it is questionable whether τὸ ὄρος appeared in Q as a setting for the Sermon. Not only is the presence of τὸ ὄρος in Mk 3:13 sufficient in itself to account for the settings of the Sermon in both Matthew and Luke, but the seemingly artless way in which these evangelists deviate in their settings suggests that the Sermon in Q was not supplied with any geographical setting at all.[16] The link between both Sermons and Mk 3.7-19 must be explained in some other way.

Others have suggested that the third evangelist derived Lk 6.12-20 not from Mark, but from Q—i.e. the Sermon in Q was introduced by an account of an ascent up a mountain, the choice of the Twelve, and a descent to the gathered multitudes.[17] If this was the case, one would expect to find here agreements between Matthew and Luke against Mark. Such agreements can be found in the accounts of the appointment of the Twelve (Lk 6.12-16; cf. Mt 10.1-6; Mk 3.13-19):[18] in the use of μαθηταί and especially ἀπόστολοι (ἀπόστολος appears nowhere else in Matthew); in the explicit designation of Andrew as the brother of Peter and the placing of Andrew immediately after Peter in the list; and in the omission of the Βοανηργές description of James and John. While these agreements are not extensive, they supply some evidence that Matthew and Luke had access to a list other than that of Mark. Such agreements, however, are not to be found elsewhere in this Lukan section. If Luke was dependent on a Q introduction to the Sermon, there is no evidence that this introduction extended beyond the account of the appointment of the Twelve and the list of their names.

But does this possibility of a more limited introduction help us at all with our problem? Indeed it does. If the Q account of the Sermon was introduced by a list of the Twelve, then it is easy to see why both Matthew and Luke would have brought the Sermon into relationship with the Markan list of the Twelve in 3.13-19. Schürmann, who holds such a position, also argues that the call of the disciples in Q took place on a mountain.[19] This is possible, but there is no separate evidence for it, and the mention of τὸ ὄρος in Mk 3.13a is sufficient to account for all the data.

The one other relevant agreement between Matthew and Luke on the setting of the Sermon is that the Sermon was addressed to the disciples in the presence of the crowds.[20] This coincidence may well be due to a similar description of the audience in Q, which would explain why both Matthew and Luke would have been eager to press the crowd of Mk 3.7-12 into service—each in his own way—as part of the audience for the Sermon.

So in summary we propose that the redactional activity of Matthew and Luke can be best explained if it is assumed that in Q the Sermon was preceeded by a list of the Twelve, and that it was addressed to the disciples in the hearing of the crowds. The source for the mountain setting of Matthew's Sermon is to be found solely in Mk 3.13a.

Our understanding of the significance of the mountain setting in Mt 5:1 is not likely to be enhanced by a form-critical study of Mk 3:13-19. Yet a few brief comments can be made about the origin and significance of the mountain setting for the appointment of the Twelve. It is unlikely that this setting originated with Mark. Although 3.13a functions as a redactional link, all of the other uses of ὄρος in Mark (6.46; 9.2, 9; 13.3) appear to be traditional, and Mark shows no interest in working these mountain scenes into any redactional motif.[21]

In the tradition contained in Mk 3.13-19, the mountain is the setting for an event of great theological significance—the summoning of the Twelve to form the foundation of the eschatological community.[22] Matthew has undoubtedly used elements of this mountain scene in his own formulations—specifically, of the gathering of the eschatological community in 4.23–5.1 and 28.16-20, and of the commissioning of the disciples in 28.16-20. Yet there does not seem to be any explicit theological significance—apart from eschatological mountain expectations of a most general nature—attached to the mountain setting in a pre-Matthean stage which may have influenced Matthew. It appears that we are dealing here with an instance of the stylized use of τὸ ὄρος to indicate what had come to be seen as a characteristic aspect of Jesus' ministry.[23]

3. *The Mountain Setting in Matthew's Redaction*

a. *In its Immediate Context*

On the basis of the foregoing source analysis we can conclude that Matthew desired to present a major example of the teaching of Jesus at an early and prominent place in his Gospel.[24] Taking advantage of Mark's first mention of διδαχή—in contrast to Luke, Matthew presents the Sermon as *teaching* (cf. Mt 5.2 and Lk 6.20)—he placed a revised and expanded version of a teaching collection known to him from Q at the outset of Jesus' ministry in Galilee. To lead into the Sermon, he constructed a massive summary statement of the ministry of Jesus among the crowds (4.23-25), concluding with a great gathering of the multitude around Jesus (4.25). The climax of the whole piece is Jesus' ascent εἰς τὸ ὄρος, where the discourse takes place. Though Matthew borrowed from Mark a number of elements (including the gathering of the crowds and the ascent up the mountain), he has pressed them into the service of an entirely different and uniquely Matthean context. Our task, then is to assess the theological and redactional significance of this mountain setting for Matthew.

The most common interpretation of the mountain setting of Mt 5–7 is that it is part of a conscious Matthean attempt to present the Sermon as Christian Torah and Jesus as the new Moses. So the mountain of the Sermon is interpreted as an antitype to Sinai. This view—that Moses and Sinai typology dominates the Sermon—has had a lengthy history in modern NT study,[25] gaining credence as a result of B.W. Bacon's thesis that the First Gospel is structured along Pentateuchal lines[26] and being adopted by many.[27]

Although Bacon's hypothesis has been largely discredited,[28] several other lines of evidence have been brought forward in support of the presence of Sinai typology in Mt 5.1.[29] (1) the unmistakable presence of Mosaic typology in Matthew's Infancy Narrative and accounts of the Temptation and Transfiguration;[30] (2) the fact that much of the Sermon deals with the law and the righteousness that the law prescribes.[31] (In fact, those aspects of the Sermon that treat the law most directly—particularly 5.17-20 and 21-48—have probably been added to the Q Sermon by Matthew.[32]) (3) The sitting posture of Jesus, which was the usual posture for studying and teaching the Torah.[33] On the strength of such evidence, it is likely that Sinai typology is at work in Mt 5.1 in some fashion. But it is to be questioned whether it plays the dominant role that has been claimed for it. A number of considerations tend to undermine the hypothesis that Sinai influence is pervasive here.

W.D. Davies, whose *The Setting of the Sermon on the Mount* is the most thorough examination of the question of Moses and Sinai typology in Matthew's Sermon, concludes, after a careful investigation of Mosaic elements in the first four chapters of the Gospel, that although such typology is clearly present, it it not dominant and has been caught up into higher christological patterns. We have discussed this phenomenon already in our treatment of the Temptation Narrative,[34] and so we need not repeat it here. Davies goes on to say that given this ambiguous state of affairs, the absence of any clear Mosaic reference in Matthew's presentation of the Sermon suggests a counsel of caution. Although Matthew deliberately presents the Sermon in legal terms (we can leave to one side for the moment the question whether the Sermon is meant to be a *nova lex*), he avoids any explicit expression of Moses or Sinai symbolism. Davies' conclusions deserve to be quoted in full:

> We cannot then doubt that the SM is the 'law' of Jesus the Messiah and Lord. Our treatment thus ends in an ambiguity. Matthew presents Jesus as giving a Messianic Law on a Mount, but he avoids the express concept of a New Torah and a New Sinai: he has cast around his Lord the mantle of a teacher of righteousness, but he avoids the express ascription to him of the honorific 'a new Moses'. Can we understand this ambiguity? Why, in a Gospel where there is much to evoke the use of these terms, where the *substance* of the New Law, the New Sinai, the New Moses, are present, is there an obvious hesitancy in giving explicit expression to them?[35]

We will return to Davies's answer to this question at a later point in our discussion. Our present concern is with his hesitancy in seeing

Sinai imagery as the controlling feature in Matthew's Sermon. While he may perhaps value explicitness more highly than necessary (NT typology is often characterized by understatement and allusion), it is nevertheless true that an allusion to Moses and Sinai could easily have been made more explicit, if this had been Matthew's intention.[36] Of more weight, though, is Davies's demonstration that wherever Moses typology is present in Matthew, it is not dominant, but is transcended and absorbed by a higher Son-christology.

Davies's hesitancy with respect to Sinai typology is further justified by several other features of Matthew's Sermon. As Wellhausen has pointed out, the parallel between 5.1 and Ex 19–20 or Ex 34 is by no means exact.[37] In the Exodus, Moses ascends the mountain alone to receive the Torah from Yahweh, and then descends to communicate it to the people. The setting of Luke's Sermon, actually, affords a clearer parallel,[38] though there appears to be very little Torah emphasis in Lk 6.17-49. If there is any parallel to be seen in Matthew at all, Jesus plays the part of Yahweh while the disciples fulfil Moses' function. One must not be pedantic where typology or symbolism is concerned. Yet since the physical setting itself is forced to bear much of the weight in a Sinai hypothesis, the lack of any clear parallel with Exodus is not without significance.

Also to be noted here is the comparison between 4.23–5.1 and 15.29-31. This second passage is another Matthean summary statement which has many features in common with 4.23–5.1. In fact, we will attempt to demonstrate later that these mountain passages form an *inclusio*, standing as they do at the beginning and end of Jesus' ministry among the Galilean crowds.[39] If this is so, one would expect both mountain scenes to have been constructed along the lines of a similar pattern. The fact that no Mosaic pattern is present in the second suggests that it is not an important feature of the first.

The Sinai interpretation works best when 5.1 is taken by itself as the introduction to the Sermon, for then it could be taken as a simple scene of Jesus giving his disciples a new law on a mountain. But when one includes 4.23-25 in the introduction to the Sermon, as one is compelled to do, one is hard put to find a place for this extended summary of Jesus' messianic activity among the gathered crowds within a Sinai pattern. Bowmann and Tapp, in fact, go so far as to say that the 'new Moses' parallelism can be carried out only by ignoring 4.23-25.[40] Thus we are forced to look further for an explanation of Matthew's use of τὸ ὄρος in 5.1. This does not mean that Mosaic

typology is completely excluded.[41] But if it is present, it is not the
controlling factor and has been taken up into something else.

The key to the meaning of the mountain setting comes with the
recognition that Matthew presents the Sermon not just as a teaching
collection but as part of an event of eschatological fulfilment. This is
evident from several considerations. The first of these concerns
Matthew's careful designation in 4.23-25 of Galilee as the area of
Jesus' ministry. Although the report of his ministry spread throughout Syria,[42] and crowds gathered to him from the whole land of
Israel,[43] Jesus himself did not pass beyond the boundaries of Galilee.
Such an emphasis on Galilee as the locus of Jesus' ministry is surely
to be seen in light of the formula citation in 4.14-16. Mt 4.23-25
represents the actualization of what was announced in these earlier
verses: the dawning of the eschatological light in the land of
Galilee.[44] In Jesus' ministry among the crowds, the eschatological
light began to shine in the land of darkness. So Matthew clearly
signals that the ministry of Jesus in Galilee in 4.23ff., which
culminates in the delivery of the mountain-top discourse, is to be
seen as an event of eschatological fulfilment.

A second consideration has to do with the terms in which Jesus'
ministry among the crowds is presented—i.e. teaching, preaching,
and healing.[45] As 11.2-6 makes clear, Matthew considered this
activity of Jesus[46] as a sign of his messianic vocation and of the
inbreaking of the kingdom (cf. 11.11-14). Although 11.2-6 was drawn
from Q, its redactional significance for Matthew can be seen from the
fact that he postponed it[47] until he was able to include examples of
Jesus' teaching, preaching and healing. Jesus' ministry among the
crowds, then—teaching included—is another indication that 4.23ff.
is to be seen as an event of eschatological fulfilment.

So Matthew has placed the Sermon in the context of a great
gathering of the people of Israel to Jesus, whose ministry among them
is a sign that the age of fulfilment has dawned. Such presence of the
crowds with Jesus on the mountain is one of the distinctive features
of Matthew's mountain scenes.[48] Recent study of οἱ ὄχλοι in
Matthew[49] reveals that far from being an amorphous and indeterminate quantity, these Jewish[50] 'crowds' form a clearly defined
group with a specific role to play in the Gospel. Although there is
some measure of ambiguity, Matthew is fundamentally well-disposed
to these followers of Jesus. More than the other evangelists, he
emphasizes that they throng around Jesus (4.25; 8.1, 18; 9.36; 13.2;

14.13; 15.30; 19.2; 20.29). They hear and acclaim his teaching
(7.28f.), they glorify God on his behalf (9.8; 15.31), and they
acknowledge Jesus in messianic terms (12.23; 21.9-11). Moreover,
they are presented as a major objective of Jesus' ministry. He carries
out his ministry of teaching, preaching and healing among them; he
has compassion on their physical and spiritual hunger (9.36; 14.14;
15.32); he speaks of them as a ready harvest and so sends his disciples
out on a mission among them (9.37–10.1).

Furthermore, Matthew clearly distinguishes οἱ ὄχλοι from both
the disciples and the Jewish leaders in their relationship to Jesus.[51]
He is careful to exclude them from denunciations addressed to the
leaders,[52] and he makes it clear that the crowds did not share in their
leaders' negative estimation of the person of Jesus.[53] At the same
time, however, they are marked off from the disciples of Jesus (e.g.
4.25–5.1; 23.1). They do not have the full understanding that has
been given to the disciples (13.10-17) and are not yet real followers of
Jesus.[54] The crowds, therefore, are those whose eschatological status
is still to be determined. Although Jesus' ministry is directed towards
them and they have been invited to join the eschatological community
of disciples, their decision has not yet been registered.[55] In all
likelihood what we have reflected here is Matthew's own attitude
towards the Jewish *am ha-aretz*, as distinct from Pharisaic Judaism.[56]

Thus the gathering to Jesus on the mountain in Galilee of the
crowds and the disciples, to whom the Sermon is addressed, should
be seen in the context of the eschatological gathering of the people of
God. The disciples are the foundation of the eschatological community called into being by the messianic activity of Jesus, and the crowds
are being invited to join their fellowship. The Sermon, then, is the
messianic interpretation of the Torah for this community[57]—the
authoritative declaration of the characteristics which this community
is called to exhibit.

At the centre of this scene, and as the locus where this eschatological gathering takes place, stands τὸ ὄρος. In 4.23–5.1 the mountain
stands at the centre of a series of concentric circles: Syria (assuming a
reference to the whole province[58]); the land of Israel; Galilee; the
crowds; the disciples; Jesus seated on the mountain. Since Matthew
presents the Sermon as an eschatological event, this mountain centre
must be seen as an eschatological site. Drawing on the widespread
tendency in Second-Temple Judaism to see 'the mountain' as a place
where eschatological events were to occur, Matthew used this

mountain setting (drawn from Mark) as the place where Jesus calls
people into eschatological fellowship and gives them the διδαχή
which provides the basis for and prescribes the characteristics of that
fellowship.

Is it possible to go further and to see specific overtones of Zion
eschatology in this passage? The broad interest in the mountain
aspect of Zion that has been documented in Chapter 5—particularly
Zion interpretations of unspecified הר/ὄρος references and the central
role of Mount Zion in eschatology—make this a legitimate question
to ask. But is there any evidence of this in the passage itself?

At the outset, one can point to the great gathering of the people of
Israel around Jesus in 4.23–5.1, described by Matthew in tones of
great solemnity. As was demonstrated above, one of the central
features of Zion eschatology in the OT and throughout the Second-
Temple period was the expectation of a great gathering of Israel to
the holy mountain of Yahweh where they would be constituted
afresh as the people of God. The gathering of the scattered flock to
the holy mountain was to be the first act in the eschatological drama.
It is not possible, of course, to make a case on this point alone. Yet the
general conformity of 4.23–5.1 to the widespread pattern of Zion
eschatology is striking—though for Matthew it is the presence on the
mountain of Jesus, and not of Jerusalem or the temple, that qualifies
it for its eschatological role. Jesus himself is the gathering point for
the people of God.

In addition, one can also point to the fact (discussed above[59]) that
in Jewish expectation one aspect of the consummation on Mount
Zion was to be a new giving of the Torah. At this point, it is useful to
return to W.D. Davies's treatment of the Sermon. After concluding
that Moses typology alone is not sufficient to account for the setting
of the Sermon, he goes on to demonstrate that in contemporary
eschatological thought it was expected that the Messiah would bring
about renewed obedience to the Torah, that he would interpret it
more clearly, and (though Davies exercises much caution at this
point) that he would even bring a new Torah.

The question of a new messianic Torah is still under discussion[60]
and is not directly relevant to our argument here. But what is
important here—a fact which Davies failed to recognize—is that all
of these Torah expectations are closely linked with Zion eschatology.
In fact, two of the three OT passages cited by Davies as evidence for a
new giving of the Torah in the Messianic Age relate this event

directly to the eschatological consummation on the mountain of God: Is 2.2-4, where the Torah is said to go out of Zion and all nations gather to 'the mountain of the house of Yahweh' to learn it; and Jer 31.31-34, where the promise of the new covenant written on the heart is found in the context of a section dealing with the gathering of scattered Israel 'to the height of Zion' (v. 12) and to the 'holy mountain' (v. 23). In the Zion eschatology of the Second-Temple period, not only is there a general expectation that an age of righteousness would accompany the restoration on Zion,[61] but there are several texts that speak explicitly of a renewed role for the Torah in connection with renewed Zion.[62] Thus it can be seen that the connection between the mountain and the law that is found in Matthew's Sermon suggests a Zion background as readily as it does a Sinai.

All of this would be idle speculation, however, were it not for the presence of 5.14b: 'a city set upon a mountain (ἐπάνω ὄρους) cannot be hidden'. This saying is found in a section (5.13-16) which has an important part to play in Matthew's redaction of the Sermon. Created from sayings gathered from several sources,[63] it forms a bridge between the Beatitudes and the rest of the Sermon. By his addition of the sayings: 'you are the salt of the earth', 'you are the light of the world', and 'let your light so shine before men . . . ', Matthew puts 5.17-7.27 into a specific context: it is not just a collection of general religious teachings, but a description of what the specific community gathered around Jesus is called to be. In fact, in 5.13-16 we have a concise statement of the intent of the whole Sermon.[64]

There is a growing body of opinion which holds that the reference to πόλις ἐπάνω ὄρους is not a secular proverb,[65] but rather an echo of the kind of Zion eschatology found in Is 2.2-4. First suggested by von Rad,[66] the idea was developed in more detail by Campbell[67] and has been widely accepted.[68] In this interpretation, the city on a mountain that cannot be hidden is none other than the new Jerusalem, established on the highest of all mountains as the centre of the restored people of God. In support of this—in addition to the striking conjunction of πόλις, ὄρος, and the notion of great visibility (a combination that suggests Zion overtones as a matter of course)—is the statement about the light of the world (v. 14a), since eschatological Jerusalem was often seen as the source of light for the world.[69]

If this is so, then the model that Jesus holds up to his disciples (and

Matthew to his own community) is that of the restored people of God on Mount Zion. This is the eschatological community into which they have been called. And if this interpretation is valid, it is but a simple step to draw the connection between the mountain of 5.14 and that of 5.1: it is this gathering of the disciples and the crowds on the Galilean mountain that has been called to be the eschatological city of God, restored Zion. The ὑμεῖς of 5.13-16 is addressed to the audience described in 5.1. The repetition of ὄρος in these two verses, then, cannot be fortuitous. The mountain setting of the Sermon is presented by the evangelist against the background of Zion eschatology—though a Zion eschatology reinterpreted in christological terms: Jesus, and not Jerusalem, is the gathering point for the eschatological people of God and the locus of the renewal of Torah.

To create the setting for his Sermon, then, Matthew has drawn on various elements of Mark—particularly Mk 3.7-19, which provided him with the mountain setting, the gathering of the crowds, and perhaps the idea of the creation of the messianic community[70] (though the mountain-top bestowal of authority is reserved until 28.16-20). Weaving these elements together in his own fashion, he presents the Sermon as an eschatological event—the messianic interpretation of the Torah for the eschatological community—in fulfilment of a christologically-reinterpreted Zion eschatology. Whatever Mosaic elements are present have been absorbed into this higher vision.[71]

b. *In the Context of the Whole Gospel*
Because of the length of the Sermon and the care that Matthew has evidently taken to place it in a prominent position at the beginning of his Gospel, there can be no doubt as to its importance for his presentation of the ministry of Jesus and of the Christian ideal for his own community. In addition, by means of the *inclusio* of 4.23 and 9.35 the words of Jesus in chs. 5-7 stand alongside the deeds of Jesus in chs. 8-9 as a two-panel depiction of Jesus' ministry.[72] But does the mountain setting itself play any larger role in the structure of the Gospel?

Kingsbury suggests that there is a connection to be seen between the Transfiguration on the mountain, where the disciples are commanded to 'hear him' (17.5), and the Sermon on the mountain, where the disciples listen to his teaching.[73] This may be true in a very general sense. But there is no real linguistic or structural evidence that any explicit connection was intended. Likewise, Frieling's view that the Sermon is to be paired with the Olivet Discourse as two mountain teaching scenes[74] fails to convince for similar reasons.

But there are two other uniquely Matthean mountain scenes where connections with 4.23–5.1 are more apparent. The first, as has been hinted at already, is the summary statement of 15.29-31 which Matthew constructed as the introduction to the second feeding miracle.[75] 4.23–5.1 and 15.29-31 both depict in summary fashion Jesus' ministry among the crowds, and they both have the same compositional function of gathering participants for the great event to follow.[76] Furthermore, these two passages are bound together by a series of explicit details: the reference to Galilee as the scene of activity; the gathering of ὄχλοι πολλοί; the presence of the sick, together with the statement καὶ ἐθεράπευσεν αὐτούς; the ascent (ἀνέβη/ἀναβάς) of Jesus εἰς τὸ ὄρος, where he sat down (καθίσαντος/ἐκάθητο); the distinction between the gathered crowds and the disciples (5.1 // 15.32).

A study of Jesus' relationship with the Galilean ὄχλοι in Matthew reveals that 15.29-39 represents the final scene of Jesus' ministry with the crowds;[77] shortly thereafter, Matthew leads us into the confession of Peter and the turning of the narrative towards Jerusalem and the passion. These two summary statements, then, also form an *inclusio*, marking the beginning and end of Jesus' ministry among the Galilean crowds and summing up this ministry in an idealized scene. It is εἰς τὸ ὄρος that the true significance of this ministry is to be seen. Here Jesus carries out his messianic ministry of teaching and healing. Here he sits in messinaic dignity. And here he calls people into the fellowship of the eschatological community.

The mountain of the Sermon points ahead not only to 15.29-31, but to the crucial closing mountain scene of 28.16-20 as well.[78] Verbal links between the two passages are present. Both speak of a 'coming' (προσῆλθαν/προσελθών) εἰς τὸ ὄρος, though in 28.16-20 the roles are reversed: it is Jesus who comes to the disciples. Jesus' reference to the ἐξουσία that has been bestowed on him (28.18) recalls the statement of the crowds with which the Sermon ends, that he taught with ἐξουσία. In both passages, a Galilee locale is mentioned. Of most significance, however, is the command of Jesus to make disciples of all nations, *teaching* them (διδάσκοντες) to observe his commandments (28.19f.). In view of Matthew's presentation of the Sermon as the prime example of the teaching of Jesus (5.1; 7.28f.; cf. Lk 6.20; 7.1), there can be no doubt that by πάντα ὅσα ἐνετειλάμην (29.20) Matthew is referring primarily to the content of the Sermon.

The link is thus not only verbal but, at a very deep level, conceptual and theological. In Matthew's view of things, the Church, whose charter is given in 28.16-20, is to be characterized by just the type of teaching found in chs. 5–7. The disciples, who have already been authorized to preach and to heal (10.1, 7), are now given the authority to transmit Jesus' teaching to the Church. The Sermon is not just a historical record of the teaching of Jesus, but the living word of the One who continues to be present with the Church and who continues to call people into discipleship.

One further link between these two passages should be noted here—one that takes us into Matthew's understanding of *Heilsgeschichte*. This link is the world-wide scope of the disciples' mission which is hinted at in 5.14 ('the light of the world') and openly commanded in 28.19 (πάντα τὰ ἔθνη). We have not commented on this yet, but in the preamble to the Sermon there are the initial stages of a tension which builds throughout Matthew between the universal scope of the gospel and its limitation to Israel. In the Gospel, statements of universalism (8.11; 10.18; 12.21; 24.14; 28.19) and particularism (10.5f.; 15.24) stand together in uneasy juxtaposition. The tension, of course, is more sharply drawn later. Yet even in these early chapters we find, on the one hand, the promise of salvation for 'Galilee of the Gentiles' (4.15), an exhortation that the new community be the 'light of the world', and (if we are correct in our identification of Zion eschatology as the background to 5.1 and 5.14) an underlying hope that the Gentiles would soon be called to join in an eschatological pilgrimage to the 'holy mountain'; while on the other hand, Jesus' ministry is restricted to Jewish lands and Jewish people. A similar tension, as we will see later, is raised by 15.29-31. This tension is only resolved by Matthew in the mountain scene at the end of his Gospel, where the risen Lord for the first time commands a mission in which Gentiles are to be included. The question raised on the Mountain of Teaching is answered on the Mountain of Commissioning.

Thus there is a *Bogen*, or over-arching connection, between these two mountain scenes as well. The mountain on which Jesus teaches points ahead to the mountain on which he commands his disciples to propagate his teaching. The one looms over the other, with the result that the teaching of Mt 5–7 is funnelled through 28.16-20 to become the standard of Christian existence for the ongoing community— both Jewish and Gentile—of Matthew's own day.

Chapter 8

THE MOUNTAIN OF FEEDING

1. *The Mountain Pericope*

The third major Matthean mountain scene is found in the summary statement of 15.29-31[1]—a 'remarkable passage' which has only begun to receive the attention it deserves.[2] Its importance for Matthew can be seen in a comparison with Mark. Matthew follows Mark closely in order and content throughout the narrative section leading up to his fourth discourse (13.53–17.27). While he omits several Markan pericopae (Mk 6.6-13, 30-31; 8.22-26) and elaborates several others (cf. Mt 14.28-31; 15.12-14; 16.2f., 17-19), 15.29-31 is one of only two fresh Matthean pericopae in the whole section (the other is 17.24-27, which concerns the payment of the temple tax). Furthermore, it is the only place in this narrative section where Matthew has replaced an entire Markan pericope with his own material (cf. Mk 7.31-37). And it is the one new Matthean pericope in the important ἄρτος-section (13.53–16.12).[3] So 15.29-31, with its setting εἰς τὸ ὄρος, occupies a unique position in this section of the Gospel.

The passage, however, cannot be studied in isolation, but must be seen in the context of its adjoining pericopae, particularly the account of the feeding of the four thousand which follows (15.32-39). In 15.29-31 there is a formal description of Jesus' ministry of healing among the crowds who have gathered to him on the Galilean mountain. Since it is precisely these crowds who are fed, vv. 29-31 are explicitly linked to the feeding account and serve as an introduction to it. Thus the significance of the mountain setting in 15.29 will have to be seen in the context of the whole passage 15.29-39. To begin with, however, it is necessary to inquire into the place and significance of τὸ ὄρος in Matthew's sources.

2. *The Mountain Setting in Pre-Matthean Tradition*

Although Matthew is largely dependent on Mark in this section, his mountain setting in 15.29 is not derived from Mark. Neither of Mark's feeding narratives (6.32-44; 8.1-10) take place on a mountain, and the suggestion that Mt 15.29-31 is modelled on Mk 3.10-13 (where τὸ ὄρος does appear) is completely unsupported by the texts.[4] While it is apparent that 15.29-31 was influenced to a certain extent by the Markan pericope which it replaces,[5] there is no reference to ὄρος in Mk 7.31-37.

This does not necessarily mean, however, that the ὄρος reference in 15.29 is purely redactional, for John's account of the feeding of the five thousand (6.1-15)—one of the few non-Passion narratives that he has in common with the Synoptics—also takes place on a mountain. Indeed, the terms in which this mountain setting is described are strikingly similar to Matthew's account of the ascent up the mountain in 15.29: cf. Jn 6.3 (ἀνῆλθεν δὲ εἰς τὸ ὄρος Ἰησοῦς, καὶ ἐκεῖ ἐκάθητο) and Mt 15.29 (καὶ ἀναβὰς εἰς τὸ ὄρος ἐκάθητο ἐκεῖ).

The issue to be decided here is this: Is John's account dependent on Matthew?—in which case we could conclude that the ὄρος setting in 15.29 was due to Matthew himself; or, Has John relied on an independent tradition at this point?—which might suggest that Matthew derived the details of the mountain setting from a tradition independent of Mark and overlapping with that of John. The other option, that 15.29 and Jn 6.3 are coincidental redactional touches,[6] is, given the similarity in language, hardly likely—particularly since John does not demonstrate any redactional or theological interest in τὸ ὄρος elsewhere in his Gospel.[7]

If one approaches the problem within the narrowest parameters, restricting the inquiry to the six feeding accounts[8] and comparing the Johannine account with those found in the Synoptics, a reasonably strong case could be made for Johannine dependence on the Synoptics. Similarities in content and wording are to be found between Jn 6.1-15 and each of the five Synoptic accounts. The most striking similarities appear in the case of Mk 6.32ff.; not only is there a long list of verbal parallels in the accounts of the feeding itself,[9] but the sequence of events in the more extended narratives of Jn 6.1-21 and Mk 6.32-52 is remarkably alike: a boat trip (Mk 6.32 // Jn 6.1); the feeding (Mk 6.33-44 // Jn 6.2-13); a retreat εἰς τὸ ὄρος (Mk 6.46 // Jn 6.15); walking on the water (Mk 6.45-52 // Jn 6.16-21). With respect to the other Synoptic accounts, in addition to the mountain setting of Mt

15.29 (the only point of contact between Jn 6.1-15 and Mt 15.29-39), there are two instances where John agrees with Matthew and Luke against Mark in the first feeding miracle,[10] several points of contact with features unique to Mark's second feeding miracle,[11] and a possible connection with a detail peculiar to Luke.[12]

While the long list of elements found only in John[13] suggests that John had access to a separate tradition, such a widespread pattern of similarities weighs heavily in favour of John's dependence on the Synoptics as well. One does not have to think of the Fourth Evangelist combining these sources in any crude mechanical fashion. Such parallels merely imply that John was conversant with the Synoptic accounts and allowed familiar phrases to slip into his own narrative.[14] If this is so, it is possible to argue that John depended on Mt 15.29 for his reference to εἰς τὸ ὄρος in 6.3.

Further support for the Matthean origin of John's mountain setting is the curious disjunction in John's account that appears between vv. 3 and 15: in v. 3 Jesus went εἰς τὸ ὄρος before the feeding, but according to v. 15 it was after the feeding that he went εἰς τὸ ὄρος.[15] This may be taken to suggest that these details have been drawn from two sources (i.e. Mk 6.46; Mt 15.29) without being fully integrated into the one narrative. Further support for this theory might be found in the fact that the presence of the crowds with Jesus on the mountain is a characteristic Matthean feature. Apart from Jn 6.3, such a situation is found only in the First Gospel. So the evidence from the narratives taken in isolation clearly suggests that John depended on the Synoptic accounts—including Mt 15.29-39—for his narrative of the feeding miracle.

When one broadens the discussion, however, to include questions about the overall relationship of John to the Synoptics, the issue is not nearly so clear. It is generally agreed that John had access to a tradition, whether oral or written, that was independent of the Synoptic tradition.[16] Johannine scholarship is divided, however, as to whether John also knew and used the Synoptic Gospels. We cannot here entertain this question in any detail. Nevertheless, the consensus from both positions is that John did not know Matthew.

John's independence of Matthew is held, of course, by those who propose that John was unfamiliar with the Synoptic tradition. Gardner-Smith, Dodd and others argue that John relied on a tradition which, though independent of the Synoptic Gospels, overlapped the Synoptic tradition at certain points.[17] But even in the older position, stated in its classic form by Streeter[18] and still advocated by many[19]—in which it is argued that John knew one or more of the Synoptics but wrote his Gospel to comment on, supplement or correct their accounts—it is generally agreed that the evidence is too slight to indicate that John had any awareness of Matthew.[20]

What does all this mean for the εἰς τὸ ὄρος reference of Mt 15.29 and Jn 6.3? If one is prepared to argue that John knew Mark and Luke, there is no *a priori* reason why he should not have know Matthew as well. While Streeter minimized the points of contact between John and Matthew, his list is sufficient to demonstrate that the striking similarity between Mt 15.29 and Jn 6.3 is not entirely unique in the comparison of these two Gospels.[21] It is more likely, however, that John was unfamiliar with the Synoptics. Still, even so, the possibility of Synoptic influence is not completely excluded, for the close verbal parallels in the feeding accounts still leaves open the possibility that, at this one point at least, the source on which John depended had been influenced by the Synoptic Gospels.[22] In other words, our problem has receded one stage to the level of John's sources: John's source either had been shaped by the Synoptic Gospels at this point, or it was an independent tradition which overlapped at this point with a tradition known to Matthew.

Admittedly, a decision cannot easily be reached in this matter. Yet it is slightly more probable that the solution is to be found in a theory of overlapping traditions—i.e. that Matthew drew not only on Mark, but also on an oral tradition that partially overlapped with the tradition available to John. That John's narrative has five thousand fed while Matthew's has four thousand presents no problem, for it is evident from the similarity in form and fluidity in detail among the various accounts that the two narratives were closely related in the transmission of the tradition.[23] In favour of a theory of overlapping traditions is the sizable list of instances where Matthew and Luke agree against Mark.[24] Unless one is prepared to call the two-source hypothesis into question, this seems to indicate that though Matthew and Luke depended extensively on Mark, they were also influenced by oral tradition. And since several of these minor agreements also appear in John,[25] it is possible that the same oral tradition influenced John as well.

It is, therefore, an open possibility that Matthew's mountain setting in 15.29 should not be considered a purely redactional feature, but was taken from traditional accounts. Given the fact that the two mountain settings studied already were derived from source materials, such a conclusion should not surprise us. It is therefore necessary to inquire as to the origin and significance of this setting in the oral period.

Form-critical study of the feeding miracles has revealed an original narrative which probably developed under the influence of the OT account of a similar miracle in the life of Elisha[26] and which then became overlaid with eucharistic[27] and Mosaic[28] elements. But there is no mountain or mountain symbolism associated with either Elisha or the Last Supper that might have served as a background for the mountain reference. And though sacred mountains figured heavily in OT accounts of the ministry of Moses, they do not appear in the wilderness–manna–prophet complex of ideas that is at work here.

John's account differs from the others in its emphasis in the conclusion to the narrative on the desire of the crowds to make Jesus king (vv. 14f.). If, as some suspect, this attempted messianic enthronement was part of the tradition received by John,[29] it is possible that the original significance of the mountain setting was that it functioned as an eschatological site—i.e. the place of enthronement of the messianic king. Such a role for τὸ ὄρος, however, was not carried over into the Fourth Gospel. The disjunction in Jn 6 between the mountain references in vv. 3 and 15, and the lack of interest in the mountain setting elsewhere in the Gospel, indicate that John incorporated a traditional detail without further theological reflection. Only in Mt 15.29 does the possibility arise of a redactional and theological role for the mountain setting of the feeding miracle.

3. The Mountain Setting in Matthew's Redaction

a. *In its Immediate Context*
It is apparent on the basis of our analysis above that Matthew did not want the end of Jesus' ministry among the Galilean crowds to go by unnoticed, but desired to remind his readers once again of the theological framework in which this ministry was to be seen. To do this, he created a new introduction to the second feeding miracle in the form of a summary statement (15.29-31) that stands at the end of a series of similar summaries with which he has punctuated his narrative (i.e. 4.23–5.1; 9.35-38; 11.1, 4-6; 12.15-21).

This summary statement, however, is not an entirely free Matthean construction. We noted the possibility that Matthew drew the mountain setting from oral tradition. Moreover, though he omitted Mk 7.31-37,[30] he made use of several features in this passage: the geographical link of v. 29a reflects Mk 7.31 (though Matthew has simplified Mark's almost impossible itinerary), and the cry of acclamation in Mk 7.37 may have inspired v. 31b. At a more subtle level, several commentators note that both Matthew and Mark appear to echo LXX Is 35.5f.—viz. Mark in his use of μογιλάλος, a term found in LXX Is 35.6 and Mk 7.32 but nowhere else in either the LXX or the NT; Matthew in his list of those who came for healing (χωλούς, κυλλούς, τυφλούς, κωφούς; cf. LXX Is 35.5f.: τυφλῶν, κωφῶν, χωλός, γλῶσσα μαγιλάλων).[31] It is possible that Matthew alluded to Is 35.5f. in the summary statement of 15.29-31[32] precisely because his attention had been drawn to the passage by the allusion in Mark. Yet, it must be insisted, all the features derived from sources have been incorporated into a coherent statement consonant with Matthew's own literary style and redactional purposes.

Before proceeding to a more direct examination of the ὄρος reference in 15.29, a further aspect of this summary passage is necessarily of interest here: the fact that in Matthew's redaction 15.29-31 serves as a connecting link between the story of the Canaanite women (15.21-28) and the account of the feeding of the four thousand (15.32-39). It has occasionally been suggested that a connection was intended by Mark between these two accounts—viz. with the dialogue between Jesus and the woman about bread and crumbs serving to anticipate the story of the multiplication of the loaves and the remaining fragments.[33] Such a connection is not implausible. Yet the connection in Mark is more ambiguous than it might have been, owing to the intervening account of the *ephphatha* healing (Mk 7.31-37). Matthew, however, omitted this intervening passage, and replaced it with the passage under consideration describing Jesus' ministry with the assembled crowd. And since it is precisely this crowd that is fed, 15.29-39 forms a unit which stands in Matthew's Gospel in direct juxtaposition with the account of the Canaanite women—a fact whose significance will become apparent as our discussion progresses.

Because 15.29-31 has been largely overlooked in scholarly discussion of the First Gospel, little attention has been paid to the significance of its mountain setting. A number of commentators

simply echo the oft-repeated opinion that the mountain is to be seen
as a place of revelation.[34] Admittedly, such a description is partially
true for some of the mountain scenes in Matthew. But it is not a
complete or adequate description of the evangelist's mountain
theology, and it is nowhere more inadequate than in this passage.
Nor, given the presence of ὄχλοι πολλοί, is it likely that the
mountain was meant to signify a place of solitude and nearness to
God.[35] And Schweizer's suggestion that the picture of Jesus εἰς τὸ
ὄρος with the sick at his feet is meant to be a reflection of Is 52.7
borders on the fanciful.[36]

Strecker comes close to the heart of the matter when he asserts
that here, as in the other Matthean mountain scenes, Jesus gathers
people to himself in eschatological fellowship.[37] As in 4.23–5.1, this
mountain setting must be seen, in the first instance, as a site for an
event of eschatological fulfilment. One indication of this is the
graphic depiction of Jesus' healing ministry which, as already noted,
is understood by Matthew as a sign of his messianic identity and of
the age of fulfilment.[38] In addition, the miraculous provision of food
must also be seen as an eschatological event.[39] In the Second-
Temple period there was a widespread expectation that the Messiah
would invite the faithful to participate in a messianic banquet.[40] And
while Matthew does not explicitly highlight such an expectation, he
seems familiar with it (cf. 8.11) and presents the feeding as a
satisfying feast of plenty[41] which points to the true identity of Jesus
(cf. 16.5-12).

So the Jewish[42] crowds who gather to Jesus and among whom his
eschatological ministry takes place, must be seen in terms similar to
those described in connection with 4.23–5.1.[43] They are those who
have been invited to join with the disciples in the fellowship of the
eschatological community. Attempts to interpret the crowds of
15.29-31 in a negative light run counter to the spirit of the text;[44]
Jesus' ministry of healing and feeding among οἱ ὄχλοι is a sign that
the age of fulfilment has broken in.

Therefore we must insist that as the place of gathering, healing and
feeding, the mountain of 15.29 functions as an eschatological site. In
keeping with a widespread Jewish interest in 'the mountain' as a
place where eschatological events would occur, Matthew has taken a
geographical reference from the tradition (which perhaps had
eschatological overtones associated with it already[45]), and used it as
the setting for an elaborate summary of the eschatological ministry of
Jesus.

As in 4.23–5.1 the picture of a massive eschatological gathering of crowds on 'the mountain' calls to mind the patterns of Zion eschatology. That this similarity was by no means coincidental, but that Matthew allowed Zion overtones to colour his presentation of the ministry of Jesus εἰς τὸ ὄρος, may be argued on the basis of a number of indications in the text. The first of these is the allusion to Is 35.5f. While it is generally agreed that these verses stand behind Matthew's list of those who came to Jesus for healing,[46] no notice has yet been taken of the fact that in the Isaiah passage this healing appears as part of the final pilgrimage of Israel to Mount Zion, when 'the ransomed of the Lord shall return, and come to Zion with singing, with everlasting joy upon their heads' (Is 35.10).[47] Since the presence of those afflicted in these ways is a common feature of Zion expectations,[48] it is to be expected that this allusion to Is 35.5f. would have called to mind the whole context of the eschatological procession to Zion.

A second indication of the presence of Zion eschatology in 15.29ff. has to do with the feeding that takes place on the mountain. Jewish eschatological thought looked forward not only to a messianic banquet, but, in at least one strand of the tradition, to a banquet that would be the culmination of the gathering on Mount Zion. The most prominent passage in this regard is Is 25.6-10a, where the banquet on the mountain is for the purpose of displaying before the nations Israel's vindication by Yahweh.[49] A Zion setting for the final banquet in which the gathered people of God partake is also found in some later Rabbinic[50] and Jewish-Christian[51] references. While it is true that Matthew does not make explicit reference to such a tradition in this passage, the combination of an eschatological feeding with a carefully-crafted mountain setting is highly suggestive.[52]

A third indication to be mentioned here has to do with the theme of the gathering of the scattered sheep. As we have been, the OT depiction of Israel as a scattered and leaderless flock is a metaphor within which all the various elements of Zion eschatology find expression.[53] In particular, we find that the scattered flock will be gathered to the mountain of God (Jer 31.10-12; Ezek 34.14), where it will be fed in abundance (Jer 31.12-14; Ezek 34.26f.). While such pastoral imagery does not appear explicitly in 15.29-31, in the wider context of 15.21-39 there can be no doubt that the crowds who gather to Jesus on the mountain—and who were described in an earlier summary statement as 'harassed and strewn about, like sheep

without a shepherd' (9.36)—are to be seen in these terms here as
well.

In the preceding account of the Canaanite woman, the 'children',
whose bread is the subject of discussion in 15.26f., are described—in
a Matthean addition—as 'the lost sheep of the house of Israel'
(15.24). There can even less doubt in Matthew than in Mark that the
debate between Jesus and the woman concerning who is to be fed is
meant to point ahead to the miraculous feeding that follows. So the
crowds who gather to be fed in v. 30 are 'the lost sheep of the house of
Israel' of v. 24.

This is further confirmed by another deft Matthean touch: the use
of ῥίπτω to describe the laying of the sick at Jesus' feet (v. 30). One
might wonder why the sick were said to be 'thrown' at Jesus' feet,
when τίθημι or βάλλω would appear to have been more appropriate
to the occasion. The verb ῥίπτω, however, is used in 9.36 in the
context of Matthew's description of οἱ ὄχλοι as sheep without a
shepherd.[54] While 9.36 depends on Mk 6.34, Matthew adds that the
crowds were ἐσκυλμένοι καὶ ἐρριμμένοι—'troubled and thrown
down/strewn about'. The RSV translation 'helpless' does not really
capture the picture of scattered disarray conveyed by ἐρριμμένοι
(from ῥίπτω). The use of this verb in both the summary statement of
9.35-38 and here in the summary statement of 15.29-31 cannot be
coincidental. So the crowds who gather to Jesus on the mountain are
the lost sheep of the house of Israel, harassed and helpless like a
leaderless flock, and Jesus, who is depicted by Matthew as the
promised Davidic shepherd of Israel (2.6),[55] heals their afflictions
and provides them with food in abundance. And this being so,
Matthew's careful creation of a mountain setting here is clearly
understandable in Zion terms.

Considered separately, such bits of evidence may not be sufficient
to demonstrate that Matthew wanted the Mountain of Feeding to be
seen in a Zion perspective. But when all these features are taken
together, the cumulative evidence is impressive. All the elements in
this passage—the gathering of the crowds; the healing of the lame,
maimed, blind and dumb; the allusion to Is 35.5f.; the feast of plenty;
echoes of the pastoral metaphor; the eschatological activity of the
'God of Israel' and, above all, the mountain setting—are part of the
Zion complex of ideas. Moreover, Matthew combined these elements
into an event whose shape conforms closely to the pattern of Zion
eschatology: a gathering of the lost sheep of Israel to 'the mountain'

where the Messiah of the God of Israel heals their infirmities and feeds them plentifully. The centre of the pattern, of course, has been transformed, for it is the presence of Christ and not the restoration of the temple that gives the event its eschatological foundation. Nevertheless, the formative influence of Zion eschatology is apparent, for the care with which Matthew has constructed the setting for 15.29-31 is evidence of its theological importance for the evangelist, and such a configuration of elements would call to mind no other theological background than that of Zion eschatology.

By his construction of 15.29-31, Matthew invites us, then, to see the feeding of the four thousand as not only an eschatological event, but, in particular, the christological fulfilment of the expectations of Zion eschatology. In Mark, it is the first of the two feeding miracles that has been imbued with OT overtones—specifically, overtones of the wilderness/new Moses complex of ideas.[56] Matthew, however, stripped this first account of its theologically significant details,[57] choosing rather to reserve his OT interpretation for the second feeding miracle. In so doing, he has created a weighty conclusion to his account of Jesus' ministry among the Galilean crowds.

b. *In the Context of the Whole Gospel*

This brings us to the question of the place of the Mountain of Feeding in the context of Matthew's wider redactional purposes. We have already demonstrated that 15.29-31 must be paired with 4.23–5.1 as the opening and closing brackets of an *inclusio*.[58] Now, on the basis of our investigation in this chapter we can emphasize what was said in connection with the Mountain of Teaching—that it is when Jesus is εἰς τὸ ὄρος that the significance of his ministry is most clearly seen, not only in *word* (4.23–7.29) but also in *deed* (15.29-39). The repetition of the mountain setting in these two passages underscores the equal emphasis that Matthew ascribes to teaching and action in Jesus' ministry.[59] The seated posture (5.1; 15.29)—not exclusively a Sinai-Torah motif—is an indication of the authority with which both aspects of his ministry are carried out. And so the mountain setting becomes a literary-theological device whereby Matthean christology is brought into focus.

Our study of the previous mountain pericopae would lead us to expect some connection also between 15.29-39 and 28.16-20. Yet such connections are not immediately apparent[60]—indeed, apart from the Galilee location and the use of εἰς τὸ ὄρος, there are no explicit verbal links at all. There is, however, the basic thematic connection concerning Matthew's deep interest in a theological basis for the salvation of the Gentiles.

The tension between universalism and particularism—a feature of Matthew's Gospel as a whole[61]—is emphatically present in Mt 15. In his redaction of the account of the Syrophoenician woman (15.21-28), Matthew made a number of changes that emphasize the contrast between Jews and Gentiles and highlight the barrier standing in the way of Gentile participation in salvation history.[62] In contrast to Mark, Matthew's identification of the woman as a Gentile is made right at the outset. Moreover, instead of using the political term 'Syrophoenician' to describe her, Matthew calls her a 'Canaanite', using the common OT term for Israel's adversaries—and thereby evoking Israel's deeply-engrained fear of and revulsion towards Gentile ways.

Furthermore, it is possible that Matthew intended to depict the encounter between Jesus and the woman as taking place on Jewish soil.[63] He omits Mark's statement that Jesus went into a (Gentile) house, and says that γυνὴ Χαναναία ἀπὸ τῶν ὁρίων ἐκείνων ἐξελθοῦσα, which could be translated: 'a Gentile woman came out of that region'. He repeats Mark's statement that Jesus went εἰς τὰ μέρη Τύρου καὶ Σιδῶνος, but the preposition εἰς can have the meaning 'towards', 'up to', as in εἰς τὴν θάλασσαν (Mt 17.27; Mk 3.7; 7.31; cf. Lk 14.23; 24.5). If this is the sense of the phrases with εἰς and ἀπό, Matthew then is describing a scene where Jesus travels in the direction of Tyre and Sidon and the woman comes out to meet him on Jewish territory. It is not possible to obtain certainty in this matter, for ἀπό can be used in adjectival phrases to denote simply a place of origin (e.g. Mt 4.25; 21.11; Lk 9.38; Acts 2.5; 6.9). But it can at least be said that here, as elsewhere, Matthew emphasizes that Gentiles seek out Jesus rather than the reverse (e.g. the Magi, the Capernaum centurion).

It is in the conversation with the woman that the barrier excluding Gentiles from salvation comes into focus most dramatically. The two most significant alterations in Matthew's account are (1) the omission of Mark's more hopeful statement 'Let the children *first* be fed' (Mk 7.27; cf. Mt 15.26)[64] and (2) the addition of Jesus' words limiting his mission to Israel: 'I was sent only to the lost sheep of the house of Israel' (v. 24). With these two changes, the priority of Israel becomes absolute, and the status of the Gentiles becomes one of complete exclusion from the benefits of Jesus' ministry. These two changes are also found in a context where Jesus' reluctance to have anything to do with the woman is emphasized. For whereas in Mark there is only one request for healing, which then leads into a dialogue between Jesus and the woman, in Matthew there are three: the first by the woman herself, to which Jesus makes no response (vv. 22f.); the second by the disciples, asking either that Jesus send her away, or, more probably, that he grant her request;[65] and, only after this, the second request by the woman, which leads into the discussion and favourable conclusion as found in Mark.

So by a series of delicate touches, Matthew emphasizes the enormity of the barrier between Jews and Gentiles, excludes the Gentiles from participation in salvation, and limits Jesus' ministry to Israel. Yet at the same time Matthew states just as emphatically that the woman's request was granted. He even describes the healing as taking place instantaneously (v. 28). Thus a sharp tension exists in the narrative between the programmatic exclusion of Gentiles from salvation on the one hand, and the participation of this one Gentile woman in messianic blessings on the other. How is such a tension to be resolved? Has Matthew built this barrier only for rhetorical purposes, breaking it down as quickly as it was erected? How was the woman able to overcome the obstacles put in her way?

The immediate answer given in the text, of course, is that the woman's request was granted because of her faith. Matthew makes it plain that her response must be seen in these terms (rather than as a mere witticism) by Jesus' acclamation of her μεγάλη πίστις (v. 28), and by several deft changes in the text emphasizing her reverential attitude.[66] But this does not solve the problem. Faith has not removed the barrier; it has only overcome it. Gentiles are not to be seen as 'house dogs' who share the same household and the same master with Israel.[67] The statement limiting Jesus' ministry to Israel (v. 24) is not rhetorical but programmatic, for it also occurs in 10.6. For Matthew, the barrier remains and is not removed until 28.16-20, when the exalted Lord gives the commandment for the mission to πάντα τὰ ἔθνη. The woman, like the centurion before her (8.5-12), must be seen as exceptions.[68] These exceptions, however, are not anomalies, but anticipations of a situation whose time has nearly come. One gets the impression in Matthew that until 28.16-20 the Gentiles are always hovering just off-camera, waiting eagerly for their time, and occasionally even bursting in to claim a share in messianic blessing before their time (2.1-12; 4.14-16; 8.5-12; 10.18; 12.21; 15.21-28). Nevertheless, until the exaltation of the risen Lord, the barrier is not removed and the tension raised by this passage is not resolved. So at the end of the account of the Canaanite woman, the status of the Gentiles is left very much hanging in the air.

Matthew, however, carefully linked the accounts of the Canaanite woman and the feeding of the multitude by means of the connective passage 15.29-31. Consequently the feeding narrative is intended by the evangelist to be seen as a prime example of Jesus' ministry mong the 'lost sheep of the house of Israel', of his provision of bread for the needs of the children. One is justified in asking, then, whether 15.29-31 plays any role in the resolution of the tension created in the previous pericope. Does the narrative of the feeding of the assembled multitudes do anything to ground the question that was left hanging?

Careful consideration reveals that it does, and in two ways. First, with respect to the OT background, Matthew constructed 15.29-31 against the background of the OT expectation of an eschatological gathering of the people of God on God's holy mountain. The feeding of the multitude is the messianic banquet on the mountain—or, at least, is a sign that the time of messianic feeding is at hand. Yet it was also expected that the Gentiles would have a share in the events taking place on the holy mountain. When restoration takes place, they too would stream in procession to the mountain to worship God (Is 2.2-4) and participate in the messianic feast (Is 25.6-10a). While for Matthew the time of fulfilment would not be complete until after the resurrection—and so Gentiles were not present at the feeding— the fact that eschatological fulfilment has begun to take place in Israel is a sign that the salvation of the Gentiles too is imminent. If the feeding of Israel is taking place, can that of the Gentiles be far behind? Thus since 15.29-31 evokes an OT context in which salvation is promised to Gentiles, by its juxtaposition with the account of the Canaanite woman it provides a partial resolution of the tension found there between the programmatic exclusion of the Gentiles and the exceptional inclusion of this one Gentile.

But resolution in this way is only partial. The passage plays a further role in resolving the tension by means of its place in the structure of Matthew. This scene εἰς τὸ ὄρος points forward to another scene εἰς τὸ ὄρος at the end of the Gospel where the resurrected Lord stands on a mountain in Galilee as the focal point of a mission that will gather πάντα τὰ ἔθνη into the community of disciples. As Wilkens observes, there is a 'secret connection' between these two mountain scenes.[69] This passage standing at the end of Jesus' ministry with the crowds in Galilee points ahead to another passage, standing at the end of Jesus' ministry on the cross in Jerusalem, in which the tension is resolved. The mountain fellowship from which Gentiles are excluded in 15.29-39 is offered to them in 28.16-20. The banquet on the mountain is a sign to the Gentiles that the time of their inclusion is near.

Chapter 9

THE MOUNTAIN OF TRANSFIGURATION

The next two major Matthean mountain references are found in passages that Matthew took over from his Markan source. In Chapter 10 we will examine the place of the Mount of Olives in the account of Jesus' final ministry in Jerusalem, with special attention given to the Olivet Discourse. Here our interest is in the Mountain of Tranfiguration (17.1-9). While the mountain settings of these two accounts are not products of redactional activity as extensive as was the case in those passages investigated in the previous two chapters, still there is evidence that each of them has been integrated into distinctive Matthean patterns that culminate in the closing mountain scene.

1. *The Mountain Setting in Pre-Matthean Tradition*

'The Transfiguration is at once the commentator's paradise and his despair.' The words are Caird's,[1] but the sentiment is widely shared. The narrative contains a series of elements—'after six days', the three disciples, the high mountain, the changed appearance, Elijah and Moses, the three tents, the cloud, the voice, the heavenly proclamation—each of which evokes a wealth of theological associations. Moreover, in its place in the Gospels, the Transfiguration has evident links with the Baptism, the Temptation, Peter's confession, Gethsemane, and Jesus' resurrection, ascension and *parousia*. Yet the task of discovering a single interpretative key that will allow all of these associations and links to be seen as parts of an overall pattern has proven to be virtually impossible.

Our interest in the Transfiguration Narrative is in the place and significance of its mountain setting in the history of the tradition, and so we will not engage in any full or systematic study of the problems that the passage presents. Nevertheless, questions concerning this setting can be answered only after considering its function in the narrative as a whole—a function which can be determined only by its relationship to other elements in the configuration. So our investigation will have to take into account scholarly study of the Transfiguration Narrative in its entirety, though in a structure and with emphases determined by our mountain interest.

As we work back from Matthew through the history of the tradition, it is evident first of all that Matthew took this narrative, with its mountain setting, from Mark (9.1ff). Admittedly, there are a half dozen or so minor agreements between Matthew and Luke[2] which have led some to postulate a second source.[3] Yet though a stronger case might be made for Luke having had access to an independent tradition,[4] it is highly unlikely that Matthew and Luke had in common any source other than Mark.[5]

Moving back another stage to the pre-Markan situation, there is scholarly consensus that the mountain setting was one element in a form of the Transfiguration Narrative available to Mark when he wrote his Gospel.[6] There is no general agreement of the form of the narrative or on the extent of Mark's editorial activity. Yet because of the integral connection between the mountain setting and other features in the narrative, and particularly because of the appearance of the same phrase εἰς ὄρος ὑψηλόν in Q (cf. Mt 4.8), it may be assumed with confidence that the mountain setting was taken over by Mark.

Our study must therefore be directed to discovering the literary and theological function of the mountain setting in the pre-Markan Transfiguration Narrative. Basic to such an inquiry, of course, is the question of the extent of the narrative as Mark received it.

It is probable that vv. 11-13 were not an essential part of this narrative. These verses are not integrally related to the Transfiguration event at all, and—while the suggestion made by some that vv. 1, 11-13 comprised a unified section into which Mark inserted his account of the Transfiguration is questionable[7]—vv. 2-10 stand together as an identifiable unit. As for vv. 9-10, in view of the apocalyptic flavour of the narrative, the element of secrecy is not as extraneous as is often maintained.[8] A striking parallel can be found in 2 Macc 2.1-8 where the hiding of the temple vessels on the top of a mountain concludes with Jeremiah's command to his followers that the place remain secret 'until God gather the people together and mercy come'.[9] It is probable, therefore, that the original Transfiguration Narrative

ended not abruptly with v. 8, but with some injunction to silence.
The present form of vv. 9-10, though, with its emphasis on the
obduracy of the disciples and its Son of Man christology, may be due
to Mark himself. The one other evident Markan addition of any
significance is the editorial comment in v. 6.[10] Other additions have
been suggested, but these are either matters of wording or highly
doubtful.[11] Thus we consider the traditional material of Mark's
Transfiguration Narrative to be Mk 9.2-5, 7-8, concluding with an
injunction to silence.

Current study of the formation and function of this narrative in
the oral period falls broadly into three categories: (1) the Transfiguration as a misplaced resurrection narrative;[12] (2) as the result of
conflicting christologies and/or the conflation of several stories;[13]
and (3) as an account that has been fashioned against the background
of a recognizable Jewish eschatological pattern.[14] It falls outside the
scope of our study to interact directly with these approaches.[15] Our
interest here is in possible explanations for the literary origin and
theological significance of the mountain setting which arise from
these approaches. At least seven such explanations can be identified
and must now be dealt with in turn.

a. *The Mountain Setting of a Misplaced Resurrection Narrative*
The mountain setting of the Transfiguration plays an important part
in arguments used to support the view that this narrative was
originally an account of a resurrection appearance that has come to
be placed in a different, pre-Easter context. These arguments are
generally of two types.[16] First, it is held that a comparison of the
Transfiguration Narrative with other accounts of post-Easter appearances, both within and outside the New Testament, reveal common
features in sufficient number to justify such an identification. In
addition to the mountain setting, the most frequently mentioned
points of contact are: the use of ὤφθη; the cloud; the changed and
glorified appearance of Jesus; the element of fear; and the explicit
temporal reference ('after six days'). As for the mountain setting, it is
noted that a mountain is the site for post-Easter appearances in Mt
28.16 and Acts 1.12. In addition, Robinson cites a list of Gnostic
references to resurrection appearances of Jesus to his disciples on a
mountain,[17] to which several other Gnostic[18] and orthodox
Christian[19] references can be added. In response to objections that
these accounts have an emphasis on the splendour and glory of the

resurrected Lord that is not present in the canonical accounts, Robinson argues that the Transfiguration Narrative—along with the accounts of the conversion of Paul—belong to a type of resurrection appearance account that was largely suppressed except in heterodox circles.[20]

Second, it is argued that the Transfiguration was known and treated in other independent traditions as a resurrection appearance. The texts used to support this argument are 2 Pet 1.16-18, where the Transfiguration is referred to in a discussion of the *parousia*, and the Ethiopic version of Apoc. Pet. 15-17, where the Transfiguration takes place as one of the events leading up to the ascension.[21] Therefore— it is argued—since a mountain setting is preserved in both of these accounts and since the mountain was a common site for resurrection appearances, ὄρος ὑψηλόν in Mk 9.2 must have originated as the setting of a post-Easter appearance.

There is, of course, an attractiveness to such an interpretation in that it provides a known category for a narrative which is otherwise difficult to classify. Yet is does not bear up under scrutiny. Dodd and Boobyer have demonstrated on the basis of a formal analysis that most of the elements of the NT appearance accounts are not found in the Transfiguration Narrative, and that many of the details of the latter need to be pared away before there is any resemblance with the former.[22] And while such formal analysis does not have any direct bearing on Robinson's thesis that the Transfiguration represents a different form of an appearance story, it is highly doubtful that his appeal to 2 Pet 1.16-18 and to extra-canonical material is valid. For though 2 Pet 1.16-18 is quite different from the Synoptic Transfiguration Narrative,[23] Baltensweiler demonstrates that it contains no detail not found already in the Synoptic accounts—which suggests that it is a compression of those accounts rather than an independent tradition.[24] And even if this passage is independent of the Synoptics, the fact that the Transfiguration is used as a *Vorspiel* of the *parousia* here by no means implies that the author knew it as a resurrection appearance.

As for Apoc. Pet. 15-17—in addition to its second century date and therefore its probable dependence on the Synoptics[25]—it is to be noted that this account of the events on the Mount of Olives includes not only the Transfiguration and Ascension, but much of the Olivet Discourse as well. This means that its author was quite prepared to place a known pre-Easter event (the Olivet Discourse) into a post-

Easter setting and suggests that the Tranfiguration was considered here as a post-Easter event no more than was the Olivet Discourse.[26] Both, evidently, were incorporated into this resurrection/ascension account for other reasons.[27] Although it is true that mountains occur frequently as settings for resurrection appearances, their recurring presence in the pre-Easter ministry of Jesus means that the mountain setting of the Transfiguration Narrative offers little support for any 'misplaced resurrection appearance' theory. Thus the argument collapses,[28] and with it this explanation for the mountain setting of Mk 9.2.

b. Θεῖος ἀνήρ *Christology*

In the assortment of conflation-theory approaches mentioned above, there are those that view the mountain setting as originating in a Hellenistic milieu. Lohmeyer, who saw the Transfiguration Narrative as a composite of Palestinian and Hellenistic layers, maintains that the secluded place and the choosing of companions are necessary parts of a Hellenistic divine epiphany story.[29] The parallels that he suggested, however, were too general and unsubstantial to be entirely convincing.

In the more recent approach to the Transfiguration Narrative that views it in its entirety as the product of a Hellenistic θεῖος ἀνήρ background, attention has been paid to the mountain setting by only a few scholars. Weeden and U.B. Müller—who take this approach—also maintain that the narrative originated as a resurrection appearance story, and so identify the mountain in the manner discussed above.[30] But Müller adds to this a suggestion that brings into relationship the ὄρος ὑψηλόν of Mk 9.2, the mountain site of Moses' death, and θεῖος ἀνήρ christology: that Moses and Elijah appear here as figures who did not die but were taken directly up into heaven, and so were θεῖοι ἄνδρες.[31] While the death of Moses is recounted in Dt 34.5-8, there was some speculation among certain Jewish interpreters that he did not really die but was translated directly from Mount Nebo into heaven. Müller points to the tradition reflected in Josephus (*Ant.* 4.323-326) that Moses was taken away in a cloud, and the tradition surfaces elsewhere as well.[32] So, though Müller did not focus attention on the mountain *per se*, it could be argued that the presence of Moses (who was treated in Hellenistic Judaism as a θεῖος ἀνήρ), the cloud which (presumably) bore Moses and Elijah away, and the transformed countenance of Jesus, all indicate that θεῖος ἀνήρ thinking generally—and Mount Nebo as the site of Moses' apotheosis specifically—provide the explanation of the mountain setting.

It is extremely doubtful, however, that θεῖος ἀνήρ christology has any real significance for the interpretation of the Transfiguration Narrative. Not only has the relevance of this concept for the development of christology in general come under increasing criticism,[33] but, as we will see below, the two elements most frequently cited in support of such a reading of the Transfiguration— the changed appearance and the term 'Son of God'—both find a more natural and plausible *Sitz im Leben* in a Palestinian milieu.[34]

As for the mountain itself, the presence of some Nebo associations cannot be ruled out. And, as we will see in the next section, the mountain does appear to function as a cosmic point of entry into the heavenly realm. But these features by no means imply θεῖος ἀνήρ connotations. In fact, the joint presence of Moses and Elijah has more natural associations with Sinai/Horeb, where both received divine revelations, than with Nebo which is associated only with Moses.

c. *An Apocalyptic Mountain of Revelation*

A more relevant background for the interpretation of the Transfiguration Narrative is that of Jewish apocalyptic literature, in which close parallels can be found for many of the characteristic features of the narrative. In various apocalyptic passages, there are references to the changed appearance that the righteous will receive to make them fit for the heavenly realm (e.g. Dan 12.3; 2 Bar 51.1-3, 10; 4 Ezra 7.97; 10.25; cf. Rev 1.16). While these passages have an emphasis on the brightness of the countenance that is more appropriate to a study of Matthew's redaction,[35] we also frequently encounter references to bright and/or white garments worn in the heavenly sphere (Dan 10.5; 1 Enoch 14.20; 62.15f.; 2 Enoch 22.8-10; Mk 16.5; Rev 3.4f.; 7.9).

Similarly, the heavenly voice is encountered as a feature of apocalyptic revelations (Dan 8.16; 1 Enoch 13.8; T. Levi 18.6; Rev 11.12). Especially important here is 2 Bar 13.1 where a voice comes to Baruch as he stands on Mount Zion. Clouds are also present in this tradition (Dan 7.13; Rev 14.4), appearing sometimes in association with mountains: in 4 Ezra 13.13, where the messianic 'Man' who comes on the clouds of heaven cuts out for himself a mountain; and especially in 2 Macc 2.7f., where it is promised that in the end times the cloud will again appear on the mountains as in the days of Moses and Solomon.

As for the mountain itself, mountains commonly appear in

apocalyptic literature as sites for revelations of heavenly matters (e.g. 1 Enoch 18.6-16; T. Levi 2.5f.; Apoc. Abr. 12; cf. *Memar Markah* 4.6; 5.3). As we saw in Chapter 5 above,[36] apocalyptic mountains of revelation combined the biblical pattern of divine theophany with the cosmic notion of the mountain as the point of entry into the heavenly realm. So on this reading of the text, the Mountain of Transfiguration is seen as an apocalyptic mountain of revelation, a cosmic mountain that brings those on its summit close to the heavenly realm.

In view of such parallels, it is not to be doubted that the description of Jesus' encounter with the heavenly personages on a mountain-top owes something to this apocalyptic background. In fact, Sabbe makes the perceptive observation that the presence in the narrative of two high points—the changed appearance and the voice from the cloud—is to be seen not as evidence of conflation but rather as the typical apocalyptic pattern of revelation and interpretation.[37] This does not mean that other mountain associations must therefore be excluded. But it does mean that if other influences have been at work in the formation of the narrative, the resultant mountain associations have also taken on some of the coloration of an apocalyptic mountain of revelation.[38]

d. *Mount Sinai*

Another common interpretation of the Transfiguration Narrative is that it was formed on the basis of a Moses typology, with the purpose of presenting Jesus as the 'new Moses' or the 'prophet like Moses'. In such an interpretation, the mountain on which Jesus was transfigured is seen as the Christian counterpart to Sinai.

In support of this interpretation, its proponents point to Sinai and wilderness parallels for virtually every detail in the account.[39] The explicit time reference 'after six days', so unusual in Synoptic materials, finds an echo in Ex 24.15-18, where God spoke to Moses from the cloud on Mount Sinai after 'the cloud covered it six days'. In that same Exodus passage, we find Moses taking three companions who are mentioned by name (Ex 24.1, 9). Moses himself, of course, appears in the Transfiguration Narrative, and Elijah, who appears with him, also had an encounter with God on Sinai/Horeb (1 Ki 19.8ff.). The cloud is an important feature in both the Sinai account (Ex 19.16; 24.15-18; 34.5) and the wilderness period generally, where it is a visible sign of God's presence (e.g. Ex 13.21f.; 33.7-11; 40.34-

38; Num 9.15-23). Especially noteworthy is the fact that the verb ἐπισκιάζω, used of the cloud in Mk 9.7, also appears with refererence to the cloud over the Tent of Meeting in Ex 40.35—one of the few occurrences of this word in the LXX. Likewise, the voice from the cloud is paralleled in Ex 24.16; the change in appearance finds its counterpart in Ex 34.29-35; and the words ἀκούετε αὐτοῦ of Mk 9.7 echo αὐτοῦ ἀκούσεσθε in Dt 18.15.

Some have also attempted to find a parallel to the σκηναί of Peter's suggestion in the Tent of Meeting which figures prominently in the wilderness accounts together with the cloud of God's presence (e.g. Ex 33.7-11; 40.34-38; Num 9.15-23).[40] The plurality of tents, however, together with the fact that in Peter's suggestion they seem to be proposed dwellings rather than places for divine encounter, make this doubtful.

In addition to this list of parallel features, appeal can also be made to the lively eschatological role played by Moses and Elijah in the cluster of wilderness/prophet eschatological ideas that looked for a return to wilderness conditions as a preliminary to the Messianic Age.[41]

True, the Moses/Sinai parallels are not always exact. In Ex 24.15-18, in contrast to the Transfiguration Narrative, the six day period was the length of time during which Moses was on the cloud-covered mountain before he heard the voice of God.[42] In Ex 24.1, 9 Moses took with him not only the three named companions, but also the seventy elders; moreover, they were all left behind when Moses made the final ascent up the mountain. Likewise, at the end of the Sinai experience Moses descended to announce to the people what he heard, but after the Transfiguration Jesus commands silence. And while the revelation in Exodus is a lengthy legal discourse, in the Gospel account there are no Torah overtones and the divine pronouncement is extremely compressed. Most of all, the Son christology of v. 7 finds no Moses/Sinai counterpart.

Nevertheless, the cumulative effect of these details suggests the presence in some form of Moses/Sinai typology.[43] Although it cannot account entirely for the christology of the passage, and though the narrative has been tinged with apocalyptic colouring, Mount Sinai plays a major typological role in this mountain scene.[44]

e. *The Binding of Isaac*

Flusser and Leaney have made the intriguing suggestion that the

Transfiguration Narrative has been informed by the Gen 22 account of the binding of Isaac—a story popular in contemporary Jewish exegesis.[45] They base this suggestion on the use in v. 7 of ἀγαπητός, arguing that the divine words of Gen 22.2 (τὸν υἱόν σου τὸν ἀγαπητόν, ὅν ἠγάπησας) provide a closer parallel to the οὗτός ἐστιν ὁ υἱός μου ὁ ἀγαπητός of Mk 9.7 than does Ps 2.7, the passage often seen as lying behind the 'Son' statement.

In the Genesis account, the binding of Isaac took place on 'one of the mountains of Moriah'. Though neither Leaney nor Flusser refer to the mountain directly,[46] we have observed the important midrashic role played by this mountain, which became known in Jewish tradition as 'Mount Moriah'.[47] Of special interest is the fact that in Targum Pseudo-Jonathan and in Rabbinic accounts of the Akedah, the presence of a cloud on the mountain is an important midrashic feature.[48] So it could be argued that the Mount Moriah site of the binding of Isaac stands behind the Mountain of Transfiguration.

It is extremely doubtful, however, that the Akedah tradition had anything to do with the Transfiguration Narrative or its Son-christology. The absence of the cloud in Jub 18 and in all Targums other than Pseudo-Jonathan makes it uncertain that this was a feature of pre-Christian tradition. And if one cannot include the cloud in the argument, it becomes difficult to sustain the interpretation on the strength of the single word ἀγαπητός—especially when neither Matthew nor Mark in their other uses of ἀγαπητός evidence any awareness of a Gen 22.2 background.[49] In fact, it is even possible that ἀγαπητός is rooted in Ps 2.7. Gundry points out that in Tg. Ps 2.2 חביב (passive participle of חבב, 'to love') is used of the Son.[50] While one cannot demonstrate conclusively the pre-Christian existence of this Targumic rendering, it is at least possible that ἀγαπητός, no less than the rest of the first part of the divine proclamation, reflects Ps 2.7. In any case, a Gen 22/Mount Moriah background for the Mountain of Transfiguration must be ruled out.

f. *The Feast of Booths*
The reference to σκηναί by Peter in Mk 9.4 has long puzzled commentators. Some, however, use it as the point of departure for an interpretation of the Transfiguration Narrative against a background of the Feast of Booths or Tabernacles. First suggested in 1922 by Lohmeyer,[51] it received its most elaborate treatment in Riesenfeld's 1947 work *Jésus transfiguré*.

Basic to Riesenfeld's thesis is the Scandinavian theory that the three Jewish autumn festivals (New Year, Atonement, and the Feast of Booths) were originally part of a single annual enthronement festival of a type common in the ancient Near East. Though this old festival disintegrated—so the argument goes—the original enthronement ideas continued to be associated with the Feast of Booths in particular—a feast that also took on eschatological overtones in the course of time. So Riesenfeld sees in the Transfiguration narrative a combination of enthronement and eschatological motifs, all of which arose out of traditions associated with the Feast of Booths.

Riesenfeld's work has been skewed by the improbability of the 'enthronement festival' thesis on which it rests.[52] But to reject a connection between the Feast of Booths and the idea of enthronement is not necessarily to invalidate the possibility of a Tabernacles background for the Mountain of Tranfiguration, especially since the feast had taken on eschatological overtones.[53] It is necessary to inquire, then, about the presence of mountain symbolism in this eschatologized Feast of Booths. Riesenfeld is content merely to appeal to the general role of the mountain in Jewish eschatological expectation.[54] But while his observations are correct in the main, they do not serve to connect a mountain setting explicitly with the feast.

Daniélou, in support of a Tabernacles thesis, points to the appearance of the Mount of Olives in Zech 14.4 in connection with the eschatological events that culminate in a celebration of the Feast of Booths.[55] Yet as Zech 14 unfolds, the scene on the Mount of Olives becomes incorporated into traditional Zion eschatology: Jerusalem 'shall remain aloft upon its site' (v. 10) and it is to Jerusalem that the nations make pilgrimage in order to celebrate the feast (v. 16). On the basis of this passage together with the general consideration of the central place of Jerusalem in all Jewish festivals, it might be possible to argue that the use of σκηναί in Mk 9.5 suggests a Zion background for the mountain setting.[56]

It is unlikely, however, that the evidence in the passage is sufficient to support a Tabernacles interpretation. Apart from σκηναί and (perhaps) the mountain setting, only the phrase 'after six days' can be brought into the discussion[57]—and then only with difficulty (i.e. as the interval between the Day of Atonement and the Feast of Booths). For the remaining features of the narrative, Riesenfeld is reduced to general statements about their eschatological connotations which, though true, do not advance his specific thesis. The most awkward factor is the mention of *three* tents. For if the conceptual framework behind Peter's suggestion was the booths of the messianic feast, one would have expected booths for the disciples as well.[58] The tents would be easier to explain if there were only one (Tent of Meeting) or six (eschatological Feast of Booths). The fact that they are proposed in the Transfiguration Narrative only for heavenly beings suggests that we have here an idiosyncratic detail whose meaning has to do with Peter's mistaken desire either to prolong the experience or to place Moses and Elijah on an equal level with Jesus. This Tabernacles approach has nothing to contribute to an explication of the mountain setting.

g. *Enthronement*

To this point we have not paid much attention to the Son-christology which is contained in the heavenly proclamation and which is really the climax of the whole narrative. A seventh approach to be considered here takes the statement οὗτός ἐστιν ὁ υἱός μου as the starting point for an interpretation of the Transfiguration Narrative that sees it as modelled on Jewish patterns of messianic enthronement.

There are two lines of argument in this approach, which combine to make a convincing case. The first has to do with the Son statement itself. Horstmann argues that 'This is my Son' is a typical enthronement formula which reflects 2 Sam 7.14 and (especially) Ps 2.7. She maintains that in these OT texts the king's ascension to the throne coincides with—indeed is made possible by—his adoption as Son by Yahweh himself.[59]

Although Ps 2.7 is frequently cited as lying behind Mk 9.7,[60] this has been flatly denied by Hahn, who argues that υἱὸς θεοῦ is a θεῖος ἀνήρ Hellenization of original παῖς/עבד terminology.[61] In his view, a messianic use of 'Son of God' would have been inconceivable in a Palestinian setting. Recent discoveries, however, have convincingly demonstrated that this is not the case. The eschatological interpretation of 2 Sam 7.10-14 in 4QFlor is solid evidence that 'Son' was coming into messianic use in pre-Christian Judaism. And though the titular 'Son of God' does not appear in 4QFlor,[62] an instance of the use of ברה די אל has turned up in a fragment also from Qumran Cave 4.[63] While this use of 'Son of God' is probably non-messianic, on the strength of 4QFlor and this text it can now be affirmed that both Son-messianology and the title 'Son of God' were present in

Palestinian usage. This being so, there are solid grounds for the assertion that the declaration οὗτός ἐστιν ὁ υἱός μου reflects OT royal ideology messianically interpreted, and that such a Son-christology was present in the earliest form of the narrative.[64]

The second line of argument has to do with the form of the narrative. Müller claims that in the three features of the changed appearance, the presence of Moses and Elijah, and the heavenly proclamation, we can see a three-fold Hellenistic enthronement form: apotheosis, presentation, enthronement.[65] His estimation of the Hellenistic origin of the narrative may be questioned. Yet, as Michel and Jeremias have shown,[66] such a three-fold formula (with the first element as elevation instead of apotheosis) is deeply rooted in Jewish tradition. And since this pattern provides a framework that accounts for all the details of the narrative, it is probable that enthronement ideas were at work not only in the content of the divine proclamation but also in the form of the narrative as a whole.

So the possibility presents itself that the mountain setting of the Transfiguration Narrative functions as a mountain of enthronement. In our study of OT Zion theology, we noticed the frequency with which the mountain is referred to as the site for the throne of Yahweh (e.g. Ps 48.2; cf. Ps 99.1-5; 146.10; Jer 8.19), or for his anointed king (e.g. Ps 2.6; cf. Ps 110.2; 132.11-18).[67] And this theme was carried over into Zion eschatology as well:[68] on that day Yahweh (Is 24.23; 52.7; Ezek 20.33, 40; Mic 4.6f.; Zech 14.8-11) or the messianic king (Ezek 17.22-24; 34.23-31; Mic 5.2-4) will reign on Mount Zion. In Second-Temple Judaism, the mountain was also seen as the seat of God's throne (Jub 1.17-29; 1 Enoch 18.8, 24.2–25.6; cf. Tob 13.11; Sib Or 3.716-720) and the place where the Messiah will exercise his rulership over the nations (4 Ezra 13; 2 Bar 40.1-4; cf. Ps Sol 17.23-51). And while the origin of the term 'the Mountain of the King' is obscure,[69] still it provides us with an indication of how deep-seated were the royal connotations associated with the mountain.[70]

The influence of Ps 2.7 on Mk 9.7 furnishes evidence of a link with the mountain of enthronement tradition. The preceding verse in Ps 2—'I have set my king on Zion, my holy mountain'—is the opening statement in the divine proclamation of enthronement. The close link between the mountain site and the Son statement in the enthronement formula of Ps 2 suggests that the mountain setting for the Son statement of Mk 9.7 should be seen in similar terms. Indeed, the use in 2 Pet 1.18 and Apoc. Pet. 15 of τὸ ἅγιον ὄρος, found also in Ps 2.6 and used frequently as an equivalent for Jerusalem/Zion,[71] indicates that the earliest commentators on the tradition interpreted it in just this way.[72] Seen from the perspective provided by v. 7, therefore, the mountain setting of the Transfiguration takes on the characteristics of a mountain of enthronement.

Our study of the Transfiguration Narrative has revealed that no single interpretative background can account for all of its features. Because of the variety and the polyvalence of the symbolic elements in the account, several prototypes within Jewish thought are evoked. This observation is applicable as well to the specific case of the mountain setting. Our study of the ὄρος ὑψηλόν in relationship to other elements of the narrative reveals definite apocalyptic, Mosaic and enthronement overtones. It remains for us to raise the question as to how these three aspects relate, given the shape of the narrative as a whole.

There can be no doubt that the key and climax to the Transfiguration account is to be found in the content of the heavenly proclamation.[73] As Pedersen astutely observes, exegesis of the passage goes awry when it is preoccupied with the change in appearance.[74] This detail has an isolated position in the story. Nothing else in the account depends on it for its meaning,[75] and, of itself, it leads only to confusion and misunderstanding, as Peter's misdirected suggestion illustrates. It is the divine proclamation, with its identification of Jesus as the Son, that overshadows and clarifies all other elements in the narrative.

Parallels drawn with Moses, then, do not serve any independent christological function, but are subordinated to the Son statement. Mosaic typology is not thereby rejected, but it is absorbed into and transcended by the larger pattern of Son-christology. One could easily imagine that the narrative assumed its present shape in a situation where there was disagreement over the relative importance of these christological conceptions.[76]

So we conclude that though there is apocalyptic colouring in the whole account, the basic shape of the narrative arises from the movement from Moses typology to Son-christology. Because of its variety of associations, the mountain functions at three levels. Taking on characteristics of an apocalyptic mountain of revelation, it serves both as a reminder of Moses typology and as the place of the exaltation of the Son—the place where Mosaic categories are transcended.

2. *The Mountain Setting in Matthew's Redaction*

In a full study of the Transfiguration Narrative, it would be necessary next to inquire as to its meaning and function in Mark's composition. But since our interest is in the significance of the mountain setting for Matthew, we will only cast sidelong glances at Mark as we attempt to answer two questions concerning the Matthean redaction: (1) How did Matthew interpret the narrative—with its mountain setting—as it came to him? and (2) What place does the mountain setting occupy in the outworking of Matthew's redactional purposes?

a. *In its Immediate Context*

A study of Matthew's redactional changes in the Transfiguration Narrative[77] reveals that each of the three aspects in the original account—apocalyptic colouring, Mosaic parallels, and enthronement of the Son—has been underscored and strengthened by Matthew. For example, the Matthean narrative has even more of the characteristics of an apocalyptic revelation than does that of Mark.[78] Matthew describes the event as a ὅραμα (v. 9), a word full of apocalyptic nuances.[79] Likewise, the emphasis on light (φῶς, φωτεινή, ἔλαμψεν) gives the narrative a stronger apocalyptic flavour. Repeatedly in apocalyptic literature it is said of those associated with the heavenly realm that they 'shone like the sun' (Dan 12.3; 1 Enoch 14.20; 4 Ezra 7.97; 10.25; Rev 1.16; cf. 2 Bar 51.1-3, 10). Matthew himself uses the phrase elsewhere in a description of the future state of the righteous (13.43). Apocalyptic parallels can also be cited for the 'bright' cloud (e.g. Ezek 1.26–2.1) and the garments 'white as light' (e.g. 1 Enoch 14.20). Furthermore, the reaction to the heavenly voice described in vv. 6-7—the disciples' falling to the ground, their fear, Jesus' touch, the command to rise, the word of assurance, and their rising and looking about—is a typical apocalyptic pattern, seen perhaps most clearly in Dan 10.7-12 (cf. Ezek 1.28–2.1; Dan 8.17; 1 Enoch 14.14-25).

There is also an increased emphasis in Matthew's narrative on Moses and Mosaic features.[80] Moses is rescued from the secondary position in which he appears in Mark, and takes his place prominently before Elijah (v. 3). Such a change suggests that the parallel between

Jesus' shining face (v. 2) and Moses' countenance after his encounter with God on Sinai (Ex 34.29-35)[81] was deliberate, so that Jesus' experience on the mountain was 'like' (cf. Dt 18.15) that of Moses. In addition, Matthew's use of φωτεινή in v. 5 parallels the combination of 'brightness' and 'cloud' found in Ex 16.10, 19.16, 24.16f. and 40.34. It is true that each of these features evocative of a Mosaic background is also paralleled in apocalyptic literature, which suggests that Mosaic typology is not as dominant as Davies maintains.[82] Nevertheless, it is probable that Mosaic themes stand alongside apocalyptic patterns as motivating factors in the Matthean redaction.[83]

Neither of these, however, was the primary motivating factor in Matthew's handling of the account. Rather, the divine proclamation, with its statement of Son-christology, is the high point of the Matthean narrative.[84] Matthew emphasized this proclamation—and the royal imagery lying behind it—in several ways. His omission of Mk 9.6 and the addition of ἔτι αὐτοῦ λαλοῦντος (v. 5) sets in sharp juxtaposition Peter's inadequate response and the voice from heaven; Peter's speech is actually broken off by the heavenly interpretation of the event. Similarly, the addition of αὐτόν in v. 8 emphasizes the superiority of Jesus, who remains, over Moses and Elijah, who disappear.

But the most significant indication of Matthew's emphasis on the heavenly proclamation appears in vv. 6-7, where the most extensive Matthean alteration to the narrative is to be found. Each evangelist mentions that the disciples reacted with fear. In Mark the fear is in response to the appearance of Moses and Elijah (Mk 9.6); in Luke to the appearance of the cloud (Lk 9.34). In Matthew, however, it is in response to the heavenly voice. So for Matthew the truly awe-inspiring feature of the narrative was the proclamation of Jesus as 'beloved Son'. By his redactional handling of vv. 6-7, he underlines this with broad strokes.

As for Matthew's interest in the content of the proclamation, particularly its Son-christology,[85] we will have occasion to say more below when we consider the place of the Mountain of Transfiguration in the whole Gospel. But there is one further redactional detail to be noted here which serves to emphasize the enthronement character of the whole event. In Mark the narrative is introduced by the statement: 'There are some standing here who will not taste death before they see the kingdom coming with power' (Mk 9.1). In Matthew, however, it reads: 'before they see the Son of Man coming in his kingdom'

(16.28). What is striking here is not the title 'Son of Man', which was just picked up from Mk 8.38 and 9.9, 12.[86] Rather, it is the direct personal reference to the kingly authority of the Son of Man—a connection between Jesus and the kingdom found elsewhere in Matthew (13.41; 25.31ff.), but rarely in the other Synoptics (Lk 22.30; 23.42). As a result of this change, the narrative to follow is no longer vaguely related to the coming of the kingdom with power; it is see, rather, as the fulfilment of the promise that Jesus himself will appear in his kingly role.[87] With this change, the enthronement character of the narrative is thrown into sharp relief.[88]

So Matthew's redaction serves to emphasize the interplay between Mosaic and 'Son' categories that was present in the original narrative. The validity of Mosaic parallels is not denied by Matthew. Indeed, he describes Jesus' experience as even more 'like' that of Moses than does Mark. Nevertheless, it is Jesus' identity as the Son, and the regal connotations surrounding this term, that take centre stage. Likewise, the heightened apocalyptic colouring of Matthew's narrative is secondary; it merely serves to assist in the basic movement from Mosaic typology to Son-christology.

Matthew does not alter in any way the description of the mountain setting as he found it in Mark. Nevertheless, his conscious involvement with the three blocks of ideas within which the mountain symbol functioned in the original narrative means that the apocalyptic, Mosaic, and particularly enthronement connotations that surrounded the mountain setting in the original narrative were probably carried over and highlighted by Matthew.

b. *In the Context of the Whole Gospel*
The primary significance of the mountain setting of the Matthean Transfiguration Narrative, however, is to be seen not with respect to its background in Jewish tradition, but in the role that it plays in the out-working of Matthew's theological themes in his Gospel as a whole—particularly his 'Son of God' christology.

We have sketched the main contours of this christological theme and the role that the Mountain of Transfiguration plays in it in our discussion of the Temptation Narrative above.[89] Jesus' identity as the Son of God, as we noted, is a two-sided concept for Matthew. On the one hand, though the declaration of Jesus' Sonship at the Baptism carries with it overtones of the triumphant king of Ps 2, for Matthew the path of Sonship into which Jesus was called led

inevitably to the cross. Satan (4.1-11), Peter (16.21-23) and onlookers
during the crucifixion (27.40, 43) attempted to deflect Jesus from
such a path, each assuming in his own way that Sonship and
suffering were incompatible. But Jesus, mindful of the failure of
God's first Son Israel, resolutely remains obedient to his calling, even
to the point of death. What Mark accomplished with his emphasis on
the suffering Son of Man, Matthew captures in his presentation of
Jesus as the obedient Son of God.

On the other hand, however, Matthew also wants to say that the
final word concerning Jesus' Sonship is not death but vindication.
The glory and Lordship suggested by the Father's earlier declaration
(3.17), offered by Satan on the Mountain of Temptation (4.8-10), and
hinted at in various pre-resurrection confessions of Jesus as Son of
God (8.29; 14.33; 16.16; 27.54), are fully bestowed and displayed in
the closing scene of the Gospel. The Transfiguration, as we argued,[90]
plays the role in Matthew of a proleptic vindication, confirming the
rightness of the path chosen by Jesus in the Temptation and
providing a foretaste of the glory to be bestowed on the risen Lord.

Now that we have looked at the Transfiguration Narrative in more
detail, we are in a position to expand on its place in Matthew's
christology. The first observation to be made is that Matthew
deliberately draws this narrative into his network of passages dealing
with the theme of Sonship. The link between the voice at the
Baptism and that at the Transfiguration is made more explicitly in
Matthew than in Mark: by means of the addition in 17.5 of ἐν ᾧ
εὐδόκησα, taken from the Baptismal account (cf. Mt 3.17; Mk 1.11),
and the alteration in Mt 3.17 from the second person of Mk 1.11 to
the third person of Mk 9.7 // Mt 17.5, the two sayings are assimilated—
with the result that Matthew leaves no doubt that, in his view, the
Transfiguration falls squarely in the path of Sonship initiated at
Jesus' Baptism and Temptation. Similarly, Matthew makes the
Sonship theme the key aspect of the link between the Transfiguration
and Peter's confession—a link already present by juxtaposition in
Mark (cf. Mk 9.1)—by means of the addition of ὁ υἱὸς τοῦ θεοῦ τοῦ
ζῶντος in Peter's confession (16.16). We must leave for the moment
the question of the significance of this change for Matthew's theology.
Suffice it to point out here that it supplies further evidence of
Matthew's active concern to bring the Transfiguration Narrative into
his pattern of christological development.

More specifically, the groundwork has now been laid to support our earlier claim that the Transfiguration Narrative plays a role in Matthew's christology that can only be described as a preliminary vindication of the Son. In the first place, as we have seen, the Transfiguration Narrative is modelled on enthronement patterns. In fact, Matthew draws attention to such regal overtones in his comment that the Transfiguration has to do with 'the Son of Man coming in his kingdom' (16.28). Because his obedience was pleasing to the Father (cf. ἐν ᾧ εὐδόκησα), Jesus was declared to be the royal Son of God.

Also to be noted is the link with 4.8 provided by the term ὄρος ὑψηλόν. While both there and here Matthew took the term from his sources, his decision to retain it in both instances suggests that the two passages are to be seen together:[91] i.e. the regal authority and Lordship that are the Son's due, but that were rejected on the ὄρος ὑψηλόν of Temptation because they were offered on Satan's terms, are bestowed on the Son by the Father on the ὄρος ὑψηλόν of Transfiguration because the Son remained faithful to his calling.

It is in the link with Peter's confession, however, that the vindication aspect of the Transfiguration is more clearly seen. Mk 9.1 indicates that even in Mark the Transfiguration was meant to play a confirming role. What is confirmed in Mark was not primarily Peter's confession (which in view of what follows was a somewhat defective confession), but Jesus' teaching about the suffering Son of Man. While Jesus is often presented by Mark as a teacher, the main content of his teaching is the necessity that the Son of Man should suffer.[92] The link between Mk 8.27-38 and 9.1-9 is provided in 9.7 by ἀκούετε αὐτοῦ:[93] what is to be heard is the description of Jesus' suffering role in 8.31ff.

In Matthew, however, though the rebuke of Peter and the teaching about the suffering Son of Man are still present, the link between Confession and Transfiguration is provided by Peter's confession of Jesus as ὁ υἱὸς τοῦ θεοῦ τοῦ ζῶντος (16.16). This is now a full christological confession, revealed to Peter by the Father himself (16.17), which by virtue of Matthew's development of the Son of God theme contains the note of obedient suffering associated in Mark with the Son of Man. So the emphasis has shifted from Mark's suffering Son of Man to Matthew's similar yet distinctive idea of the obedient Son of God. And now it is the truth of Peter's confession of Jesus as Son that is confirmed by the Transfiguration, as the Father who revealed Jesus' Sonship to Peter demonstrates this Sonship in

dramatic fashion.[94] Thus the Transfiguration Narrative, with its
enthronement overtones, its links with the third temptation, and its
ratification of Peter's confession serves to vindicate the Son in his
path of humble obedience to the Father.

Yet the Transfiguration was not a full vindication, for the path of
obedience had not yet run its full course. In both Mark and Matthew
the Transfiguration points ahead to events on the far side of the
cross. In Mark's Gospel, it is probably not appropriate to attempt any
specific or exclusive choice of the event (resurrection, ascension,
parousia) of which the Transfiguration is an anticipation.[95] While it
may be true that the glorious appearance of Jesus may be more
apropos of a *parousia* reference, and that the *parousia* of the Son of
Man is referred to in the framework of the Markan narrative (8.38),
at the end of the account the reader is pointed ahead to the
resurrection (9.9f.). The anticipatory role of the Transfiguration in
Mark is further complicated by the problem of the ending of the
Gospel, though it is likely that the author intended that it conclude at
16.8 with no explicit appearance scene.[96]

In brief, it is probable that the Transfiguration plays a dual role in
Mark. The predominantly *parousia* characteristics of the Markan
narrative[97] suggest that it functions there as an anticipated *parousia*.
At the same time, however, in the structure of Mark's Gospel the
Transfiguration appearance to the disciples after the confession of
Jesus as the Christ (8.29) appears to be the counterpart of the
promised post-resurrection appearance to the disciples (14.28; 16.7)
after the confession of Jesus as Son of God (15.39)—an appearance
that in all likelihood was intended by the author to take place 'off-
stage'. This does not necessarily mean that the promised Galilee
encounter was meant by Mark to be a reference to the *parousia* which
his own Galilean community should expect soon to experience.[98]
Sharp distinctions between the resurrection, exaltation, and *parousia*
evidently were not drawn, so that a promised Galilean appearance
could act as the counterpart to an anticipated *parousia* experience in
the Transfiguration, without replacing the *parousia* completely.

The post-resurrection counterpart of the Transfiguration which
occurs off-stage in Mark is presented in explicit terms by Matthew as
the climax of the drama. Although the Transfiguration in Matthew
still shows signs of an anticipated *parousia* (16.27f.), it primarily
points ahead to the mountain-top appearance of the risen Lord in
28.16-20. This is not a *parousia* scene (cf. ἕως τῆς συντελείας τοῦ

αἰῶνος, v. 20); nevertheless, Jesus is here fully endowed with the dignity and authority that will be his at his coming. The reality which underlies both scenes will be fully present only at the close of the age. Yet the emphasis is firmly placed in Matthew on the present reality of the authority of the risen Lord.

There are several other explicit redactional details serving to bind 17.1-9 and 28.16-20 together.[99] The most apparent is the use in 17.7 and 28.18 of προσέρχομαι with Jesus as subject. While this is a favourite word in Matthew's vocabulary (Mt 53 times; cf. 6 for Mk, 11 for Lk) which is often used of others coming to Jesus (34 times), the only two places where it is said that Jesus comes to someone are the two passages under discussion.[100] Nor is the similarity limited to the term alone, for the scenes themselves are strikingly similar: in addition to a mountain setting, in both the disciples are on their knees, doubting and afraid; in both Jesus comes to them with a word of assurance.[101]

Such a structural similarity is reinforced by the presence in both passages of the combination of teaching and authority: in the Transfiguration Narrative in the words ἀκούετε αὐτοῦ (the only element of the divine proclamation not assimilated to the Baptism); in the consummation scene by the declaration of authority and the command to teach.[102]

Thus, in view of the 'deep correspondence' between the Transfiguration Narrative and the closing commissioning scene in Matthew,[103] one is justified in concluding that the mountain settings of these scenes are also to be brought into correspondence. The enthronement of the Son which is glimpsed in a visionary way on the ὄρος of 17.1 is fully displayed on the ὄρος of 28.16. Further, the vindication of the path of Sonship which is proleptically announced on the Mountain of Transfiguration is fully declared on the Mountain of Commissioning.

Recalling the correspondence that exist between each of these mountains and the Mountain of Temptation,[104] one can go even further. On these three mountains Matthew has depicted for us in bold but economical fashion the whole pattern of the path of obedient Sonship and its outcome.[105] On the Mountain of Temptation, which stands at the end of a section where Jesus' Sonship is declared and then tested (3.13–4.11), Jesus chooses obedience to the Father rather than the Lordship due him as Son. On the Mountain of Transfiguration, after making clear to his disciples that the path of obedient Sonship must lead to the cross, the disciples receive a foretaste of the vindicatory enthronement that will be his. And on the Mountain of Commissioning, the path of obedience having been followed to its end, Jesus appears as the fully enthroned Lord of heaven and earth.

Chapter 10

THE MOUNT OF OLIVES AND THE OLIVET DISCOURSE

1. *The Mount of Olives and Matthew's Mountain Motif*

In his presentation of Jesus' final ministry in Jerusalem, Matthew took over three instances from Mark where the Mount of Olives appears: the triumphal entry (21.1; cf. Mk 11.1), the Olivet Discourse (24.3; cf. Mk 13.3), and the logion on the scattered flock (26.30; cf. Mk 14.26). While there can be little doubt that the traditional eschatological overtones associated with the Mount of Olives[1] helped to determine the royal-messianic character of the account of the triumphal entry,[2] and while the Mount of Olives may have had some part to play in the structure of Mark's Gospel,[3] at first glance there does not appear to be any pressing reason for the inclusion of these references in a discussion of the mountain motif in Matthew. They stand somewhat apart from the other ὄρος passages in Matthew in that they refer to a specified geographical site.[4] Moreover, in his handling of these three Markan passages, Matthew shows no editorial interest in the mountain setting *per se*. He appears merely to share in a common Synoptic tendency to see the Mount of Olives as Jesus' chosen place of retreat and base of operations during his last days in Jerusalem.[5]

Yet a hasty dismissal of these passages from our discussion of Matthew's mountain motif would be unwise, for on closer inspection two explicit links between these Mount of Olives passages and the closing mountain scene become evident. First, in Mt 26.30-32 // Mk 14.26-28 it is on the Mount of Olives that Jesus promises to meet his disciples in Galilee after the resurrection.[6] In Mark, of course, this anticipated meeting is not recounted. In Matthew, however, the promise made on τὸ ὄρος τῶν ἐλαιῶν (26.30-32) is fulfilled on τὸ ὄρος οὗ ἐτάξατο αὐτοῖς ὁ Ἰησοῦς (28.16-20). A second connection is indicated in 24.3 where Matthew recasts the disciples' question asked

of Jesus on the Mount of Olives so that it specifically mentions
συντέλεια τοῦ αἰῶνος. This phrase, found in the Synoptics only in
Matthew,[7] appears also in 28.20 in a strikingly similar context: Jesus
on a mountain giving instructions to his disciples for the period
leading up to the close of the age. So it is apparent that in Matthean
thought these two mountain scenes were linked together.

There is little more that can be said about the Mount of Olives
reference in the logion of 26.30-32, apart from what has been and will
be said elsewhere in this study about the endings of Matthew and
Mark.[8] But this link between the Mount of Olives in 26.30-32 and
the Mountain of Commissioning in 28.16 provides subsidiary support
for the argument that Matthew, by means of his use of ὄρος and
συντέλεια τοῦ αἰῶνος in both 24.3 and 28.16-20, intended these two
passages be read together. We will direct our attention in this
chapter, then, to a study of the mountain setting of the Olivet
Discourse, beginning with the pre-Matthean situation.

2. *The Mountain Setting in Pre-Matthean Tradition*

The study of Mk 13 has raised a vast complex of problems which
have engendered a great deal of discussion.[9] Approaches taken to the
literary history of this eschatological discourse, however, generally
fall into one of two main categories. On the one hand, there has been
a widespread tendency to see Mk 13 as constructed out of a pre-
existing apocalyptic document of one sort or other. In one form of
this 'little apocalypse' theory, it is held that Mk 13 is just an edited
and expanded version of a Jewish apocalypse that originated in
response to Caligula's threat to erect a statue of himself in the
Jerusalem temple (AD 40).[10] The expression 'little apocalypse' has
also been used in the case of those who hold to a Jewish-Christian
origin for the tradition adapted by Mark.[11] Even Beasley-Murray,
who attempts to refute such 'little apocalypse' theories and to argue
for the essential authenticity of the discourse, can be included among
those who see an earlier apocalypse lying behind Mk 13, in that he
sees Mk 13 as having been built up on an original shorter discourse of
Jesus by means of the inclusion of sayings uttered on other occasions.[12]
When the distinction between questions of authenticity and tradition
history has been recognized, he can be classed with many other
commentators who argue that a pre-existing apocalyptic 'fly-sheet'
can be extracted from vv. 5-27.[13]

The other main approach lays emphasis on the disparate nature of the sources lying behind Mk 13 and the redactional activity of Mark. Here it is held that the evanglist assembled apocalyptic material from a variety of sources in order to address a 'word of the Lord' to his own Christian community at the time of the Jewish war with Rome.[14] A modification of this approach, which differs from the first category only in emphasis, sees one of these scattered sources as an apocalyptic 'fly-sheet'.[15]

We are interested here in the literary history of the Olivet Discourse only in so far as that history helps us to discover the origin and significance of its mountain setting. In view of the eschatological nuances associated in Jewish tradition with the Mount of Olives,[16] this mountain would have been quite fitting for a discourse of such a nature.[17] As for the literary origin of the setting, if the discourse was just a Markan compilation of scattered sayings, then its mountain setting was due to Mark's redactional activity. It is much more likely, however, that Mk 13 is based on a connected apocalyptic source. The wide variety in the attempts to isolate such a source discourages one from any attempt to be overly specific about its extent. Nevertheless, Hartman's demonstration that vv. 5b-8, 12-16, 19-22, 24-27 all resonate with themes drawn from Daniel, and his consequent argument that the earliest form of Mk 13 was an eschatological midrash on Daniel represented by these verses, is probably as close to the truth as our sources will allow us to come. So we may posit that the Eschatological Discourse was first put into literary form as an interpretation of Jesus' eschatological teaching in the light of the prophecies of Daniel and in the context of the threatened desecration of the temple by Caligula,[18] and that Mark supplemented this core apocalypse with other eschatological sayings—just as Matthew did after him.

To take such a position, however, is not necessarily to argue for a pre-Markan mountain setting. In fact, most scholars who hold to an underlying apocalyptic fly-sheet theory see vv. 1-4 as largely a Markan construction designed to link the eschatological discourse with the traditional logion concerning the destruction of the temple (v. 2).[19] The mountain setting, in fact, is often viewed as part of the expression in the passage of Mark's typical secrecy motif (cf. the inner group of disciples, κατ' ἰδίαν).[20] And if some Lukan commentators are correct in asserting that, in his composition of the Eschatological Discourse, Luke drew heavily on another source in

addition to Mk 13,[21] then the absence of a mountain setting in Luke
may point to its absence in this second source as well. This is not a
necessary inference, but it could serve as one indication among
others of a Markan origin of the mountain setting in Mk 13.3.

The evidence of Mark's redactional hand in vv. 1-4 cannot easily
be denied. Yet on the other hand, the mountain setting must not
simply be explained as a secrecy device, for it bears a striking
resemblance to the mountains of revelation frequently encountered
in apocalyptic literature. We think here not so much of mountains as
cosmic points of entry into the heavenly realm, as of those passages
where revelations of the End are vouchsafed on mountains. Included
among such passages (discussed fully in Chapter 5 above[22]) are 2
Bar 13.1, where Baruch receives a revelation of the final events while
standing on Mount Zion; Tg. Ps.-J. Dt 34.1 and *Memar Marqah* 5.3,
where Moses receives a similar revelation on Mount Nebo;[23] and
Apoc. Abr. 21-31, where Abraham has outlined for him on Mount
Horeb the course of history from the Fall until the punishment of the
heathen and the ingathering of Israel. One could also mention
Jubilees, which presents itself as a revelation—concerned at least in
part with future events—given to Moses on Mount Sinai.

It has often been pointed out that Mk 13 deviates in certain ways
from traditional apocalyptic forms: some typical apocalyptic features
are missing, and the parenetic emphasis that runs through the
chapter is seldom paralleled in apocalyptic literature.[24] Yet apocalyptic was a fluid literary form, and the undeniably apocalyptic features
of the discourse, particularly in its earliest stratum, are sufficiently
numerous that the usual categorization of this discourse as apocalyptic is quite justified.[25] This being so, it is probable that its mountain
setting was intended as a mountain of revelation of the type common
in Jewish apocalyptic literature. This does not necessarily imply that
such a setting could not have been provided by Mark himself. But
Mark's evident intention in ch. 13 to modify apocalyptic fervour with
parenetic instruction[26] suggests that such an apocalyptic feature as
the mountain setting was already present in the tradition as he
received it.

Such an understanding of the origin and significance of the Mount
of Olives setting for Mk 13 is held as a possibility by Pesch, who
points to the frequent parallel mountain scenes of revelation in later
(especially Gnostic) literature as evidence that the mountain was an
established apocalyptic setting.[27] While this can be more firmly

established on the basis of Jewish apocalyptic material itself, his arguments for the mountain setting as an essential, and pre-Markan, feature of the Eschatological Discourse are persuasive. By contrast, Gaston's citation of such extra-canonical mountain settings—particularly the Mount of Olives—as evidence that Mk 13 originated as a post-Easter discourse, has nothing to commend it.[28]

We conclude, then, that a Mount of Olives setting for the Olivet Discourse of Mk 13 was present in the apocalyptic source which underlies it, and that it probably functioned in typically apocalyptic fashion as the site of a revelation of future events. This was a function for which the eschatological nuances associated with the Mount of Olives made it eminently suitable.

3. *The Mountain Setting in Matthew's Redaction*

As noted already, Matthew took over Mark's three Mount of Olives references without placing any apparent theological emphasis on the mountain *per se*. He may have perceived that apocalyptic/eschatological nuances were present in the Olivet Discourse of Mk 13, but he made no attempt to underline or modify them in his version of the discourse. The redactional significance of the Mount of Olives setting in 24.3, therefore, lies in its literary function in the Gospel as a whole, and not in any specifically theological function within the Eschatological Discourse itself. So our interest here will be primarily in the link between Matthew's Olivet Discourse (chs. 24–25) and his Great Commission (28.16-20), for which the mountain setting is one indication.

The key to the linkage is provided by συντέλεια τοῦ αἰῶνος, appearing in 24.3 and 28.20. This term was current in apocalyptic circles,[29] and may have been suggested to Matthew by the use of συντελεῖσθαι in Mk 13.4. The appearance of this term in two important Matthean passages dealing with the nature of the period between Jesus' passion and the end of the age cannot be coincidental. Matthew's redactional hand can also be seen in his widening of the audience for the discourse to include all οἱ μαθηταί (v. 3), and not just the select four of the Markan account. By so doing, Matthew indicates that both the Olivet Discourse and the Great Commission are addressed to the disciples of Jesus (cf. οἱ ἕνδεκα μαθηταί in 28.16)—and hence, from the evangelist's perspective, to the Church in his own day.[30] So both passages describe the nature of the

Church's existence in the world and its relationship with its Lord during the 'interim period' between the cross and the *parousia*. Our task, therefore, will be to discover what it is that Matthew wanted to convey by means of his evident linking of these passages.

The nature of this interim period as described in 28.16-20 is reasonably straightforward. The Church lives in a world that has been placed under the authority of the risen Jesus, whose presence with the Church is promised until the End. Her task is to invite 'all nations' to acknowledge Jesus' authority by becoming disciples and Church members. Although the duration of this period is not given, there is no indication that the End is imminent. But the nature of the interim period described in Matthew's redaction of the Olivet Discourse[31] is not so immediately evident, and needs to be examined in more detail.

In order to determine the nature of the interim period leading up to the *parousia* in Mt 24–25, it is necessary first to be clear about the relationship in Matthean thought between the *parousia* or close of the age and the destruction of the Jerusalem temple—the two events mentioned in the introduction to the discourse (24.2f.). The crux of the problem is found in 24.29, where Matthew inserted εὐθέως into the description of the *parousia* of the Son of Man (24.29-31; cf. Mk 13.24-27). If, as is often assumed and the text itself seems to suggest, vv. 15-22 refer to the siege of Jerusalem and the destruction of the temple, the insertion of εὐθέως appears to imply that for Matthew the *parousia* and the destruction of the temple are bound together in a tight temporal sequence (vv. 23-28 being essentially parenthetical). In fact, there is a school of thought among (mainly older) commentators that argues on the basis of just such considerations that Matthew was written either immediately before or shortly after AD 70 and that he expected the *parousia* to arrive hard on the heels of the fall of Jerusalem.[32] In such a reading of the text, there is no interim period at all, except in the past tense; Matthew's expectation in this interpretation of 24.29 was that the *parousia* and the close of the age were to appear momentarily.

If this was Matthew's view, however, not only does it contrast sharply with the vista of a Church age that opens up in 28.16-20, but it is a surprising development from the interpretation of the destruction of the temple found in Mk 13. Critical study of Mark's discourse has resulted in a consensus that Mark's purpose was to dampen apocalyptic enthusiasm and wild speculation being stirred up in some quarters by the events of the war in Palestine.[33] The tone of the passage is set by cautions against too-soon expectations of the End (vv. 7, 8, 10, 32, 35), warnings about false teachers who would lead astray the faithful by announcing the arrival of Christ prematurely (vv. 5f., 21-23), and exhortations to watchfulness in view of the uncertain hour of Jesus' coming (vv. 32-37). In a perceptive study, Conzelmann notes how Mk 13 differs from usual apocalyptic patterns in its refusal to announce a direct and unambiguous link between current historical events and the arrival of the End.[34] Both a period of tribulation leading up to the destruction of the temple (vv. 5-23) and the coming of the Son of Man with its preliminary tribulations (vv. 24-27) are described in the chapter, and the eschatological relationship between the two is recognized (vv. 28-31). Yet, as Conzelmann points out, any direct chronological relationship between the two is broken by means of vv. 24 and 32. Thus Mark describes the destruction of the temple and the coming of the End in two related but clearly differentiated panels of material, thereby being able both to correct certain false apocalyptic speculations that arose in connection with the Roman-Jewish war and to draw out the parenetical-eschatological implications of that event.

If Matthew depends on Mark for much of his Eschatological Discourse—and if, as is likely, he wrote some years after the events of AD 70[35]—it is difficult to see why he would have blurred the careful Markan differentiation between thee events.[36] In fact, from the two-fold nature of the question in 24.3 it appears that Matthew made, in the disciples' question itself, the distinction between the war with Rome and the *parousia* that in Mark appears only in Jesus' answer.[37] Is there, then, some other understanding of the orientation of Matthew's discourse vis-à-vis the destruction of the temple that will solve the problems raised by the insertion of εὐθέως in v. 29?

Among commentators who recognize the problem,[38] one approach has been to deny that vv. 15-22 have anything to do with the destruction of Jerusalem at all.[39] If it is insisted on the basis of vv. 1-3 that the discourse must contain some reference to the events of the Jewish war, adherents of this position reply that allusions are to be found only in vv. 4-14 and that vv. 15-22 refer in a symbolic way to events still in the future—perhaps to a threatened imposition of Emperor worship.[40]

Such an approach, of course, releases the tension from v. 29 by allocating all of vv. 15-31 to the indefinite future. Yet the position cannot be sustained. For Matthew's reference to the temple in v. 15 (ἐν τόπῳ ἁγίῳ), together with the Palestinian flavour of vv. 15-22, weigh heavily in favour of the view that in these verses there is the answer to the first half of the disciples' question—i.e. that these verses deal with the time of the destruction of the temple. Meier's modification of this approach, suggesting that in vv. 15-22 there is a double reference wherein the fall of the temple serves as a paradigm for an anticipated future tribulation,[41] does not really meet this objection.

Another approach to the problem differs from the first by a full 180 degrees. Gaston, Brown and others[42] argue that both vv. 15-22 (the fall of Jerusalem) and vv. 29-31 (the *parousia* of the Son of Man) refer to events lying in the past for Matthew. Verses 29-31 are held to refer in a symbolic way to the destruction of the temple in AD 70 and the Gentile mission. In Gaston's words:

> Mark has said that the parousia of the Son of Man would occur with the destruction of the temple and that the mission to the Gentiles was an eschatological event associated with the temple. It seems that Matthew has agreed with him and said that indeed the parousia occurred while the temple was in flames.[43]

Only at v. 32, or perhaps at v. 36, does Matthew's attention shift to the future.

But though this interpretation eliminates the problem raised by the insertion of εὐθέως, it too is highly unlikely. Apart from the *prima facie* difficulty of seeing vv. 29-31 as historical,[44] the inclusion in 24.3 of both παρουσίας and συντελείας τοῦ αἰῶνος—the latter of which is definitely a future event (cf. 28.20)—under the single article τῆς,[45] suggests strongly that for Matthew the *parousia* and the close of the age are one and the same (future) event. Furthermore, elsewhere in Matthew the sending out of the gathering angels (cf. 24.31) is an event which takes place at the συντέλεια τοῦ αἰῶνος (13.40-43, 49). Consequently, the identification of 24:31 with a Gentile mission which was already in progress is virtually impossible to maintain. In addition, it is also to be noted that the *parousia* of the Son of Man is also referred to in 24.37, as part of a section that begins with the declaration: 'But of that day and hour no one knows', and goes on to urge the reader to 'watch'. But if the *parousia* is past, the injunctions to watch lose all of their force, and the whole discourse collapses. One could also point to the 'mourning of the tribes of the earth' in v. 30. How could this possibly have been intended as a reference to an event (the fall of Jerusalem) that was surely greeted by the 'tribes of the earth' with relief and even joy? There can be no doubt that vv. 29-31 refer to a future *parousia*, so that in these verses Matthew gives an answer to the second part of the disciples' question: i.e. that the sign of the *parousia* and end of the age is the coming of the Son of Man himself.[46]

What relationship, then, is there in Matthew's perspective between the destruction of the temple and the *parousia?* The key to his thinking appears in the vague time reference μετὰ τὴν θλῖψιν τῶν ἡμερῶν ἐκείνων (v. 29; cf. Mk 13:24). For Matthew, what immediately precedes the *parousia* is not the fall of Jerusalem itself, but a period of tribulation of which the βδέλυγμα τῆς ἐρημώσεως ... ἑστὸς ἐν τόπῳ ἁγίῳ forms a part. That this is the case is evident from vv. 9-14— Matthew's unique description of the period leading up to the arrival of τὸ τέλος—where θλῖψις is used (v. 9; cf. συνέδρια in Mk 13.9) in an emphatic way to describe the whole period. So the fall of Jerusalem is an indication that the second phase of events has begun (vv. 15-28, 29-31 are epexegetic of vv. 9-14a, 14b respectively), but that second phase will be brought to a close only by the temporally uncertain (cf. v. 36) *parousia* of the Son of Man.[47]

In view of this analysis, the significance of εὐθέως becomes clear. It serves as an indication of the suddenness or unexpectedness with which the End arrives, not of its immediate appearance after some known and datable event. As Lagrange observes, similar terms are frequently used in apocalyptic to indicate a new stage in the unfolding of a vision or a shift from one period to the next.[48]

For Matthew, then, the Church finds itself in an interim period between the resurrection and (more recently) the fall of Jerusalem, on the one hand, and the *parousia* and close of the age, on the other. But what are the characteristics of this period in Matthew's view, and what is his message to the Church as it lives 'between the times'?

Looking at Mt 24–25 on its own terms, we can say that the interim period is characterized by three things: (1) tribulation from without, as the Church faces suffering and persecution at the hands of the nations (24.9, 21-22); (2) apostasy and faithlessness within, as the Church is threatened by false prophets, ἀνομία, and love grown cold (24.10-12, 23-26); and (3) the mission to πάντα τὰ ἔθνη, which must be carried out before the End can come (24.14). This whole period lies under the shadow of an imminent *parousia*, which will bring a time not only of judgment for the nations (24.30; 25.31-46), but also of judgmental separation within the Church itself (24.40-42, 48-51; 25.11-13, 26-30). Consequently, Matthew urges the Church to be watchful, so that when the Lord returns he will find them faithfully observing his commands (24.37–25.30).

With the exception of the presentation of the Church as a *corpus mixtum*, all of this is also present in Mark. But a comparison with Mark makes clear Matthew's distinctive emphases,[49] which are most in evidence in his unique sections of 24.9-14 and 24.37–25.46. With the amplified description of internal problems facing the Church (24.10-12) and the lengthy elaboration of the Markan theme that the nearness yet indeterminacy of the time of the End demands that the Church be vigilant (24.37–25.30), the emphasis of Matthew's discourse falls more decidedly than in Mark on the nature of Christian existence in the period leading up to the End. During the absence of the master, it is necessary for the servants to remain faithful to his commands. Because it is possible for a Church member to say 'Lord, Lord' without doing the will of the heavenly Father, a question about the *parousia* can lead for Matthew only to a consideration of the necessity for watchfulness (which in his terms means obedience) in view of the prospect of possible judgment. And as is the case throughout the Gospel—and especially in each of the discourses— eschatology is pressed into the service of parenesis, as the Church's existence is seen as conditioned by the nearness of the End.[50]

We have suggested that by means of their mountain settings and the phrase συντέλεια τοῦ αἰῶνος Matthew indicates his intention that chs. 24–25 and 28.16-20, the two passages dealing with the Church's life in the period before the close of the age, be read together. If this is so, what can be said about eschatology, history and the Church in Matthean perspective on the basis of such a parallel reading?

A comparison of these two passages reveals not only similarities in their depiction of the interim period and the Church's role in it, but also striking differences in tone and content. In addition to the features that drew our attention to the passages in the first place— their mountain settings, the presence of Jesus with his disciples, discourses about the period leading up to the close of the age—two additional items of similarity deserve mention. First, in both passages the time leading up to the End is characterized by a mission to πάντα τὰ ἔθνη. In the Olivet Discourse this appears in 24.14, where

Matthew has expanded the brief mention found in Mk 13.10, has given it an emphatic position at the end of the paragraph, and has made explicit the intimate relationship between this mission and the coming of the End (v. 14b; cf. Mk's more vague πρῶτον). In 28.18-20 the instructions concerning the Gentile mission comprise the long central section of the three-fold declaration of the risen Lord, with that mission command being the only injunction laid on the Church by her Lord for the interim period. Second, though it is expressed in different terms, in both passages we are presented with a view of discipleship centred on the necessity of obedience to the Lord's commands.

But once the connection between the two passages is seen, it is the differences that are more striking. In place of the sense of urgency and tension that pervades the Eschatological Discourse of chs. 24–25, the concluding statement of the risen Lord is characterized by a calmness and confidence that leaves no room for the terrors of an apocalyptic future. The life of the Church in the time before the close of the age is determined by the present status of its risen Lord rather than by any threat of future judgment. But most significantly, while the Son of Man is very much the absent master in the Olivet Discourse—a presupposition which underlies the whole concluding section of Matthew's discourse (esp. 24.43–25.30)[51]—the Great Commission concludes with a ringing declaration of the presence of the Lord with his disciples until the end of the age.

In view of such differences, it cannot be said that Matthew intended the two passages to be mere repetitions of each other. As one moves from the Olivet Discourse to the Commission, there is a real advance in the depiction of the interim period. This does not mean that Matthew's message in chs. 24–25 is somehow denied or cancelled by 28.16-20. The Commission, no less than the Olivet Discourse, emphasizes the ethical imperatives that derive from eschatological expectations. In fact, since elsewhere in Matthew the phrase συντέλεια τοῦ αἰῶνος is used only in the context of the threat of final judgment, its appearance in 28.20 may well mean that overtones of eschatological judgment are present in the concluding declaration as well.

But while there are parenetical concerns and judgmental overtones in both passages, Matthew's emphasis in the closing verses of his Gospel lies elsewhere. Because of the abiding presence of the risen Lord with his Church, the interim period is seen in a whole new perspective. Many of the benefits that before the resurrection were associated only with the *parousia* have now in this interim period become operative in a proleptic way for the Church. The theme of the presence of the Lord was sounded earlier in 1.23 and 18.20. But since such a presence can in reality be founded only on the resurrection and exaltation of Jesus, Matthew waits until these events have taken place before announcing its full significance for the Church in the interim period. Just as 28.16-20 represents an advance in the sphere of the authority of Jesus (no longer just authority on earth; cf. 9.6), and an advance in the scope of the disciples' mission (no longer just to Israel as in 10.5 and 15.24—though like the theme of Christ's presence the universality of the mission has been anticipated throughout the Gospel; cf. 4.15; 8.11f.; 12.21; 24.14), so it represents a new understanding of the relationship of the Church to her Lord in the period leading up to the End. Mt 24–25, therefore, is not the evangelist's last word on this period. By linking these chapters with the closing scene of the Gospel, Matthew points the reader ahead to that passage in which the existence of the Church during πᾶσαι αἱ ἡμέραι ἕως τῆς συντελείας τοῦ αἰῶνος is most completely and finally described.

Conzelmann argues that though Mark leaves the interim period as an undefined and generally negative quantity, by refusing to allow any close temporal link between the Jewish war with Rome and the inbreaking of the eschatological era he prepared the way for further theological reflection on the nature and significance of this hitherto unforeseen period.[52] Our argument here is that such further reflection has been carried out by Matthew, and is to be seen not primarily in his redaction of the Olivet Discourse itself, but in 28.16-20, the passage to which this discourse looks forward. In 28.16-20 the proleptic enjoyment of the benefits of the *parousia*—the universal sovereignty of the risen Lord and the presence of the Lord with his people—defines for the Church the nature of the interim period during which it seeks to proclaim his sovereignty among the nations.

It would appear, then, that we are justified in seeing the Olivet Discourse in Matthew as part of a mountain motif in the Gospel which finds its key and culmination in the closing mountain scene. Although the eschatological and apocalyptic nuances traditionally associated with the Mount of Olives, and in particular its function as a mountain of revelation, are not foreign to Matthew's purposes here, his interest in the mountain setting of the discourse is primarily in its value as a literary symbol by means of which the link with the closing scene may partially be established. By means of this symbol Matthew is able to gather up the description of the interim period found in the Olivet Discourse and incorporate that description into the larger and more profound view of the Church's place in salvation history that comes to expression in the closing mountain scene.

Chapter 11

THE MOUNTAIN OF COMMISSIONING

1. *The Mountain Pericope*

The final mountain in the Matthean chain is the mountain on which the Resurrected One meets with his band of disciples and commands them to undertake—on the basis of his authority and with the assurance of his presence—a universal discipling mission. This passage (28.16-20) came into our discussion of the other mountain scenes in a secondary way, as we attempted to demonstrate that each of these contains themes that are gathered up and brought to consummation in this all-important closing pericope. But it is now time to address the passage directly.

What we have observed about the relationship between 28.16-20 and the other mountain scenes in the Gospel is consistent with what has been discovered about the function of this closing passage in the Gospel as a whole. There is general and widespread agreement among scholars that 28.16-20 was carefully crafted in accordance with the evangelist's particular theological interests in such areas as christology, ecclesiology and salvation history, and that it serves as a summary and climax of these themes as they are developed throughout the Gospel.[1]

The fact that the mountain motif is also summarized and brought to a high point in the closing scene suggests that the ὄρος of 28.16 is not just an incidental detail but an important element in what is by all accounts a carefully constructed passage. This raises the question of the significance of the ὄρος setting within the passage itself. While it is being increasingly realized that vv. 18-20 cannot be understood in isolation from vv. 16f.,[2] relatively little attention has been paid to the place and meaning of the mountain setting. Before addressing this question, however, it is necessary to look at the place of the ὄρος reference in pre-Matthean tradition.

2. *The Mountain Setting in Pre-Matthean Tradition*

Although the strong concentration in 28.16-20 of characteristically Matthean vocabulary[3] indicates extensive redactional activity, most commentators recognize that the passage was built up on the basis of traditional material. This conclusion is not unanimous,[4] but it is sufficiently widespread that we can speak of a scholarly consensus. Leaving to one side for the moment the question of the setting, underlying traditional materials are most commonly suggested for vv. 18b, 19b, and 20b—i.e. for the declaration of exaltation, the mission and baptismal command, and the promise of divine assistance.[5]

A consensus has not yet been reached, however, on the question of the form in which this traditional material came to Matthew. Michel's argument that—since parallels exist to the three individual sayings but not to the passage as a whole—it was Matthew who first joined these originally independent sayings together[6] has received significant endorsement.[7] Strecker, however, arguing that each of the three statements must have existed in a liturgical setting, maintains that they were already linked together in Matthew's church as a tripartite word of revelation.[8]

Hubbard's work on the passage represents a significant advance, not only on the question of its form in Matthew, but also on the nature of the pre-Matthean tradition.[9] Recognizing that the passage is at its most basic level a commissioning formulation centred on vv. 19-20a, he argues with considerable success that 28.16-20 is the Matthean redaction of a primitive post-resurrection commissioning that also lies behind other NT commissioning statements (Lk 24.36-49; Jn 20.19-23; Mk 16.14-18). His reconstruction is weakened, however, by a failure to include any ἐξουσία or exaltation statement in the original commissioning. Meier suggests that Acts 1.6-11—a commissioning statement curiously disregarded by Hubbard[10] but containing both exaltation (vv. 9-11) and a mission command (v. 8)—provides support for the idea that the ἐξουσία statement in 28.18b is based on a traditional feature.[11] While the mission command of Acts 1.6-11 is not as clearly predicated on a statement of exaltation as that of Mt 28.16-20, the evidence from the Acts passage is sufficient to suggest that behind Mt 28.16-20 lies an early commissioning statement consisting of: (1) a declaration of exaltation or enthronement; (2) a mission and baptismal command; and (3) a promise of continuing divine support, perhaps with reference to the Holy Spirit.[12]

The ὄρος of 28.16, then, is the setting for a statement containing a combination of traditional and redactional elements. Many commentators argue that, since Matthew shows a preference elsewhere in his Gospel for mountains as 'places of revelation', the mountain setting for the final commissioning must be included among the redactional elements.[13] Such an argument loses much of its force, however, when it is realized that—as we demonstrated in the preceding pages—each of the earlier Matthean mountain settings is rooted in the Gospel tradition in one way or another. Nowhere else has Matthew created a mountain setting *ex nihilo* in order to further his redactional purposes. This does not necessarily argue against his having done so here. But an argument in favour of such a possibility cannot appeal to the other mountain scenes in the Gospel for support; these lead us to expect just the opposite.

On the other side of the discussion there are two lines of approach to the traditional nature of the ὄρος setting that prove to be no more convincing. The first is the attempt to set 28.16-20 alongside the Transfiguration Narrative, 2 Pet 1.16-18, and later non-canonical accounts[14] in order to argue for a primitive mountain-top resurrection appearance form on which all these passages depend. While we will have more to say presently about the non-canonical material,[15] the difficulties with such an approach were dealt with in our discussion of the Transfiguration Narrative[16] and need not be repeated here.

The other line of approach to be set aside is the argument that Matthew depended for a number of the aspects of his final chapter—including the ὄρος reference in v. 16—on a lost ending of Mark. This was argued at length by Allen, who even attempted a reconstruction of the ending in general terms,[17] and it has more recently been suggested—albeit in different forms—by Linnemann and Strobel.[18] But even if one should grant the questionable hypothesis of a lost ending, the argument will not stand. The fact that a mountain was not mentioned as part of the instructions for the post-resurrection Galilee meeting in Mk 14.28 and 16.7 makes it quite unlikely that Mark would have abruptly introduced a mountain setting for the meeting—particularly if it is assumed that the phrase οὗ ἐτάξατο αὐτοῖς ὁ Ἰησοῦς is Markan. Appeal to the lack of preparation in Matthew's Gospel for the appearance of ὄρος in 28.16 does not make a Markan mountain setting any more likely, for the absence of any reference to ὄρος in Mt 26.32, 28.7, and—by extension—28.10 must be attributed to Matthew's dependence on his Markan *Vorlage*.[19]

When such superficial and unfounded arguments have been cleared away, however, the remaining considerations tend to favour the traditional nature of the ὄρος reference. Three pieces of evidence must be considered here. The first of these is the cryptic phrase οὗ ἐτάξατο αὐτοῖς ὁ Ἰησοῦς (v. 16). While it is possible that this phrase was Matthew's own clumsy attempt to soften the abruptness with which the mountain setting was being introduced into the narrative, it is more probable that the phrase was taken from some other source.[20] The language is not Matthean,[21] and the phrase 'the mountain where Jesus appointed for them (to meet him)' appears to require some other context for its meaning than what is provided in the Gospel of Matthew.[22] It is likely, therefore, that we are dealing here with the vestige of some longer account of a post-resurrection meeting of Jesus with his disciples.

A second piece of evidence arises from the reference to the Mount of Olives in Acts 1.12. We have already noted similarities between the two commissioning narratives of 28.16-20 and Acts 1.6-11. But we have yet to take account of the fact that both are placed in a mountain setting. Since many of the differences between the two accounts—particularly the geographical difference (Galilee versus Jerusalem and environs)—can be attributed to the redactional interests of Matthew and Luke, it is at least within the realm of possibility that lying behind both passages is a single scene of commissioning which took place on an unspecified mountain that Matthew and Luke localized according to their own special concerns.[23] But even if we give full weight to the geographical and other differences and see these passages as representing two separate sources of information, Acts 1.12 at least supplies evidence that extra-Matthean traditions of mountain-top resurrection appearances existed.

A third area of evidence to be considered here concerns the numerous passages in later Gnostic and non-canonical Christian material where a mountain serves as the setting for a post-resurrection discourse.[24] These passages, it was argued, represent a later form, which developed on the basis of such passages as Mt 28.16-20, Acts 1.6-12 and Mk 13 // Mt 24–25—under the influence of the apocalyptic mountain of revelation form—and as such do not preserve independent early tradition. Nevertheless, the frequency with which such scenes occur and the wide variety of mountains mentioned (Olives, Amalech, Gaugelan, Jericho, as well as several unnamed mountains) indicate how deeply the idea of mountain-top resurrection appearances had penetrated popular Christian consciousness by the second century. It may be possible, of course, to account for such a phenomenon entirely on the basis of factors already mentioned, together with other second-century considerations. But one wonders whether this resurrection appearance form could have gained such a foothold on the basis of Mt 28.16 and Acts 1.12 alone. Might it not suggest that behind the canonical passages was a widespread first-century belief that Jesus appeared after the resurrection on a mountain?—i.e. that although these later mountain passages do not preserve any specific independent *tradition*, they reflect a more widespread first-century *form*? While one cannot answer this question with any degree of certainty, the evidence from later literature is at least consistent with such a possibility. But even leaving this consideration out of account, the phrase οὗ ἐτάξατο αὐτοῖς ὁ Ἰησοῦς and the evidence from Acts 1.12 suggest that the mountain setting of Matthew's concluding scene of commissioning was dependent on an earlier report of a mountain-top resurrection and commissioning appearance.[25]

With the nature of the tradition lying behind 28.16-20 so much a matter of doubt, it is difficult to speak with assurance of any theological or typological function played by a mountain setting in pre-Matthean accounts of resurrection appearances. There is certainly not enough solid data here to justify Strobel's assertion that the mountain lying behind 28.16 and Acts 1.12 is an antitype to Sinai.[26] The most that can be said is that the literary accounts of the event owe something to an apocalyptic background.[27] More specifically, on the assumption that the tradition behind 28.16-20 was a mountain scene of commissioning, some influence might be detected from the second type of apocalyptic mountain of revelation discussed above— viz. the mountain as a place for the revelation of the divine will.[28] The parallels, however, are not exact.[29] Indeed, it is to be expected that it would have been impossible to recount such an unprecedented event as the resurrection entirely within already-existing forms of expression. And given the evidence of Matthean redaction through-out 28.16-20, the significance of the mountain setting in v. 16 will be determined largely by its context in the Gospel.

3. *The Mountain Setting in Matthew's Redaction*

a. *In its Immediate Context*

Mt 28.16-20 was carefully crafted by the evangelist as the key and climax of his Gospel. The ὄρος setting in v. 16, therefore, is not to be casually dismissed as an incidental detail introduced into the narrative in an awkward and haphazard manner.[30] Rather, the awkward disjunction between v. 16 and the preceding narrative testifies to the evangelist's desire to conclude his Gospel with a mountain scene—even though the Gospel of Mark which lay before him did not adequately prepare for it.

In our study of Matthew's earlier mountain scenes, we discovered at least part of his purpose in concluding his Gospel on a mountain: the mountain of 28.16 functions as a literary symbol that binds each of the other mountain scenes, and themes developed in them, to the closing scene of the Gospel. In those earlier passages, however, ὄρος was not simply a literary symbol, but played a variety of typological and theological roles within the passages themselves. One would expect to find the same situation in the closing mountain scene as well.

To raise this possibility, however, is to run headlong into the most vexing problem in the interpretation of the passage. For despite the wide measure of agreement that the various elements of 28.16-20 function individually as the culmination of identifiable redactional motifs and theological themes developed through the Gospel as a whole, no satisfying explanation has yet been given of the relationship between the various elements within the passage itself. There has been no agreement among the many scholars who have tackled the problem as to an underlying *schema* or theological framework on which the passage was constructed. At least four approaches have been taken to the problem. Three of these (the form-critical, the christological, and the attempt to find a clearly defined OT background) are interrelated, while a fourth (the attempt to find the germ of the passage solely within the Synoptic tradition itself) stands somewhat apart. We will look briefly at each of these approaches in turn.

The most common attempt to discover the theological heart of the passage is that which seeks to ascertain the literary form into which it has been cast. There is general agreement that the words of the risen Lord fall into three parts—the proclamation of authority (v. 18b), the commission (vv. 19-20a), and the promise of the abiding presence (v. 20b). And there is growing realization that vv. 16f. have to be taken into account in any discussion of form. But beyond this, the forms that have been suggested are bewildering in their variety. They include: (1) an 'enthronement hymn' such as is found in Phil 2.9-11,

1 Tim 3.16 and Heb 1.5-14;[31] (2) a 'divine utterance' (*Gottesrede*);[32] (3) an 'official decree' modelled on 2 Chron 36.23;[33] (4) a 'covenant renewal formulation';[34] (5) part of a 'theophanic form' modelled on the Sinai theophany;[35] (6) a 'commissioning *Gattung*'.[36]

Detailed discussion of the form-critical problem falls outside the scope of this study. Yet since the command in vv. 19-20a forms the core of the saying (the proclamation and the promise only give the conditions under which the command is given and in which it is to be carried out), it is likely that Hubbard's isolation of a commissioning *Gattung* provides the closest parallel. But even this does not account for all the features of the passage.[37] Therefore it is probably more accurate to say that, while the passage describes a scene of commissioning and while there are numerous OT echoes, Matthew's redaction of the tradition was not carried out here within the confines of any recognizable form. The passage is of a *sui generis* nature which defies classification.[38]

But if the question of form remains problematic, it is possible that the theological content of the pericope (as distinct from its form) was shaped by an identifiable OT *Vorlage*. The strongest case for such a *Vorlage* has been made for LXX Dan 7.13f., and it is with this passage that the discussion of the place of the OT in the construction of 28.16-20 has been concerned.

The verbal similarities between the two passages are striking. LXX Dan 7.14 begins with καὶ ἐδόθη αὐτῷ ἐξουσία, which, except for the change in person, differs from v. 18b only in the absence of the word πᾶσα. We also find the important phrase πάντα τὰ ἔθνη in both passages. In addition to such strictly linguistic considerations, Dan 7.13f. resembles 28.18-20 more generally in its description of the unlimited ἐξουσία of the Son of Man and in its explicit mention of the inclusion of the Gentiles within his sphere of authority. So on the basis of such considerations, Michel argues that 28.18-20 was constructed as an explicit fulfilment of LXX Dan 7.13f.,[39] and he is followed in this by others.[40]

This position, however, has come under sharp attack by Vögtle, who argues that since Dan 7.13f. deals with the *parousia* of the Son of Man after the destruction of the kingdoms of the world, this passage is not at all relevant for 28.16-20, which in its Matthean perspective still looks forward to the parousia.[41] He sees 28.16-20 rather as a fulfilment of the promise accentuated by the evangelist in 26.64. Vögtle has been justly criticized for not allowing the possibility that

Matthew creatively reinterpreted the Daniel passage in order to present the post-resurrection commissioning as a proleptic *parousia*.[42] Nevertheless, further study reveals a number of other significant conceptual differences which tend to support the conclusion that while Matthew may have made use of some Danielic language, he did not intend his closing pericope to be a fulfilment of Dan 7.13f., so that the Daniel passage was not the controlling factor in its construction.[43]

Many important features of Dan 7.13f. are missing in 28.16-20: the coming on the clouds of heaven, βασιλεία, δόξα, and especially the term Son of Man itself. The emphasis in the Matthean passage falls not on the handing over of ἐξουσία as in Dan 7, but on the world-wide mission of the disciples—who, as well, find no counterpart in Dan 7. Moreover, the nations in Dan 7.14 are present in an entirely subservient role; the picture here is of the subjugation of πάντα τὰ ἔθνη rather than of their becoming disciples. It is possible, of course, to argue that Matthew transformed the role of the ἔθνη in accordance with more positive hopes found elsewhere in Jewish and Christian traditions. But this just emphasizes further the inadequacy of Dan 7 in the interpretation of the passage. Finally, the closing promise of v. 20b, while rich in OT echoes, has no parallel in Daniel at all.

So while Dan 7.13f. may have had some influence on Matthew's choice of vocabulary in 28.16-20, it is of no real help in discovering the theological core of the passage. And what is true of Dan 7.13f. is true of other suggested OT texts as well. No single OT passage has yet been found which provides a unifying principle for all features of 28.16-20.

Another approach to the construction of the passage is the attempt to discover an underlying christological conception that animates the whole. This approach overlaps considerably with the one just discussed, and therefore it is not surprising that it too proves to be rather inconclusive. For while it is generally agreed that christological ideas of exaltation and enthronement play an important part in the passage, the specific christological title in view here is a matter of some dispute.

Echoes of Dan 7.13f. in v. 18b have led many to suppose that the heart of the passage is to be found in ideas of the exaltation of the Son of Man.[44] But the absence of the term itself in 28.16-20, the uncertainty of the relevance of Dan 7.13f. to these verses, and the fact that elsewhere in Matthew it is the Son (of God) rather than the Son of Man who is seen as the object of exaltation (e.g. 3.16f.; 17.1-8), make such a view highly doubtful. No more convincing is the suggestion that the passage is based on κύριος-christology.[45] That title does not appear in the passage either, and there is nothing else to indicate a background in Ps 110.1.

New ground on the christology question has been broken by Kingsbury.[46] Taking issue with those who say that there is no christological title present in the passage, he points out that in v. 19b the title 'the Son' appears, and argues from this that Matthew constructed 28.16-20 'in large part with a view to his Son-of-God christology'.[47] He observes further than Son (of God) is the only christological conception that is to be found in connection with Matthew's other mountain scenes (cf. 4.8; 14.23, 33; 17.5).

Kingsbury's suggestion deserves further consideration. Verse 19b is often dismissed as a liturgical formula with no christological import, or even as a late intrusion into the text.[48] But if we read the passage afresh—in its Matthean context rather than in the context of later trinitarian formulations—it becomes apparent that ὁ υἱός here can be given its full christological weight. Elsewhere in Matthew the Holy Spirit is mentioned in passages where Father–Son conceptions are to the fore (e.g. in the Baptism and Temptation Narratives). This suggests that the combination of these three terms in vv. 19b indicates the presence of Son-christology in this final mountain passage as well.

Nevertheless, it must also be recognized that this Son saying does not occupy a prominent position in the passage. It appears in connection with the baptismal command alone, and is not explicitly brought into relationship with the wider themes of the passage as a whole. Son-christology is certainly present in the passage. But Kingsbury has not proved his contention that it is the controlling idea.

Finally, there is a handful of scholars who forgo all attempts to explain 28.16-20 in terms of extra-Synoptic categories, preferring rather to see the passage as a Matthean reformulation of texts and ideas found elsewhere in the Synoptic tradition. The most thoroughly worked-out example of this approach is that of Lange, who argues that 28.16-20 is a new edition of the Q saying in Mt 11.27a, designed by the evangelist as a positive counter-representation of the temptation on the mountain, now incorporated in 4.8-10.[49] In similar fashion, Gibbs sees the passage as Matthew's reformulation of the commissioning scene found in Mk 3.13-19,[50] and Daniel argues that it was built out of features found in the Transfiguration Narrative.[51]

Some connections, of course, are to be found between 28.16-20 and these suggested Synoptic passages—especially the earlier mountain scenes of Temptation and Transfiguration.[52] Yet none of the passages is capable of explaining more than one or two of the features of the final pericope.[53] So it can be concluded that though 28.16-20 gathers up themes found elsewhere in Matthew's Gospel, it was not modelled on or inspired by any identifiable passage found elsewhere in the Synoptic tradition.

Our discussion of the last few pages is not meant to deny the significance of questions of form, of OT and Synoptic dependence, or of christology—nor to suggest that solid results have not been obtained in any of these areas. The point being made here is that none of these investigations has uncovered an underlying *schema* or theological framework on which the passage has been constructed and within which the significance of the mountain setting might be found.

It may be, of course, that an answer to this question cannot be found; 28.16-20 may perhaps be *sui generis* not only in form but also in its pattern of thought, so that the passage finds its unity only in view of the Gospel whose themes it summarizes. In this case its mountain setting would be a purely literary pointer to themes brought to their climax in the closing passage. But rather than abandoning the question, we suggest that what is needed is a fresh approach. Let us turn the question around: What light is thrown on the theology of the passage if we begin not with the statement of the risen Lord but with the mountain setting in which this statement is uttered?

The question of a possible theological or typological significance for the mountain setting has been largely ignored in discussions of the theology of the passage. Verses 18-20 are often treated in isolation, and even where vv. 16f. are included they are generally viewed as a preamble or an introductory feature of secondary importance.[54] Where the mountain is discussed more directly it is treated either as a place of revelation,[55] or as the result of Sinai typology at work in the passage.[56] But to speak of the mountain merely as a place of revelation in the First Gospel is ultimately an unhelpful suggestion. And while some Sinai overtones may be detected—the charge to keep Jesus' commands is expressed in language reminiscent of Deuteronomy[57] and the appointment of the mountain as the place of rendezvous perhaps recalls arrangements for the Sinai encounter (Ex 3.12; 19.11)[58]—their significance is muted by the fact that wherever Mosaic typology appears elsewhere in the Gospel, it is transcended by and absorbed into some higher christological pattern. Moreover, it is only the middle section of the logion (i.e. vv. 19-20a) that can be brought into a Sinai constellation of ideas, and even here the commissioning of the disciples and the inclusion of the Gentiles find no counterpart in a Sinai pattern. So Sinai parallels alone do not supply a framework that is able to draw the other elements of the passage into a unity.

In our investigation of the mountain as a religious site and theological symbol in the Second-Temple period, we discovered that 'the mountain' frequently functioned as a site for eschatological events and that Mount Zion in particular was at the centre of hopes for an eschatological restoration of the people of God. Now Matthew's closing scene on the mountain in Galilee is a highly eschatological pericope, for it inaugurates an age in which Jesus exercises universal authority and in which the long-anticipated (cf. 8.11; 12.21), but formerly-prohibited (cf. 10.5f.; 15.24), mission to the Gentiles is to take place. Is it possible, therefore, that Zion overtones are present in this closing mountain scene? In the discussion that follows, we hope to demonstrate that each of the three segments of the saying of the risen Lord in vv. 18-20 resonate with themes drawn from eschatological traditions associated with Mount Zion, and so to conclude that the mountain reference in v. 16 leads us into the theological heart of the passage.

Let us look first at the ἐξουσία statement of v. 18b. While it is unlikely that the whole of vv. 18-20 was modelled on the pattern of an enthronement hymn,[59] enthronement ideas undoubtedly are present in the declaration concerning the bestowal of authority in v. 18b.[60] In Second-Temple Judaism as we have seen, the mountain—especially Mount Zion—was intimately tied up with the eschatological enthronement of Yahweh or his Anointed One.[61] But is it possible to go beyond this general observation to discover more tangible links between the mountain statement of v. 18b and the Zion enthronement traditions? In view of enthronement motifs based on Ps 2 which we have found to be at work in the earlier Temptation and Transfiguration Narratives, and in view of the evident parallels between these narratives and Matthew's final mountain scene, such a background for v. 18b appears plausible. Is there, however, evidence in the passage itself that would turn plausibility into likelihood?

It may be objected at the outset that the enthronement language of v. 18b echoes Dan 7.13f., where Son of Man rather than Zion eschatology is the controlling conception. Yet even if this were unambiguously the case, the interweaving of elements from Dan 2 and 7 into the vision of 4 Ezra 13 that is centred on the eschatological mountain of Zion[62] demonstrates that such a mixture of traditions is possible for this Matthean scene as well.

But the link between v. 18b and Dan 7.13f. is not unambiguous. The phrase διδόναι τινὶ ἐξουσίαν was sufficiently common[63] to suggest that its presence in Dan 7.14 and Mt 28.18, even in a similar passive form, is not enough to establish an exclusive link. It is true that ἐξουσία is a word particularly characteristic of Daniel.[64] But while ἐξουσία used to describe royal or divine authority came into the LXX only at its latest stages of translation,[65] the term could easily have been used elsewhere in the LXX where the same idea is rendered with other terminology reflecting the more vivid language of the MT.[66] In particular, the essential meaning of ἐδόθη μοι πᾶσα ἐξουσία is found in Ps 2.8: δώσω σοι ἔθνη τὴν κληρονομίαν σου, καὶ τὴν κατάσχεσίν σου τὰ πέρατα τῆς γῆς. Here, in a manner similar to Mt 28.18b, διδόναι is used, with God as agent, to express the bestowal of world-wide sovereignty on God's royal Son, a bestowal taking place on Zion, God's holy mountain.

It is not necessary, however, to rely on διδόναι alone in order to establish a Ps 2 background for v. 18b. The term ἐξουσία may also provide evidence of the influence of Ps 2.8 on the thought of the evangelist here. In Rev 2.26f. there is striking evidence for the fact that ἐξουσία was being used in connection with Ps 2.8:

δώσω αὐτῷ ἐξουσίαν ἐπὶ τῶν ἐθνῶν καὶ ποιμανεῖ αὐτοὺς ἐν ῥάβδῳ σιδηρᾷ, ὡς τὰ σκεύη τὰ κεραμικὰ συντρίβεται.

Here Ps 2.8 is paraphrased using the same construction διδόναι τινὶ ἐξουσίαν as is found in 28.18b. And since Ps 2.9 appears in full in the passage cited from Revelation, with only minor variations from the LXX,[67] it is possible that we have here not just an *ad hoc* paraphrase of the psalm but a quasi-'Targumic' rendering which enjoyed wide currency. In any case, the use of ἐξουσία here in connection with Ps 2 is striking, and lends support to a position which views the mountain setting, the terms ἐδόθη and ἐξουσία, and (if Kingsbury is correct) the Son-christology as pointers to a Zion background for the enthronement declaration of v. 18b. This is not a necessary conclusion, but it is a plausible one. And its probability increases with the accumulation of evidence for Zion overtones in the other two sections of the passage.

Verses 19-20a contain more than just a mission command. With the terms μαθητεύσατε, βαπτίζοντες, διδάσκοντες and ἐνετειλάμην we are brought into the centre of Matthew's ecclesiology. In this command to make disciples who adhere to Jesus' teachings and who are visibly identified with him in baptism, we have the charter of the Church, the constitution of the eschatological people of God. In our study of Zion eschatology we found that it was to Mount Zion that the scattered people were to be gathered in the last days and that there they would be newly constituted as God's people. And in our investigation of earlier Matthean depictions of mountain-top gatherings (the Sermon, the feeding), we found reasons for believing that in Matthew's view the disciples and crowds were being invited to participate, albeit in a preliminary way, in the type of eschatological fellowship that had been anticipated for the restored people of God on Zion, God's holy mountain. Is there evidence in vv. 19-20a that the mountain setting of this command was similarly intended to provide a link with the Zion expectations developed in Second-Temple Judaism?

Such a link between these verses and the theme of the eschatological establishment of the people of God on Mount Zion is to be found, we suggest, in the command in v. 19 for the inclusion of πάντα τὰ ἔθνη into the fellowship of the Church. Admittedly, this phrase is found in Dan 7.14. But this was not the source of the background to Matthew's thought here, for Dan 7.14 is part of a broad stream of OT tradition that looked for the eventual subjugation of the nations and their subservience to Israel.[68] For the same reason, Ps 2 is also to be ruled out. There is, however, a more positive strand of tradition in the OT and the literature of the Second-Temple period in which it was expected that the Gentiles would participate in the salvation of the last day. The salvation of the Gentiles, as we have seen,[69] was most frequently connected in Jewish thought with the restoration of Zion: when Yahweh restores his people on Zion, his holy mountain, then the Gentiles will be invited to come and share in the eschatological blessings. In fact, apart from a few scattered references,[70] wherever we find passages in which Gentiles are assigned a positive role in the events of the End, Zion eschatology is invariably present. Our immediate interest, though, is with the phrase πάντα τὰ ἔθνη. A study of the occurrence of this term in the LXX reveals that virtually every time that it appears in connection with a description of the eschatological salvation of the Gentiles, it is in a passage which deals explicitly with the themes of Zion eschatology.[71] Of particular interest are those passages in Isaiah where πάντα τὰ ἔθνη and τὸ ὄρος occur together: Is 2.2f., where πάντα τὰ ἔθνη come to the gloriously exalted τὸ ὄρος κυρίου, there to learn the Torah; Is 25.6, where Yahweh makes a great feast for πάντα τὰ ἔθνη on τὸ ὄρος τοῦτο; and Is 56.7, where πάντα τὰ ἔθνη come to worship in the house of prayer on τὸ ὄρος τὸ ἅγιόν μου. In addition, the term πάντα τὰ ἔθνη appears in other LXX passages describing the salvation of the nations at Zion where ὄρος is not used.[72] And of course there are many other passages in the OT and the literature of Second-Temple Judaism which deal with these same themes without using this terminology.[73]

In Mt 28.16-20, the risen Jesus meets with his disciples on a mountain in Galilee and gives the command that the Gentiles be invited to participate in their fellowship and to learn the ways of a disciple. The command is eschatologically based—i.e. the age in which the gospel was restricted to Israel has been brought to an end by the death, resurrection and exaltation of Jesus (note the οὖν in v. 19), and a new age has dawned in which Gentiles are to be included in salvation.[74] And the whole passage is deeply rooted in OT phraseology and thought. So in view of what has been said about the salvation of πάντα τὰ ἔθνη in Jewish tradition, the appearance of both τὸ ὄρος and πάντα τὰ ἔθνη in 28.16-20 cannot help but suggest that the mountain fellowship into which the Gentiles are being invited is to be seen against the background of Zion eschatology. Of particular significance for 28.16-20 is LXX Is 2.2f., for here, in addition to the centrality of τὸ ὄρος in the eschatological salvation of πάντα τὰ ἔθνη, there is a Torah emphasis reminiscent of Jesus' command that the Gentiles become disciples and be taught to observe his commands. In Is 2.2f., as in Mt 28.16-20, the nations are gathered into a mountain-centred fellowship to learn the ways of the Lord.

But, it may be objected, is not the action in Zion eschatology centripetal—i.e. the nations come to God's holy mountain—whereas in 28.16-20 the action is centrifugal—i.e. the disciples are sent out

from the mountain to the nations? Do we not have here two
essentially different patterns of salvation? Such an objection might
be dismissed as being overly pedantic, demanding of the Gospel
writer a literalism such as would leave no room for any creative
reinterpretation of Scripture in the context of a new historical
situation. And, in fact, at least one important OT passage, Is 2.2f.,
contains not only centripetal action ('let us go up to the mountain of
the Lord'), but centrigfugal action as well ('for out of Zion shall go
forth the law'). But even apart from this, a closer consideration of
28.16-20 in the light of this objection reveals two important things
about the passage and Matthew's christological reinterpretation of
Zion eschatology.

The first is that the emphasis in the passage is not on 'going' at all.
There is a curious permanence about the situation described in the
closing scene. Matthew does not describe the breaking up of this
mountain fellowship; Christ promises to be continually present with
his disciples, yet there is no account of his or his disciples' departure
from the mountain. The Gospel leaves us with a picture of the
Church as a mountain-top gathering with Christ at the centre. As for
the presence of πορευθέντες in the mission command, the participial
form of πορεύεσθαι is often used in Matthew (and elsewhere) in
conjunction with an imperative in such a way that the participle has
no independent syntactical function.[75] The idea of 'going' is not
stressed, and indeed is present only in so far as it is necessary to 'go'
in order for the command to be fulfilled.

The command in vv. 19-20a, then, is to make disciples of all
nations. In order that this command be fulfilled, it will be necessary,
of course, for the disciples to go. But the passage places no emphasis
on going. Gentiles are to be called into the fellowship inaugurated on
the mountain in Galilee and centred around Christ—who, without
leaving the mountain, promises his abiding presence with his people.
The impression one gains from the passage, though it is not stated
expressly, is that gathering, not going, is what is primarily in mind.

This leads into a second and more fundamental observation: that
the gathering point throughout the Gospel for the eschatological
people of God is not the mountain, but Christ himself. For Matthew,
Christian experience is not merely a matter of replacing one mountain in Jerusalem with another mountain in Galilee. It is Christ who
has replaced Zion as the centre of eschatological fulfilment, and the
mountain motif in Matthew acts as a vehicle by which Zion
expectations are transferred to Christ.

Such an interpretation is borne out by several redactional features found elsewhere in the Gospel. One is the statement in 12.6, found nowhere else in the Gospels, that in the person of Jesus 'something greater than the temple is here'. While Matthew acknowledges the special religious significance of Jerusalem,[76] only in his Gospel do we find such a direct contrast between Christ and the temple—with the implication being that religious significance has passed from one to the other. Matthew does include unique references to eschatological events—the coming of Zion's long awaited king (21.5, 15), healing (21.14), resurrection (27.53)—taking place in the temple or city. But these events take place only by virtue of Christ's presence. As the one 'greater than the temple', Christ himself has become the locus of eschatological fulfilment.

Another piece of redactional evidence has to do with the account of the coming of the Magi to Jesus. Although Matthew probably depended on earlier sources for this account, his version makes unmistakable allusion to the OT expectation that Gentiles would make procession to Jerusalem to give gifts to the royal Son (Ps 72) or to a restored Zion itself (Is 60).[77] Among the gifts which in Isaiah the nations would bring as a tribute to Zion are those which in Matthew the Magi bring as a tribute to Jesus (χρυσίον καὶ λίβανον, Is 60.6; cf. χρυσὸν καὶ λίβανον καὶ σμύρναν, Mt 2.11; see also Sib Or 3.772-775). In Matthew's case, the ultimate destination of the procession of the Gentiles is not Jerusalem or even Bethlehem, but Jesus himself. So Matthew reinterpreted the eschatological procession to Zion in christological terms.

Finally, we note the logion found only in 18.20: 'For where two or three are gathered (συνηγμένοι) in my name, there am I in the midst of them'. Not only does this logion relate the promise of the abiding presence (cf. 28.20) to a centripetal gathering to Jesus, but it does so using a term (συνάγω) that had become virtually a technical term for the eschatological gathering of the scattered people of God.[78] For Matthew, therefore, Christ has replaced Zion at the centre of the gathered people of God.

All these bits of redactional evidence point in the same direction. As one who is greater than the temple, Jesus replaces Zion as the centre of eschatological fulfilment. He is the one around whom the people are to gather and to whom the Gentiles will make procession.[79] The journey of the Magi to Jesus at the beginning of the Gospel is but an anticipation of the great gathering of πάντα τὰ ἔθνη commanded

at the end. The mountain setting of the command is the principal
means by which Matthew indicates that Zion expectations have been
transferred to and fulfilled in Christ.[80]

The validity of this interpretation is further confirmed by an
investigation of the third element in the passage—the promise of
Jesus' abiding presence. Jesus' promise to his disciples that he would
be with them (μεθ' ὑμῶν) until the end of the age is made in terms
whose roots go deep into OT thought. Frequently throughout the OT
Yahweh promises to be 'with'[81] individuals[82] or the people as a
whole,[83] thereby pledging his assistance, comfort and strength.
Almost stereotypical is the recurring refrain: 'Fear not, for I am with
you'. Indeed, this promise of God's presence was one of the most
fundamental features of Israel's covenant existence (cf. Hag 2.4f.). In
fact, as Clements demonstrates,[84] the theme of the divine presence,
expressed in 'with'-terminology and related concepts (especially שׁכן),
provides an organizing principle around which much of the material
of the OT can be discussed.

The culmination of this strand of OT thought is to be found in the
belief that God was present with his people on Zion, 'the mountain
which God desired for his abode' (Ps 68.16). It is Zion (Ps 135.21;
Joel 3.21) or Mount Zion (Ps 74.2; Is 8.18) or the holy mountain (Ps
43.3; Joel 3.17) that is the place where God dwells. Because Jerusalem
is 'the holy habitation of the Most High', Israel can declare: 'The
Lord of Hosts is with us (עמנו), the God of Jacob is our refuge' (Ps
46.4, 7, 11).

Such a doctrine, of course, carried with it the ever present danger
that God's presence would come to be seen in a static and cultic way,
unrelated to the demands of the covenant—i.e. that the possession of
the sanctuary would be taken as a guarantee of God's presence and
blessing. It was this that led to the Deuteronomic tendency to speak
guardedly of 'the place where Yahweh has chosen to set his name'[85]
and to the prophets' warnings about a coming destruction of Zion.[86]
Still, in the prophetic vision of the eschatological future, Zion is
repeatedly encountered as the place where Yahweh will dwell, the
place where once again he will be 'with' his people. In fact, the theme
of the eschatological presence of God is not really developed at all
apart from Zion eschatology.

'With'-terminology is encountered in this connection in a number
of important passages in the OT and the literature of Second-Temple
Judaism. Ezek 34, which deals with the re-establishment of the

scattered flock of God on the 'mountain height of Israel',[87] ends with the declaration: 'And they shall know that I, the Lord their God, am *with* them (אתם), and that they, the house of Israel, are my people' (v. 30). In Zech 8.23, Gentiles beg to be allowed to accompany Israelites on their procession back to Jerusalem, 'for we have heard that God is *with* you'. In Jub 1.17f. God declares that when the sanctuary is renewed on Mount Zion (cf. vv. 27f.) then 'I will dwell *with* them, and I will be their God, and they shall be my people'. Similarly Life of Adam and Eve 29.7 speaks of the restored house of God where he 'will dwell *with* men on earth'. And in Rev 21.2f., John, seeing 'the holy city, new Jerusalem' descending to 'a great, high mountain', hears a voice declare: 'Behold, the dwelling of God is *with* men, and he will dwell *with* them, and they shall be his people and God himself will be *with* them'.

In addition to such passages in which the term 'with' appears explicitly, we find the theme of the presence of God in eschatological Zion treated in several other ways. One of the central themes of Ezekiel is the departure of the divine presence from Jerusalem and its return to the restored temple. In Ezek 37.26f. we have the promise that when God rebuilds his sanctuary in the midst of the people, 'my dwelling place will be among them (LXX ἐν αὐτοῖς; MT עליהם), and I will be their God and they shall be my people'. When Ezekiel sees the new city of God on the high mountain, a city which is named 'Yahweh is there' (יהוה שמה; Ezek 48.35), he is told: 'Son of Man, this is the place . . . where I will dwell (אשכן) in the midst of the people of Israel for ever' (Ezek 43.7). Similar ideas are found in Zech 2.10-12 in connection with the inclusion of the Gentiles into the eschatological people of God, and in Zech 8.3, where the term 'holy mountain' is also encountered.[88]

So it can be concluded that the eschatological hope of the renewed presence of God with his people, whether expressed by means of 'with'-terminology or in some other way, was intimately bound up with the hope for the restoration of Zion. Of particular note is the frequency with which mountain terminology occurs in the relevant passages. Given this background, there can be little doubt that the mountain-top declaration of the abiding presence of the risen Lord in Mt 28.20 is meant to recall the promise of the renewal of עמנו אל fellowship on Zion, the holy mountain of Yahweh. Matthew is declaring that this long-anticipated promise has come to fulfilment not with the restoration of Zion, but with the resurrection and exaltation of Jesus. God is with his eschatological people, not when they gather to Zion, but when they gather to Jesus, who is himself called Immanuel (1.23; cf. 18.20).[89]

There is solid evidence, therefore, to indicate that each of the three statements in 28.16-20 is deeply rooted in the eschatological expectations connected with Mount Zion. Matthew's closing passage is not to be seen merely as a compilation of Matthean themes with no inner cohesiveness—as something of a table of contents to the material of the Gospel. Rather, the mountain setting of v. 16 provides the clue to the connective thread running through the various elements of the passage and binding them tightly together. The passage as a whole partakes in a profound unity provided by Matthew's christological reinterpretation of Zion eschatology: the exalted Jesus is the gathering point for the eschatological people of God and the locus of God's presence with his people. The mountain setting functions as the vehicle by which these Zion expectations are transferred to Christ in whom they find their fulfilment. Whatever apocalyptic and Sinai overtones are present have been gathered up into this larger vision.

b. *In the Context of the Whole Gospel*

With this analysis of the closing mountain scene, we are able to see more clearly the relationship between 28.16-20 and the other mountain scenes in Matthew's Gospel. Each of these earlier scenes deals with themes which anticipate and culminate in Matthew's closing pericope. There is no need to repeat here the documentation of these links. But we can review the overall picture from the perspective of these closing verses and make some observations on the place of the Mountain of Commissioning in the whole pattern.

Generally speaking, there are three major themes or strands which run throughout the Matthean mountain scenes and culminate in this final passage. The first of these is the christological theme. The Mountains of Temptation, of Transfiguration and of Commissioning are parts of a developed Son (of God) motif in Matthew in which the Son, who was called into a life of humble obedience to the Father, resisted all attempts to deflect him from the path which led inevitably to the cross, but was finally vindicated by the Father in resurrection and exaltation. On the Mountain of Temptation the Son refused the world-wide sovereignty that was his due, because it was offered on terms incompatible with his vocation of filial devotion. On the Mountain of Transfiguration Jesus' chosen path was proleptically vindicated, as his Sonship was reaffirmed and the authority of his words proclaimed. And on the Mountain of Commissioning world-wide sovereignty is declared as having been bestowed on the Son, not by the devil but by the Father, and Jesus commands that his words be taught among all nations. So the closing pericope serves as the culmination of this theme, not only by virtue of the linguistic and structural considerations discussed above, but more fundamentally because in the closing mountain scene there is the same Mount Zion–enthronement–Ps 2 complex of ideas (along with subordinated apocalyptic and Sinai overtones) as in the earlier passages.

The second is the ecclesiological theme. The uniquely Matthean mountain scenes in 4.23–5.1, 15.29-39 and 28.16-20 deal with the gathering of the eschatological community and its constitution as the Church. The first two of these passages describe in ideal fashion the ministry of Jesus with his disciples among the crowds, as they gather to him on the mountain to participate in the eschatological blessings of healing, teaching and feeding. But though eschatological fellowship was initiated in these mountain scenes and though the nature of the eschatological community was described in Jesus' teaching of chs. 5–7, what is lacking is a presentation of the formal constitution of the eschatological community. The eschatological blessings were antici-patory, and several issues—notably the question of the participation of the Gentiles, raised most acutely in 15.29-39—were left unresolved. It is only in the final mountain scene, where the disciples enjoy עמנו אל fellowship and where Jesus commands a discipling mission of teaching and baptizing in which the Gentiles are to be included, that we find the formal constitution of the eschatological community, the Church. The fellowship experienced in a preliminary way in the earlier passages is fully present in the closing pericope. So this pericope serves as a culmination of the ecclesiological theme (as also the christological theme) not only by virtue of linguistic and structural considerations, but also because all three mountain scenes are deeply rooted in the same Jewish tradition of the eschatological gathering of the people of God on his holy mountain.

The final theme to be mentioned here is that of salvation history. In Matthew's view, with Jesus' reception of universal authority and his consequent establishment of the Church with its world-wide mission, a new period of salvation history has begun that is to last until the close of the age. Because of this, 28.16-20 is able to gather up and place on a christological and ecclesiological foundation not only the intimations in 4.23–5.1 and 15.29-39 that the eschatological age was breaking in, but also the description in the Olivet Discourse of the interim period between the Matthean present and the close of the age. In the process, the apocalyptic vision of Mt 24–25 is complemented and corrected by the more realized eschatology which Matthew is able to declare on the basis of the exaltation of the risen Lord. There are, of course, no Zion overtones in the Olivet Discourse. Nevertheless, this closing mountain pericope, because of its salvation-historical nature, is able to gather up the earlier mountain passage into the pattern of which it is the keystone.

Matthew's final mountain scene not only gathers up themes developed in earlier mountain passages, but grounds them in a christologically reinterpreted vision of Zion eschatology. Since, with the exception of the Olivet Discourse, these earlier passages also reverberate with Zion motifs, the mountain scenes in Matthew are linked together at a deeper level than has yet been realized. So we can conclude that the mountain pattern in the First Gospel—of which 28.16-20 is the key and culmination—is not a mere surface literary motif, but rests on foundations deep in Matthean theology.

PART IV
CONCLUSIONS

Chapter 12

THE MOUNTAIN MOTIF IN MATTHEW'S GOSPEL

On the basis of our exegesis of the Matthean mountain scenes, we can conclude that ὄρος functions in the First Gospel as a motif—having both literary and theological aspects—which the evangelist used to highlight and develop several important theological themes. The distinction between the literary and the theological aspects of this symbol arose in the course of our formulation of the problem because of the possibility that the mountain setting plays a compositional role within the Gospel itself without necessarily carrying any typological overtones or acting as a pointer to any extra-Matthean categories or content.[1] The distinction between 'literary device' and 'theological symbol', therefore, lies in the idea that, while in both cases τὸ ὄρος functions as a recurring motif which helps to give shape and definition to some aspect of the Gospel, the literary device—unlike the theological symbol—does so without introducing its own independent meaning into the text. In the final analysis, however, the theoretical possibility which necessitates such a distinction is not realized in the First Gospel. While it is possible, due to the nature of the case, to speak with more confidence about the literary function of the mountain motif, there are sufficient grounds for the assertion that the literary pattern of Matthew's mountain scenes is based on a profound theological conception for which ὄρος serves as an indicator.

Let us look first at the literary pattern. Since Matthew depends to a greater or lesser extent on his sources for his mountain scenes (none of them has been created *ex nihilo*), there is an evident diversity in these six passages, not only in the terminology by which the mountain is designated, but also in the nature and content of the scenes themselves. This diversity, however, has been brought into a unity by means of the closing mountain scene. By means of a series of linguistic and structural details, Matthew has linked each of the first five mountain occurrences to the Mountain of Commissioning. Each mountain scene anticipates in some way or other the concluding scene, and each deals with themes that are brought to culmination there.

The *Mountain of Temptation* was in all likelihood found in the Q account, where it functioned as one of three eschatological sites in which was put to the test Jesus' faithfulness to the vocation of humble obedience into which he had been called as Son. In the First Gospel this mountain stands in antithetical parallelism to the Mountain of Commissioning. While in the first mountain appearance of Jesus the devil promises to give him world sovereignty on the condition that Jesus worship him, in his final mountain appearance he announces that universal authority has been given to him by the Father, and he rather than the devil receives the worship that is his due. The first and last Matthean mountains stand as literary brackets within which the drama of the obedient, suffering, yet finally vindicated Son is played out. It is even possible that this contrasting correspondence between the end of the Temptation Narrative and the end of the Gospel is the result of a deliberate inversion on the part of the evangelist of the order of the final two temptations as they appeared in the Q source.

The *Mountain of Teaching*—the setting for the Sermon on the Mount—has been fashioned by Matthew on the basis of Mark's account of the mountain-top commissioning of the Twelve. Since he had plans to conclude his Gospel with a mountain-top commissioning scene of his own, Matthew omitted this Markan pericope, but used its depiction of a gathering of Jesus with his disciples εἰς τὸ ὄρος as the nucleus of a scene of teaching which he inserted at the first mention of Jesus' teaching ministry in the Markan outline. On this mountain Jesus gives to his disciples (the core of his new community) and to the crowds (those who were being invited to respond to the signs of eschatological activity that were being worked in their midst and to join the company of disciples) an extended body of teaching concerning the nature of the eschatological community that he had come to call into being. The real foundation of this community, though, is to be found in the closing scene of commissioning, where Jesus authorizes a universal discipling mission in which obedience to his teaching—together with baptism—would serve as hallmarks of the fellowship that would be thereby created. The teaching which was given on the former mountain was, by means of the instructions given on the final mountain, made the basis of life in the Church.

The *Mountain of Feeding*—the setting for Matthew's account of the Feeding of the Four Thousand—probably originated as an item of oral tradition, as the appearance of εἰς τὸ ὄρος in Jn 6.3 suggests. In Matthew's Gospel, however, it appears as part of a massive summary statement of Jesus' ministry among the ὄχλοι which both introduces the account of the miraculous feeding that follows and links this account with the closely related narrative of the Canaanite woman. This mountain has evidently been introduced by the evangelist at least in part to be paired with the Mountain of Teaching to form an *inclusio* within which Jesus' ministry among the Galilean ὄχλοι takes place. In addition, while the link between this mountain passage and the final one is not as readily apparent as in the other instances, we have seen that by constructing this mountain pericope as the redactional link between the two narratives with which it is flanked, Matthew raises the problem of the grounds on which the Gentiles can participate in salvation—a problem which is resolved only in the final mountain scene. The whole of Mt 15.21-39 is to be seen as a unit in which the salvation of this Gentile woman is brought into tension with Jesus' statement that his ministry of feeding was limited to 'the children', 'the lost sheep of the house of Israel'. This tension, however, is released at the end of the Gospel when the limitations are at last removed and the Gentiles are invited to participate fully in salvation. The mountain fellowship which was reserved for the lost sheep of the house of Israel in the former instance is made available to πάντα τὰ ἔθνη in the latter.

The main contours of the *Mountain of Transfiguration* have been taken over by Matthew from his Markan source. By means of several deft redactional touches, however, Matthew has integrated this passage into his carefully developed theme of the Son who suffers as a result of his obedience, but who is ultimately vindicated by the Father. On this mountain, just after the imminent consequences of this way of obedience have been revealed in all their harshness (Mt 16.21-27), Jesus' path of Sonship is vindicated in a preliminary way as the Father's pleasure in the Son is reaffirmed and the consequent authority of the Son (cf. 'hear him'; Mt 17.5) is proclaimed. The Mountain of Transfiguration is thus linked both with the Mountain of Temptation—on which the issues of obedience, sovereignty and Sonship first became clear—and with the Mountain of Commissioning—where the sovereignty of the obedient Son is fully manifested.

The *Mountain of the Eschatological Discourse*, which is also taken over from Mark, stands somewhat apart from the other Matthean mountains in that it is a specifically designated geographical site. But instead of following the course which was chosen by Luke and omitting the mountain setting altogether, Matthew incorporated this passage as well into the pattern anchored by the final mountain pericope. Both passages deal with the nature of the Church's existence in the period of time leading up to the συντέλεια τοῦ αἰῶνος. By linking these two passages together, Matthew set the Eschatological Discourse within the more complete vision of the place of the Church in *Heilsgeschichte* that was able to be articulated only after the resurrection.

Thus the frequency of mountain settings in the First Gospel is not to be dismissed as coincidental, nor is it merely a random and disjointed Matthean idiosyncrasy. Rather, the mountain passages are linked together in a clearly discernible pattern, and ὄρος serves as a literary motif with the aid of which Matthew develops several of his distinctive theological themes. The fact that each of these mountain references was in all probability taken from traditional sources merely serves to illustrate that the evangelists, Matthew included, expressed their theological viewpoints by shaping and reinterpreting the tradition that they had received.[2]

More specifically, the mountain motif in Matthew serves to focus characteristic Matthean themes in the areas of christology, ecclesiology and salvation history. The christological theme of the nature of true Sonship and the path of obedience that the Son must follow to receive sovereignty is set out principally in the Temptation and Transfiguration Narratives and brought to culmination in the closing scene—though the authority of Jesus is also in view in the Sermon on the Mount (cf. Mt 7.28f.). The ecclesiological theme of the gathering of the eschatological community and its constitution as the Church is developed in the Sermon, in the second feeding miracle, and ultimately in the final commissioning passage—though the community is also in view in the command to 'hear him' in Mt 17.5. These two themes together form the basis for Matthew's development of salvation history, in that the vindication of the Son ushers in an age of fulfilment in which the Church finds its existence. It is into this theme of salvation history that the Eschatological Discourse has been incorporated.

Thus the mountain in Matthew serves as a place for Jesus and his community.[3] Jesus' conflict with his opponents, so much a feature of the Matthean narrative elsewhere, never intrudes into the mountain scenes. The encounter with the devil on the Mountain of Temptation is no real exception, since the vital issue in this passage is the nature of Sonship. On the other hand, the crowds—those who were being invited to join the ranks of the disciples—do participate in eschatological fellowship with Jesus in mountain settings. Such mountain-top events in which crowds are included are not really encountered in the Gospels apart from Matthew.[4] In Matthean perspective, therefore, it is when Jesus is 'on the mountain' that his significance and the nature of his mission are most clearly seen. Consequently it can be said that mountains in Matthew function not primarily as places of revelation or isolation, but as eschatological sites where Jesus enters into the full authority of his Sonship, where the eschatological community is gathered, and where the age of fulfilment is inaugurated.[5]

The results of our investigation allow us to go one step further and to conclude that ὄρος in Matthew's Gospel functions not only as a literary device, but as a theological symbol as well. Of course, by saying that the mountain is a literary device which aids in Matthew's development of key theological themes, we are saying that it is a term with theological significance. We have been using the term 'theological symbol', though, to refer to a term which introduces its own independent theological content into a text by means of its allusion to biblical or other forms of sacred mountain conceptions. Our studies have shown that the literary ὄρος motif is worked out in Matthew on the basis of theological mountain ideas that were mediated to Matthew via the religious and exegetical traditions of Second-Temple Judaism.

Speaking first in general terms, our investigation of the literature of this period allows us to say that Jesus ministered and the Gospels took shape in a milieu in which there was a vibrant and widespread interest in the mountain as a religious site and theological symbol. This was evidenced both in a 'horizontal' way, as mountains were retrojected into the salvation-historical past and projected into the eschatological future, and in a 'vertical' way, as mountains took on increasing cosmic dimensions as the *Weltnabel* or the point of entry into the heavens. In particular, we observed the frequency with which mountains appeared as eschatological sites—especially in the case of Mount Zion, which was at the centre of most of Israel's hopes for the future.

Turning to the occurrences of the ὄρος setting in the Gospels, a number of factors—the appearance of mountain settings in all strata of the tradition, the wide variety of these mountain scenes, and the highly stylized use of the articular but unspecified τὸ ὄρος in Gospel narratives—suggest that the mountain setting was characteristic of Jesus' ministry. While the question of the *Sitz im Leben Jesu* has not been addressed in this redactional study, it is apparent that such a preference for mountain settings is to be interpreted against the background of the widespread contemporary interest in the mountain as a sacred—and especially eschatological—site and symbol.

As the Gospel tradition took shape, specific aspects of the theological mountain traditions of Second-Temple Judaism were incorporated in recognizable ways into narratives for which τὸ ὄρος served as the setting. We have discovered the influence of the cosmic-eschatological mountain of apocalyptic literature in the Temptation and Transfiguration Narratives, and perhaps as well in the account of a resurrection appearance lying behind Mt 28.16-20. In the Temptation and Transfiguration Narratives, both Moses–Sinai and Zion–enthronement ideas have also been at work. The eschatological traditions associated with the Mount of Olives made it an appropriate setting for the Eschatological Discourse, and the mountain—together with the desert and the temple—function in the Temptation Narrative as three eschatological sites in which temptation takes place.

By taking up the Temptation and Transfiguration Narratives as well as the Eschatological Discourse, and by building up his final scene on the basis of an earlier report of a mountain-top resurrection appearance, Matthew has carried over this diversity of theological mountain symbolism into his Gospel. Not only does he carry it over, but by creating two new summary statements concerning Jesus' ministry with the crowds εἰς τὸ ὄρος (Mt 4.23–5.1; 15.29-31) which reflect OT conceptions of the eschatological gathering on Mount Zion, he adds to it as well.

But diversity is not the final word to be said about Matthew's mountain symbolism. The passages in which such symbolism occurs are drawn into a theological unity by Mt 28.16, not only by virtue of purely literary considerations, but also as a result of the eschatological Zion conceptions which lie at the heart of this all-important passage. In the case of Matthew's first four mountain scenes, the theological link is forged directly, in that the overriding theological symbolism associated with the mountain in each of these cases has been drawn from the same collection of Zion traditions as is at work in the final passage. With respect to the Temptation and Transfiguration Narratives, we have seen that even in the pre-Matthean situation the overriding theological conception which provided these mountain settings with their significance was a Son-christology depending on the 'enthronement on Zion' ideas of Ps 2. That Matthew was not unaware of such a dependence can be seen from the fact that these two passages have been incorporated into an extended humiliation–vindication pattern of Son-christology which reaches its climax in the enthronement statement of Mt 28.18b—a statement which probably reflects a similar Zion–enthronement–Ps 2 background. Moreover, it is apparent that the command in Mt 28.19-20a to gather a community of disciples in which Gentiles were to be included and the promise in v. 20b of Jesus' abiding Immanuel presence with this eschatological community are deeply rooted in the same OT expectations of the gathering of the eschatological community on Zion that lie behind Matthew's special constructions in Mt 4.23–5.1 and 15.29-31.

In the case of the Olivet Discourse the theological link with Mt 28.16-20 is less direct. Though the two passages do not share a common background in Zion eschatology, the fact that Matthew's concluding mountain scene—influenced as it is by the expectations of Zion eschatology—inaugurates an era of salvation history that is to last until the end of the age and in which these expectations come to at least partial fulfilment, means that it is able to gather up, complement and place on a more profound christological footing the description of the period leading up to the end of the age that is found in the earlier discourse on the Mount of Olives.

In the final analysis, then, the mountain in Matthew is able to carry out its role as an eschatological site—specifically as the place of the enthronement of the Son, of the establishment of the end-time community, and of the inauguration of the new age—because of Matthew's consistent and undergirding christological reinterpretation of Zion eschatology for which Mt 28.16-20 provides the most certain indication.

So, when Matthew's mountain motif is viewed from the perspective of the final mountain in the chain, the true significance for Matthew of 'Jesus on the mountain' can be seen: in Jesus and his ministry all of the hopes which had been associated with Zion have been fulfilled. He is the promised messianic Son whose enthronement to universal

sovereignty had long been anticipated. He was the one to whom the
people gathered for healing, feeding, teaching and eschatological
fellowship. Not only was he the one around whom the eschatological
community gathered, but in a more profound sense Jesus was himself
the fulfilment of the hopes for the restoration of Israel. Matthew
defines Jesus' Sonship in terms not only of royal messianology but
also of true Israel. In the opening chapters of the Gospel, Jesus is
depicted as the one who was called to recapitulate in his own life the
path of obedient Sonship that God's Son Israel had failed to
complete. In Jesus' vindication on the Mountain of Commissioning,
therefore, we see the fulfilment of the hopes of the restoration on
Mount Zion: it was to Jesus, rather than to restored Israel—or better,
to Jesus as the restored Son Israel—that the Gentiles were to gather
to participate in eschatological salvation. This being the case, there
was no continuing need for the temple. In Jesus rather than the
temple is to be found the long-awaited fulfilment of the promise of
'God-with-us'. With Jesus something 'greater than the temple' has
arrived (Mt 12.6). The procession of the Gentile Magi with their
eschatological gifts has as its goal not Jerusalem nor the temple, but
Jesus himself (Mt 2).

This vision of Christ comes to its most complete expression in Mt
28.16-20, and it is this passage which provides the framework in
which the other mountain scenes find their place. Like so much else
in the First Gospel, Matthew's mountain theology is to be understood
von hinten her.[6] When this perspective has been grasped, it can be
recognized that the mountain motif is a device used by the evangelist
to make the christological statement that Christ has replaced Zion as
the centre of God's dealings with his people; in him all the hopes
associated with Zion have come to fruition and fulfilment.

Matthew's theological construction here can perhaps be more
clearly outlined when it is compared with other early Christian
reinterpretations of Zion eschatology. In the NT and other literature
of the Ante-Nicene period, Zion eschatology is reinterpreted in the
light of Christian belief in at least four distinct ways.

a. One approach was to incorporate elements of Zion eschatology
into Christian hopes for the future. In this interpretation, the
fulfilment of Zion eschatology is transferred in a straightforward
manner to the future *parousia* of Christ. In the NT, such an
interpretation is found in the Apocalypse—especially in Rev 14.1,
where Jesus the Lamb stands on Mount Zion with a great gathered

company of the saints, and in Rev. 21.9–22.5, where John sees the New Jerusalem, the Bride of the Lamb, coming down to a 'great high mountain'. In similar fashion, Irenaeus cites 1 Bar 4.36ff. and Rev. 21 to argue for a literal future millennial fulfilment of a Jerusalem-centred kingdom on earth (*Ag. Her.* 5.35.1-2), and a future messianic banquet on Zion is described in 5 Ezra 2.38-48 (*NTApoc*, II, p. 695).

b. Other interpretations looked back on the Christ event, seeing it in one way or other as the fulfilment of expectations traditionally associated with Zion. The most literal of these approaches found such a fulfilment in the facts that salvation was accomplished in Jerusalem and that it was from there that the Gospel message went out to all the nations. Such a conception may well underlie Luke's emphasis on Jerusalem and the temple. Of particular interest is his account of the Pentecost sermon in Acts 2, where the beginning of the Church is described as the result of the preaching of the gospel message to a gathering of Jews 'from every nation under heaven' (v. 5). Is 2.2-4 was also often seen in later literature as fulfilled in the progress of the gospel outwards from Jerusalem to all nations.[7]

c. In a less literal way, characteristics pertaining to Mount Zion were sometimes attributed to specific mountains in Jesus' ministry. The clearest example of this is the use of τὸ ἅγιον ὄρος—a term associated almost exclusively in the OT and later literature with Mount Zion—to refer to the mountain of the transfiguration.[8] Several other OT mountains are brought into association with Jesus' mountain ministry in similar fashion.[9]

d. Finally, we encounter the purely symbolic use of Zion conceptions and terminology with respect to Christ—where Christ is said to replace Zion, to be Zion, or to be the fulfilment of Zion hopes—without any attempt being made to construct links with either Jerusalem or actual mountains on which Jesus ministered. The most striking passage in this regard is Heb 12.18-24, where Sinai and Zion are used to effect a contrast between the old covenant and the new: those who have come to Christ have come not to Mount Sinai with its terrors, but 'to Mount Zion and to the city of the living God, the heavenly Jerusalem' (v. 22). Also to be mentioned here is Jn 4.19-26, where Jesus himself appears as the replacement for both Mount Gerizim and Jerusalem. To these NT texts, a collection of patristic passages can be added.[10]

Our analysis suggests that Matthew's mountain motif has aspects in common with both (c) and (d) above. As in category (c), Matthew has taken elements usually associated in Jewish thinking with the eschatological role of Mount Zion and incorporated them into his treatment of specific mountains in the ministry of Jesus. But unlike 2 Pet 1.16-18, Matthew shows little interest in the mountain itself. For Matthew, there is no thought of a 'holy mountain'—a Christian Zion to rival the temple mount, to do for the Church what Gerizim did for Samaritanism. Jesus himself, and not any mountain on which he ministered, is for Matthew the Christian replacement for Zion. Zion theology has floated free of its Jerusalem moorings to become attached, not—as elsewhere in the Judaism of the period—to another mountain,[11] but to a person. The mountain in Matthew has significance only because Jesus is there.[12] Matthew uses it in the framework of his christological portrait where it functions as a vehicle by means of which Zion hopes are transferred to—and seen as fulfilled in—Jesus of Nazareth.

So, though Matthew makes use of specific mountains, he has much in common with the way of thinking that animates the symbolic approach of category (d). His mountain motif is a presentation in narrative form of the theological statement found in Heb 12.18-24; Matthew is saying in effect that those who gather to Jesus have come to the faithful Son (cf. Heb 3.1-6) in whom all the hopes associated with Mount Zion and the heavenly Jerusalem have come to fulfilment.

Chapter 13

THE MOUNTAIN MOTIF
AND THE MATTHEAN REDACTION

1. *Christology, Ecclesiology and Salvation History*

The themes of christology, ecclesiology and salvation history which come to expression in Matthew's mountain scenes are not limited to these passages but—as contemporary study of the First Gospel makes abundantly clear—are central to the theology of Matthew as a whole. The question arises, therefore, of the place of the mountain motif within the broader pattern of the evangelist's development of these key themes.

Recent discussion of Matthean christology consists largely of the attempt to discover which christological title or combination of titles is determinative for Matthew.[1] In the course of this discussion virtually every christological term to appear in the First Gospel—*Kyrios*, Son of Man, Son of God, Son of David, Messiah—has been assigned primary importance by one commentator or another.[2]

Our study of Matthew's mountain scenes throws fresh light on one of these terms—Son/Son of God. We discovered that not only is this term closely associated with the mountain motif—indeed, it is the primary christological category to appear in connection with the ὄρος setting in the First Gospel—but this motif serves to focus a characteristic aspect of Matthew's development of Son-christology. In this christological development the idea of the royal messianic Son is fused with and modified by that of Israel as God's Son: the Son who is enthroned in universal sovereignty is of necessity first of all the obedient Son who follows to its end the path of humility that Israel was not able to complete. The enthroned Son is at the same time true Israel; and only because he has remained true to his vocation of humble obedience to the Father is he enthroned. The three mountain scenes of the Temptation, the Transfiguration and the final comissioning serve as anchor points for Matthew's development of this theme.

It would be foolish to attempt to draw conclusions concerning the question of Matthew's preferred christological term(s) on the basis of such a narrow segment of material as has been canvassed here. But our study of the christological aspect of the mountain motif is relevant to the larger question of Matthean christology in a less direct way. The fact that virtually every christological term of any importance has been put forth as determinative for Matthew suggests that an approach based on terminological considerations alone has reached an impasse. Even Kingsbury's impressive argument for the pre-eminence of Son-christology founders on the fact that, while 'Son' appears in the all-important christological statement of 28.16-20, it does so in such a peripheral way as would not be expected were Son-christology as decisive for Matthew as he argues. Perhaps what is needed is a shift of emphasis from the single terms themselves to larger christological patterns built up on the basis of terminological and other elements—a shift from isolated titles to governing conceptions that draw various materials into a christological unity.

Such an approach is carried out by Blair, who argues that the idea of authority is the organizing principle in Matthew's portrait of Christ.[3] But while the importance of ἐξουσία for the First Gospel is not to be doubted, another category has been suggested by Frankemölle which is more fundamental to Matthean thought and into which the idea of authority can be incorporated—that of fulfilment.[4] A study of Matthew's use of πληρόω and related concepts reveals good grounds for the assertion that 'fulfilment' is a central conception in his presentation of Christ. Of particular importance in this regard is the series of formula quotations with which he punctuated his narrative in order to draw attention to the fulfilment of Scripture that he saw in Jesus' ministry.[5] πληρόω is also used of Jesus in significant ways in connection with 'the law and the prophets' (5.17) and 'all righteousness' (3.15). And if our analysis of the mountain scenes is correct, the evangelist used this motif at least in part in his presentation of Jesus as the one in whom the expectations of Zion eschatology come to fulfilment.

If the christological question is approached within such a frame-work, our study of Matthew's mountain motif can be of value in the explication of his christology not by providing evidence favouring this or that christological term, but by serving as a paradigm of the way in which Matthew combined christological terms, OT citations, and other typological and narrative elements to form a comprehensive picture of Jesus as the fulfilment of OT hopes and ideals. The mountain settings that came to Matthew in the Gospel tradition comprise one element among many which the evangelist pressed into the service of this central christological conception.

The other two theological themes under discussion—ecclesiology and salvation history—are important concerns in the First Gospel, going to the heart of Matthean theology. Looking first at ecclesiology, not only is the term ἐκκλησία found in the Gospels only in Matthew (16.18, twice in 18.17), but a recognition that this Gospel was written in the context of a specific church, shaped by ecclesiastical needs and concerns, and characterized by a particular vision of what the Church should be, has provided the basis for great advances in the understanding of the Gospel.[6] This raises the theological question of the nature and foundation of the Church in Matthew's thought, especially with regard to the Church's relationship with God's OT people Israel.

The contours of Matthean salvation history are to be found in the tension which is created in the body of the Gospel between anticipated universalism (e.g. 4.15; 8.11; 10.18; 12.21; 24.14) and strict particularism (10.5f.; 15.24), but which is released in the final verses as the command is given to 'make disciples of all the nations' (28.19). Since this bears all the marks of a deliberate Matthean construction,[7] the question arises: What occasioned the shift from particularism to universalism? On what grounds were the restrictions against preaching the gospel to the Gentiles removed?

Despite vigorous discussion, there is no consensus on these two questions.[8] Nevertheless, it is fair to say that the position gaining the widest following among redaction critics is that ecclesiology and salvation history are closely tied together in Matthew's thought by virtue of the fact that they are both fundamentally rooted in the rejection of Israel. Such a position finds its starting point in those passages which, in Clark's estimation, exhibit a 'Gentile bias'[9]— especially such 'rejection parables' as 21.33-46 and 22.1-14.[10] While not all who can be included in this category see the Gentiles as the exclusive beneficiaries of the rejection of Israel,[11] this position overlaps for the most part with the approach to the *Sitz im Leben* question that sees the Gospel as arising from a Gentile Christian community now totally separated from Judaism. Its main contours can be summarized as follows:[12] (1) Jesus' earthly ministry, which confirmed his identity as the promised Messiah, was restricted to

Israel. (2) Despite such an unprecedented opportunity, Israel refused the gospel and rejected Christ. (3) Consequently, Israel's salvation-historical fate was sealed: it was rejected by God and would figure in his purposes no longer. (4) Israel was to be replaced in *Heilsgeschichte* by the Church—a 'new' or 'true' Israel, drawn (at least in the majority view) only from the Gentile world. (5) Salvation history thus consists of three epochs: the preparatory age of Israel; the time of Jesus, brought to an end by Israel's rejection of him at the trial before Pilate; and the time of the Church, in which Israel's position is taken by (Gentile) Christianity. So the foundational role played in this approach to Matthew's ecclesiology and salvation history by the idea of the rejection of Israel is readily apparent: it is the rejection of Israel which provides the basis and necessary presupposition for the existence of the Church and which clears the path for the opening of the kingdom to the Gentiles.

Our study has revealed that the themes of ecclesiology and salvation history come to expression in Matthew's sequence of mountain passages. The idea of the rejection of Israel, however, did not enter into our discussion of the mountain motif at all, for it is nowhere to be found in these passages. Consequently, we are faced with an alternative: either the mountain motif is really peripheral to Matthew's development of these themes, the crucial texts for which are to be found elsewhere; or the idea of the rejection of Israel plays a less central role in Matthean ecclesiology and salvation history than Walker, Strecker and others would have us believe.

Now there can be no doubt that in Matthew's perspective the ministry of Jesus and John the Baptist provoked what Trilling describes as a crisis in Israel.[13] Moreover, the presence in the First Gospel of a long series of pericopae dealing with themes of judgment, rejection and replacement[14] clearly indicates that in Matthean thought the Jewish opponents of Jesus and his Church have—because of their opposition—been rejected by God. But whether it is possible to speak without further qualification of the rejection of Israel—particularly when this rejection is seen in ethnic Jew-Gentile terms—and whether the idea of rejection plays the pivotal role in Matthew's ecclesiology and salvation history that has been claimed for it, are issues that are open to serious question. Let us look at them in turn.

First, it is overstepping the evidence to say that Matthew views Israel as a monolithic whole that has been rejected as a *massa*

perditionis in favour of a Gentile Church.[15] Such an interpretation—
with its assumption that opposition to Pharisaism implies an alienation
from Judaism—exhibits a historical naïveté that fails to take account
of the diversity and 'crisis of identity' which characterized first-
century Judaism. But even more tellingly, it can be squared with the
First Gospel only by ignoring or arbitrarily excluding important
aspects of the data.

A study of the terminology for the various groups that appear in
Matthew—μαθηταί, Φαρισαῖοι, Σαδδουκαῖοι, γραμματεῖς, ἀρχιερεῖς,
ἔθνη, Ἰσραήλ, λαός, ὄχλοι—reveals that the major line of division in
the Gospel is drawn not between Jew and Gentile, but between the
Jewish leaders on the one hand and Jesus with his disciples and John
the Baptist on the other.[16] Matthew, in fact, includes in his Gospel
several *logia* in which τὰ ἔθνη are held up as examples of activity that
does not please God (6.7f., 32; 20.25). What makes the phrase 'the
rejection of Israel' somewhat misleading is the fact that Matthew
does not treat non-Christian Judaism as an undifferentiated mass
that can be unambiguously assigned to the negative side of the line of
division. As we have already had occasion to observe,[17] a comparison
with the other Synoptics reveals that Matthew made a sharp
distinction between the leaders and the ὄχλοι. The ὄχλοι generally
differ from the leaders in their response to Jesus,[18] and Matthew
carefully isolated the leaders from the crowds whenever words of
condemnation and rejection were to be spoken.[19]

It is true that Matthew does not depict the ὄχλοι as full-fledged
followers of Jesus. They are blind to the true secret of the kingdom
(13.10-17) and, in the Passion Narrative, join with their leaders in
calling for and accepting responsibility for the death of Jesus (27.20-
25). But it is not possible to see here a progressive deterioration of the
attitude of the crowds to Jesus—moving from initial enthusiasm to
final rejection so that in the end the distinction between leaders and
crowds is abolished and πᾶς ὁ λαός (cf. 27.25) stand as one rejected
mass.[20] The fact that Matthew sees a Jewish mission continuing to
the *parousia* (10.23), the emphasis in the Passion Narrative on the
influence of the leaders over the ὄχλοι,[21] and the hope expressed
even after the crucifixion (albeit in ironic terms) that the λαός would
believe in the resurrection (27.64)—all indicate that for Matthew the
eschatological status of the crowds remains open to the end. While he
is not unaware of the possibility that they might finally succumb to
the influence of the leaders (Matthew does not present οἱ ὄχλοι as a

remnant whose existence is necessary for the onward movement of salvation history), he hopes that they will even yet join the ranks of the disciples. The positive treatment of the ὄχλοι arises from Matthew's genuine interest in the Jewish mission, rather than from any purely literary or historicizing motives. Just as the Jewish leaders and the disciples function in the First Gospel as transparencies for the Judaism of Matthew's day and for his own church respectively, so the crowds represent a segment of Judaism for whose salvation the evangelist still holds out hope.[22]

When this aspect of Matthew is taken into account,[23] the statement that Matthew develops a 'rejection of Israel' theme needs to be qualified in two ways. First, since the rejection theme is concentrated on the Jewish leadership, the Israel that is rejected is not ethnic Jewry *per se*, but official Judaism as it is constituted under the leadership of the opponents of Jesus. Though there is no longer any hope, in Matthew's perspective, that the house of Israel as it is currently constituted will recognize Jesus, the 'lost sheep of the house of Israel'—i.e. those who have not yet fully aligned themselves with the leaders—are still viewed as potential Church members. The rejection of Israel is for Matthew primarily a rejection of the Jewish leaders. Second, while the Church has opened its doors to the Gentiles, this is not for Matthew its defining characteristic. With the Jewish mission continuing until the *parousia* (10.23), the Church is not an exclusively Gentile institution. A Church which is open to τὰ ἔθνη—but not consisting entirely of τὰ ἔθνη—is for Matthew the beneficiary of the rejection of Israel.[24]

But even in this more moderate reformulation, it is doubtful that the concept of the rejection of Israel plays a foundational role in Matthean ecclesiology and salvation history. Admittedly, texts can be cited that seem to support such a position (ecclesiology: 21.43; salvation history: 8.11f.). However, in Matthew's clearest and foundational statements on ecclesiology (16.13-20; 18.20; 28.18-20) and salvation history (28.18-20) the idea of rejection is absent. This suggests that while the rejection theme plays a part, it is not the starting point for the understanding of these aspects of Matthean thought.

While we have not yet stated the matter in precisely these terms, our study of these themes in the mountain scenes of the First Gospel leads to the result that for Matthew both ecclesiology and salvation history find their fundamental basis and starting point in christology.

The relevance of this insight, we would suggest, is not restricted to the mountain motif, for it provides the key to a more convincing picture of the whole Matthean construction of ecclesiology and salvation history—a picture within which the rejection theme finds its proper, and subsidiary, place.

Let us look first at ecclesiology. By saying that our study demonstrates the christological basis of Matthean ecclesiology, we are thinking not primarily of the centrality of Jesus in the life of the Church—i.e. that he is the gathering point for the eschatological people of God; that it is constituted by baptism in his name and obedience to his commands; that he is present in its midst. We are thinking rather of the more fundamental fact that from the outset of his Gospel Matthew presents Jesus himself as God's true Son Israel, who was obedient where Israel was disobedient and who for this reason was vindicated where Israel was judged. In Matthean thought, Jesus himself is *das wahre Israel*—a fact which issues positively in the existence of the Church, the eschatological community of Jews and Gentiles who obey his commands and gather in his name, and negatively in the rejection of the group identified with the Jewish leaders, which demonstrates by its rejection of Jesus that it is pseudo-Israel. The existence of the Church and the rejection of Israel, then, are related only indirectly through the mediation of Matthew's christology of fulfilment. The Church owes its existence not to the rejection of Israel but to the fulfilment of the Israel ideal in Christ. The rejection of Israel, in turn, is not the necessary presupposition of the Church, but the result of the refusal of pseudo-Israel to see in Christ the fulfilment of its own calling. In Matthean thought, ecclesiology and the rejection of Israel are related indirectly as the positive and negative consequences of the same christological conception.

A christological foundation is even more clearly evident in the case of Matthean *Heilsgeschichte*. It is recognized by all observers that 28.16-20, where the prohibition of a mission to the Gentiles is finally removed, marks an important salvation-historical turning point. But what has been overlooked in the fascination with the rejection theme is the fact that this passage actually provides the key to Matthew's pattern of *Heilsgeschichte*.[25] The closing pericope of Matthew's Gospel not only serves as a marker for the transition from one period of salvation history to another, but it provides a reason and a basis for this transition as well. The new age has dawned not because of the

rejection of Israel—indeed, once it is realized that Matthew's rejection
theme does not preclude a continuing Jewish mission, this idea loses
much of its ability to explain the Gentile mission—but because of the
vindication of Christ. The operative word in the passage is οὖν
(v. 19a): the resurrected Jesus has received universal authority;
therefore the Gentile mission can begin. Matthean *Heilsgeschichte* is
thus fundamentally grounded in christology.[26]

Our analysis of the themes that are focussed by Matthew's
mountain motif and that shine most brightly in this final mountain
scene enable us to see this connection between christology and
salvation history in broader perspective. In contemporary Jewish
thought, it was expected that the salvation of the Gentiles would be a
by-product of the restoration of Israel. When Israel was gathered to
God's holy mountain and reconstituted there as his people, the
Gentiles would be invited to share in eschatological blessings. In
Matthew's Gospel, this expectation has been reinterpreted in
christological terms. The mountain motif serves to underline the
conviction that in Jesus all the eschatological hopes associated with
Zion have come to fulfilment. In the particular matter of the
Gentiles, it is the mountain-top vindication and enthronement of
Jesus, rather than the mountain-top restoration of Israel, which in
Matthew's perspective initiates the era of Gentile salvation. Or—in
view of the 'true Israel' foundation of Matthew's Son-christology—it
can be said that the salvation-historical transition is grounded on the
restoration of Jesus, God's true Son Israel. In Matthean perspective,
Christ himself plays the role in *Heilsgeschichte* that elsewhere in
Jewish Christianity might have been assigned to the Jewish mission
or a Jewish Christian remnant.[27] As in the case of Matthean
ecclesiology, the rejection of Israel does not play a foundational role,
but stands with the salvation of the Gentiles as parallel salvation-
historical consequences of the central christological fact.

So the basic conception in Matthew's pattern of *Heilsgeschichte* is
the fulfilment in Christ of the OT hope. While this process of
fulfilment reaches its decisive moment in the post-resurrection
commissioning declaration, Matthew makes clear by his series of
formula quotations that the whole of Jesus' ministry was characterized
by fulfilment.[28] Consequently, there is no need to see the earthly
ministry of Jesus and the age of the Church as separate salvation-
historical epochs. Together with the *parousia*, they stand as three
phases ('preparation', 'inauguration' and 'consummation') of one

period of fulfilment. Matthean *Heilsgeschichte* can therefore be most accurately described as consisting of the two epochs of promise (the OT period up to the time of John the Baptist; cf. 11.11-13) and fulfilment (including Jesus' earthly ministry, the age of the Church, and the *parousia*).[29] A three-stage schema—especially as predicated on the idea of the rejection of Israel—is foreign to Matthew's way of thinking and open to the criticism of too uncritical a dependence on Conzelmann's study of Luke.[30]

2. *Life Setting*

In the opening pages of this study, we presented reasons for the assumption that Matthew's Gospel arose in the context of a church which, while open to the Gentile mission as long as safeguards against antinomian extremes were erected, was Jewish-Christian in its foundation and was involved in the process of consolidating its own life and identity during the period after the Roman war when a resurgent and increasingly anti-Christian Pharisaism was carrying out the reconstruction of Judaism in such a way as to exclude the Jewish-Christian community from the institutions and structures of Jewish life. Though the verification of this assumption has not been an explicit aim of this study, the circular nature of the redaction-critical process demands that we return to the *Sitz im Leben* question to re-examine initial assumptions in light of our investigations.

Speaking first in general terms, no aspect of Matthew's mountain motif is inconsistent with this picture of the Matthean church. In fact, while the conflict with Pharisaism is not reflected in the passages studied here, the evident interest in questions of ecclesiology and salvation history which these passages evince seems to reveal a community being forced to re-examine its identity and place in God's historical purposes in just the manner that has been proposed for Matthew's church.

Yet it is possible to be more precise about Matthew's church situation on the basis of the christological reinterpretation of Zion eschatology which, we have argued, the mountain motif in large measure represents. We begin with Brown's perceptive reconstruction of the life setting of the First Gospel, which takes as its starting point the presence in Matthew of two distinct—and even conflicting—descriptions of the Church's mission—the Israel-centred mission of ch. 10 and the unrestricted universal mission of 28.16-20.[31] He suggests that, while 28.16-20 expresses the evangelist's own view, ch. 10 represents the traditional approach of the Matthean church. This church originated in Palestine, where its understanding of its mission developed as a Jewish Christian analogue to current Jewish eschatological thinking: i.e. the task of the Church was to preach to Israel; the Gentiles would be included—if at all—on God's initiative alone and only after the *parousia*. But, according to Brown, events associated with the war—a move from Palestine into a Greek-speaking area (Syria?), the flight of the Jerusalem church, the destruction of the temple, and increasing alienation from Judaism due to the Pharisaic resurgence—conspired to make such a view of mission anachronistic and to lead some members of Matthew's church in the direction of a growing openness towards the Gentile mission. It was to encourage his church to embrace this wider view of mission that Matthew wrote his Gospel.

Brown's reconstruction is not entirely convincing as it stands. His reluctance to see any salvation-historical framework behind Matthew's treatment of these two views of mission[32] misses what we have seen to be an important aspect of Matthean thought. And he is almost certainly wrong in his main contention that major segments of Matthew's church needed to be convinced of the appropriateness of the Gentile mission, for in such a situation the question of circumcision would surely have arisen. His response to this objection—that since the Gentile mission was by definition a circumcision-free enterprise, this did not have to be addressed as a separate issue but was understood to be part of the package being advocated—fails to convince. But if the issue which Matthew was facing is seen as having to do not with the appropriateness of the Gentile mission itself but with the theological framework within which the mission was to be carried out, Brown's identification of these two understandings of mission provides us with a way forward.

The position being argued here is that in its beginning stages Matthew's church inherited (perhaps via the mediation of Peter) the Israel-centred view of salvation history with its corresponding conception of the Church and its mission which in all probability characterized the moderate element in the Jerusalem church,[33] but that (like Peter and James in Acts 15 and Gal 2) it had come to accept the validity of the Gentile mission without making any radical alteration in its understanding of salvation history. In other words, as long as its relations with Judaism and the uninterrupted progress of the Jewish mission allowed the continuation of the belief that the conversion of Israel was the key to salvation history, it was able to accept the hitherto unanticipated fact of the present-day inclusion of the Gentiles. The basis of such an inclusion was still seen as the fulfilment of the promises to Israel, even though this fulfilment had not yet come to completion. Although the salvation of the Gentiles had been expected to be a future event, only a minor adjustment was needed to accept it as a present reality.

The events associated with the war against Rome, however, provoked a crisis of understanding for Matthew's church. As it became apparent that Israel in its official structures and institutions had rejected Christ and that it was becoming increasingly difficult for the Jewish Church to see itself as the crest of the future within Judaism, the Israel-centred view of the nature of the Church, of salvation history, and of the Gentile mission was being stretched to the breaking point. What was needed was a more secure theological foundation for the life and mission of the Church.

It is against such a background that Matthew's development of a christological basis for ecclesiology and salvation history is to be seen. In place of the anticipated fulfilment of eschatological hopes on Zion as the foundation for Christian existence, Matthew proposed the realized fulfilment of every Zion expectation in Christ. The Church was to find its identity in its identification not with national Israel, but with Jesus, God's true Son Israel. The mission to the Gentiles was to be carried out not as an anticipatory consequence of the restoration of Israel on Mount Zion, but on the basis of the vindication of Christ announced on the mountain in Galilee. So Matthew's purpose was not to convince his community to embark on the Gentile mission, but to provide a firmer and more profoundly Christian anchor point for his church and its mission in a situation where the old mooring lines were no longer holding.

Perrin describes the accomplishment of the rabbis in Jamnia as that of providing for Judaism in the Torah a foundation for existence that, with the temple in ruins, could no longer be found in Zion.[34] The suggestion being made here is that Matthew responded to the same set of circumstances by attempting to provide for the Church a secure and independent foundation in Christ. The degree to which his Gospel has guided and inspired the Church in its life and mission through the centuries is the degree to which it can be said that he succeeded.

NOTES

Notes to Chapter 1

1. Though we must leave a discussion of the literature until later, the pervasiveness of this observation can be seen by the number of commentators who mention in passing Mt's interest in mountains without making any attempt to characterize or explain it; e.g. W.F. Albright and C.S. Mann, *Matthew* (Anchor Bible; Garden City, N.Y.: Doubleday, 1971), p. 32; W. Grundmann, *Das Evangelium nach Matthäus* (THKNT, 1; Berlin: Evangelische Verlaganstalt, 1968), p. 102; F.V. Filson, *A Commentary on the Gospel according to St. Matthew* (London: A. & C. Black, 1960), p. 75; H. Frankemölle, *Jahwebund und Kirche Christi* (Münster: Verlag Aschendorff, 1974), p. 42; J. Schreiber, *Theologie des Vertrauens: Eine redaktionsgeschichtliche Untersuchung des Markusevangeliums* (Hamburg: Furche-Verlag, 1967), p. 167; J.D. Kingsbury, 'The Composition and Christology of Matt. 28.16-20', *JBL* 93 (1974), 575; C.H. Giblin, 'A Note on Doubt and Reassurance in Mt. 28.16-20', *CBQ* 37 (1975), 71; J.A. Kirk, 'The Messianic Role of Jesus and the Temptation Narrative: A Contemporary Perspective', *EvQ* 44 (1972), 95.

2. Mt 4.8; 5.1; 8.1; 14.23; 15.29; 17.1, 9; 21.1; 24.3; 26.30; 28.16. ὄρος also appears in sayings material (Mt 5.14; 17.20; 18.12; 21.21; 24.16), but we will be interested in these occurrences only obliquely (see below, pp. 11f.).

3. Mt 14.23; 21.1; 26.30. On 14.23, see below, p. 12 and p. 283 n.5; on 21.1 and 16.30, see below pp. 157f.

4. For Mt 8.1, cf. 5.1; for 17.9, cf. 17.1.

5. See below, pp. 275f. n.1.

6. Both τὸ ὄρος and ὄρος ὑψηλὸν (λίαν) appear.

7. Mk 3.13; 5.11; 6.46; 9.2, 9; 11.1; 13.3; 14.26; Lk 4.29; 6.12; 8.32; 9.28, 37; 19.29, 37; 22.39.

8. The significance of this observation is not diminished by the fact that Mt has probably depended on tradition in some way or other for each of these mountain settings; see the discussion in Chapters 6, 7, 8, and 11 below.

9. Mk 6.46 // Mt 14.23; Mk 9.2, 9 // Mt 17.1, 9; Mk 11.1 // Mt 21.1; Mk 13.3 // Mt 24.3; Mk 14.26 // Mt 26.30. As we shall see below (pp. 106-11), the mountain setting in Mk 3.13 has been adapted for use in the Sermon on the Mount.

10. Mk 5.11; cf. Mt 8.30. Mt replaces Mk's ἐκεῖ πρὸς τῷ ὄρει with μακρὰν ἀπ' αὐτῶν.

11. Though Mauser attempts to force Mk's references to ὄρος, as well as to θάλασσα, into an over-arching wilderness/place of retreat motif, Mk 5.1-13 and 13.1ff. preclude such a possibility; see U. Mauser, *Christ in the Wilderness* (SBT, 39; London: SCM, 1963), pp. 108-19. His motivation for this attempt seems to be the fact, embarrassing for his thesis, that Markan references to ἔρημος do not appear beyond Mk 6.35. Lk emphasizes mountains as places of prayer (Lk 6.12; 9.28). But the presence of Lk 4.29 means that this idea is not as consistently worked out as Conzelmann maintains; H. Conzelmann, *The Theology of St. Luke*, trans. G. Buswell (London: Faber and Faber, 1960), p. 29.

12. Carrington's argument for a three-mountain structure to Mk's messianic secret is scarcely convincing; see P. Carrington, *The Primitive Christian Calendar* (Cambridge: University Press, 1952), esp. pp. 6-8.

13. Mark: the wilderness as a place of retreat, Galilee as a land of salvation, and Jerusalem as the centre of opposition; Luke: the journey from Galilee to Jerusalem (and then from Jerusalem to Rome).

14. Those works which focus their attention in more than a passing way on the significance of the ὄρος references for Matthew are few. The only publication completely devoted to the topic is that by J.-B. Livio, 'La signification théologique de la "montagne" dans le premier évangile', *Bulletin du Centre Protestant d'Etudes* 30 (1978), 13-20; he responds to a comment made by Bonnard to the effect that Mt's mountain references are to be seen as only random bits of traditional detail. The most extensive work is that of Lange, who studies Mt's mountain scenes in the context of his explication of Mt 28.16-20: J. Lange, *Das Erscheinen des Auferstandenen im Evangelium nach Matthäus* (Forschung zur Bibel, 11; Würzburg: Echter Verlag, 1973), pp. 392-445. Also to be mentioned is W. Schmauch's *Orte der Offenbarung und der Offenbarungsort im Neuen Testament* (Göttingen: Vandenhoeck und Ruprecht, 1956), pp. 67-77; though this work tends to waver between a historicist and a biblical theology viewpoint, it occasionally has valuable insights of a redactional nature. Covering the same grounds but from a quasi-devotional perspective is C. Kopp, *The Holy Places of the Gospels*, trans. R. Walls (New York: Herder & Herder, 1963). J.D. Kingsbury has a brief section in his *Matthew: Structure, Christology, Kingdom* (Philadelphia: Fortress, 1975) dealing with the place of the mountain in Matthean christology (pp. 56-58). Also to be included is the attempt by R. Frieling to find a literary pattern in Mt's mountain scenes, though his work is superficial and uncritical in the extreme; *Die Verklärung auf dem Berge: Eine Studie zum Evangelienverständnis* (Stuttgart: Verlag Urachhaus, 1965), pp. 53-57.

15. There is no need to attempt an exhaustive list of all those who characterize Mt's mountain scenes in this way. The statement is frequently

found in the commentaries: e.g. E. Lohmeyer, *Das Evangelium nach Matthäus*, ed. W. Schmauch (MeyerK; 4 Aufl.; Göttingen: Vandenhoeck und Ruprecht, 1967), p. 414; Grundmann, *Matthäus*, pp. 379, 576; Filson, *Matthew*, p. 180; J.P. Meier, *Matthew* (NT Message, 3; Wilmington, Del.: Michael Glazier, 1980), p. 367; F.W. Beare, *The Earliest Records of Jesus* (New York, Nashville: Abingdon, 1962), pp. 142, 243; D. Hill, *The Gospel of Matthew* (New Century Bible; London: Oliphants, 1972), p. 361. Similar statements are found in more specialized works as well: e.g. B.J. Hubbard, *The Matthean Redaction of a Primitive Apostolic Commissioning: An Exegesis of Mt. 28.16-20* (SBLDS, 19; Missoula: Scholars Press, 1974), p. 73; G. Bornkamm, 'Der Auferstandene und der Irdische. Mt. 28.16-20', in *Zeit und Geschichte*, ed. E. Dinkler (Tübingen: J.C.B. Mohr [Paul Siebeck], 1964), p. 171; R.H. Fuller, *The Formation of the Resurrection Narratives* (New York: Macmillan, 1971), p. 81; B. Rigaux, *Dieu l'a ressuscité. Exégèse et théologie biblique* (Gembloux: Duculot, 1973), p. 254; J. Zumstein, 'Matthieu 28.16-20', *RThPh* 22 (1972), p. 16; J.M. Gibbs, 'The Son of God as the Torah Incarnate in Matthew', *StEv* 4 (1968), 45.

16. Occasionally vague references can be found to mountains of revelation in the OT (e.g. Gibbs, 'The Son of God as the Torah Incarnate', 45), especially Sinai (Lohmeyer, *Matthäus*, pp. 24f.). But whether Sinai, with its covenantal role in the establishment of the people of God, can be adequately described simply as a 'mountain of revelation', and whether it is a suitable parallel for Mt when characterized in this way, are matters which require further elaboration and qualification to be convincing.

17. So F. Rienecker, *Das Evangelium des Matthäus* (Wuppertal: Verlag R. Brockhaus, 1953), p. 216; J. Schniewind, *Das Evangelium nach Matthäus* (NTD; 8 Aufl.; Göttingen: Vandenhoeck und Ruprecht, 1956), p. 185; W. Trilling, *The Gospel according to St. Matthew*, trans. K. Smyth (New York: Herder & Herder, 1969), II, p. 109.

18. J. Wellhausen, *Das Evangelium nach Matthäus* (Berlin: G. Reimer, 1904), p. 13.

19. *Orte der Offenbarung*, pp. 71-74.

20. No teaching takes place in Mt 15.29-31; the element of authority implicit in Jesus' sitting posture is not enough to imply that it does (*contra* Schmauch, *Orte der Offenbarung*, p. 72; R.H. Gundry, *Matthew: A Commentary on His Literary and Theological Art* [Grand Rapids: Eerdmans, 1982], p. 317).

21. G. Strecker, *Der Weg des Gerechtigkeit* (FRLANT, 82; 2 Aufl.; Göttingen: Vandenhoeck und Ruprecht, 1966), p. 98.

22. 'La signification théologique de la "montagne"'; he argues that on the mountain there comes into focus the One who is greater than a New Moses or a New Israel.

23. T.J. Ryan, 'Matthew 15.29-31: An Overlooked Summary', *Horizons* 5 (1978), 39; the mountain is the place where Jesus speaks and acts with authority.

24. F.H. Daniel, 'The Transfiguration: A Redaction Critical and Traditio-historical Study' (Ph.D. Dissertation, Vanderbilt University, 1976), p. 115; Kingsbury, *Matthew*, pp. 56-58. Both Daniel and Kingsbury see the mountain as the place of the manifestation of Jesus as Son of God.

25. *Die Verklärung auf dem Berge*, pp. 53-57. There are correspondences between Mt 4.8 and 28.16, and to a lesser extent between 5.1 and 24.3. But no similarity is to be found between 14.23 and 17.1, and in no way can 15.29 serve as the centrepiece of the whole pattern.

26. Similar links have been suggested by various scholars in individual cases (see the discussion of the Matthean passages below), but Schmauch and Lange are the only ones who have moved in the direction of seeing an overall pattern based on 28.16-20; see Schmauch, *Orte der Offenbarung*, pp. 71f.; Lange, *Das Erscheinen des Auferstandenen*, pp. 393-440.

27. Specifically his inclusion of 14.23 and exclusion of 24.3; see also below, p. 12.

28. Lange, *Das Erscheinen des Auferstandenen*, pp. 441-45. See also Born-kamm, 'Der Auferstandene und der Irdische', 171; P. Nepper-Christensen, *Das Matthäusevangelium: ein judenchristliches Evangelium?* (Aarhus: Universi-tetsforlaget, 1958), pp. 163-79, esp. 174-77.

29. On the allusive citations in Mt, see R.H. Gundry, *The Use of the Old Testament in St. Matthew's Gospel* (Leiden: Brill, 1967).

30. See the literature cited in Chapter 4 below.

31. The mountain occasionally comes into the discussion when such related concepts as 'temple' and 'navel of the earth' are being treated; see Chapter 5 below. But direct investigation of the use of ὄρος/רה/טור in this period is rare. See H. Riesenfeld, *Jésus transfiguré. L'arrière-plan du récit évangélique de la transfiguration de Notre-Seigneur* (Copenhagen: Ejnar Munksgaard, 1947), pp. 217-22; K.M. Campbell, 'The New Jerusalem in Matthew 5.14', *SJT* 31 (1978), 335-63, esp. 346-52; Gibbs, 'The Son of God as the Torah Incarnate', 45.

32. A Sinai background to Mt's mountain scenes is frequently suggested in individual cases; see, e.g., the literature cited in the case of the Sermon on the Mount below (pp. 111f.). Others see Sinai behind Mt's whole mountain motif, though not necessarily as the overriding feature: Hubbard, *The Matthean Redaction*, pp. 92-94; Livio, 'La signification théologique de la "montagne"', 13-20; Schmauch, *Orte der Offenbarung*, pp. 76f. Cf. also R.E. Brown, *The Gospel according to John* (Anchor Bible; Garden City, N.Y.: Doubleday, 1966), pp. 232, 1093, who suggests that τὸ ὄρος was seen throughout the Gospel tradition as a Christian counterpart to Sinai.

33. See W.D. Davies, *The Setting of the Sermon on the Mount* (Cambridge: University Press, 1964), pp. 92-108; Kingsbury, *Matthew*, pp. 82-92; and below, pp. 98f.

34. *Orte der Offenbarung*, p. 77. Schmauch is vigorously opposed by Lange at this point (*Das Erscheinen des Auferstandenen*, p. 441 n. 101). In a

review of Lange's book, though, E.L. Bode has called for more work to be done on this possibility (*CBQ* 37 [1975], 125f.).

35. Ten occurrences in the Gospels: Mk 3.13 // Lk 6.12; Mk 6.46 // Mt 14.23; Mt 5.1; 15.29; 28.16; Lk 9.28; Jn 6.3, 15.

36. W. Foerster, 'Ὄρος', *TDNT*, V, pp. 475-87, esp. 484f.

37. G. Dalman, *Sacred Sites and Ways*, trans. P.P. Levertoff (London: SPCK, 1935), p. 155; M. Black, *An Aramaic Approach to the Gospels and Acts* (2nd edn; Oxford: Clarendon Press, 1954), p. 96; see also B. Lindars, *The Gospel of John* (New Century Bible; London: Oliphants, 1972), p. 240; P. Bonnard, *L'Evangile selon Saint Matthieu* (2nd edn; Neuchâtel: Delachaux et Niestlé, 1970), pp. 54, 234; Filson, *Matthew*, p. 180; B.W. Bacon, *The Sermon on the Mount* (New York: Macmillan, 1902), p. 66; J. Murphy-O'Connor, 'The Structure of Matthew XIV–XVII', *RB* 82 (1975), 372; and the RSV, NEB, JB, and NIV translations.

38. Foerster cites several classical references (Herodotus 1.104; Xenophon, *Anab.* 1.2.22; and Demosthenes, *Or.* 55.10), and Bauer–Arndt–Gingrich adds Diodorus Siculus 20.58.2. In these refences, ὄρος does mean 'mountain range', though there is no parallel to the absolute τὸ ὄρος of the Gospels (the Herodotus reference is τὸ καυκάσιον ὄρος; the other three are all anarthrous). Liddell–Scott does not include this meaning in its treatment of ὄρος, except in the case of papyrological usage. The papyri provide some evidence that ὄρος was used to describe both the large desert plateaus overhanging the Nile Valley and the hilly approaches to those plateaus, though the relevance of this Egyptian usage for the geographically different Palestinian situation is questionable; see H. Cadell and R. Rémondon, 'Sens et emplois de τὸ ὄρος dans les documents papyrologiques', *Revue des Etudes Greques* 80 (1967), 343-49.

39. For הר, see Brown–Driver–Briggs, pp. 249-51; for טור, see Black, *Aramaic Approach*, p. 96; G. Dalman, *Aramäisch-Neuhebräisches Handwörterbuch* (2 Aufl.; Frankfurt: J. Kauffmann Verlag, 1922), p. 168; but cf. M. Jastrow, *Dictionary of the Targumim, the Talmud Babli and Yerushalmi, and the Midrashic Literature* (New York: Pardes Publishing House, 1950 [1903]), I, p. 526; and J. Levy, *Wörterbuch über die Talmudim und Midraschim*, ed. J. Goldschmidt (2 Aufl.; Berlin und Wien: Benjamin Harz Verlag, 1924), II, p. 148—neither of whom include this wider meaning.

40. A few other terms, such as βουνός and γῆ occur once.

41. E.g. Gen 19.17; Josh 11.3; 12.8; 17.16; Judg 1.19.

42. 1 Macc 4.18, 19; 9.38, 40. For some uncertainty with respect to the meaning of τὸ ὄρος, however, cf. the translation of 4.18f. with that of 9.38, 40 in J.A. Goldstein, *I Maccabees: Introduction and Commentary* (Anchor Bible; Garden City, N.Y.: Doubleday, 1976), pp. 258, 378.

43. There are eleven instances where the singular ὄρος is rendered by the plural 'hills' or an equvalent in Thackeray's Loeb translation; a check with the concordance indicates that this is an inclusive list. In five of these (*War*

3.158; *Ant.* 5.87; 5.257; 13.19; 15.364) the singular gives just as plausible a reading. Two other references are to specific ranges of mountains (*War* 4.452; *Ant.* 4.83). In the other four cases (*War* 1.419; *Ant.* 5.177; 13.159; 20.121), only one of which has the article, the meaning 'hill country' is clearly indicated by the context.

44. For the normative situation, see the Greek version of Judith, where the substantive ὀρεινή is used for 'hill country', ὄρη for 'mountains', and ὄρος for 'mountain'.

45. Cf. also εἰς τὸ ὄρος τῶν ἐλαιῶν—Mk 13.3 // Mt 24.3; Mk 14.26 // Mt 26.30; Mt 21.1; Lk 19.29, 37; 21.37; 22.39.

46. Schmauch rejects Foerster's translation solely on the basis of the typological significance which he finds in the term: *Orte der Offenbarung*, p. 79. While this argument is not totally circular, it is safer to establish the meaning of τὸ ὄρος in the Gospels on linguistic grounds before considering the theological evidence.

47. So, e.g., H. Montefiore, 'Revolt in the Desert? (Mark vi.30ff.)', *NTS* 8 (1961–62), 135; and most commentaries.

48. Johannes Jeremias, *Der Gottesberg: Ein Beitrag zum Verständnis der biblischen Symbolsprache* (Gütersloh: C. Bertelsmann, 1919), pp. 142f., interprets it as the anonymous divine mountain common in ancient Near Eastern thought; in view of the lack of any extended narrative interest in the mountain itself, this is unlikely. Allen's explanation of τὸ ὄρος in Mt 5.1 as reflecting a traditional association of the Sermon with a mountain fails to explain any of the other occurrences of the term; W.C. Allen, *A Critical and Exegetical Commentary on the Gospel according to St. Matthew* (3rd edn; ICC; Edinburgh: T. & T. Clark, 1912), p. 38.

49. See below, p. 198.

50. Mt 17.20 and 21.21 depend on Mk 11.23, and Mt 24.16 on Mk 13.14. The parable of Mt 18.10-14 is taken from Q (cf. Lk 15.3-7). But where Mt has ἐπὶ τὰ ὄρη, Lk has ἐν τῇ ἐρήμῳ; though Bussby argues that the deviation is to be explained as a misunderstanding of the Aramaic term דּוּרָא ('walled compound') which arose in the process of oral tradition (F. Bussby, 'Did a Shepherd Leave Sheep upon the Mountains or in the Desert? A note on Matthew 18.12 and Luke 15.4', *ATR* 45 [1963], 93f.), it is more likely that Mt's choice of ὄρη reflects his familiarity with the OT pastoral metaphor (see, e.g., Ezek 34, and below, pp. 47f.). On the source of Mt 5.14, see below, p. 255 n.63.

51. Mt 5.14; see below, p. 117.

52. Below, pp. 123f.

53. Below, p. 283 n.5.

54. *Das Erscheinen des Auferstandenen*, p. 392.

55. Below, pp. 157f. Livio includes Mt 24.3 in his survey of Mt's mountain theology; 'La signification théologique de la "montagne"', 19.

Notes to Chapter 2

1. For a still-helpful survey from a comparative religions perspective, see J.A. MacCulloch, 'Mountains, Mountain Gods', *Encyclopaedia of Religion and Ethics*, ed. J. Hastings (Edinburgh: T. &. T. Clark, 1908–1926), VIII, pp. 863-68. For studies of sacred mountain concepts in broader perspective, see M. Eliade, *Cosmos and History: The Myth of the Eternal Return*, trans. W.R. Trask (New York: Harper & Row, 1959), esp. pp. 12-17; E.A.S. Butterworth, *The Tree at the Navel of the Earth* (Berlin: Walter de Gruyter, 1970). That such concepts are not just ancient or primitive phenomena can be seen, for example, from the place of the 'Hill of Cumorah' in traditions surrounding the origin of Mormonism; e.g. R. Mullen, *The Latter-Day Saints: The Mormons Yesterday and Today* (Garden City, N.Y.: Doubleday, 1966), pp. 11-15.

2. Mt. 1.22f.; 2.15, 17f., 23; 4.14-16; 8.17; 12.17-21; 13.35; 21.4f; 27.9f.

3. For a more complete list, see W.G. Kümmel, *Introduction to the New Testament*, trans. H.C. Kee (London: SCM, 1975), pp. 112-14.

4. Eusebius quotes Origen as saying that Mt 'was prepared for the converts from Judaism, and published in the Hebrew language' (*H.E.* 6.25.4). The situation before the onset of Redaction Criticism is ably represented by B.H. Streeter, *The Four Gospels* (London: Macmillan, 1924), pp. 511-16; B.W. Bacon, *Studies in Matthew* (New York: Henry Holt, 1930), pp. 131-42; and E. von Dobschütz, 'Matthäus als Rabbi und Katechet', *ZNW* 27 (1928), 338-48.

5. This approach is taken, with varying emphases, by E.P. Blair, *Jesus in the Gospel of Matthew* (New York: Abingdon, 1960), pp. 145-61; B. Rigaux, *The Testimony of St. Matthew*, trans. P.J. Oligny (Chicago: Franciscan Herald Press, 1968), pp. 136-43; P.F. Ellis, *Matthew: His Mind and His Message* (Collegeville: Liturgical Press, 1974), pp. 2-25; Kümmel, *Introduction*, pp. 117-20; K. Stendahl, *The School of St. Matthew and its Use of the Old Testament* (Philadelphia: Fortress, 1954), pp. 11-35; Davies, *Setting*, pp. 256-315; R. Hummel, *Die Auseinandersetzung zwischen Kirche und Judentum im Matthäusevangelium* (München: Chr. Kaiser Verlag, 1966), pp. 28-30; R.P. Martin, 'St. Matthew's Gospel in Recent Study', *ExpT* 80 (1968–69), 132-36; J.P. Martin, 'The Church in Matthew', *Int* 39 (1975), 41-56. While these authors would generally see the separation between church and synagogue as more or less complete and final, Bornkamm and his pupils take the Jewish-Christian approach one step further, asserting, on the basis of such passages as Mt 17.24-27, that the church had not yet broken with Judaism—the debate was still *intra muros*; see G. Bornkamm, G. Barth, and H.-J. Held, *Tradition and Interpretation in Matthew*, trans. P. Scott (Philadelphia: Westminster, 1963), pp. 21-24, 159-64. It is possible that the difference between these two approaches is more semantic than substantial; cf. J.P. Meier, *Law and History in Matthew's Gospel* (AnBib, 71; Rome: Biblical Institute Press, 1976), pp. 9f.

6. For the suggestion that Mt works on two fronts, countering both Pharisaism and antinomianism, see Barth, 'Matthew's Understanding of the Law', in *Tradition and Interpretation*, pp. 62-105; Bornkamm, 'Der Auferstandene und der Irdische', 180; Hummel, *Auseinandersetzung*, pp. 66-75.

7. The term is that of K.W. Clark, who pioneered this new approach; see his article 'The Gentile Bias in Matthew', *JBL* 66 (1947), 165-72.

8. See esp. Strecker, *Der Weg der Gerechtigkeit*, pp. 29-35; W. Trilling, *Das wahre Israel: Studien zur Theologie des Matthäusevangeliums* (Leipzig: St. Benno-Verlag, 1959), pp. 191f.; J. Rohde, *Rediscovering the Teaching of the Evangelists*, trans. D.M. Barton (London: SCM, 1968), pp. 111f.

9. See G. Strecker, 'The Concept of History in Matthew', *JAAR* 35 (1967), 219-30; Meier, *Law and History*, pp. 21-23; R. Walker, *Die Heilsgeschichte im ersten Evangelium* (FRLANT, 91; Göttingen: Vandenhoeck und Ruprecht, 1967), pp. 88f.

10. See also Nepper-Christensen, *Das Matthäusevangelium*; S. van Tilborg, *The Jewish Leaders in Matthew* (Leiden: Brill, 1972); L. Gaston, 'The Messiah of Israel as Teacher of the Gentiles: The Setting of Matthew's Christology', *Int* 29 (1975), 24-40.

11. For more detail, see Kümmel, *Introduction*, pp. 114-19; also our discussion of the 'rejection of Israel' motif below, pp. 205-208.

12. Cf. S. Brown, 'The Two-fold Representation of the Mission in Matthew's Gospel', *StTh* 31 (1977), 27.

13. See below, pp. 281f. n.74.

14. E.g. Strecker, *Der Weg der Gerechtigkeit*, pp. 30f.

15. *Auseinandersetzung*, esp. pp. 26-33.

16. M. Hengel, *Judaism and Hellenism*, trans. J. Bowden (London: SCM, 1974).

17. Though OT scholars will have to decide the relevance of Childs's 'canonical criticism' for OT studies, his insights are of great value for the place of the OT in historical-critical study of the NT; see B.S. Childs, *Introduction to the Old Testament as Scripture* (Philadelphia: Fortress, 1979).

18. For this 'horizontal-vertical' terminology, see W.G. Thompson, *Matthew's Advice to a Divided Community: Mt 17.22–18.35* (AnBib, 44: Rome: Biblical Institute Press, 1970), pp. 6f. These two aspects have also been called 'redaction criticism' and 'composition criticism' respectively; see N. Perrin, *What is Redaction Criticism?* (Philadelphia: Fortress, 1970), pp. 65-67. In the present study, as in Perrin's work, 'Redaction Criticism' refers to the procedure which encompasses both aspects.

19. R. Bultmann, *History of the Synoptic Tradition*, trans. J. Marsh (New York: Harper & Row, 1963), p. 5.

20. There have always been those who see no need for the Q hypothesis, arguing that Lk was dependent for his 'Q' material on Mt alone; e.g. A.M. Farrer, 'On Dispensing with Q', in *Studies in the Gospels*, ed. D.E. Nineham

(Oxford: Blackwell, 1955), pp. 55-86. More recently, however, the continuing problem of the minor agreements of Mt and Lk against Mk, and the demonstration that the argument from order is fallacious, have led to several new attempts to establish Markan dependence on Mt: for a revival of the Augustinian order, see B.C. Butler, *The Originality of St. Matthew* (Cambridge: University Press, 1951); for a neo-Griesbach hypothesis, see W.R. Farmer, *The Synoptic Problem: A Critical Analysis* (New York: Macmillan, 1964).

21. Farmer has complained that redaction critics turn a blind eye to this new discussion of the source question; W.R. Farmer, 'The Two-Document Hypothesis as a Methodological Criterion in Synoptic Research', *ATR* 48 (1966), 380-96, esp. 391-93. For examples of attempts to construct a redaction-critical methodology that is independent of any source hypothesis, see O.L Cope, *Matthew: A Scribe Trained for the Kingdom of Heaven* (CBQMS, 5; Washington: Catholic Biblical Association, 1976), pp. 2-9; Thompson, *Matthew's Advice*, pp. 4-6.

22. Bultmann, commenting on Redaction Criticism in the foreword to R. Bultmann and K. Kundsin, *Form Criticism: Two Essays on New Testament Research*, trans. F.C. Grant (New York: Harper & Bros, 1962), reaffirmed his earlier position that the composition of the Gospels 'involves nothing in principle new, but only completes what was begun in the oral tradition'; cf. *History of the Synoptic Tradition*, p. 321. See also Strecker, *Der Weg der Gerechtigkeit*, pp. 9f.; K. Koch, *Was ist Formgeschichte? Methoden der Bibelexegese* (3 Aufl.; Neukirchen-Vluyn: Neukirchener Verlag, 1974), esp. pp. 72-74.

23. For generally similar views, see G. Schille, 'Der Mangel eines kritischen Geschichtbildes in der neutestamentlichen Formgeschichte', *TLZ* 88 (1963), cols. 491-502; Rohde, *Rediscovering*, pp. 16-21; R.H. Stein, 'What is Redaktionsgeschichte?', *JBL* 88 (1969), 45-56; and in Matthean studies, Cope, *Matthew*, pp. 5-9.

24. For more detailed formulations, see W. Marxsen, *Mark the Evangelist*, trans. J. Boyce *et al.* (Nashville, New York: Abingdon, 1959), pp. 15-29; Rohde, *Rediscovering*; and Perrin, *What is Redaction Criticism?*

Notes to Chapter 3

1. For Mesopotamian and Babylonian religion, see R.J. Clifford, *The Cosmic Mountain in Canaan and the Old Testament* (HSM 4; Cambridge, Mass.: Harvard University Press, 1972), pp. 9-25, along with the literature cited there; also E. Burrows, 'Some Cosmological Patterns in Babylonian Religion', in *The Labyrinth*, ed. S.H. Hooke (London: SPCK, 1935), pp. 45-70. For Canaanite religion, see Clifford, *The Cosmic Mountain*; F.M. Cross, *Canaanite Myth and Hebrew Epic* (Cambridge, Mass.: Harvard University Press, 1973). For Persian tradition, see, e.g., the retreat of Zoroaster

(Zarathustra) to a mountain: Dio Chrysostom 19(36).40. For Hellenism, see below, pp. 79-81.

2. See S.N. Kramer, *Sumerian Mythology* (2nd edn; New York: Harper & Row, 1961), p. 39; Burrows, 'Some Cosmological Patterns'; S. Talmon, 'הר', *TDOT*, III, 436f.; Clifford, *The Cosmic Mountain*, pp. 9-25.

3. E.g. Burrows, 'Some Cosmological Patterns'; R.J. McKelvey, *The New Temple: The Church in the New Testament* (Oxford: University Press, 1969), p. 189.

4. See Clifford, *The Cosmic Mountain*, pp. 9-25.

5. For a vigorous defence of the *Weltberg* idea in response to Clifford, see B. Margulis, '*Weltbaum* and *Weltberg* in Ugaritic Literature: Notes and Observations on RŠ 24.245', *ZAW* 86 (1974), esp. 19-23. Margulis's use of the term *Weltberg*, however, seems to be almost equivalent to Clifford's 'cosmic mountain' and to bear little resemblance to the Mesopotamian concept; it appears that he has misunderstood Clifford.

6. For extensive bibliography, see S. Terrien, 'The Omphalos Myth and Hebrew Religion', *VT* 20 (1970), 315-38; also A.J. Wensinck, *The Ideas of the Western Semites Concerning the Navel of the Earth* (Amsterdam: Johannes Müller, 1916); Butterworth, *The Tree at the Navel of the Earth*; W. Müller, *Die Heilige Stadt: Roma quadrata, himmlisches Jerusalem und die Mythe vom Weltnabel* (Stuttgart: W. Kohlhammer Verlag, 1961); Talmon, 'הר', pp. 437f.

7. The Omphalos Stone, recovered in archaeological excavations at Delphi, was thought to mark the spot which Zeus had determined was the centre of the earth; see H.W. Parke, *A History of the Delphic Oracle* (Oxford: Blackwell, 1939), p. 9.

8. See below, pp. 59f.

9. Wensinck's work (*The Navel of the Earth*) is methodologically unsound. He draws conclusions with respect to the OT on the basis of material found in Rabbinic literature, and he assumes that the appearance of concepts associated with the *Weltnabel* (e.g. mountains, sanctuary) implied an underlying use of the navel concept, without attempting to show the link. The arguments of Childs and Terrien are more rigorous; see B.S. Childs, *Myth and Reality in the Old Testament* (London: SCM, 1960), pp. 83-93; Terrien, 'The Omphalos Myth'.

10. The usual anatomical terms שׁר (Ezek 16.4) or שׁרר (Cant 7.2) are never used in this geographical sense. The two instances of טבור ('centre'; Judg 9.37; Ezek 38.12) are translated in the LXX by ὀμφαλός, which suggests the influence of the *Weltnabel* concept in the third century BC. Wright, Anderson and others have argued that טבור in Judg 9.37 should be translated 'navel' and taken as evidence that Shechem was seen as a *Weltnabel*; see G.R.H. Wright, 'The Mythology of Pre-Israelite Shechem', *VT* 20 (1970), 75-82; B.W. Anderson, 'The Place of Shechem in the Bible', *BA* 20 (1957), 10-19; Terrien, 'The Omphalos Myth'; Wensinck, *The Navel of the Earth*,

p. 1. Judg 9.37, however, is apparently devoid of mythological overtones, and it is doubtful that this passage shows evidence of the Omphalos myth; cf. Clifford, *The Cosmic Mountian*, pp. 135, 183. Such influence is more probable in Ezek 38.12. In view of the description of Jerusalem in Ezek 5.5 as 'the centre of the nations' (בתוך הגוים), the appearance of טבור הארץ in Ezek 38.12 may owe something to *Weltnabel* cosmology; but cf. Talmon, 'הר', 437f.

11. Clifford does not mention it; see also R.L. Cohn, 'The Sacred Mountain in Ancient Israel' (Ph.D. Dissertation, Stanford University, 1974), p. 209.

12. See W. Eichrodt, *Ezekiel: A Commentary*, trans. C. Quin (London: SCM, 1970), pp. 88, 524.

13. For generally similar definitions of 'cosmic mountains', see Cohn, 'The Sacred Mountain', pp. 192-95; Clifford, *The Cosmic Mountain*, pp. 2-8. Talmon unnecessarily restricts the term 'cosmic mountain' to the mountain as the home of the gods; 'הר', 439-42. For a broader treatment in which the mountain is seen as one of several forms of cosmic centre, see Eliade, *Cosmos and History*, pp. 3-12.

14. Metzger's attempt, however, to interpret Zion theology in terms of the *axis mundi* concept is unconvinving; see M. Metzger, 'Himmlische und irdische Wohnstatt Jahwes', *UF* 2 (1970), 139-58.

15. E.g. H. Schmidt, *Der heilige Fels in Jerusalem* (Tübingen: J.C.B. Mohr [Paul Siebeck], 1933), esp. pp. 78-85.

16. E.g. Ps 48.2; Is 14.13. See Cohn, 'The Sacred Mountain', p. 130; R.E. Clements, *God and Temple* (Oxford: Blackwell, 1965), pp. 3-11; S. Talmon, 'The Biblical Concept of Jerusalem', *JES* 8 (1971), 308; Margulis, '*Weltbaum* and *Weltberg*', 15.

17. *The Cosmic Mountain*.

18. In his attempt to explain Zion theology solely on the basis of David's historical activity and the mountain symbolism already at work in Israel's tradition, Cohn does not sufficiently recognize the importance of this background; R.L. Cohn, 'Mountains and Mount Zion', *Judaism* 26 (1977), 97-115, esp. 111.

19. For more detailed methodological treatments which take these limitations into account, see B.M. Metzger, 'Methodology in the Study of the Mystery Religions and Early Christianity', in his *Historical and Literary Studies: Pagan, Jewish, and Christian* (Grand Rapids: Eerdmans, 1968), pp. 1-24; S. Sandmel, 'Parallelomania', *JBL* 81 (1962), 1-13. For critical comments on Clifford's methodology specifically, see J.D. Levenson, *Theology of the Program of Restoration of Ezekiel 40–48* (HSM 10; Missoula: Scholars Press, 1976), pp. 17, 28f.

20. See below, pp. 33, 38, 42f., 50.

21. This eschatological aspect of Mount Zion (see below, pp. 41-49) is also an OT distinctive.

22. See below, pp. 34, 39-41.

23. See Cohn, 'The Sacred Mountain', pp. 21-26; and below, p. 30.
24. See below, pp. 33, 36f.

Notes to Chapter 4

1. For a survey, see Cohn, 'The Sacred Mountain', pp. 1-58.
2. In the OT there are more than five hundred occurrences of הר, and sixty of גבעה. הר appears in every OT book except Ruth, Ecclesiastes, Esther and Ezra.
3. E.g. Mount Carmel as a symbol of beauty and fertility (Cant 7.5; Is 25.2; Jer 50.19); snowy Mount Hermon associated with life-giving rainfall (Ps 133.3); Tabor joining with Hermon in praise of the creator (Ps 89.12).
4. They appear as symbols of fertility and prosperity (e.g. Ps 104.10, 13; 147.8; 148.9; Joel 3.18; Amos 9.13). The 'everlasting hills' are a symbol of permanence (Gen 49.26); to have been in existence before the mountains is noteworthy (Ps 90.2; Prov 8.25). They are also figures of stability, but usually in the imagery of divine shaking or destruction (Ps 18.7; 46.2f.; 97.5; Hab 3.10); that is to say, God's activity is so fearful that it causes even the unshakable to tremble. They appear also as typical places both for refuge and security (Gen 19.17; Josh 2.16; Ps 11.1; Hos 10.8; Am 9.2f.) and of desolation and lostness (2 Chron 18.16; Jer 13.16).
5. The mountains were the first things to emerge from the primal waters (Ps 104.6-9); their roots reach down to Sheol (Jon 2.6).
6. See Cohn, 'The Sacred Mountain', pp. 21-26.
7. E.g in the common phrase 'on every high hill and under every green tree', found with minor variations in Dt 12.2; 1 Ki 14.23; 2 Ki 16.4; 17.10; Is 30.25; 57.5, 7; 65.7; Jer 2.20; 3.6, 13; 17.2; Ezek 6.13; 20.28; Hos 4.13; 2 Chron 28.4. In fact, גבה, רם, and נשא are almost never predicated of mountains and hills apart from the context of the worship of foreign gods; see Cohn, *ibid.*, p. 22.
8. For the place of Bethel in Israel's religious history, see Clements, *God and Temple*, pp. 12-14.
9. See Gen 12.8; 1 Sam 13.2; cf. 1 Ki 12.32. Later Jewish and Samaritan tradition placed greater emphasis on the mountain setting of biblical Bethel; see below, pp. 70, 78.
10. See Wright, 'The Mythology of Pre-Israelite Shechem', 75-82.
11. J. Boehmer, 'Der Gottesberg Tabor', *BZ* 23 (1935-36), 339.
12. M. Noth, *The History of Israel*, trans. P.R. Ackroyd (2nd edn; New York: Harper & Row, 1960), p. 66.
13. These four archaic poetic passages (Dt 33.2; Judg 5.4f.; Ps 68.7f.; Hab 3.3-6) depict Yahweh as a 'Man of War' marching in aid of his people, either in or from southern mountainous areas variously designated as Seir, Edom, Paran, Teman and Sinai. Though mountains are mentioned in all these passages, the term הר סיני does not appear.

14. מדבר סיני appears thirteen times as a place of encampment for Israel, usually in connection with the giving of the law (e.g. Ex 19.1f.; Num 1.1). On the various uses of סיני in the OT, see Cohn, 'The Sacred Mountain', pp. 60-65; Clifford, *The Cosmic Mountain*, pp. 108-19.

15. *Ibid.*, p. 122.

16. See R.A. Carlson, 'Elie à l'Horeb', *VT* 19 (1969), 416-39.

17. Cf. G. von Rad, *Old Testament Theology*, trans. D.M.G. Stalker (Edinburgh & London: Oliver & Boyd, 1962), I, 187: 'Nowhere else in the Old Testament is there to be found such a huge presentation of traditions, made up of so many strands, and attached to one single event (the revelation at Sinai)'.

18. 'The Sacred Mountain', p. 95.

19. Though some believe that the reference to fire and smoke implies volcanic terminology (e.g. Noth, *The History of Israel*, p. 13), it is generally agreed that the passage has made use of storm imagery; see Clifford, *The Cosmic Mountain*, p. 120; J. Bright, *A History of Israel* (2nd edn; London: SCM, 1972), p. 122; cf. E.C. Kingsbury, 'The Theophany *TOPOS* and the Mountain of God', *JBL* 86 (1967), 205-10.

20. Cf. Clements, *God and Temple*, pp. 25, 27. Clements's work is a masterful treatment of the development of Israel's attempts to deal with the paradox of their belief in both God's transcendence and his presence with his people.

21. See von Rad, *Old Testament Theology*, I, p. 10; Bright, *A History of Israel*, pp. 123-25; G.E. Mendenhall, 'Covenant Forms in Israelite Tradition', *BA* 17 (1954), 50-76; W. Beyerlin, *Origins and History of the Oldest Sinaitic Traditions*, trans. S. Rudman (Oxford: University Press, 1965), p. 169.

22. See G. von Rad, 'The Form-Critical Problem of the Hexateuch', in his *The Problem of the Hexateuch and Other Essays*, trans. E.W. Trueman Dicken (Edinburgh & London: Oliver & Boyd, 1966), pp. 20-26; Beyerlin, *The Oldest Sinaitic Traditions*, pp. 167f.; Clements, *God and Temple*, pp. 22, 63.

23. In Noth's proposal, 'Israel' was an amalgamation in Canaan of a number of different tribes, each with its own traditions; *The History of Israel*, pp. 64-68.

24. 'The Form-Critical Problem', pp. 1-8.

25. 'Covenant Forms in Israelite Tradition'.

26. *The Oldest Sinaitic Traditions*.

27. A. Weiser, *Introduction to the Old Testament*, trans. D.M. Barton (London: Darton, Longman and Todd, 1961), pp. 81-99.

28. E.W. Nicholson, *Exodus and Sinai in History and Tradition* (Richmond: John Knox Press, 1973).

29. See von Rad, *Old Testament Theology*, I, p. 306.

30. Even the 'March in the South' hymns are by all accounts early, though there is no consensus as to whether they developed out of the Sinai event or

the Sinai motif was incorporated into a pre-existent tradition. Cohn argues the latter on the basis of the diversity of names, but admits that scholarly opinion favours the former; 'The Sacred Mountain', pp. 63f.; cf. Clifford, *The Cosmic Mountain*, p. 119.

31. See below, pp. 36f., 41, 45f., 50.

32. Though 'Zion' originally referred to the fortified hill south of the temple site between the valleys of Kidron and Tyropoeon (cf. 2 Sam 5.7), the term was later transferred to the site of the temple which is its usual OT meaning. Modern day 'Mount Zion' in the SW section of the city is a Christian designation which goes back no earlier than the fourth century AD. See G.A. Barrois, 'Zion', *IDB*, IV, pp. 959f.

33. Reading the singular here with the LXX and the Targum. See below, n. 81.

34. There is some dispute whether the reference in Ex 15.17 is to Zion or not. Cross and Freedman argue for a pre-conquest setting for the hymn; Childs represents the more likely and majority opinion when he asserts that the conquest is presupposed throughout. See B.S. Childs, *Exodus: A Commentary* (London: SCM, 1974), pp. 240-53; Clements, *God and Temple*, pp. 52f.

35. The figure, which we have no desire to verify, is that of Talmon in his 'The Biblical Concept of Jerusalem', 301.

36. The Deuteronomic concept of 'the place which the Lord your God will choose' (e.g. Dt 12.5) is somewhat beyond our area of interest; but cf. Clements, *God and Temple*, pp. 88-99.

37. Recognizing the importance of the concept of election, Schreiner devotes the first third of his study of Zion theology to 'Jerusalem, der erwählte Ort'; see J. Schreiner, *Sion–Jerusalem: Jahwes Königssitz. Theologie der heiligen Stadt im Alten Testament* (München: Kösel Verlag, 1963).

38. Although Dahood holds that this mountain was Sinai, Sinai is nowhere described as Yahweh's abode. The majority opinion, that the mountain referred to here is Zion, is more likely. See M. Dahood, *Psalms II: 51–100* (Anchor Bible; Garden City, N.Y.: Doubleday, 1968), pp. 130-32, 142f.; cf. A. Weiser, *The Psalms: A Commentary*, trans. H. Hartwell (Philadelphia: Westminster, 1962), I, pp. 487f.

39. Cf. Clements, *God and Temple*, pp. 50-52. See also Ps 78.54, where 'holy land' and 'mountain' are parallel concepts.

40. Even without the common emendation in which סיני בם is replaced by בא מסיני, it is apparent that Sinai in this Psalm is merged into the theology of the sanctuary; see Weiser, *Psalms*, I, p. 488; A.A. Anderson, *The Book of Psalms* (New Century Bible; London: Oliphants, 1972), I, p. 491; cf. Dahood, *Psalms II*, p. 143.

41. See Cohn, 'The Sacred Mountain', pp. 142-45.

42. I.e. Ps 2, 18, 20, 21, 45, 72, 89, 101, 132; see the discussion in von Rad, *Old Testament Theology*, I, p. 319.

43. The king in view here is clearly Yahweh; see M. Dahood, *Psalms I: 1–50* (Anchor Bible; Garden City, N.Y.: Doubleday, 1966), p. 290; Anderson, *Psalms*, I, p. 369.

44. On the footstool motif, see Metzger, 'Himmlische und irdische Wohnstatt Jahwes'.

45. For discussions, see J.H. Hayes, 'The Tradition of Zion's Inviolability', *JBL* 82 (1963), 419-26; Clifford, *The Cosmic Mountain*, p. 153; Clements, *God and Temple*, p. 71.

46. E.g. Ps 11.4. See also Clements's chapter on the presence of God in Israel's worship; *God and Temple*, pp. 63-73.

47. See above, n. 4.

48. *God and Temple*, p. 76.

49. See M. Noth, 'Jerusalem and the Israelite Tradition', in his *The Laws in the Pentateuch and Other Studies*, trans. D.R. Ap-Thomas (Philadelphia: Fortress Press, 1967), pp. 132-44.

50. The work by G. Wanke, *Der Zionstheologie der Korachiten* (BZAW; Berlin: Töpelmann, 1966), a study of Psalms 42–49, is a recent exception.

51. For summaries of the Jebusite theory, see Clements, *God and Temple*, pp. 43-48; Clifford, *The Cosmic Mountain*, pp. 131-60; Hayes, 'Zion's Inviolability'.

52. Cf. Clifford, *The Cosmic Mountain*, pp. 35-57.

53. See H.H. Rowley, 'Zadok and Nehushtan', *JBL* 58 (1939), 113-41.

54. See J.J.M. Roberts, 'The Davidic Origin of the Zion Tradition', *JBL* 92 (1973), 329-44; Cohn, 'Mountains and Mount Zion'.

55. *The Cosmic Mountain*, p. 181.

56. For the development in the geographical term 'Zion' which accompanied this change in the location of the ark, see above, n. 32.

57. Cf. Noth, 'Jerusalem and the Israelite Tradition', p. 134; N.W. Porteous, 'Jerusalem–Zion: The Growth of a Symbol', in *Verbannung und Heimkehr*, ed. A. Kuschke (Tübingen: J.C.B. Mohr [Paul Siebeck], 1961), p. 235.

58. 'Jerusalem and the Israelite Tradition'.

59. Cf. Cohn, 'Mountains and Mount Zion', 111-15.

60. Cf. Weiser, *Psalms*, I, pp. 23-52.

61. See von Rad, *Old Testament Theology*, I, p. 319.

62. For this position, see N.H. Snaith, *The Jewish New Year Festival: Its Origin and Development* (London: SPCK, 1947); A.R. Johnson, *Sacral Kingship in Ancient Israel* (Cardiff: University of Wales Press, 1955).

63. See Anderson, *Psalms*, II, pp. 847f.; S. Mowinckel, *The Psalms in Israel's Worship*, trans. D.R. Ap-Thomas (Oxford: Blackwell, 1962), II, p. 208.

64. The most significant passages are Is 2.2-4; 18.7; 25.6-10a; 27.13; 35.1-10; 56.6-9; 60.1-22; 66.20; Jer 3.14-18; 31.1-40; 50.4-7; Ezek 17.22-24; 20.33-44; 34.1-31; 37.21-28; 40.1–48.35; Mic 4.1-7; Hag 2.6-9; Zech 8.1-23; 14.10f., 16-21.

65. *Old Testament Theology*, II, pp. 295, 296.

66. It was central from the time of the exile onwards. In the pre-exilic period, however, it was the nations rather than Israel who would take part in the pilgrimage to Zion; cf. Is 2.2-4, and below, pp. 48f.

67. See J. Bright, *Jeremiah* (Anchor Bible: Garden City, N.Y.: Doubleday, 1965), pp. 284-87.

68. *The Program of Restoration*, pp. 7-19, 90; cf. Eichrodt, *Ezekiel*, p. 282.

69. Cf. von Rad, *Old Testament Theology*, II, p. 293.

70. See Is 18.7; 60.1-22; 66.18-21; Hag 2.21f.

71. 'This mountain' of Is 25.6 undoubtedly refers back to the appearance of Mount Zion in 24.23; see O. Kaiser, *Isaiah 13–39: A Commentary*, trans. R.A. Wilson (London: SCM, 1974), p. 199.

72. For the importance of this concept of eschatological salvation, see R.A. Martin-Achard, *A Light to the Nations*, trans. J.P. Smith (London: Oliver & Boyd, 1962), esp. pp. 61-75; J. Jeremias, *Jesus' Promise to the Nations*, trans. S.H. Hooke (SBT, 24; London: SCM, 1958), pp. 55-62; H.H. Rowley, *The Missionary Message of the Old Testament* (London: Carey Press, 1944); B. Sundkler, 'Jésus et les païens', *RHPR* 16 (1936), 485-88; Campbell, 'The New Jerusalem', 344; Kaiser, *Isaiah 13–39*, p. 200; McKelvey, *The New Temple*, pp. 12-15.

73. See Is 30.23; 61.6; 62.8f.; 65.21; Joel 2.26; 3.18; Amos 9.13-15.

74. For the connections between Mount Zion and the Garden of Eden, see Levenson, *The Program of Restoration*, pp. 37-49; cf. Clifford, *The Cosmic Mountain*, pp. 158f.

75. See above, pp. 36f.

76. See R. de Vaux, 'Jerusalem and the Prophets', in *Interpreting the Prophetic Heritage*, ed. H.M. Orlinsky (New York: Ktav, 1969), p. 296; Clifford, *The Cosmic Mountain*, pp. 157f.

77. *Old Testament Theology*, II, pp. 211f.

78. *The Program of Restoration*, pp. 37-49.

79. *Ibid*, p. 87.

80. Cf. de Vaux, 'Jerusalem and the Prophets', pp. 285f.

81. Though the MT has the plural (בהרי מרום ישראל), the singular is found in the LXX (ἐν τῷ ὄρει τῷ ὑψηλῷ Ἰσραήλ) and the Targum (בטור קודשא דישראל). In view of the presence of the singular phrase in Ezek 17.23 and 20.40, Levenson is probably correct in choosing the singular reading here; *The Program of Restoration*, pp. 8, 85, 90. In any case, since the passage goes on to speak of the dwelling place of the flock as the 'places around my hill' (MT—גבעתי; LXX—τοῦ ὄρους μου; v. 26), it cannot be doubted that the holy mountain is the place of gathering for the scattered flock in Ezek 34.14.

82. As observed by de Vaux, 'Jerusalem and the Prophets', pp. 287f.

83. See n. 64.

84. See von Rad, *Old Testament Theology*, II, p. 157; Clements, *God and*

Temple, p. 81; H. Wildberger, 'Die Völkerwallfahrt zum Zion. Jes. 2.1-5', *VT* 7 (1957), 62-81.

85. See G. von Rad, 'The City on the Hill', in his *The Problem of the Hexateuch*, pp. 233-35; *Old Testament Theology*, II, p. 295; Wildberger, 'Die Völkerwallfahrt zum Zion'; de Vaux, 'Jerusalem and the Prophets', p. 296; A. Causse, 'Le mythe de la nouvelle Jérusalem du Deutéro-Esaïe à la IIIe Sibylle', *RHPR* 18 (1938), 377. But cf. O. Kaiser, *Isaiah 1–12: A Commentary*, trans. R.A. Wilson (London: SCM, 1972), pp. 24f.; Childs, *Introduction*, p. 435.

86. I.e. Jer 3.11-18 and 31.1-14, where both Judah and Israel are to be gathered together to Yahweh on Mount Zion.

87. Cf. Causse, 'Le Mythe de la nouvelle Jérusalem', 396-98; Porteous, 'Jerusalem–Zion', p. 236.

88. See Clements, *God and Temple*, pp. 123-27.

89. See below, p. 238 n.106.

Notes to Chapter 5

1. E.g. 1 Macc 14.15; 2 Macc 1.18; 2.16-18. For a discussion of the place of Zion in Hasmonaean eschatology, see below, pp. 65f.

2. See Zech 4.10; Tob 14.5; 1 Enoch 89.73; 2 Bar 4.2-6.

3. E.g. 1QpHab 12.7f. The Qumran community apparently saw itself as a replacement for the temple; see below, p. 65.

4. The developing wisdom tradition, for example, became attached to Zion: 'Moreover in Zion was I established; in the holy city likewise he caused me to rest, and in Jerusalem was my authority' (Sir 24.10b-11).

5. E.g. the Tannaitic saying: 'The Holy One, blessed be He, considered all cities, and found no other city wherein the temple might be built, other than Jerusalem' (Lev R. 13.2).

6. Zion is generally described as the place where the Shekinah dwells, rather than the abode of God himself.

7. Cf. C.E. L'Heureux, 'The Biblical Sources of the "Apostrophe to Zion"', *CBQ* 29 (1967), 60-74. L'Heureux asserts that terms ordinarily reserved for God are in this psalm addressed to Zion. Though he may have exaggerated the point (cf. W.D. Davies, *The Gospel and the Land* [Berkeley, Los Angeles, London: University of California Press, 1974), p. 142], the psalm is lavish in its praise for Zion. See also 1QM 12.9-15.

8. For an introductory survey, see McKelvey, *The New Temple*, pp. 9-57.

9. טורא קדישא (1QapGen 19.8); for the (unlikely) suggestion that this is not a reference to Zion, see below, n. 28.

10. הר מרום ישר[אל (4Q171 3.11); cf. Ezek 17.23; 20.40.

11. Allegro's reconstruction of 4Q171 3.11 as הר מרום ישר[אל וב]קורשו (*DJD*, V, p. 44) has been criticized by J. Strugnell ('Notes en marge du volume V des "Discoveries in the Judean Desert of Jordan"', *RevQ* 7 [1969–72], 214)

and D. Pardee ('A Restudy of the Commentary on Psalm 37 from Qumran Cave 4', *RevQ* 8 [1973–75], 185), both of whom argue that the lacuna should be reconstructed as אל בהר. In view of the facts that the phrase הר מרום ישראל occurs in the OT only in Ezekiel (17.23; 20.40; cf. 34.14), and that in Ezek 20.40 it is in parallel with הר קדשי, the reconstruction of Strugnell and Pardee (i.e. 'his holy mountain') is most probably correct. Cf. H. Stegemann, 'Der Pešer Psalm 37 aus Höhle von Qumran (4QpPs37)', *RevQ* 4 (1963–64), 252, who reads ו]בקודשו הר מרום יש[ראל.

12. 4Q163pIsa^c, frag. 24 reads; בהר י]; Allegro suggests the probable reconstruction בהר יהוה (*DJD*, V, p. 25).

13. Of the ten grades of holiness leading up to the Holy of Holies, the temple mount represents the fourth (Kelim 1.6-9; cf. Yoma 12a; Meg. 26a).

14. Given the Targumic rendering, it is unlikely that the LXX preserves a textual variant. The most probable reconstruction of the Hebrew is למה צערו רשעים קדשך.

15. Such replacement of symbol and metaphor with prosaic interpretation is a common feature of the Targums. See, e.g., Tg. Jer 3.14-18; 23.1-8, where the shepherd metaphor disappears completely.

16. For a Rabbinic parallel, see Sukk. 49a.

17. A somewhat related tendency might be seen in the occasional reluctance of the Targumist to use טור of Mount Gerizim; e.g. in Tg. Amos 6.1, where the MT has 'the mountain of Samaria', we find 'the capital (כרכא) of Samaria'.

18. Aboth 6.10; Pesaḥ. 87b; Mek. Shir. 9.122; 10.13f.

19. See above, p. 31.

20. Tg. Ps.-J. Dt 1.7, 11.24; Tg. 2 Ki 19.23; Tg. Jer 22.20, 26; Tg. Hos 14.8; Tg. Hab 2.17; Tg. Zech 10.10; Tg. Cant 4.8, 15.

21. Yoma 21b, 39b; Ex R. 23.5; Num R. 11.3, 12.4; Cant. R. 3.10 §3, 4.8 §1; Aboth R. Nat. 4.5 (20a).

22. Aboth R. Nat. 4.5 (20a).

23. G. Vermes, *Scripture and Tradition in Judaism: Haggadic Studies* (Leiden: Brill, 1961), pp. 26-39.

24. Given the absence of any reference in Dt to the temple or the temple mountain, most interpreters are no doubt correct in translating הר as 'hill country' in Dt 3.25.

25. E.g. Giṭ. 56a-b; Ber. 48b; Gen R. 16.2; Ex R. 35.1; Lev R. 1.2; Cant R. 7.5 §3; Midr. Ps 104.13; Sifre Dt 71b (§28).

26. 'That good mountain and the place of the sanctuary' (Onkelos); 'this good mountain and the mountain of the sanctuary' (Neophyti); 'that good mountain on which is builded the city of Jerusalem, and Mount Lebanon, where the Shekinah will dwell' (Pseudo-Jonathan).

27. See below, p. 78.

28. Despite Fitzmyer's hesitation, this identification—made by Dupont-Sommer, Lehmann, and van der Woude—is virtually certain, especially

since it is also found in Rabbinic tradition (Gen R. 39.16). Fitzmyer appears to equate this mountain with the mountain between Bethel and Ai (Gen 12.8); note that Bethel itself is also said to be a mountain in 1QapGen 21.7) on which Abraham built an altar; in 1QapGen 19.8-10, however, Abraham *leaves* Bethel in order that he might go to the 'holy mountain'. See the discussion in J.A. Fitzmyer, *The Genesis Apocryphon of Qumran Cave 1* (2nd edn; Rome: Biblical Institute Press, 1971), p. 106.

29. E.g. Gen R. 55.7; Lam R. Proem §24; Midr. Ps 68.9; Pesiḳ. R. 39.2; 43.2; Pirke R. El. 31.

30. Targum Pseudo-Jonathan and Pirke de R. Eliezer are closely related; see G. Friedlander (trans. and ed.), *Pirke de R. Eliezer* (New York: Hermon Press, 1965), p. xix.

31. Tg. Ps.-J. Gen 2.7, 15; cf. Pirke R. El. 11, 12; Gen R. 14.8; Midr. Ps 92.6. Since there are traditions that Adam's dust was taken from the four corners of the earth which do not mention the temple mountain (e.g. Sanh. 38a-b), Schäfer may be right in suggesting that the Targum has fused two separate traditions of Adam's origin—one of dust from the temple mountain, and the other of dust from the whole world; see P. Schäfer, 'Temple und Schöpfung. Zur Interpretation einiger Heiligtumstraditionen in der rabbinischen Literatur', *Kairos* 16 (1974), 130.

32. Tg. Ps. -J. Gen 8.20; in Pirke R. El. 23, the altar is said to have been built by Cain and Abel.

33. An alternate reading is 'the mountain on which the glory of the Shekinah of the Lord was revealed'; see A. Díez Macho, *Neophyti 1* (Madrid, Barcelona: Consejo superior de investigaciones cientificas, 1970), II, p. 416.

34. See also Midr. Ps 87.3: 'Jerusalem is the foundation of the world by virtue of two holy mountains, Mount Sinai and Mount Moriah'.

35. See below, p. 73.

36. Of the Targums, the traditions concerning Adam, Noah, Isaac and Jacob are found only in Pseudo-Jonathan, a Targum which, though containing some early material among its unique traditions, is a later Babylonian recension; cf. J. Bowker, *The Targums and Rabbinic Literature* (Cambridge: University Press, 1969), pp. 26-28; M. McNamara, *Targum and Testament* (Grand Rapids: Eerdmans, 1972), pp. 179f. Though R. Eliezer lived in the early Tannaitic period, the final redaction of the work attributed to him is much later, perhaps the eighth century—though it too contains much material that is early; see Friedlander's comments in the introduction to *Pirke de R. Eliezer*, pp. liii-lv.

37. See the excellent methodological discussion in Vermes, *Scripture and Tradition*, pp. 1-10.

38. See McKelvey, *The New Temple*, p. 191; cf. Pirke R. El. 20.

39. See J.H. Charlesworth, *The Pseudepigrapha and Modern Research* (Missoula: Scholars Press, 1976), p. 74; L.S.A. Wells, 'Books of Adam and Eve', *APOT*, II, p. 127.

40. See R.H. Charles, *The Book of Jubilees* (London: A. & C. Black, 1902), p. 39.

41. A tradition which probably lies behind that of the primeval mountain dwelling in the *Cave of the Treasures*; see below, n. 142.

42. See above, p. 50.

43. See below, pp. 70f.

44. See above, pp. 26-29, 50; cf. the statement by W.D. Davies who, while recognizing the presence of cosmic ideas in the OT, says: 'In no way do they belong to the peculiarity of the Biblical understanding of the land' (*The Gospel and the Land*, pp. 9f.).

45. For a description of the various elements of cosmic mountain mythology, see above, p. 26.

46. And into its eschatology as well, as can be seen in the cosmic elements of apocalyptic; see below, pp. 66f., 71f.

47. See above, p. 26.

48. *War* 3.52. For a discussion of the cosmic symbolism which Josephus and Philo saw in the temple (though with no mention of the mountain), see J. Daniélou, 'Le symbolisme cosmique du temple de Jérusalem chez Philon et Josèphe', in *Le symbolisme cosmique des monuments religieux* (Rome: Istituto Italiano per Il Medio ed Estremo, 1957), pp. 83-90.

49. See R.H. Charles, *The Book of Enoch* (London: SPCK, 1917), p. 54. For a parallel in a Jewish work of the second century AD, see Sib Or 5. 249-250: 'the godlike heavenly race of the blessed Jews, who dwell around the city of God at the centre of the earth'.

50. In Jub 4.26 a fourth cosmic 'place of the Lord' is mentioned, viz. the Mount of the East. It is omitted in Jub 8.19 no doubt because in the geo-cosmic scheme of the author it falls outside the territory of Shem.

51. Pirke R. El. 35; Midr. Ps 91.7. For a discussion of the foundation stone and the Omphalos myth, see R. Patai, *Man and Temple in Ancient Jewish Myth and Ritual* (London, New York: Thomas Nelson, 1947), pp. 54-104, esp. p. 85.

52. E.g., Sanh. 37a; Num R. 1.4; Cant R. 7.3 §1; Pesiḳ. R. 10.2.

53. Pirke R. El. 11; the identification of this place with Mount Moriah is found in Pirke R. El. 20.

54. E.g., Num R. 12.4; Lam R. 3.58-64 §9; Pesiḳ. R. 10.2; 12.10.

55. Pesiḳ. R. 10.2. See also Num R. 1.4; Midr. Ps 91.7.

56. For the various elements associated with the Omphalos myth, see Wensinck, *The Navel of the Earth*, p. xi.

57. E.g., Num R. 12.4; Cant R. 3.10 §4; Midr. Ps 11.2; 91.7.

58. E.g., Yoma 54b; Lev R. 20.4; Num R. 12.4; Pirke R. El. 35. Though Schäfer's assertion that this tradition dates from before AD 70 ('Tempel und Schöpfung', 125) remains unproven, it goes back at least to the early Tannaitic period (cf. Yoma 54b; Lev R. 20.4).

59. See Midr. Ps 87.3: 'Jerusalem is the foundation of the world by virtue

of two holy mountains, Mount Sinai and Mount Moriah'. There was also a tradition that the world was created from the outside inwards (Yoma 54b).

60. Zebaḥ. 54b; Ḳid. 69a; Cant R. 7.5 §3; Sifre Dt 69b (§23).

61. Gen R. 33.7; Lev R. 31.10; Cant R. 1.15 §4; Pirke R. El. 23; cf. Bowker, *The Targums and Rabbinic Literature*, p. 170. Standing over against this tradition is the Rabbinic reply to similar claims made by the Samaritans about Mount Gerizim, to the effect that *all* mountains, high and low, were submerged by the flood; Gen R. 32.10; Dt R. 3.6.

62. Gen R. 33.7; Lev R. 31.10; Tg. Ps.-J. Gen 8.11. In Etheridge's translation of this Targumic passage, he mistakenly rendered מוור מישחא (the Mount of Olives) as 'the mountain of the Meshiha' (i.e. 'Messiah'; apparently reading it as מוור משיחא); J.W. Etheridge, *The Targums of Onkelos and Jonathan ben Uzziel on the Pentateuch with the Fragments of the Jerusalem Targum* (New York: Ktav, 1968 [1862–65]), p. 182.

63. Lev R. 31.7; cf. Schäfer, 'Temple und Schöpfung', 128-30.

64. See below, pp. 71f.

65. Ascribed to R. Simeon b. Yohai, a third generation Tanna.

66. In midrashic interpretations of Gen 28.17; e.g. Midr. Ps 91.7; Pirke R. El. 35.

67. Gen R. 55.7; Num R. 4.13; Cant R. 3.10 §4; 4.4§9.

68. See Midr. Ps 91.7; Pirke R. El. 35; Tg. Ps.-J. Ex 28.30. Cf. Patai, *Man and Temple*, pp. 54-58; Schäfer, 'Tempel und Schöpfung', 125-27.

69. For pre-Rabbinic references to the heavenly Jerusalem/temple, see T. Levi 5.1; Wisd 9.8; 2 Enoch 55.2; 2 Bar 4.2-6; 59.4; 4 Ezra 9.38–10.57; and these Qumran references: 1QM 12.1f.; 1QSb 3.25f.; 1Q32; 2Q24; 4QShir-Shab; 5Q15; 11QJNar. The concept is frequently found in Rabbinic literature: Ta'an. 5a; Ḥag. 12b; Gen R. 55.7; 69.7; Num R. 4.13; Cant R. 3.10 §4; 4.4 §9; Midr. Ps 30.1; 122.4; Pesiḳ. R. 40.6; Mek. Shir. 10.24-28. For discussions of the development of this tradition, see K.L. Schmidt, 'Jerusalem als Urbild und Abbild', *ErJb* 18 (1950), 207-48; Clements, *God and Temple*, pp. 126f.; McKelvey, *The New Temple*, pp. 25-41; D. Flusser, 'Two Notes on the Midrash on 2 Sam 7', *IEJ* 9 (1959), 99-109; M. Baillet, 'Fragments Araméens de Qumrân 2: Description de la Jérusalem nouvelle', *RB* 62 (1955), 222-45; J. Strugnell, 'The Angelic Liturgy at Qumran–4Q serek širôt 'ôlat haššabàt', *VTSup* 7 (1960), 318-45; Patai, *Man and Temple*, pp. 130-32.

70. See below, n. 106.

71. See above, p. 51.

72. Even the mountain of God's throne which Enoch sees on his cosmic journey is identified as an earthly mountain (probably with its summit in heaven, i.e. an *axis mundi*); 1 Enoch 25.3-6.

73. See above, pp. 41-48.

74. For a thorough discussion, see D.S. Russell, *The Method and Message of Jewish Apocalyptic* (Philadelphia: Westminster, 1964).

75. The important role played by Zion eschatology in countering the

forces of oppression and disintegration during this period has been recognized by Causse, 'Le mythe de la nouvelle Jérusalem', esp. pp. 396-98. See also J.J. Collins, *The Sybylline Oracles of Egyptian Judaism* (SBLDS, 13; Missoula: Scholars Press, 1974), pp. 44-55; Campbell, 'The New Jerusalem', 346.

76. Other extended passages with similar themes include Tob 13.7-18; 1 Bar 5.1-9; Ps Sol 17.28-35; 1 Enoch 90.28-36; Sib Or 3.652-731, 772-795.

77. See also 2 Bar 4.2-4; Jub 1.15-17; Adam and Eve 29.1-10; Ex R. 15.21; Lev R 24.4; Cant R. 7.5 §3; Midr. Ps 14.6, 36.6; Pesiḳ. R. Kah. 21.4.

78. E.g. 1 Bar 4.36f.; Ps Sol 11.1-3; 17.50; Jub 1.15-17; Apoc Ab 23; Pesaḥ. 88a; Gen R. 56.2; 98.2; Ex R. 23.5; Num R. 16.25; Cant R. 4.8 §2; Pirke R. El. 17; Sifre Dt §1.

79. See Tg. Jer 31.23; Tg. Is 4.3; 6.13; 33.24; 35.6; 42.7; 46.11; 53.5; 54.15; 60.8; 66.9.

80. See 2 Macc 1.27; 2.17f.; Ps Sol 8.33f. See also Benedictions 10, 14 and 17 of the Shemoneh 'Esreh, all of which date from before AD 70; for the dating, see L. Finkelstein, 'The Development of the Amidah', *JQR* n.s. 16 (1925–26), 1-43.

81. Tob 13.11; Sib Or 3.772-795; Gen R. 78.12, 97; Ex R. 35.5; Esth R. 1.4; Midr. Ps 87.6; Tg. Is 16.1.

82. Ps Sol 17.34; Cant R. 4.8 §2; Midr. Ps 87.6.

83. E.g. Tob 13.1-18; 14.3-7; Sib Or 3.710-719, 772-795; 1 Enoch 90.33; LXX Is 54.15; LXX Am 9.12; Aboth R. Nat. 36.1(31b); Ex R. 15.21; Num R. 8.9; Midr. Ps 36.6; Pesiḳ. R. Kah. 21.4; cf. Gen R. 98.9. There are also numerous positive references to the Gentiles in the Testaments of the Twelve Patriarchs; e.g. T. Levi 4.4, 18.9; T. Zeb. 9.8; T. Ash. 7.3; T. Ben. 9.2; 10.5. Their evidential value is sharply limited, however, due to the presence in T. 12 Patr. of frequent Christian interpolations, and to the possibility that many of the Testaments, with the exception of the Aramaic Levi and Hebrew Naphtali, are later and perhaps Christian works. See M. de Jonge, *The Testaments of the Twelve Patriarchs* (Assen: van Gorcum, 1953); id., 'Once More: Christian Influence in the Testaments of the Twelve Patriarchs', *NovT* 5 (1962), 311-19; 'Christian Influence in the Testaments of the Twelve Patriarchs', in *Studies in the Testaments of the Twelve Patriarchs*, ed. M. de Jonge (Leiden: Brill, 1975), pp. 191-246; cf. M. Philonenko, *Les Interpolations chrétiennes des Testaments des Douze Patriarches et les manuscrits de Qumran* (Paris: Presses Universitaires de France, 1960).

84. Ps Sol 17.32-34; 2 Bar 72.1-6; Apoc Ab 23; Tg. Is 25.6-10; cf. Gen R. 21.1; 41.9; 83.5; Lev R. 27.5; Num R. 2.13; Dt R. 1.25; Cant R. 7.3 §3; Pesaḥ. 68a. Perhaps the reference in Rev 16.16 to Ἀρμαγεδών as the site of God's final battle with the nations should be included here as well. Since Jerusalem has always been seen as the site for this battle in Jewish tradition, Cheyne, Charles, Bowman and others may be right in supposing that this term refers not to the city of Megiddo (near Mount Carmel), but—as a transliteration of הר מגדו ('his fruitful mountain') or something similar—to Zion itself. See

R.H. Charles, *A Critical and Exegetical Commentary on the Revelation of St. John* (ICC; Edinburgh: T. & T. Clark, 1920), II, pp. 50f.; J.W. Bowman, 'Armageddon', *IDB*, I, pp. 226f.

85. This statement is true not only with respect to the eschatological pilgrimage, but to the wider treatment of Gentiles as well; cf. Jub 1.9; 6.35; 23.23; 24.28; 30.11-14; and the Qumran literature generally. For the Rabbinic attitude towards the Gentiles, see B.W. Helfgott, *The Doctrine of Election in Tannaitic Literature* (New York: King's Crown Press, 1954): W.G. Braude, *Jewish Proselytizing in the First Five Centuries of the Common Era* (Providence, R.I.: Brown University, 1940).

86. Jub 1.28; Ps Sol 17.23-51; Ex R. 35.5; Midr. Ps 11.6.

87. E.g. Lev R. 24.4; Pesiḳ. R. 41.2; Sib Or 3.710-719; Jub 1.15-29. See also below, pp. 116f.

88. Ex R. 25.8; Pesiḳ. R. 41.5.

89. Above, p. 53.

90. In Midr. Ps 42/43.5 we find an eschatological interpretation of the 'holy mountain' of Ps 43.3f. Ex 15.17 is linked with the eschatological verses Ezek 17.23; 20.40 by means of the *Stichwort* הר (Mek. Shir. 10.13f.). Is 2.2 is interpreted as the restoration of Mount Moriah (Midr. Ps 68.9) or in terms of eschatological Jerusalem sitting on top of Sinai, Tabor and Carmel, which God will bring together for this purpose (Midr. Ps 36.6; Pesiḳ. R. Kah. 21.4).

91. 1QS 5.5; 8.5-19; 9.3-6; 4QFlor 1.1-7; 4Q164pIsa[d]. Though McNicol attempts to minimize this aspect of Qumran thought (A.J. McNicol, 'The Eschatological Temple in the Qumran Pesher 4Q Florilegium 1.1-7', *OJRS* 5 (1977), 133-41), its importance has been generally recognized. See B. Gärtner, *The Temple and Community in Qumran and the New Testament* (SNTSMS, 1; Cambridge: University Press, 1965); McKelvey, *The New Temple*, pp. 46-53; J. Neusner, 'Judaism in a Time of Crisis: Four Responses to the Destruction of the Second Temple', *Judaism* 21 (1972), 313-27.

92. 1QS 5.5f.; 8.5-10. Though there is some uncertainty as to the interpretation of מבשר in 1QS 9.4, there can be no doubt that a spiritualized view of sacrifice is intended; cf. P. Wernberg-Møller, *The Manual of Discipline* (Leiden: Brill, 1957), p. 133.

93. 1QS 8.5f. It appears that the latter term was reserved for 'Aaron' (i.e. the priests), while the former referred to the laity; cf. Wernberg-Møller, *The Manual of Discipline*, pp. 124f.

94. 4QFlor 1.6f. This phrase has been variously interpreted: 'a man-made sanctuary' (Allegro, *DJD*, V, p. 54); 'a sanctuary of men' (G. Vermes, *The Dead Sea Scrolls in English* [Harmondsworth: Penguin, 1968], p. 246); 'a sanctuary amongst men' (Flusser, 'Two Notes on the Midrash on 2 Sam 7', 102; McNicol, 'The Eschatological Temple', 138f.). Since this passage equates 'works of the Torah' with 'smoke of incense', a straightforward reading of the term (i.e. a sanctuary consisting of men) is probably to be preferred.

95. See 11QTemple 29.7-10; and the passages cited by McNicol, 'The Eschatological Temple', 139. See also below, n. 106.

96. See especially 11QTemple 29.7-10; and Y. Yadin, 'The Temple Scroll', *BA* 30 (1967), 135-39; J. Milgrom, 'The Temple Scroll', *BA* 41 (1978), 114; and the review of Y. Yadin, *The Temple Scroll* (Jerusalem: Israel Exploration Society, 1977), by J.M. Baumgarten (*JBL* 97 [1978], 588).

97. For this position and a criticism of Yadin's interpretation, see B.E. Thiering, '*Mebaqqer* and *Episkopos* in the Light of the Temple Scroll', *JBL* 100 (1981), 60f.

98. In light of the continuing eschatological interest at Qumran in Jerusalem and the temple, the 'community-as-temple' belief should be seen as an interim measure for the period before the end, rather than as an early belief which gave way to a more thoroughly eschatological expectation, as is argued by McNicol ('The Eschatological Temple', 140). If 11QTemple is early and represents an(other) interim measure, as Yadin argues, then perhaps the 'community-as-temple' belief was a subsequent doctrine, developed as the deterioration of relationships with Jerusalem began to preclude all hopes of an interim temple in Jerusalem.

99. There is, however, no evidence from Qumran of the traditional expectation of the gathering of the exiles. Since the sect saw itself alone as true Israel, there was no place for such an expectation.

100. *1 Maccabees*, p. 304.

101. See, e.g., the hymn of praise to Simon the High Priest in 1 Macc 14.4-15. As Goldstein demonstrates, this passage is studded with sentences and phrases lifted word for word from OT prophetic passages. A comparison of v. 8 with Zech 8.12, Ezek 34.27, and of v. 12 with Mic 4.4, reveals that the only significant difference is in the tenses of the verbs. What was future for the prophets has already begun to take place for the writer of 1 Maccabees (cf. also v. 9 with Zech 8.4); see Goldstein, *1 Maccabees*, pp. 490-92. Now the author of 1 Maccabees was well aware of Simon's sad end (1 Macc 16.16), so that it is not correct to say that he saw Simon as *the* Messiah in any individual sense. Rather, we see here a form of realized eschatology applied to the whole Maccabean/Hasmonaean house: in the Maccabean victories and in the glories of the Hasmonaean reign the eschatological tide had turned and the Messianic Age had dawned. This Messianic Age was therefore a this-worldly, immanent (rather than imminent!) and gradually developing situation, inaugurated by the Hasmonaean ruler-priests.

A similar situation is found in Jubilees. Jubilees' support for the Hasmonaeans can be seen in its emphasis on the house of Levi (31.12-17), in its positive use of the term 'priests of the Most High God' (32.1)—the Melchizedekian term (Gen 14.18) used by the Hasmonaeans of themselves (Ass Mos 6.1; Jos. *Ant.* 16.163; Roš. Haš. 18b)—and perhaps by the curious lacuna at Jub 13.25 just as the narrative begins to pick up the story of Melchizedek (a story which some later scribe may have found to be too supportive of the then-discredited Hasmonaean house); cf. Charles, *Jubilees*, p. lxxiii. In Jub 23.26-31, the zeal for the law and for righteousness displayed in the Maccabean revolt (v. 26) leads gradually ('shall begin to'; vv. 26, 27) to an age of longevity (v. 27), of messianic bliss (v. 29), of judgement upon Israel's enemies (v. 30), and of the absence of the works of Satan (v. 29)—i.e. the Messianic Age; see R.H. Charles, 'Jubilees', *APOT*, II, pp. 9, 48f.; Russell, *Method and Message*, p. 292; but cf. Hengel, *Judaism and Hellenism*, I, p. 226. Since the author of Jubilees also looked forward to a new creation (Jub 4.26), we should probably see here an early example of the distinction between the Messianic Age and the Age to Come.

102. *Ant.* 13.215-217; *War* 5.139. In the former reference the levelling was said to have been accomplished by Simon, whereas in the latter passage it was by 'the Hasmonaeans', i.e. one of Simon's successors. Since according to 1 Macc 14.37 Simon fortified the hill, it is more likely that the earlier statement in *War* 5.139 is correct, and that the action was taken during the more secure reign of John Hyrcanus.

103. A similar, though more poetic, attitude towards the place of Jerusalem in the last days is to be found in several pseudepigraphic passages which, while not using mountain terminology, call on Jerusalem to 'stand upon the height' in order to see the returning exiles as they flock to Zion (1 Bar 5.5; Ps Sol 11.3; cf. Is 40.9; 60.4). See also Ps Sol 17.32; ἐν ἐπισήμῳ is difficult, but the passage probably speaks of the Messiah in Jerusalem glorifying God 'in a place which is conspicuous for all the earth' and may well be an allusion to Is 2.2 (so G.B. Gray, 'Psalms of Solomon', *APOT*, II, p. 650).

104. See above, n. 101.

105. For discussion of the eschatology of Jubilees, with recognition of the important role played by Mount Zion, see Charles, *Jubilees*, p. 10; R.G. Hamerton-Kelly, 'The Temple and the Origins of Jewish Apocalyptic', *VT* 20 (1970), 1.

106. Though there are a few references to the human origin of the final temple (Tob 14.5; Tg. Onk. Gen 49.10), the belief was growing in this period that the temple would be of divine construction—even a heavenly temple come to earth (1 Enoch 90.28f.; 4 Ezra 9.38–10.57; 2 Bar 4.2-6; 11QTemple 29.7-10; Ex R. 15.21; Pesiḳ. R. 20.3; 28.1; cf. Sib Or 5.414-433; Gen R. 97; Num R. 13.2; Cant R. 4.16 §1; where the temple is built by the Messiah). See McKelvey, *The New Temple*, pp. 25-41; Flusser, 'Two Notes on the Midrash on 2 Sam 7', 99f.; Gärtner, *The Temple and the Community*, pp. 16f.

107. Unless it is the 'place' of 2 Bar 36.6.

108. Cf. G.H. Box, 'IV Ezra', *APOT*, II, p. 617; L. Hartman, *Prophecy Interpreted: The Formulation of Some Jewish Apocalyptic Texts and of the Eschatological Discourse*, trans. N. Tomkinson (Lund: Gleerup, 1966), pp. 96-98.

109. Cf. Tg. Ezek 17.22 where the 'high and lofty mountain' is interpreted as the Messiah himself, and Pirke R. El. 11 where the mountain of Dan 2.35 is seen as a reference to the Messiah.

110. See M.E. Stone, 'The Concept of the Messiah in IV Ezra', in *Religions in Antiquity*, ed. J. Neusner (Leiden: Brill, 1968), pp. 303f.

111. For the possibility that Daniel's 'mountain' grew out of Zion eschatology, see E.F. Siegman, 'The Stone Hewn from the Mountain (Daniel 2)', *CBQ* 18 (1956), 364-79.

112. 'The Messiah in IV Ezra', p. 306.

113. See above, pp. 55-59.

114. 1 Enoch 26.1-6, a passage considered above, pp. 59f.

115. Several passages (e.g. 4 Ezra 3.17f.; Mek. Baḥ. 4.45-47) speak of God bowing down the heavens to touch Sinai; in the Palestinian Targum (both Frag. and Neoph.) on Dt 30.12, Moses is said to have ascended to heaven to receive the law. See also Apoc Abr 12; *Ant.* 2.264; 3.76, 82.

116. For Jubilees, see Jub 1.1-5, 26; 6.19; 48.2. For 11QTemple, although the first column is missing, it is apparent that it introduced the book as a Sinai revelation; see Milgrom, 'The Temple Scroll', 109. Moreover, in 11QTemple 51.6f. there is a parenthetical reference to 'those things which I am declaring to you on this mountain' (בהמה אשר אני מגיד לכה בהר הזה) which definitely identifies the whole as a Sinai revelation.

117. See Tg. Ps.-J. Dt 34.1. This tradition appears later in Samaritan material as well; see *Memar Marqah* 5.3.

118. Sinai was chosen over all other mountains (Soṭ. 5a; Lev R. 13.2)—especially over lofty Tabor and Carmel, which, because of their pride, were refused as sites for the giving of the law (Num R. 13.3; Midr. Ps 68.9; Pesiḳ. R. 7.3; cf. Meg. 29a).

119. Passages such as Ps 24.3; 68.16-18 are often interpreted as references to Sinai, as in Dt R. 11.2; Midr. Ps 24.7; 92.2; Mek. Baḥ. 4.17-25; cf. Cant R. 2.9 §1; 4.4 §1; Midr. Ps 68.9; 87.4.

120. 2 Macc 2.1-9; 2 Bar 6.1-10; 80.1-3; Life Jer. 9-15; Yoma 53b-54a; Num R. 15.10; cf. Soṭ. 9a; Ruth R. Proem 7.

121. Angels (2 Bar 6.1-10; 80.1-3) and Jeremiah (Life Jer. 9-15; 2 Macc 2.1-9) are mentioned.

122. See, e.g., the range of Rabbinic opinion in Yoma 53b-54a.

123. For the first century dating of the Lives of the Prophets, see C.C. Torrey, *The Lives of the Prophets* (SBLMS, 1; Philadelphia: SBL, 1946), pp. 11f.; Charlesworth, *Pseudepigrapha*, pp. 175-77. Although the Jeremiah work stands somewhat apart from the others (e.g. in its Egyptian orientation) and shows evidence of Christian reworking (7f, 10), it is clear that it is basically a Jewish work and that the passage cited here is a Jewish tradition.

124. Pp. 77-79.

125. See C.H. Kraeling, *The Synagogue*, Part I of *The Excavations at Dura-Europos. Final Report VIII*, ed. A.R. Bellinger et al. (New Haven: Yale University Press, 1956); the panel in question appears on plate LXIX, discussed by the author on p. 182.

126. Perhaps a related tradition is the Rabbinic belief that the Mount of

Olives was the last resting place of the Shekinah before it departed from the earth (Lam R. Proem 25; Pesik̠. R. Kah. 13.11; cf. Roš. Haš. 31a); i.e. the place from which the Shekinah departed the earth becomes the place at which the resurrection age will arrive.

127.　See Men. 87a; Gi̠t. 55b, 57a; Ber. 44a; y.Ta'an. 69a; y.Dem. 22c, 24d; Lam R. 2.2 §4; Mek. Amal. 2.41-45; Sifre Dt §6; Tg. Judg 4.5. For the currency of this term in Tannaitic times, see A. Büchler, 'Die Schauplätze des Bar-Kochbakrieges und die auf diesen bezogenen jüdischen Nachrichten', *JQR* o.s. 16 (1904), 180-84.

128.　Messianic possibilities, however, were not overlooked by later Jewish Christianity. In the third or fourth century Acts of Pilate and the related Descent of Christ into Hell, we find references to Christ and his disiples sitting on a mountain called Μαμίλχ or Malech (Acts Pil. 14.1, 15.1; *NTApoc*, I, p. 462), and to the sudden appearance of Christ with a great multitude 'ex monte Amalech' (Desc. Chr. 1.6; *NTApoc*, I, p. 479). Though the number of textual variants (Μαμβήχ, Μαλήκ, Μοφήκ, Μομφή, Mambre) suggests that the original significance of the term became lost in translation, there can be little doubt that the term originated in Jewish Christian circles as the highly suggestive הר המלך was borrowed and applied to Christ.

129.　Since there is no evidence that any Hasmonaean proclaimed himself king before the short-lived reign of Aristobulus, the son of John Hyrcanus (104 BC; see *Ant.* 13.301), the term probably does not go back as far as Hyrcanus. Note the connection, however, between this term and Alexander Jannaeus in Gi̠t. 57a and Ber. 44a.

130.　E.g. Tg. Ezek 34.14; 37.22.

131.　Cf. Jub 1.28; 1 Enoch 25.3-6; 4 Ezra 13.5-13.

132.　For earlier works, see the bibliography in J. Macdonald, *The Theology of the Samaritans* (London: SCM, 1964), pp. 457-63. Recent study has been greatly facilitated by the work of J. Bowman and his students at the University of Leeds, who are responsible for translating much of the Samaritan material into English, particularly the *Memar Marqah* (see *Memar Markah: The Teaching of Marqah*, trans. J. Macdonald [BZAW, 84; Berlin: Töpelmann, 1963]—and the Defter (S. Brown, 'A Critical Edition and Translation of the Ancient Samaritan Defter [i.e. Liturgy]' [Ph.D. Dissertation, University of Leeds, 1955]).

133.　See H.H. Rowley, 'The Samaritan Schism in Legend and History', in *Israel's Prophetic Heritage*, ed. B.W. Anderson and W. Harrelson (New York: Harper & Bros., 1962), pp. 208-22; Macdonald, *The Theology of the Samaritans*, pp. 11-40; J.D. Purvis, *The Samaritan Pentateuch and the Origin of the Samaritan Sect* (Cambridge, Mass.: Harvard University Press, 1968); R.J. Coggins, *Samaritans and Jews: The Origins of Samaritanism Reconsidered* (Oxford: Blackwell, 1975); J. Bowman, *The Samaritan Problem: Studies in the Relationship of Samaritanism, Judaism, and Early Christianity*, trans. A.M. Johnson (Pittsburgh: Pickwick Press, 1975). As far as relationships between Samaritanism and Judaism in the Rabbinic period is concerned, though contacts continued (cf. Gen R. 32.10; Dt R. 3.6; etc.), Rabbinic understanding of Samaritanism was faulty (e.g. Ḥul. 6a)—especially with respect to the Samaritan doctrine of resurrection (Kuth. 2.7 [61b]). This suggests that the separation by this time was virtually complete.

134. Cf. Bowman, *The Samaritan Problem*, p. 30. Bowman points out that in the Hasmonaean era, Zadokites, Essenes and Samaritans had much common ground in their opposition to the Jerusalem temple establishment.

135. See Coggins, *Samaritans and Jews*, p. 164.

136. On the Jewish roots of Samaritan eschatology, see Macdonald, *The Theology of the Samaritans*, pp. 359f.

137. The main sources are: (1) the Samaritan Pentateuch, whose recension undoubtedly goes back to pre-Christian times (see M. Gaster, *The Samaritans* [London: Oxford University Press, 1925], pp. 128f.; Purvis, *The Samaritan Pentateuch*); (2) The *Memar* (or teaching of) *Marqah*; and (3) the *Defter* (or liturgy). Though the latter two sources—both of which were compiled in the fourth century AD—are too late to be of direct relevance for a study of the pre-AD 70 situation, they provide valuable corroborative material, particularly when they contain full-blown versions of traditions available to us in pre-AD 70 sources.

138. Translated by Brown, 'Defter', p. 61.

139. See J.A. Montgomery, *The Samaritans* (New York: Ktav, 1968 [1907]), p. 207; cf. Brown, 'Defter', pp. 34, 209.

140. For the text with an English translation, see Gaster, *The Samaritans*, pp. 185-90.

141. See also Brown, 'Defter', p. 313.

142. See, e.g., the fourth century AD *The Cave of Treasures*, translated by E.A.W. Budge (London: Religious Tract Society, 1927), as well as the citation from *Kitab alMajal* 123a-b in Bowker, *The Targums and Rabbinic Literature*, p. 230. Note especially the thorough study by J. Jeremias, 'Golgotha und der heilige Felsen: Eine Untersuchung zur Symbolsprache des Neuen Testaments', Αγγελος 2 (1926), 74-128. In this tradition, which was well established by the time of Origen (cf. *Commentary on Matthew* 126; on Mt 27.33), Golgotha was seen both as a cosmic centre (navel of the earth, point of entry into the underworld, etc.) and as the central site of *Heilsgeschichte* (site of Adam's creation and burial, of Abraham's offering of Isaac, etc.). In keeping with this Christian appropriation of Zion legends, Golgotha came to be seen as a mountain (cf. Mount Calvary) from the fifth century AD onwards; see C. Warren, 'Golgotha', *Dictionary of the Bible*, ed. J. Hastings (New York: Scribners, 1903), II, pp. 226f.

143. Above, p. 74.

144. Brown, 'Defter', p. 87; see also *Memar Marqah* 4.11, 12; Macdonald, *The Theology of the Samaritans*, pp. 365-71.

145. 'Defter', p. xxvi.

146. *Ant.* 2.264; 3.76, 82.

147. E.g. the 'mount of God' in the burning bush incident (*Mos.* 1.65); Mount Nebo, the site of Moses' death (*Mos.* 2.288); cf. *Mig.* 139; *Q. Ex* 2.52, 82, 90.

148. Although he shows a reverence for Jerusalem and the temple (e.g. *Mos.* 2.71-74; *Leg.* 281), the term Zion is scarce.

149. E.g. in his discussion of the Sinai revelation, though he finds allegorical interpretations for the lightning, thunder, cloud and fire, he does not mention the mountain (*Dec.* 44-49).

150. E.g. *Q. Gen* 4.46; *Q. Ex* 2.27-29, 40; cf. *Mig.* 139; *Ebr.* 128.

151. See M.P. Nilsson, *Greek Piety*, trans. H.J. Rose (Oxford: Clarendon Press, 1948), p. 3.

152. See Parke, *A History of the Delphic Oracle*, p. 9.

153. See above, pp. 26, 59-62.

154. E.g. Antiochus attempted to install Zeus worship on Mount Zion. Zeus was also identified with the *bel* of Mount Kasios in Syria; see F.W. Beare, 'Greek Religion and Philosophy', *IDB*, II, p. 491.

155. Mountains are not mentioned at all in R. Reitzenstein, *Hellenistic Mystery-Religions*, trans. J.E. Steely (Pittsburgh: Pickwick Press, 1978).

156. *PetPhil* (CG VIII,2) 133.13-16, 134.9-17.

157. Acts of John 97-102 (*NTApoc*, II, pp. 232-35).

158. *SJC* (CG III,4) 90.14ff. This Nag Hammadi text is a Christianized version of the pagan *Eugnostos the Blessed*, which was Christianized by means of the addition of the introductory mountain setting.

159. *Questions of Mary*; preserved in Epiphanius *Pan.* 26.8.2f. (*NTApoc*, I, p. 339).

160. *1ApocJas* (CG V,3) 30.18–31.2.

161. *Apocryphon of John*. This writing is found in Codex I of the Nag Hammadi literature; the first part of the text, however, in which the mountain setting is described, is missing, but is found in Papyrus Berolinensis 8502, 19.6–22.17 (*NTApoc*, I, p. 321).

162. *ApocPaul* (CG V,2) 19.10-14.

163. Acts of John 97 (*NTApoc*, II, p. 232).

164. *GEgypt* (CG III,2) 68.2–69.6.

165. Apoc. Pet. 1 (*NTApoc*, II, p. 668); Quest. Barth. 3f. (*NTApoc*, I, pp. 494f.); Acts Pil. 14.1; 15.1 (*NTApoc*, I, p. 462), Desc. Chr. 1.6 (*NTApoc*, I, p. 479).

Notes to Chapter 6

1. The presence of εἰς ὄρος ὑψηλόν in a number of texts at Lk 4.5 (א corr A W Θ 0102 f¹ Byz syrᴾ it vg copˢᵃ,ᵇᵒ) and of εἰς ὄρος ὑψηλὸν λίαν in a few others (D f¹³) is the result of the influence of Mt 4.8. The shorter version of א B C is without a doubt the original reading.

2. The use of Mk by Mt in the framework of the narrative can be seen in these agreements against Lk: εἰς τὴν ἔρημον (Mt 4.1 // Mk 1.12); καὶ . . .

ἄγγελοι . . . διηκόνουν αὐτῷ (Mt 4.11 // Mk 1.13). The use of Mk by Lk can be seen especially in this long agreement against Mt: ἐν τῇ ἐρήμῳ ἡμέρας τεσσεράκοντα πειραζόμενος ὑπὸ τοῦ (Lk 4.2 // Mk 1.13). The use by Mt and Lk of a source other than Mk is evidenced by these agreements against Mk: Ἰησοῦς (Mt 4.1 // Lk 4.1); the use of the passive (Mt 4.1 // Lk 4.1); διαβόλου (Mt 4.1 // Lk 4.1); ἐπείνασεν (Mt 4.2 // Lk 4.2); the departure of ὁ διάβολος (Mt 4.11 // Lk 4.13).

3. S. Schulz (*Q: Die Spruchquelle der Evangelisten* [Zürich: Theologischer Verlag, 1972], p. 186) and Schniewind (*Matthäus*, p. 29) argue that since there is no evidence of Q influence in the Matthean and Lukan accounts of the baptism, Q can not have contained a baptism account. Such influence can be seen, however, in the agreement of Mt and Lk in the use of ἀνοίγω rather than σχίζω (Mt 3.16 // Lk 3.21) and in the use of Ἰησοῦς with the aorist participle of βαπτίζω (Mt 3.16 // Lk 3.21). In addition, though it does not constitute proof, the Temptation Narrative in its Q form with its emphasis on Son-christology appears to assume the baptism account; so Streeter, *The Four Gospels*, p. 188; V. Taylor, *Behind the Third Gospel* (Oxford: Clarendon Press, 1926), p. 76; I.H. Marshall, *The Gospel of Luke* (NIGTC; Grand Rapids: Eerdmans, 1978), p. 165. Although it is not our purpose to engage in a full source analysis and reconstruction of Q, such analysis and reconstruction will be carried out at those points where it is relevant to our discussion. For more thorough treatments of the sources of the Temptation Narrative, see A. Harnack, *The Sayings of Jesus*, trans. J.R. Wilkinson (London: Williams & Norgate, 1908), pp. 41-48; T.W. Manson, *The Sayings of Jesus* (London: SCM, 1949), pp. 41-46; Schulz, *Q: Die Spruchquelle*, pp. 177-90.

4. λίαν is probably Matthean, as in Mt 8.28; 27.14.

5. So Lohmeyer, *Matthäus*, p. 60; M.-J. Lagrange, *Evangile selon Saint Matthieu* (Paris: Gabalda, 1948), p. 62; Conzelmann, *Theology of St. Luke*, p. 29; P. Hoffmann, 'Die Versuchungsgeschichte in der Logienquelle: Zur Auseinandersetzung der Judenchristen mit dem politischen Messianismus', *BZ* 13 (1969), 209; Schulz, *Q: Die Spruchquelle*, p. 177; J. Dupont, *Les tentations de Jésus au désert* (StudNeot, 4; Bruges: Desclée de Brouwer, 1968), p. 24; H. Schürmann, *Das Lukasevangelium* (HTKNT; Freiburg, Basel, Wien: Herder, 1969), I, p. 210.

6. See Allen, *Matthew*, p. 33; A.H. M'Neile, *The Gospel according to Matthew* (London: MacMillan, 1938), pp. 40f.; Hill, *Matthew*, p. 101.

7. It is true that the desert is mentioned only in the introductory section and thus, theoretically, may have been found only in Mk. As Schulz points out, however, the details of the first temptation—i.e. the reference to hunger (definitely in Q), the temptation to make bread from stones, and the reply from Dt 8—all assume a wilderness setting; *Q: Die Spruchquelle*, p. 178.

8. E.g. the long speech of Satan in v. 6; cf. Harnack, *Sayings*, p. 47.

9. Of the 23 NT occurrences, 20 are in Luke–Acts.

10. Conzelmann (*The Theology of St. Luke*, p. 29) and Schulz (*Q: Die Spruchquelle*, p. 180) are incorrect in seeing Lk's omission of ὄρος as stemming from his desire to reserve the mountain for Jesus as a place of prayer. Given the presence in Lk of references in which the mountain is the setting for an attempt on Jesus' life (4.29) and for an encounter with demons and swine (8.32; cf. Mk 5.11), such a thesis cannot be maintained.

11. Of the rest, in addition to those who opt for Luke's order (see below, n. 24), a few see in the variations in order evidence for separate sources: e.g. Allen, *Matthew*, p. 31; Lohmeyer, *Matthäus*, p. 53; Albright, *Matthew*, p. 32.

12. M. Dibelius, *From Tradition to Gospel*, trans. B.L. Woolf (New York: Scribners, 1935), p. 275.

13. *Matthieu*, p. 60.

14. See, e.g., A. Farrer, *The Triple Victory: Christ's Temptations according to Matthew* (London: Faith Press, 1965), p. 64.

15. See, e.g. Harnack, *Sayings*, pp. 42f.; Farrer, *The Triple Victory*, p. 63; F. Smyth-Florentin, 'Jésus, le Fils du Père, vainqueur de Satan. Mt 4,1-11; Mc 1,12-13; Lc 4,1-13', *AssSeign* 14 (1973), 61; C.E. Carlston, 'Interpreting the Gospel of Matthew', *Int* 29 (1975), 11.

16. P. Gaechter, *Das Matthäus Evangelium* (Innsbruck: Tyrolia Verlag, 1963), pp. 109f.

17. *Q: Die Spruchquelle*, p. 177.

18. *Les tentations de Jésus*, p. 35.

19. Smyth-Florentin, 'Jésus, le Fils du Père, vainqueur de Satan', 56-60; W.R. Stegner, 'Wilderness and Testing in the Scrolls and in Matthew 4.1-11', *BR* 12 (1967), 26f.; cf. J.A.T. Robinson, 'The Temptations', in his *Twelve New Testament Studies* (London: SCM, 1962), 53-60.

20. There is, however, some uncertainty as to the Exodus passage lying behind Dt 6.13; of those authors mentioned in the previous note, Smyth-Florentin suggests Ex 23.20-33, while Robinson argues for Ex 34.

21. E.g. Manson, *Sayings*, pp. 42f.; J.A. Findlay, 'Luke', *Abingdon Bible Commentary* (Nashville, New York: Abingdon, 1929), p. 1036; cf. Carlston, 'Interpreting the Gospel of Matthew', 11.

22. *The Theology of St. Luke*.

23. Cf. Dibelius, *From Tradition to Gospel*, p. 275; E. Percy, *Die Botschaft Jesu* (Lund: Gleerup, 1953), p. 18. The other reason given in the pre-Conzelmann period for Lk's change was that he wanted to reduce the number of scene changes; see Schmid, *Matthäus*, p. 62.

24. For the position that Lk's order was original, see Dalman, *Sacred Sites and Ways*, p. 97; Schmauch, *Orte der Offenbarung*, p. 69; Percy, *Die Botschaft Jesu*, p. 18; Schürmann, *Lukasevangelium*, I. pp. 211, 218; J.P. Comisky, '"Begone, Satan!"', *BibTod* 58 (1972), 622; B. Przybylski, 'The Role of Mt 3.13–4.11 in the Structure and Theology of the Gospel of Matthew', *BTB* 4 (1974), 234f.; Grundmann, *Matthäus*, p. 100. Cf. also A.G. Bowden-Smith, 'A Suggestion towards a Closer Study of the Significance of

the Imagery of the Temptation', *ExpT* 47 (1935–36), 408-12; and G.S. Freeman, 'The Temptation', *ExpT* 48 (1936–37), 45, where the interest is in the order not of Q, but of the original events in the life of Jesus.

25. See Dalman, *Sacred Sites and Ways*, p. 97; Schmauch, *Orte der Offenbarung*, p. 69.

26. *Lukasevangelium*, I, p. 218.

27. See above, n. 20.

28. This has often been recognized, and will be demonstrated at length below, pp. 101-104.

29. See Bultmann, *History of the Synoptic Tradition*, p. 254; B. Gerhardsson, *The Testing of God's Son (Mt 4.1-11): An Analysis of an Early Christian Midrash*, trans. J. Toy (Lund: Gleerup, 1966), p. 17; Percy, *Die Botschaft Jesu*, p. 17; and below, p. 94.

30. Independent accounts have been suggested by Mauser, *Christ in the Wilderness*, p. 97; C.K. Barrett, *The Holy Spirit and the Gospel Tradition* (London: SPCK, 1947), p. 46; Schniewind, *Matthäus*, p. 28; Lohmeyer, *Matthäus*, p. 60.

31. The former position is argued by Percy, *Die Botschaft Jesu*, p. 14; P. Pokorný, 'The Temptation Stories and their Intention', *NTS* 20 (1973–74), 122; Smyth-Florentin, 'Jésus, le Fils du Père, vainqueur de Satan', 69f. The latter position is taken by Gerhardsson, *The Testing of God's Son*, p. 10; P. Doble, 'The Temptations', *ExpT* 72 (1960–61), 91; A. Feuillet, 'L'épisode de la tentation d'après l'Evangile selon Saint Marc (1,12-13)', *EstBib* 19 (1960), 73; H.A. Kelly, 'The Devil in the Desert', *CBQ* 26 (1964), 190; Schulz, *Q: Die Spruchquelle*, p. 182. The details of the angels and beasts, mentioned in Mk but not in Q, and the absence of any mention of fasting in Mk, are difficult to account for in any theory of direct relationship.

32. Cf. J. Dupont, 'L'origine du récit des tentations de Jésus au désert', *RB* 73 (1966), 45. Dupont argues that the origin of the story is to be found in Jesus himself, and this position is taken in varying ways by others: e.g. M. Albertz, *Die synoptischen Streitgespräche* (Berlin: Trowitzsche & Sohn, 1921), p. 48; R.E. Brown, 'Incidents that are Units in the Synoptic Gospels but Dispersed in St. John', *CBQ* 23 (1961), 155; P.G. Bretscher, 'The Temptation of Jesus in Matthew' (Th.D. Dissertation, Concordia Seminary, 1966), p. 246; J.A. Kirk, 'The Messianic Role of Jesus and the Temptation Narrative: A Contemporary Perspective', *EvQ* 44 (1972), 23f.; Gaechter, *Matthäus*, p. 110. Though this question lies outside our area of interest here, the similarity between the Temptation Narrative and 'temptations' during Jesus' career (e.g. the rebuke of Peter, the requests for a sign, messianic pressure) provides support for such a view.

33. For a discussion of the early development of this position by H.J. Holtzmann and J. Weiss, see Bretscher, 'Temptation', pp. 38-45. This position is taken, in varying ways, by Dibelius, *From Tradition to Gospel*, pp. 274f.; Pokorný, 'The Temptation Stories', 125; F.C. Grant, *An Introduction to New Testament Thought* (New York, Nashville: Abingdon / Cokesbury, 1950), p. 207; Manson, *Sayings*, pp. 43-45; Barrett, *The Holy*

Spirit and the Gospel Tradition, pp. 48f.; H. Riesenfeld, 'Le caractère messianique de la tentation au désert', in *La Venue du Messie: messianisme et eschatologie* (RechBib, 6; Bruges: Desclée de Brouwer, 1962), pp. 51-63; Hoffman, 'Die Versuchungsgeschichte'; Kirk, 'The Messianic Role of Jesus'; Schniewind, *Matthäus*, p. 29; Gaechter, *Matthäus*, p. 114.

34. See *History of the Synoptic Tradition*, pp. 254-57.

35. See *Theology of the New Testament*, trans. K. Grobel (New York: Scribners, 1951), I, pp. 26f.

36. E.g. Percy, *Die Botschaft Jesu*, pp. 14f.; Schulz, *Q: Die Spruchquelle*, pp. 186-88; G. Bornkamm, 'End Expectation and Church in Matthew', in *Tradition and Interpretation*, pp. 36f.; G.H.P. Thompson, 'Called–Proved–Obedient: A Study in the Baptism and Temptation Narratives of Matthew and Luke', *JTS* 11 (1960), 5f.; R.A. Edwards, *A Theology of Q* (Philadelphia: Fortress Press, 1976), pp. 82-84; F. Hahn, *Christologische Hoheitstitel: ihre Geschichte im frühen Christentum* (Göttingen: Vandenhoeck und Ruprecht, 1964), pp. 301-303. For O. Cullmann, the first two temptations reflect the θεῖος ἀνήρ idea, while the third is messianic; *The Christology of the New Testament*, trans. S.C. Guthrie and C.A.M. Hall (2nd edn; Philadelphia: Westminster, 1964), pp. 276f. Lohmeyer, by contrast, sees the absence of 'Son of God' from the mountain temptation as evidence that this temptation—in contrast to the other two—was of Jesus as a pious man rather than as Messiah; *Matthäus*, p. 59. Bonnard (*Matthieu*, p. 43), Schmid (*Matthäus*, p. 66), and Farrer (*The Triple Victory*, pp. 18f.) also see the temptations as paradigmatic.

37. And it is unlikely that the third temptation account ever existed apart from the other two; see Dupont, *Les tentations de Jésus*, p. 34; cf. Bultmann, *History of the Synoptic Tradition*, pp. 254-57; Lohmeyer, *Matthäus*, p. 60.

38. See Gerhardsson, *The Testing of God's Son*, p. 22; E. Lövestam, *Son and Saviour: A Study of Acts 13.32-37* (Lund: Gleerup, 1961), pp. 94-101; Grundmann, *Matthäus*, p. 103; Schmid, *Matthäus*, p. 64; Gaechter, *Matthäus*, p. 114.

39. See below, p. 96.

40. See Gerhardsson, *The Testing of God's Son*; Dupont, *Les tentations de Jésus*, pp. 12-16; Riesenfeld, 'Le caractère messianique de la tentation'; Lövestam, *Son and Saviour*, pp. 94-101.

41. This was argued unsuccessfully by Doble, 'The Temptations'; Robinson, 'The Temptations'; W. Powell, 'The Temptation', *ExpT* 72 (1960–61), 248; cf. R. Holst, 'The Temptations of Jesus', *ExpT* 82 (1970–71), 343f.

42. Cf. A. Mason, 'The Temptation in the Wilderness: A Possible Interpretation', *Theol* 4 (1922), 128; Albright, *Matthew*, pp. 32f.; Marshall, *Luke*, p. 168.

43. So Dibelius, *From Tradition to Gospel*, pp. 274f.; E. Schweizer, *The Good News according to Matthew*, trans. D.E. Green (London: SPCK, 1976), pp. 60, 64-66; Pokorný, 'The Temptation Stories', 125.

44. So Hoffmann, 'Die Versuchungsgeschichte', 219; H. Baltensweiler, *Die Verklärung Jesu: Historisches Ereignis und synoptische Berichte* (Zürich: Zwingli Verlag, 1959), pp. 58f.

45. See further 2 Macc 2.4; *Memar Marqah* 5.1-4. One can only speculate on the place of the mountain in the lost ending of the Assumption of Moses.

46. In Gen 13.14-18, Abraham is dwelling at the place where he had built the altar (Gen 13.3-4) which, according to Gen 12.8, was on a mountain. In 1QapGen 21, though טור does not appear, there are several indications of height—סלק, חצור, רמת, רמתא. Cf. Mek. Amal. 2.75-90.

47. Cf. Robinson, 'The Temptations', 57, where it is argued that Moses typology is at work in the passage, but in terms of Sinai rather than Nebo.

48. So Manson, *Sayings*, p. 44; Barrett, *The Holy Spirit and the Gospel Tradition*, p. 52; Dupont, *Les tentations de Jésus*, p. 24; Gerhardsson, *The Testing of God's Son*, pp. 61-64; H.M. Teeple, *The Mosaic Eschatological Prophet* (SBLMS, 10; Philadelphia: SBL, 1957), pp. 75-77; Riesenfeld, 'Le caractère messianique de la tentation', 61; Smyth-Florentin, 'Jésus, le Fils du Père, vainqueur de Satan', 60f.; Przybylski, 'The Role of Mt 3.13–4.11', 233; Bretscher, 'Temptation', pp. 222-25; Schweizer, *Matthew*, p. 64; Grundmann, *Matthäus*, p. 102; Schmid, *Matthäus*, p. 67; Lohmeyer, *Matthäus*, pp. 53f.; E. Klostermann, *Das Matthäusevangelium* (HNT; Tübingen: J.C.B. Mohr [Paul Siebeck], 1971), p. 28; Hill, *Matthew*, p. 101; Gundry, *Matthew*, pp. 54, 57.

49. Cf. LXX Dt/Mt: ἔδειξεν αὐτῷ / δείκνυσιν αὐτῷ; πᾶσαν τὴν γῆν / πάσας τὰς βασιλείας τοῦ κόσμου; δώσω αὐτὴν / ταῦτα πάντα δώσω. See Dupont, *Les tentations de Jésus*, p. 25; Hill, *Matthew*, p. 101.

50. Cf. Gen. 22.1f. and Jub 17.16; see Dupont, *ibid.*, p. 15.

51. 'The Devil in the Desert'.

52. See above, pp. 59-61, 71f.; also Riesenfeld, 'Le caractère messianique de la tentation', 61; Jeremias, *Der Gottesberg*, p. 149.

53. K.H. Rengstorf, 'Old and New Testament Traces of a Formula of the Judean Royal Ritual', *NovT* 5 (1962), 241.

54. See above, p. 91.

55. E.g. Smyth-Florentin, 'Jésus, le Fils du Père, vainqueur de Satan', 65, who sees the third approach by Satan as arising from Jesus' reference to 'the Lord your God' (Mt 4.7); cf. Bretscher, 'Temptation', pp. 222-25.

56. So Lövestam, *Son and Saviour*, pp. 100f.; Doble, 'The Temptations', 92; Farrer, *The Triple Victory*, pp. 67f.; Schürmann, *Lukasevangelium*, I, p. 211; Kingsbury, *Matthew*, p. 51; Schweizer, *Matthew*, p. 64; Grundmann, *Matthäus*, p. 103; Schmid, *Matthäus*, p. 64; Klostermann, *Matthäusevangelium*, p. 28; Gaechter, *Matthäus*, p. 114.

57. Cf. J. Wilkens, *Der König Israels: Eine Einführung in das Evangelium nach Matthäus* (Berlin: Furche Verlag, 1934), I, p. 76, where this mountain is designated 'der Berg der Herrschaft'.

58. Above, pp. 66, 68f.

59. See LXX Is 40.9; Ezek 17.22; 20.40; 34.14; 40.2; Ep. Arist. 83f.; cf. 4 Ezra 13.6. This term is not used exclusively of Zion; see, e.g., 1 Enoch 17.2; 22.1; 25.3 where it is used of other unnamed cosmic mountains.

60. For an unsuccessful attempt to relate the temple scene to the wilderness experience of Israel, see Riesenfeld, 'Le caractère messianique de la tentation', 60.

61. To this point, this has been recognized only by Grundmann; cf. *Matthäus*, pp. 103f.: 'Die Versuchungen in der Wüste, im Tempel und auf dem hohen Berg umfassen die Orte, die in Israel mit besonderen eschatologisch-apocalyptischen Erwartungen verbunden sind'. For another attempt to view the three settings as a unity, see Lohmeyer, *Matthäus*, pp. 53f.

62. Note also the prominence of the wilderness in the activity of Josephus's messianic prophets (*War* 2.258-263; *Ant.* 20.169-172). For discussions of the wilderness and related concepts, see Mauser, *Christ in the Wilderness*; W.A. Meeks, *The Prophet-King: Moses Traditions and the Johannine Christology* (Leiden: Brill, 1967); Teeple, *The Mosaic Eschatological Prophet*.

63. Above, pp. 62-64.

64. See Schweizer, *Matthew*, p. 63; Kirk, 'The Messianic Role of Jesus', 92.

65. See *War* 6.283-287; *Ant.* 20.169-172.

66. See above, especially pp. 73-76.

67. We have already cited several scholars who feel that this is a more logical sequence on *geographical* grounds (above, n. 25); here we are suggesting that it may be more logical on the grounds of eschatological expectations as well.

68. See Roš. Haš. 31a; cf. Lam. R. Proem 25; Pesiḳ. R. Kah. S.13.11. In the latter reference, the divine presence waits for three and a half years on the Mount of Olives.

69. The tradition of Roš. Haš. 31a is attributed to R. Joḥanan b. Nappaha, an Amoraitic Rabbi.

70. *War* 2.261-263; *Ant.* 20.169-172. For the importance of these passages for the eschatological significance of the mountain setting, see above, p. 75.

71. Though there are texual variants for these additions in vv. 4 and 10, the readings given here in (b) and (c) are virtually certain.

72. Since these are the only words spoken by Jesus which are not taken from the OT, they are undoubtedly a Matthean addition.

73. See above, pp. 88-90, 97f.

74. See, e.g., Blair, *Jesus in the Gospel of Matthew*, p. 134; Farrer, *The Triple Victory*, pp. 15f.; Przybylski, 'The Role of Mt 3.13–4.11', 231; Smyth-Florentin, 'Jésus, le Fils du Père, vainqueur de Satan', 62; Dupont, *Les tentations de Jésus*, p. 27; Allen, *Matthew*, p. 30; Schniewind, *Matthäus*, p. 29; Wilkens, *Der König Israels*, p. 75; Gundry, *Matthew*, p. 57.

75. Gerhardsson, *The Testing of God's Son*, p. 42. See also Nepper-

Christensen, *Das Matthäusevangelium*, pp. 163-79, for the argument that no typological patterns of thought appear in Matthew at all.

76. We will have occasion later to speak of Mosaic parallels in the Sermon on the Mount and the Transfiguration. For Moses typology in Mt 1.1–4.16, see R.E. Brown, *The Birth of the Messiah* (Garden City, N.Y.: Doubleday, 1977), pp. 112-16, 214-17; Teeple, *The Mosaic Eschatological Prophet*, pp. 74-84; Blair, *Jesus in the Gospel of Matthew*, pp. 124-37; Davies, *Setting*, pp. 14-108; D.M. Crossan, 'Structure and Theology of Mt 1.18–2.23', *CahJos* 16 (1968), 119-35.

77. For the alternate suggestion that the account of Jesus' flight to Egypt was modelled on midrashic accounts of Jacob's journey to Egypt, see D. Daube, *The New Testament and Rabbinic Judaism* (London: Athlone Press, 1956), pp. 189-92; C.H. Cave, 'St. Matthew's Infancy Narrative', *NTS* 9 (1962–63), 382-90; M.M. Bourke, 'The Literary Genus of Matthew 1–2', *CBQ* 12 (1960), 160-75.

78. Mt 2.20: τεθνήκασιν γὰρ οἱ ζητοῦντες τὴν ψυχὴν τοῦ παιδίου; cf. Ex 3.19: τεθνήκασιν γὰρ πάντες οἱ ζητοῦντές σου τὴν ψυχήν.

79. Davies, *Setting*, pp. 92-108; Kingsbury, *Matthew*, pp. 82-92.

80. Teeple argues for a Mosaic parallel; *The Mosaic Eschatological Prophet*, p. 75.

81. Cf. Hoffmann, 'Die Versuchungsgeschichte', 208.

82. See Kingsbury, *Matthew*, pp. 42-83; D. Senior, *The Passion Narrative according to Matthew: A Redactional Study* (Louvain: Leuven University Press, 1975); *id.*, 'The Death of Jesus and the Resurrection of the Holy Ones (Mt 27.51-53)', *CBQ* 38 (1976), 322-25. Though the question of Matthew's christology has not been completely answered (see Kingsbury, *Matthew*, pp. 40-42, and below, pp. 203-205), the importance of Son-christology in the First Gospel cannot be denied.

83. Cf. Senior, 'The Resurrection of the Holy Ones', 323: 'The prime issue of the death scene has become a challenge to Jesus' Sonship. While the mockers question Jesus' identity as Son—or perhaps more accurately, the quality of his sonship—Jesus himself is portrayed as the obedient Son who prays in the face of death and who dies with an attitude of reverent obedience.'

84. See Wellhausen, *Matthäus*, p. 10; J.C. Fenton, *The Gospel of Saint Matthew* (Baltimore: Penguin Books, 1963), p. 64.

85. See Schniewind, *Matthäus*, pp. 30f.

86. See Pokorný, 'The Temptation Stories', 125; T.H. Robinson, *The Gospel of Matthew* (London: Hodder & Stoughton, 1951), p. 22.

87. Senior, 'The Resurrection of the Holy Ones', 312-29; also J.P. Meier, 'Salvation History in Matthew: In Search of a Starting Point', *CBQ* 37 (1975), 207-10.

88. See below, pp. 177f.

89. Kingsbury, 'Composition and Christology', 573-84.

90. See, e.g., Lange, *Das Erscheinen des Auferstandenen*, p. 418.

91. Those who specifically mention the mountain setting include Schmauch, *Orte der Offenbarung*, p. 71; Frieling, *Die Verklärung auf dem Berge*, p. 54; Kingsbury, *Matthew*, pp. 56-58; Lange, *Das Erscheinen des Auferstandenen*, pp. 168, 393, 404f.; Kirk, 'The Messianic Role of Jesus', 95; Przybylski, 'The Role of Mt 3.13–4.11', 225, 228-31; Riesenfeld, 'Le caractère messianique de la tentation', 62; Allen, *Matthew*, p. 33; Schweizer, *Matthew*, p. 64; Grundmann, *Matthäus*, pp. 103, 576. To this list, add these scholars who note the parallels but do not mention the mountain: Carlston, 'Interpreting the Gospel of Matthew', 11; Lohmeyer, *Matthäus*, p. 60.

92. *Das Erscheinen des Auferstandenen*, pp. 168, 404f.

93. Cf. Lange, *ibid.*, p. 168: 'Das ἐδόθη μοι, die ἐξουσία, die πᾶς– Terminologie, dazu auch die Szenerie des Berges und wohl auch die Proskynese in Mt 28.16-20, sind also auch zu sehen als letzte Antworte des Theologen Matthäus auf die Herausforderung von Mt 4.8ff.';.

94. So most commentators; e.g. Schulz, *Q: Die Spruchquelle*, p. 180. But cf. Lange, *Das Erscheinen des Auferstandenen*, pp. 91-93; Gundry, *Matthew*, p. 58.

95. See Lk 12.5, 11; 19.17; 20.20; 22.53; 23.7—all unique to Luke.

96. An opinion held by many; see above, n. 91.

97. *Matthew*, p. 33.

98. See Schmauch, *Orte der Offenbarung*, p. 71; Frieling, *Die Verklärung auf dem Berge*, p. 54.

99. See below, pp. 189f., 209-11.

100. The connection, according to Kingsbury, is so close that the use of the term ὄρος implies Son-christology, even where 'Son' does not appear; *Matthew*, pp. 56-58; 'Form and Message of Matthew', 21.

Notes to Chapter 7

1. W.D. Davies's *The Setting of the Sermon on the Mount* is a good example. Despite some rather strong statements on the inadequacy of any study of the Sermon 'in stark separation from the rest of the Gospel' (see pp. 13f.), he pays almost no attention to its immediate setting in Matthew.

2. See, e.g., H.-W. Bartsch, 'Feldrede und Bergpredigt: Redaktionsarbeit in Luk. 6', *TZ* 16 (1960), 74; Gaechter, *Matthäus*, p. 136.

3. It is often asserted that Mt's Sermon is addressed to the disciples alone: e.g. H.B. Carré, 'Matthew 5.1 and Related Passages', *JBL* 42 (1923), 39-48; Bartsch, 'Feldrede und Bergpredigt', 7f.; Manson, *Sayings*, p. 47; J.W. Bowmann and R.W. Tapp, *The Gospel from the Mount* (Philadelphia: Westminster, 1957), p. 21; Albright, *Matthew*, p. 45. But in view of Mt's interest in οἱ ὄχλοι in general, and of 7.28-29 in particular, this cannot be maintained. So P. Hoffmann, 'Die Stellung der Bergpredigt im Matthäusevangelium. Auslegung der Bergpredigt I', *BibLeb* 10 (1969), 59; G. Eichholz,

Auslegung der Bergpredigt (2nd edn; Neukirchen-Vluyn: Neukirchener Verlag, 1970), pp. 22-24; H. Windisch, *The Meaning of the Sermon on the Mount*, trans. S. MacL. Gilmour (Philadelphia: Westminster, 1941), p. 64; Klostermann, *Matthäusevangelium*, p. 32; Schmid, *Matthäus*, p. 74; Bonnard, *Matthieu*, p. 53; Schniewind, *Matthäus*, p. 36; Schweizer, *Matthew*, p. 77; Wellhausen, *Matthäus*, p. 13.

4. So Bowmann and Tapp, *The Gospel from the Mount*, p. 19; Grundmann, *Matthäus*, p. 111. There are no literary grounds whatsoever for Lohmeyer's division between 4.24 and 4.25; see Lohmeyer, *Matthäus*, p. 74.

5. See, e.g., Hoffmann, 'Die Stellung der Bergpredigt', 61; W.G. Thompson, 'Reflections on the Composition of Mt 8.1–9.34', *CBQ* 33 (1971), 366; D. Senior, *Invitation to Matthew* (Garden City, N.Y.: Doubleday, 1977), p. 57; Grundmann, *Matthäus*, p. 110; Schmid, *Matthäus*, p. 72; Bonnard, *Matthieu*, p. 51; Lagrange, *Matthieu*, p. 71; Schniewind, *Matthäus*, p. 8; Schweizer, *Matthew*, p. 69.

6. *Matthew*, p. 9.

7. Mt specifies in contrast to Mk that it was οἱ ὄχλοι who were amazed, and adds αὐτῶν to Mk's οἱ γραμματεῖς.

8. This placing of the Sermon in the Markan outline is not universally recognized, especially in the Gospel synopses. Huck, impressed by the use of Mk 1.39 in 4.23, places the Sermon at that point in Mk's outline. Aland, noting the dependence of 4.25–5.1 on Mk 3.7-13a, places the Sermon at Mk 3.13; also Bacon, *Studies in Matthew*, p. 165; Marshall, *Luke*, p. 237; G.E.P. Cox, *The Gospel according to St. Matthew* (London: SCM, 1952), p. 44. Although the verbal parallels with Mk 1.39, 3.7-13a are not to be denied, the parallel of *order* is with Mk 1.21f.; see A. Farrer, *St. Matthew and St. Mark* (2nd edn; Westminster, Dacre Press, 1966), p. 198; Bartsch, 'Feldrede und Bergpredigt', 6; Lange, *Das Erscheinen des Auferstandenen*, p. 394; Allen, *Matthew*, p. xv; Klostermann, *Matthäusevangelium*, p. 32; Schmid, *Matthäus*, p. 72; M'Neile, *Matthew*, p. 48; and especially F. Neirynck, 'The Sermon on the Mount in the Gospel Synopsis', *EThL* 52 (1976), 350-57.

9. Such dependence on Mk is generally recognized by commentators. See, e.g., Lange, *Das Erscheinen des Auferstandenen*, pp. 399-403.

10. There are only three insertions into the Markan sequence in the section under consideration: the genealogy (Lk 3.23-38); the teaching in the Nazareth synagogue (Lk 4.16-30); and Lk's own account of the call of the first disciples (Lk 5.1-11).

11. Rarely does it come up for discussion in the commentaries; exceptions among Mathean commentators include Schweizer, Johnson, and Cox, though Cox incorrectly states that Mt and Lk located the Sermon at the same place in Mk (*Matthew*, p. 44). See also F. Neirynck, 'The Argument from Order and St. Luke's Transpositions' *EThL* 49 (1973), 784-815, in which he argues strenuously in favour of the two-source hypothesis and against Schürmann's hypothesis of a Q source for Lk 6.12-16, without any

recognition of the problem that this passage poses for the two-source theory. For discussions of these passages which recognize the issue, see L. Vaganay, 'L'absence du sermon sur la montagne chez Marc', *RB* 58 (1951), 5-46; T. Schramm, *Der Markus-Stoff bei Lukas* (Cambridge: University Press, 1971), p. 113; Schürmann, *Lukasevangelium*, pp. 318f.; Taylor, *Behind the Third Gospel*, pp. 81-83; Bacon, *The Sermon on the Mount*, p. 124; and H. Marriott, *The Sermon on the Mount* (London: SPCK, 1925), p. 44.

12. As does Vaganay, who calls these passages 'la ruine du système'; 'L'absence du sermon', 16.

13. *Ibid.*, 5-46.

14. Which included, in all likelihood, the preaching of John, the Temptation, the Sermon, the healing of the centurion's servant, and the question of John's disciples; see W.L. Knox, *The Sources of the Synoptic Gospels. II: St. Luke and St. Matthew*, ed. H. Chadwick (Cambridge: University Press, 1957), p. 7; and discussions by Bartlett and Streeter in *Oxford Studies in the Synoptic Problem*, ed. W. Sanday (Oxford: Clarendon Press, 1911), pp. 187, 327f.

15. See, e.g., Marshall, *Luke*, p. 241.

16. On the question of the setting of the Sermon in Q, an original mountain setting is maintained by Knox, *Sources of the Synoptic Gospels*, II, p. 7; A.R.C. Leaney, *A Commentary on the Gospel according to St. Luke* (London: A. & C. Black, 1958), p. 132; Schweizer, *Matthew*, p. 77. The absence of any setting is supported by Bultmann, *History of the Synoptic Tradition*, p. 333; Carré, 'Matthew 5.1', 39-48; J. Mánek, 'On the Mount— On the Plain (Mt 5.1—Lk 6.17)', *NovT* 9 (1967), 124-31. Mánek's suggestion, however, that Lk's avoidance of mountain settings is somehow connected with his lengthened citation of Is 40.3-5 in 3.4-6, is not convincing. For those who favour the originality of Lk's setting, see the next paragraph.

17. So Taylor, *Behind the Third Gospel*, pp. 81-83; Marriott, *The Sermon on the Mount*, p. 44; Schramm, *Der Markus-Stoff bei Lukas*, p. 113. Cf. Davies (*Setting*, p. 99), who states, without elaboration, that the Sermon in Q was delivered after Jesus descended from the mountain, as in Lk. 6.17.

18. See, e.g., Vaganay, 'L'absence du sermon', 14f.

19. *Lukasevangelium*, p. 319.

20. For Mt, see 5.1f.; 7.28f.; for Lk, see 6.17-20; 7.1.

21. See above, pp. 4f.

22. Cf. D.E. Nineham, *The Gospel of Mark* (Harmondsworth: Penguin Books, 1963), p. 114.

23. See above, p. 11.

24. Cf. Hoffmann, 'Die Stellung der Bergpredigt', 58; J. Dupont, *Les Béatitudes. I* (Louvain: Nauwelaerts, 1958), p. 9; F. Neirynck, 'La rédaction matthéenne et la structure du premier évangile', *EThL* 43 (1967), 67; Davies, *Setting*, p. 107.

25. It was being discussed at the turn of the century in Germany (cf.

Wellhausen, *Matthäus*, p. 13) and England (cf. Allen, *Matthew*, p. 70)... For an immense bibliography on the Sermon, see W.S. Kissinger, *The Sermon on the Mount: A History of Interpretation and Bibliography* (Metuchen, N.J.: Scarecrow Press, 1975).

26. See 'The "Five Books" of Matthew against the Jews', *Exp*, 8th ser., 15 (1918), 56-66; and *Studies in Matthew*, pp. 81f. Though Bacon refers to the Sermon as the 'New Torah' (e.g. *The Sermon on the Mount*, p. 23; *Studies in Matthew*, p. 177), he does not develop Moses or Sinai typology in his discussion of the Sermon, and interprets τὸ ὄρος as meaning merely 'hill country' (*The Sermon on the Mount*, p. 66).

27. Including Bornkamm, 'End-Expectation and Church in Matthew', in *Tradition and Interpretation*, p. 35; Barth, 'Matthew's Understanding of the Law', *ibid.*, pp. 157f.; Blair, *Jesus in the Gospel of Matthew*, p. 134; G.D. Kilpatrick, *The Origins of the Gospel according to St. Matthew* (Oxford: Clarendon Press, 1946), p. 108; Knox, *The Sources of the Synoptic Gospels*, II, p. 7; Farrer, *St. Matthew and St. Mark*, pp. 174-78; Teeple, *The Mosaic Eschatological Prophet*, pp. 77-80; Eichholz, *Auslegung der Bergpredigt*, p. 25; E.M. Skibbe, 'Pentateuchal Themes in the Sermon on the Mount', *LuthQ* 20 (1968), 44-51; M. Schoenberg, 'The Location of the Mount of Beatitudes', *BibTod* 1 (1962–63), 232-39; Klostermann, *Matthäusevangelium*, p. 33; Senior, *Invitation*, p. 59; Grundmann, *Matthäus*, p. 114; Schniewind, *Matthäus*, p. 38; Lohmeyer, *Matthäus*, pp. 75f.; Fenton, *Matthew*, p. 77; A.W. Argyle, *The Gospel according to Matthew: Commentary* (Cambridge: University Press, 1963), p. 44; Johnson, *Matthew*, p. 279; Wilkens, *Der König Israels*, p. 83; Gundry, *Matthew*, pp. 66, 138.

28. For discussions of Matthew's structure and Bacon's hypothesis, see Kingsbury, *Matthew*, pp. 3-24; J.-C. Ingelaere, 'Structure de Matthieu et histoire du salut: Etat de la question', *Foi et Vie* 78 (1979), 10-33; Davies, *Setting*, pp. 17-25.

29. For the most complete discussion of the evidence, see Davies, *Setting*, pp. 25-108. The attempts by Farrer (*St. Matthew and St. Mark*, pp. 174-78) and Skibbe ('Pentateuchal Themes') to find a Mosaic motif in the structure of the Sermon itself, are not persuasive enough to be mentioned here.

30. See above, pp. 98f.; below, pp. 149f.

31. See, e.g., Schniewind, *Matthäus*, p. 38.

32. Note also Mt's addition of δικαιοσύνη in 5.6 and 6.33.

33. E.g. Pirke Aboth 1.4; 3.3, 8; cf. Mt 23.2. For references to Moses sitting on Mount Sinai, see Pirke R. El. 46; *Memar Marqah* 4.6. Cf. Davies, *Setting*, p. 8. Lachs points out that the phrase היה יושב ודורש was commonly used by the end of the first century AD in connection with the study of the Torah, and he cites this passage from Meg. 21a: 'Our Rabbis taught: From the days of Moses up to Rabban Gamaliel the Torah was learned only standing. When Rabban Gamaliel died, feebleness descended upon the world and they learned the Torah sitting.' See S.T. Lachs, 'Some Textual Observations on

the Sermon on the Mount', *JQR* 69 (1978), 98-111. The significance of this quotation lies not in the reference to a shift in practice, but in its assumption that sitting to study the Torah was a tradition in need of explanation. For a passage in which the stone on which R. Eliezer sat to teach in his Beth ha-Midrash is compared to Mount Sinai, see Cant R. 1.3 §1.

34. See above, pp. 98f.

35. *Setting*, p. 108.

36. Lagrange draws attention, for example, to the contrast between Mt's Sermon and the typological treatment of Sinai in Heb 12.18-21, with its explicit mention of such Sinai features as fire, darkness, the voice from heaven, the sound of a trumpet, and the injunction to remain at a distance; Lagrange, *Matthieu*, p. 82; cf. Hill, *Mathew*, p. 109.

37. *Matthäus*, p. 13. He is surely wrong, however, in his assertion that in Exodus only God was on the mountain.

38. As suggested by Neirynck, 'St. Luke's Transpositions', 809; Schürmann, *Lukasevangelium*, p. 241; cf. Knox, *The Sources of the Synoptic Gospels*, II, p. 7.

39. See below, p. 119.

40. *The Gospel from the Mount*, p. 20.

41. Gibbs can deny that there is any Moses typology at all in Matthew only by ignoring such a passage as 2.20; Gibbs, 'The Son of God as the Torah Incarnate', 38-46.

42. The whole province, rather than the region to the north and east of Galilee. This is the more usual meaning of the term (cf. Bonnard, *Matthieu*, p. 52; Lagrange, *Matthieu*, p. 72). And the more natural reading of v. 24a is that the author is describing the *whole* area over which the fame of Jesus spread, i.e. inclusive of Palestine.

43. In contrast to Mk 3.7f., Mt's list of territories in 4.25 comprises the four quadrants of Jewish-occupied Palestine (excluding Samaria); cf. Trilling, *Das wahre Israel*, p. 135; Thomson, 'The Composition of Mt 8.1–9.34', p. 367 n. 6; Lohmeyer, *Matthäus*, p. 75.

44. Cf. P.S. Minear, 'The Disciples and the Crowds in the Gospel of Matthew', *ATRSup* 3 (1974), 39.

45. This triple designation is unique to Mt, occurring in 4.23 and 9.35, but nowhere else in the Gospels.

46. In light of the reference to διδάσκειν καὶ κηρύσσειν in 11.1, the absence of any reference to teaching in 11.2-6 is not important.

47. From Lk 7.1-10 it is apparent that the account of John's question immediately followed the Sermon and the healing of the centurion's servant.

48. The contrast between Mt and Mk in this regard has been noted by R. Pesch, *Naherwartungen: Tradition und Redaktion in Mk 13* (Düsseldorf: Patmos-Verlag, 1968), p. 97.

49. See Minear, 'The Disciples and the Crowds', 28-44; J.D. Kingsbury, *The Parables of Jesus in Matthew 13* (Richmond, Va.: John Knox Press, 1969), pp. 24-28; van Tilborg, *Jewish Leaders*, pp. 142-65.

50. It is clear from, e.g., 7.29 ('*their* scribes') that οἱ ὄχλοι are Jewish; see Kingsbury, *Parables*, p. 25.

51. For more thorough studies that we are able to carry out here, see the works by Minear, Kingsbury and van Tilborg cited in n. 49.

52. Cf. 3.7 ('many of the Pharisees and Sadducees') with Lk 3.7 ('the crowds').

53. See 9.1-8, 32-34; 12.22-29; 21.14-17, 46; 22.32f.; 23.1f., where a comparison with Mt's sources reveals his desire to make such a distinction between the crowds and their leaders.

54. Cf. J.D. Kingsbury, 'The Verb *Akolouthein* as an Index of Matthew's View of His Community', *JBL* 97 (1978), 56-73.

55. Cf. Gibbs, 'The Son of God as the Torah Incarnate', 45.

56. Rather than seeing them as a transparency for Church members, as does Fenton (*Matthew*, p. 74) and Gundry (*Matthew*, pp. 65, 138f.). Despite 27.25, Mt's openness to the crowds continues to the end of his Gospel (cf. 27.64). It is not possible to see in 13.10-17 and 27.25 evidence for a progressive deterioration of Mt's attitude toward them; see van Tilborg, *Jewish Leaders*, p. 159; Eichholz, *Auslegung der Bergpredigt*, p. 23.

57. Rather than a *nova lex*; if Mt had wanted to describe a *new* law here, Mk's διδαχὴ καινή (1.27) was close to hand.

58. See above, n. 42.

59. See above pp. 45f., 64.

60. For bibliography on the current discussion, see B.F. Meyer, *The Aims of Jesus* (London: SCM, 1979), p. 152. Note also that Davies' work on the messianic Torah in Judaism was anticipated somewhat by Bacon (*The Sermon on the Mount*, pp. 45ff.).

61. E.g. Tob 14.4-6; 1 Enoch 90.28-36; Ps Sol 17.28-35; Jub 1.15-17; 1 Bar 5.1-9; 2 Bar 40.1-4; 4 Ezra 13.25-36.

62. In Sib Or 3.710-719, the nations, attracted by the glories of restored Israel, want to make procession to the temple in order to 'ponder the law of the Most High God'. Jub 1.15-29 looks forward to an age of restoration that will be centred on Mount Zion, in which the people will be righteous (v. 17) and will keep the commandments from the heart (vv. 23-25). In Rabbinic literature as well, Is 2.2-4 is cited as evidence that in the Messianic Era Mount Zion would be the source of Torah for Israel (B. Bat. 21a; Lev R. 24.4; Pesiḳ. R. 41.2; Sifre Dt. §1), and the Davidic Messiah who gathers the scattered flock is expected to cause the Torah to prosper (Tg. Jer 23.5).

63. V. 13 appears independently in Mk 9.49f., and v. 15 in Mk 4.21. Mt was perhaps not entirely responsible for this collection of sayings, however, for the sayings concerning the city on a mountain and the lamp on a lampstand are found in sequence in the Gospel of Thomas (31, 32; the city saying is preserved as well in Oxy. Pap. I.15-20 [recto]). If, therefore, as is widely suspected, the Gospel of Thomas is independent of the Synoptics, it is possible that Mt found vv. 14b and 15 together.

64. In a perceptive article, O. Riethmueller sees the whole Sermon as a code of life for the 'city on the mount', i.e. the new 'peoplehood' called into being by Christ; 'The City on the Mount', *Student World* 30 (1937), 203-12. For the significance of 5.13-16, see also R. Schnackenburg, "'Ihr seid das Salz der Erde, das Licht der Welt." Zu Mt 5.13-16', in his *Schriften zum Neuen Testament* (München: Kösel-Verlag, 1971), 177-200; J. Dupont, *Les Béatitudes. III* (Paris: Gabalda, 1973), p. 320; J.B. Souček, 'Salz der Erde und Licht der Welt: Zur Exegese von Matth. 5.13-16', *TZ* 19 (1963), 169-79.

65. A proverbial origin is suggested by Johnson, *Matthew*, p. 290.

66. 'The City on the Hill', pp. 232-42.

67. 'The New Jerusalem', 335-63.

68. E.g. Schnackenburg, "'Ihr seid das Salz der Erde, das Licht der Welt"', p. 191; Jeremias, *Jesus' Promise to the Nations*, p. 66; H.-T. Wrege, *Die Überlieferungsgeschichte der Bergpredigt* (Tübingen: J.C.B. Mohr [Paul Siebeck], 1968), p. 31; Souček, 'Salz der Erde und Licht der Welt', 175; Grundmann, *Matthäus*, p. 139; also accepted as a possibility by Schweizer, *Matthew*, p. 99; Fenton, *Matthew*, p. 84; Hill, *Matthew*, p. 116; Gundry, *Matthew*, p. 77.

69. E.g. Is 60.1-3; Tob 13.11; B. Bat. 4a; Gen R. 59.5; Lev R. 31.7; Cant R. 1.3; Pesiḳ. R. Kah. 21.4; cf. Schäfer, 'Tempel und Schöpfung', 128-30.

70. Cf. Nineham, *Mark*, p. 114.

71. For other examples of the absorption of Sinai elements by Zion theology, see above, pp. 36f.

72. See above, p. 106.

73. *Matthew*, p. 69.

74. *Die Verklärung auf dem Berge*, p. 54.

75. Schmauch also notes connections between 4.23–5.1 and 15.29-31, but he errs in describing both passages as teaching scenes; *Orte der Offenbarung*, pp. 71f.

76. Cf. Trilling, *Das wahre Israel*, p. 136.

77. 17.14-20 is no real exception, as the incident has to do with an individual and the disciples, and not the crowds as a whole.

78. This has been observed by Lange, *Das Erscheinen des Auferstandenen*, p. 403; Kingsbury, *Matthew*, p. 69; Hoffmann, 'Die Stellung der Bergpredigt', 62-65; Eichholz, *Auslegung der Bergpredigt*, p. 24; Cox, *Matthew*, pp. 43f.

Notes to Chapter 8

1. We have already presented reasons for not including 14.23 as a major object of investigation (above, p. 12; cf. below, p. 283 n. 5), though it will come into discussion in this chapter.

2. R.H. Lightfoot (*Locality and Doctrine in the Gospels* [London: Hodder & Stoughton, 1938], p. 128) described 15.29-31 as a 'remarkable passage', but did not elaborate. Commentators have been aware that these verses

make contact with significant Matthean themes; e.g. Strecker, *Der Weg der Gerechtigkeit*, p. 98; Wilkens, *Der König Israels*, pp. 209f.; Grundmann, *Matthäus*, p. 379; H.B. Green, *The Gospel according to Matthew* (Oxford: University Press, 1975), p. 148; Senior, *Invitation*, p. 155. But the article by Ryan ('Matthew 15.29-31: An Overlooked Summary') is the first extensive treatment of the passage.

3. So called because the theme of 'bread' or 'loaves' comes up repeatedly; cf. L. Cerfaux, 'La section des pains (Mc 6.31–8.26; Mt 14.13–16.12)', in *Synoptische Studien*, ed. J. Schmid and A. Vögtle (München: Karl Zink Verlag, 1953), 64–77; Schmid, *Matthäus*, p. 231.

4. Lange so argues, pointing to the use of θεραπεύειν in Mk 3.10 and the cry of acclamation in 3.11b; cf. *Das Erscheinen des Auferstandenen*, pp. 408-10. However, in view of Mt's fondness for θεραπεύειν (4.23, 24; 9.35; 10.1; 12.22; 14.14; 17.16, 18; 21.14), it is scarcely necessary to look for a Markan background here; with respect to Mk 3.11b, it is the demons and not the crowds who are speaking.

5. Cf. Schweizer, *Matthew*, p. 331; below, p. 127.

6. Proponents of such a view can be found among both those who see Jn as dependent on Mk and those who see an independent tradition lying behind Jn's account. Among the former group, Barrett insists that Jn is independent of Mt at this point but drew the εἰς τὸ ὄρος phrase from Mk (perhaps 6.46) and used it as a substitute for εἰς ἔρημον τόπον in Mk 6.31; C.K. Barrett, *The Gospel according to St. John* (2nd edn; London: SPCK, 1978), pp. 271-73. See also M.-J. Lagrange, *Evangile selon Saint Jean* (Paris: Gabalda, 1925), p. 161. Representing the latter opinion, Lindars (*John*, p. 240) argues that just as the phrase εἰς τὸ ὄρος occurs at a number of points in the Synoptic tradition, it occurred as well in John's tradition, but not in connection with the feeding account. R. Schnackenburg (*Das Johannesevangelium* [Freiburg: Herder, 1971], II, pp. 17f.) and R. Bultmann (*The Gospel of John: A Commentary*, trans. G.R. Beasley-Murray [Oxford: Blackwell, 1971], p. 211) contend that Jn picked up the reference from the end of the account as he received it and transferred it to the beginning.

7. Apart from the references in Jn 6.3, 15, ὄρος appears only in 4.21 with reference to Samaritan worship on Mount Gerizim. See also Kysar's summary of various Johannine source theories, which indicates that most scholars who postulate sources behind Jn's Gospel see ὄρος in 6.3 as traditional; R. Kysar, 'The Source Analysis of the Fourth Gospel: A Growing Consensus?', *NovT* 15 (1973), 140.

8. I.e. Mk 6.32-44 // Mt 14.13-21 // Lk 9.10-17; Mk 8.1-10 // Mt 15.32-39; Jn 6.1-15.

9. I.e. (1) πολὺς ὄχλος (Jn 6.5 // Mk 6.34); (2) ἀγοράσωμεν (Jn 6.5 // Mk 6.37), though in Mk the word is on the lips of the disciples rather than of Jesus; (3) διακοσίων δηναρίων ἄρτοι (Jn 6.7 // Mk 6.37); (4) πέντε ἄρτους (Jn 6.9 // Mk 6.38, 41); (5) δύο fish (Jn 6.9 // Mk 6.38, 41); (6) the command

to make the crowd sit down (Jn 6.10 // Mk 6.39); (7) χόρτος (Jn 6.10 // Mk 6.39); (8) ἄνδρες ... πεντακισχίλιοι (Jn 6.10 // Mk 6.44); (9) δώδεκα κοφίνους κλασμάτων (Jn 6.13 // Mk 6.43).

10. (1) ἠκολούθει αὐτῷ (Jn 6.2; cf. Mt 14.13; Lk 9.11), though both Mt and Lk have the plural ὄχλοι and hence the plural verb; (2) ὡς (Jn 6.10; cf. Mt 14.21; Lk 9.14 where we find ὡσεί).

11. I.e. (1) τῆς θαλάσσης τῆς Γαλιλαίας (Jn 6.1 // Mk 7.31); (2) like Mk, Jn does not include the fish in the action of thanksgiving (Jn 6.11 // Mk 8.6; cf. Mk 6.41); (3) εὐχαριστήσας (Jn 6.11/Mk 8.6); (4) as in the Markan account, Jesus takes the initiative (Jn 6.5 // Mk 8.2).

12. I.e. the placing of the reference to the number of men present. Unlike Mk and Mt who do not mention the size of the crowd until the end, Lk and Jn have this reference in the middle of their accounts, though at slightly different places (Jn 6.10 // Lk 9.14).

13. I.e. (1) the crowd followed because of Jesus' healing activity (v. 2; but cf. Mt 14.14; 15.30f.; Mk 7.31-37); (2) the proximity of Passover (v. 4); (3) no indication of the passing of time (cf. evening, three days); (4) the roles of Philip, Andrew and the boy; (5) the testing (v. 6); (6) loaves of *barley* (v. 9); (7) the term for fish—ὀψάρια (v. 9); (8) no mention of the breaking of the bread (v. 11); (9) no mention of the disciples' role in distributing the bread (v. 11); (10) the command to gather up the fragments (v. 12); (11) the motive for Jesus' retreat εἰς τὸ ὄρος: i.e. the crowd perceive him as prophet-king (vv. 14f.).

14. The process is not nearly so difficult to imagine as Dodd makes it out to be; cf. C.H. Dodd, *Historical Tradition in the Fourth Gospel* (Cambridge: University Press, 1963), p. 209.

15. Cf. Brown, *John*, I, p. 235; Bultmann, *John*, p. 211 n. 5.

16. For bibliography and concise accounts of the history of the discussion, see C.K. Barrett, 'John and the Synoptic Gospels', *ExpT* 85 (1973–74), 228-33; Kümmel, *Introduction*, pp. 200f.

17. P. Gardner-Smith (*Saint John and the Synoptic Gospels* [Cambridge: University Press, 1938]) pioneered this position, though E.R. Goodenough ('John a Primitive Gospel', *JBL* 64 [1945], 145-82) claims to have reached a similar position independently. C.H. Dodd argues strongly for such a position in his *Historical Tradition in the Fourth Gospel*, and *The Interpretation of the Fourth Gospel* (Cambridge: University Press, 1954). Also W. Wilkens, 'Evangelist und Tradition im Johannesevangelium', *TZ* 16 (1960), 81-90; D.M. Smith, 'John 12.12ff. and the Question of John's Use of the Synoptics', *JBL* 82 (1963), 58-64; Brown, *John*, I, pp. xliv-xlvii; R. Schnackenburg, *The Gospel according to John*, I, trans. K. Smith (New York: Herder & Herder, 1968), pp. 28-34; L. Morris, *Studies in the Fourth Gospel* (Grand Rapids: Eerdmans, 1969), 15-63; Lindars, *John*, pp. 25-28; Kysar, 'The Source Analysis of the Fourth Gospel', 134-52.

18. *The Four Gospels*, pp. 395-426.

19. Most recently, Kümmel, *Introduction*, p. 204; Barrett, *John*, pp. 45f. See also Lagrange, *Jean*, pp. lxxvii-lxxviii; J.H. Barnard, *A Critical and Exegetical Commentary on the Gospel according to Saint John* (ICC; Edinburgh: T. &. T. Clark, 1928), I, p. xcvi; E.C. Hoskyns, *The Fourth Gospel*, ed. F.N. Davey (London: Faber & Faber, 1940), p. 87; W.F. Howard, *The Fourth Gospel in Recent Criticism and Interpretation*, rev. C.K. Barrett (London: Epworth Press, 1955), pp. 128-43; R.H. Lightfoot, *St. John's Gospel: A Commentary*, ed. C.F. Evans (Oxford: Clarendon Press, 1956), p. 29.

20. For a presentation of the possible points of contact, see Streeter, *The Four Gospels*, pp. 408-16. Of the authors listed in the previous note, only Lagrange, Hoskyns and Lightfoot argue for Johannine knowledge of Matthew.

21. Streeter, of course, found the similarity between Mt 15.29 and Jn 6.3 embarrassing for his thesis. But his argument that Mk 7.31 originally contained the phrase ἀναβὰς εἰς τὸ ὄρος ἐκάθητο ἐκεῖ, which was later omitted in an error of homoeoteleuton (*The Four Gospels*, pp. 413f.), must be dismissed as a case of special pleading. That *two* lines would have been omitted in this way is highly unlikely.

22. See, e.g., Lange, *Das Erscheinen des Auferstandenen*, p. 411 n. 42. Even some who argue for independence are prepared to see Jn 6.1-21 as an exception of some sort. According to Goodenough, 'some sort of literary relation is highly probable, unless the story was conventionalized in the telling as was no other in the NT'; 'John a Primitive Gospel', 156; also Dodd, *Historical Tradition in the Fourth Gospel*, p. 196.

23. The prevailing opinion is that we are dealing with a doublet of the same event; e.g. Dibelius, *From Tradition to Gospel*, pp. 71, 78; Bultmann, *History of the Synoptic Tradition*, p. 217; H. Clavier, 'La multiplication des pains dans le ministère de Jésus', *StEv* 1 (1959), 441-57; P.G. Ziener, 'Die Brotwunder im Markusevangelium', *BZ* 4 (1960), 282-85; B. van Iersel, 'Die wunderbare Speisung und das Abendmahl in der synoptischen Tradition', *NovT* 7 (1964), 167-94; Brown, *John*, I, pp. 236-39. But even if there were two original events, as argued by M.-J. Lagrange (*Evangile selon Saint Marc* [Paris: Gabalda, 1947], pp. 203f.) and J. Knackstedt ('Die beiden Brotvermehrungen im Evangelium', *NTS* 10 [1963–1964], 309-35), the two accounts have become closely assimilated in the oral tradition.

24. For a complete list, including common omissions, see W.R. Stegner, 'Lucan Priority in the Feeding of the Five Thousand', *BR* 21 (1976), 19-28.

25. I.e. ἠκολούθει αὐτῷ; the use of ὡς with the number πεντακισχίλιοι; the references to healing; the omission of the reference to 'sheep without a shepherd'; the omission of the statement that the crowds arrived ahead of Jesus.

26. 2 Ki 4.42-44. Cf. E. Haenchen, *Der Weg Jesu* (2nd edn; Berlin: de Gruyter, 1968), p. 284; Nineham, *Mark*, p. 178; F. Quiévreux, 'La récit de la multiplication des pains dans le quatrième évangile', *RevSR* 41 (1967), 97-108.

27. Although disputed by G.H. Boobyer ('The Eucharistic Interpretation of the Miracle of the Loaves in St. Mark's Gospel', *JTS* 3 [1952], 161-71), the feeding miracle is clearly connected in all accounts with the Last Supper and the Eucharist. The connection is spelled out explicitly in Jn 6.25-59 (esp. vv. 53-58), and it appears from verbal similarities between Synoptic accounts of Jesus' actions over the bread and fish and the accounts of the Last Supper (Mt 26.26; Mk 14.22; Lk 22.19; 1 Cor 11.23f.; cf. also ὀψίας δὲ γενομένης in Mt 14.15 and 26.20) that Jn was just making explicit what was implicit in the other Gospels. See E. Lohmeyer, 'Das Abendmahl in der Urgemeinde', *JBL* 56 (1937), 217-52; Ziener, 'Die Brotwunder im Markusevangelium', 282-85; T. Suriano, 'Eucharist Reveals Jesus: The Multiplication of the Loaves', *BibTod* 58 (1972), 642-51; van Iersel, 'Die wunderbare Speisung und das Abendmahl', 167-94; cf. R.H. Hiers and C.A. Kennedy, 'The Bread and Fish Eucharist in the Gospels and Early Christian Art', *PRS* 3 (1976), 20-47.

28. A new Moses/new manna interpretation is made explicit by Jn, not only in the dialogue with 'the Jews' that follows (esp. 6.31-33, 48-51), but also in the conjunction of prophet and king in vv. 14f.; see Meeks, *The Prophet-King*, pp. 91-96. A similar background is present in Mk. He makes explicit reference to the wilderness setting (εἰς ἔρημον τόπον; Mk 6.31, 32; cf. v. 35), his mention of the leaderless flocks probably reflects Num 27.17, and he probably intended a parallel with Moses' grouping of the people of Israel in the desert (Ex 18.13-27) with his reference to the seating of the crowds 'by hundreds and fifties' (6.40); cf. CDC 13.1; 1QS 2.21; 1QSa 1.14f.; 1QM 4.1-5; and E. Stauffer, 'Zum apokalyptischen Festmahl in Mc 6.34ff.', *ZNW* 46 (1955), 264-66; Ziener, 'Die Brotwunder im Markusevangelium', 283f.; J.-M. van Cangh, 'Le thème des poissons dans les récits évangéliques de la multiplication des pains', *RB* 78 (1971), 80. If Jn and Mk represent independent accounts, it is likely that this interpretation predates the written Gospels.

29. Cf. Dodd, *Historical Tradition in the Fourth Gospel*, pp. 213-17, 222; Montefiore, 'Revolt in the Desert?', 139.

30. Perhaps because he wanted to avoid the disobeyed command of Mk 7.36 (cf. Allen, *Matthew*, p. 170), or because he disliked the 'magical' features of the Markan passage (cf. Schweizer, *Matthew*, p. 331; note that Mt omitted Mk 8.22-26, a passage with similar features).

31. See Fenton, *Matthew*, p. 257; Albright, *Matthew*, p. 187; Hill, *Matthew*, p. 255; Schweizer, *Matthew*, p. 331.

32. While it is not possible to be certain about the role of Mk here, there is no doubt about the influence of Is 35.5f.; see G. Bertram, 'Θαῦμα', *TDNT*, III, p. 37; Ryan, 'Matthew 15.29-31: An Overlooked Summary', 38; Rienecker, *Matthäus*, p. 216; Schniewind, *Matthäus*, p. 185; Bonnard, *Matthieu*, p. 234; Albright, *Matthew*, p. 187; Hill, *Matthew*, p. 255; Schweizer, *Matthew*, p. 331.

33. E.g. G.H. Boobyer, 'The Miracles of the Loaves and the Gentiles in St.

Mark's Gospel', *SJT* 6 (1953), 82; A. Farrer, 'Loaves and Thousands', *JTS* 4 (1953), 2f.; T.A. Burkill, 'The Syrophoenician Woman: The Congruence of Mark 7.24-31', *ZNW* 57 (1966), 30-32.

34. E.g. Hubbard, *The Matthean Redaction*, p. 73; J.P. Meier, *The Vision of Matthew: Christ, Church and Morality in the First Gospel* (New York, Toronto: Paulist Press, 1979), p. 105; Lohmeyer, *Matthäus*, p. 258; Grundmann, *Matthäus*, p. 379; Filson, *Matthew*, p. 180.

35. As proposed by Ryan, 'Matthew 15.29-31: An Overlooked Summary', 39; Rienecker, *Matthäus*, p. 216; Schniewind, *Matthäus*, p. 185.

36. *Matthew*, p. 331.

37. *Der Weg der Gerechtigkeit*, p. 98.

38. Cf. Mt 11.1-6; 12.15-21; see above, p. 114.

39. So Stauffer, 'Zum apokalyptischen Festmahl'; A. Schweitzer, *The Quest of the Historical Jesus*, trans. W. Montgomery (2nd edn; London: A. & C. Black, 1911), pp. 374f.

40. The concept is encountered at Qumran (1QSa 2.17-22; cf. J.F. Priest, 'The Messiah and the Meal in 1QSa', *JBL* 82 [1963], 95-100), in the NT (Mt 8.11; 22.1-12; 25.1-13; Lk 22.29f.; Rev 19.6-9), and frequently in Rabbinic literature (Shab. 153a; Ex R. 25.7-8; 45.6; Lev R. 13.3; Num R. 13.2; Eccl R. 9.8 §1; Midr. Ps 14.7; Pesiḳ. R. 41.5; Tg. Ps.-J. Num 11.26). In variations on the theme, one finds the statement that Behemoth or Leviathan are being reserved for the banquet (B. Bat. 75a; Midr. Ps 18.25; Pirke R. El. 11; Tg. Ps.-J. Gen 1.21), or that wine has been kept for the banquet since the days of creation (e.g. Sanh. 99a). The expectation of miraculous productivity is also found in 2 Bar 29.4-8.

41. Mt's few changes to Mk's account emphasize the size of the crowd and the abundance of the food: ἄρτοι τοσοῦτοι, ὄχλον τοσοῦτον (15.33); πάντες, πλήρεις (15.37); women and children (15.38).

42. It is often asserted that Mt has a Gentile crowd in view in 15.29-31; e.g. Wilkens, *Der König Israels*, p. 210; M'Neile, *Matthew*, p. 232; Johnson, *Matthew*, p. 443; Rienecker, *Matthäus*, p. 216; Lohmeyer, *Matthäus*, p. 257; Schniewind, *Matthäus*, p. 185; Schmid, *Matthäus*, p. 241; Gaechter, *Matthäus*, p. 505; Tasker, *Matthew*, p. 153; Fenton, *Matthew*, p. 257; Hill, *Matthew*, p. 255; Gundry, *Matthew*, pp. 317-19; Davies, *Setting*, p. 328. This may be true of Mk 6.32-44, but the reasons given for such an interpretation of the parallel passage in Mt are scarcely adequate. The term 'the God of Israel', for example, does not imply a Gentile speaker here any more than it does in the Psalms (e.g. 41.13; 59.5; 68.35; 69.6; 72.18; 106.48) or in Lk 1.68. Mt is just using biblical phraseology in keeping with the formal nature of his summary statement. Nor is the argument from Jesus' itinerary any more persuasive. In fact, Mt revised Mk's itinerary to avoid having Jesus enter Gentile territory (Tyre, Sidon, the Decapolis; cf. Mt 15.29 and Mk 7.31). Here, as elsewhere in Mt, οἱ ὄχλοι are Jewish crowds; so Meier, *The Vision of Matthew*, p. 105; Trilling, *Das wahre Israel*, pp. 109f.; A. Plummer, *An*

Exegetical Commentary on the Gospel according to St. Matthew (London: R. Scott, 1909), p. 218; Lagrange, *Matthieu*, p. 311; Grundmann, *Matthäus*, p. 378; Bonnard, *Matthieu*, p. 234; Schweizer, *Matthew*, p. 331.

43. Above, pp. 114f.

44. Ryan ('Matthew 15.29-31: An Overlooked Summary', 31-42) and Murphy-O'Connor ('The Structure of Matthew XIV–XVII', 372-74) interpret this passage within a framework of blindness and rejection. The emphasis, however, is on the participation of the crowds in the eschatological ministry of Jesus.

45. See above, p. 126.

46. See above, n. 32.

47. For a discussion of this passage, see above, pp. 43f.

48. E.g. Jer 31.8, where the blind and lame are part of a great company being consoled by Yahweh as he leads them back to 'the height of Zion'; Mic 4.6f., where the lame and afflicted are made into a remnant and a strong nation on Mount Zion. Though Jer 31.8 is absent from the LXX textual tradition, it is present in the Targum. In the Micah passage, the vocabulary is not χωλός/חסם, but συντετριμμένην (LXX; from συντρίβω, 'to break, shatter, smash')/הצלעה (MT; 'the limping'). See also above, p. 45.

49. For a discussion of this passage, see above, pp. 44f.

50. Most notably Ex R. 25.8; see also Num R. 13.2; Pesiḳ. R. 41.5.

51. Though both the banquet and the gathering on Mount Zion are found in Revelation (Rev 19 and 14.1, respectively), they are not brought together. The banquet on Mount Zion is found, however, in 5 Ezra 1.38-48 (*NTApoc*, II, p. 695).

52. Cf. Jeremias, *Der Gottesberg*, p. 143, where it is argued that Is 25.6 lies behind Jn 6.3.

53. See above, pp. 47f. See also 1 Enoch 89–90 where sheep/shepherd imagery forms the basis for this apocalyptic vision of the future.

54. The only other occurrence in Mt of ῥίπτω is in 27.5, referring to Judas' throwing down the betrayal money. The verb appears elsewhere in the NT only in Lk–Acts (4 times).

55. Mt 2.6 is taken from Mic 5.2 and 2 Sam 5.2. It is to be noted that Mic 5.2 is part of a larger section (4.1–5.9) which contains many of the major elements of Zion eschatology.

56. See above, n. 28.

57. Mt transfers the statement about the leaderless flock to the introduction of his mission discourse (9.36), and omits entirely the description of the division of the crowd into groups.

58. See above, p. 119.

59. Cf. Lange, *Das Ercheinen des Auferstandenen*, p. 407.

60. Lange, who argues that 28.16-20 provides a recapitulation of the earlier mountain scenes, can find here only a vague connection in the area of discipleship; cf. *ibid.*, p. 413.

61. Above, p. 120.

62. All the differences between the two accounts can be explained in this way. There is no reason to suppose, with Streeter (*The Four Gospels*, p. 260), that Matthew's was the more primitive account.

63. So R.A. Harrisville, 'The Woman of Canaan: A Chapter in the History of Exegesis', *Int* 20 (1966), 279f.; S. Légasse, 'L'épisode de la Cananéene d'après Mt 15.21-28', *BLE* 73 (1972), 24f.; Allen, *Matthew*, p. 168; M'Neile, *Matthew*, p. 230; Lagrange, *Matthieu*, p. 308; Hill, *Matthew*, p. 146.

64. Mk's use of 'first' suggests a subsequent 'feeding' of the Gentiles. Two interpretations are possible: either the feeding of the five thousand is the 'first' feeding of the Jewish 'children', so that the second feeding miracle is for Gentiles (many commentators see the crowd of Mk 8.1 as Gentile), or the abundance of leftovers from each feeding is destined for the Gentiles.

65. The verb ἀπολύω used by the disciples in their request to Jesus (v. 23) can mean either 'set free, release' or 'send away, dismiss'. If the disciples' request was that he send the woman away, it is difficult to understand Jesus' reply to the disciples in v. 24, unless this reply is to be seen as directed to the woman. But the woman does not seem to be aware of this statement and does not reply to it. Rather she makes a fresh request. So it is likely that Jesus' statement about being sent only to the lost sheep of the house of Israel was directed to the disciples in response to their request that he free the woman from her load of concern; so Harrisville, 'The Woman of Canaan', 282; Légasse, 'L'épisode de la Cananéene', 28.

66. I.e. the honorific titles κύριε, υἱὸς Δαυίδ (v. 22), κύριε (v. 25), the use of προσεκύνει for προσέπεσεν (v. 25; cf. Mk 7.25); and the change from 'children's crumbs' to 'masters' table', which puts the focus on the woman's relationship to God rather than to Israel.

67. Such an interpretation of the diminutive κυναρίον is rightly rejected by Harrisville ('The Woman of Canaan', 283) and T.A. Burkill ('The Historical Development of the Story of the Syrophoenician Woman (Mark vii,24-31)', *NovT* 9 [1967], 169-73).

68. So Grundmann, *Matthäus*, p. 378; Bonnard, *Matthieu*, pp. 230f.

69. Wilkens, *Der König Israels*, p. 210. The objection of Nepper-Christensen to Wilkens's comment here is due to his own (unjustifiable) aversion to typology; *Das Matthäusevangelium*, p. 175 n. 60. See also Green, *Matthew*, p. 231; though his suggestion that the crowd in 15.29-31 is Gentile is questionable, he is nevertheless correct in seeing a concern for the salvation of the Gentiles as the link between these two mountain scenes.

Notes to Chapter 9

1. G.B. Caird, 'The Transfiguration', *ExpT* 67 (1955–56), 291.

2. For lists of these, see R.H. Stein, 'Is the Transfiguration (Mk 9.2-8) a Misplaced Resurrection-Account?', *JBL* 95 (1976), p. 95 n. 75; Allen, *Matthew*, pp. 185f.

3. E.g. T.W. Manson (*The Teaching of Jesus* [Cambridge: University Press, 1931], p. 32) holds that this account was also in Q.

4. See Stein, 'A Misplaced Resurrection-Account?', 95; but cf. Baltensweiler, *Die Verklärung Jesu*, pp. 125f.

5. In several of the 'agreements', the differences between Mt and Lk are more striking (the description of Jesus' face, the substitution for ῥαββί); cf. Allen, *Matthew*, p. 185. The rest could easily have happened independently (e.g. the order 'Moses and Elijah'; καὶ ἰδού, λέγουσα).

6. Daniel, who states at the outset of his study that the Transfiguration Narrative was a Markan composition rather than a unit of tradition taken over by Mark, is only an apparent exception, for he states later that Mark made use of many traditional elements, including the mountain setting ('The Transfiguration', p. 220).

7. Suggested by M. Horstmann, *Studien zur markinischen Christologie* (Münster: Verlag Aschendorf, 1969), p. 72. Cf. J. Wellhausen (*Das Evangelium Marci* [2nd edn; Berlin: G. Reimer, 1909], p. 69), who sees vv. 2-8 inserted between 9.1 and 9.9. While it is true that v. 11 follows v. 1 more naturally than does vv. 1-10, v. 1 is also a high point on which a narrative might reasonably have been expected to end.

8. Horstmann (*Studien zur markinischen Christologie*, p. 73), Dibelius (*From Tradition to Gospel*, p. 276) and U.B. Müller ('Die christologische Absicht des Markusevangeliums und die Verklärungsgeschichte', *ZNW* 64 [1973], 176f.) are representative of many who see vv. 9-10 as Markan.

9. For a thorough discussion of the esoteric element in apocalyptic, see Russell, *Method and Message*, pp. 107-18.

10. So F. Hahn, *The Titles of Jesus in Christology*, trans. H. Knight and G. Ogg (London: Lutterworth Press, 1969), p. 337; T.J. Weeden, *Mark— Traditions in Conflict* (Philadelphia: Fortress Press, 1971), p. 123; E. Lohmeyer, 'Die Verklärung Jesu nach dem Markus-Evangelium', *ZNW* 21 (1922), 186.

11. Many argue that ἀκούετε αὐτοῦ is a Markan insertion, designed to direct attention back to Mk 8.31-38; see Horstmann, *Studien zur markinischen Christologie*, p. 96; Müller, 'Die christologische Absicht', 175; W. Schmithals, 'Der Markusschluss, die Verklärungsgeschichte, und die Aussendung der Zwölf', *ZTK* 69 (1972), 393. In view of the Moses-typology elsewhere in the narrative, however (see below, pp. 142f.), this echo of Dt 18.15 is quite probably original.

12. First suggested by Wellhausen (*Das Evangelium Marci*, p. 69), the idea found an influential proponent in Bultmann (*The History of the Synoptic Tradition*, pp. 259f.) and has gained a substantial following; see, e.g., C.E. Carlston, 'Transfiguration and Resurrection', *JBL* 80 (1961), 233-40; H.D. Betz, 'Jesus as Divine Man', in *Jesus and the Historian*, ed. F.T. Trotter (Philadelphia: Westminster Press, 1968), p. 120; J.M. Robinson, 'On the *Gattung* of Mark (and John)', in *Jesus and Man's Hope*, ed. D.G. Buttrick

(Pittsburgh: Pittsburgh Theological Seminary, 1970), pp. 116-18; Schmithals, 'Der Markusschluss'; M. Coune, 'Radieuse Transfiguration. Mt 17.1-9; Mc 9.2-10; Lk 9.28-36', *AssSeign* 15 (1973), 51; Müller, 'Die christologische Absicht'; F.R. McCurley, '"And After Six Days" (Mk 9.2): A Semitic Literary Device', *JBL* 93 (1974), 79f.; Schniewind, *Matthäus*, p. 193. For further bibliography, see Stein, 'A Misplaced Resurrection-Account?', p. 79 n. 2.

13. This category draws together a variety of approaches which would explain the complexity of the Transfiguration Narrative by seeing it as the result of a tension between two conflicting christological views, two independent traditions that have been woven into one narrative, or a combination of the two. E. Lohmeyer's 1922 article, 'Die Verklärung Jesu nach dem Markus-Evangelium', was the first of several attempts to interpret the narrative as a composite—the union of two separate and independent narratives. The starting point for such interpretations is generally the observation that there appear to be two high points in the narrative—the change in Jesus' appearance and the voice from the cloud—neither of which seems to presume or require the other. In some of these reconstructions, both traditions are seen as arising within a Palestinian milieu; e.g. J.M. Nützel, *Die Verklärungserzählung im Markusevangelium* (Würzburg: Echter Verlag, 1973); H.-P. Müller, 'Die Verklärung Jesu', *ZNW* 51 (1960), 56-64. For Lohmeyer, Hahn (*Titles of Jesus*, pp. 334-46) and Masson (C. Masson, 'La Transfiguration de Jésus (Marc 9,2-13)', *RThPh* 97 [1964], 1-14), however, the narrative is stratified chronologically into Palestinian and Hellenistic elements; the use of μεταμορφόω in v. 2, along with various other details (for Lohmeyer, the whole of vv. 2-3; for Masson, vv. 2c-3, 7) are seen as evidence for the reinterpretation of a Palestinian story according to Hellenistic categories—which Hahn defines more explicitly as θεῖος ἀνήρ christology. Taking this approach one step further, Weeden (*Mark—Traditions in Conflict*, pp. 159-63) and Müller ('Die christologische Absicht') feel that the whole narrative originated as a θεῖος ἀνήρ resurrection account, but argue that Mk, who wrote to combat such views, undercut his opponents by pre-dating it and subordinating it to his suffering Son of Man christology. This is basically a refinement of Dibelius's earlier characterization of the narrative as the reflection of a 'Christ-myth'; *From Tradition to Gospel*, pp. 268-76.

14. Although most commentators in this group see a variety of influences, several backgrounds receive emphasis: (1) apocalyptic revelation: E. Lohmeyer, *Das Evangelium des Markus* (Göttingen: Vandenhoeck & Ruprecht, 1967 [1937]), pp. 178-81, who here reverses his earlier position; H.C. Kee, 'The Transfiguration in Mark: Epiphany or Apocalyptic Vision?', in *Understanding the Sacred Texts*, ed. J. Reumann (Valley Forge, Pa.: Judson Press, 1972), pp. 135-52; B. Trémel, 'Des récits apocalyptiques: Baptême et Transfiguration', *LumVie* 23 (1974), 70-83; S. Pedersen, 'Die

Proklamation Jesu des eschatologischen Offenbarungsträgers (Mt xvii 1-13)', *NovT* 17 (1975), 241-64; (2) Mosaic/Sinai typology: J.A. Ziesler, 'The Transfiguration Story and the Markan Soteriology', *ExpT* 81 (1969–70), 263-68; M. Sabbe, 'La redaction du récit de la transfiguration', in *La Venue du Messie*, ed. E. Massaux (RechBib, 6; Bruges: Desclée de Brouwer, 1962), pp. 65-100; Davies, *Setting*, pp. 50f.; (3) the Feast of Tabernacles: Riesenfeld, *Jésus transfiguré*; Baltensweiler, *Die Verklärung Jesu*; J. Daniélou, 'Le symbolisme eschatologique de la Fête des Tabernacles', *Irénikon* 31 (1958), 26; Albright, *Matthew*, p. 207; cf. W.R. Roehrs, 'God's Tabernacles among Men: A Study of the Transfiguration', *CTM* 35 (1964), 18-25; (4) the Binding of Isaac: D. Flusser, *Jesus*, trans. R. Walls (New York: Herder & Herder, 1969), pp. 96f.; A.R.C. Leaney, *The Christ of the Synoptic Gospels* (Auckland: Pelorous Press, 1966), pp. 19-28; (5) messianic enthronement: Horstmann, *Studien zur markinischen Christologie*, pp. 90-96; Riesenfeld, *Jésus transfiguré*.

15. The question of the *Sitz im Leben Jesu* also lies outside our purposes in this redactional study. Yet the work by Baltensweiler (cited above) has shown that it should be taken seriously and is by no means beyond solution. For another geographical suggestion in addition to the traditional sites of Tabor or Hermon, see W.L. Liefeld, 'Theological Motifs in the Transfiguration Narrative', in *New Dimensions in New Testament Study*, ed. R.N. Longenecker and M.C. Tenney (Grand Rapids: Zondervan, 1974), p. 167.

16. For comprehensive surveys of the arguments, see the articles by Carlston (pro) and Stein (con) cited above.

17. *PS* 2; *ApocryJn* (BG 2) 20.1; *1ApocJas* (CG V,3) 30.19; *PetPhil* (CG VIII,2) 133.14; see 'On the *Gattung* of Mark (and John)', 117.

18. *SJC* (CG III,4) 90.14; *ApocPaul* (CG V,2) 19.11f.; *Acts of John* 97-102. For the phenomenon of the mountain setting in Gnosticism, see P. Perkins, *The Gnostic Dialogue* (New York, Toronto: Paulist Press, 1980), esp. pp. 31, 42; also above, pp. 80f.

19. Apoc. Pet. 1 (*NTApoc*, II, p. 668); Quest. Barth. 3, 4 (*NTApoc*, I, pp. 494f.); Acts Pil. 14.1, 15.1 (*NTApoc*, I, p. 462); Desc.Chr. 1.6 (*NTApoc*, I, p. 479).

20. 'On the *Gattung* of Mark (and John)', 117f.

21. E.g. Schmithals, 'Der Markusschluss', 395-97.

22. See C.H. Dodd, 'The Appearance of the Risen Christ: An Essay in Form-Criticism of the Gospels', in *Studies in the Gospels*, ed. D.E. Nineham (Oxford: Blackwell, 1955), 9-35; G.H. Boobyer, *St. Mark and the Transfiguration Story* (Edinburgh: T. &. T. Clark, 1942), pp. 11-16.

23. For a list of differences, see J.H. Neyrey, 'The Apologetic Use of the Transfiguration in 2 Peter 1.16-21', *CBQ* 42 (1980), 509.

24. *Die Verklärung Jesu*, p. 27; see also Coune, 'Radieuse Transfiguration', 46; Sabbe, 'La redaction du récit de la transfiguration', 75.

25. Bultmann concedes that Apoc. Pet. is dependent on the Synoptics; *History of the Synoptic Tradition*, p. 259.

26. There is no hint in other early references to the Transfiguration that it was seen as a post-Easter event; see *Acts of John* 90-91; *Acts of Peter* 20; cf. Perkins, *The Gnostic Dialogue*, p. 39.

27. Cf. Stein, 'A Misplaced Resurrection-Account?', 87f.

28. For other refutations of this approach, see Beare, *Earliest Records*, pp. 141f.; J.E. Alsup, *The Post-Resurrection Appearance Stories of the Gospel Tradition* (Stuttgart: Calwer Verlag, 1975), p. 142; Baltensweiler, *Die Verklärung Jesu*, pp. 91-95.

29. 'Die Verklärung Jesu', 203.

30. Weeden, *Mark—Traditions in Conflict*, pp. 160f.; Müller, 'Die christologische Absicht', 159-73. See above, pp. 138-40.

31. 'Die christologische Absicht', 182-85. For similar estimations of the significance of Moses and Elijah here, though without the θεῖος ἀνήρ aspects, see M.E. Thrall, 'Elijah and Moses in Mark's Account of the Transfiguration', *NTS* 16 (1969-70), 314; W. Gerber, 'Die Metamorphose Jesu, Mk 9,2f. par.', *TZ* 23 (1967), 388f.; Argyle, *Matthew*, p. 132.

32. See the texts discussed by J. Jeremias ('Μωϋσῆς', *TDNT*, IV, p. 855); also *Memar Markah* 5.3.

33. See, e.g., M. Hengel, *The Son of God*, trans. J. Bowden (Philadelphia: Fortress Press, 1976), pp. 31f.; W.L. Lane, '*Theios Anèr* Christology and the Gospel of Mark', in *New Dimensions in New Testament Study*, pp. 144-61; C.R. Holladay, *Theios Aner in Hellenistic Judaism: A Critique of the Use of This Category in New Testament Christology* (SBLDS, 40; Missoula: Scholars Press, 1977).

34. For the changed appearance, see p. 141; for 'Son of God', see pp. 146f.; cf. Kee, 'The Transfiguration in Mark', 137-39.

35. Cf. Mt 17.2; see also below, pp. 149f.

36. P. 82.

37. 'La redaction du récit de la transfiguration', 83.

38. Cf. Sabbe, *ibid.*, 84; Thrall, 'Elijah and Moses', 312; Leaney, *The Christ of the Synoptic Gospels*, p. 22.

39. For a concise summary, see Davies, *Setting*, p. 50.

40. So Beare, *Earliest Records*, p. 142; Ziesler, 'Transfiguration Story', 265-67; Caird, 'The Transfiguration', 293.

41. For surveys of this strand of Jewish eschatology, see Teeple, *The Mosaic Eschatological Prophet*; Meeks, *The Prophet-King*. The associations of Moses and Elijah with both wilderness eschatology and Sinai/Horeb provide a better explanation for their presence in the Transfiguration Narrative than the notion that they represent the law and the prophets (suggested by Pedersen, 'Die Proklamation Jesu', 255; Meier, *Matthew*, p. 190; Trilling, *Matthew*, p. 110; Filson, *Matthew*, p. 192).

42. Few will be convinced by McCurley's suggestion that this time reference stood originally in v. 7; '"And After Six Days"', 80.

43. Cf. Nützel, *Die Verklärungserzählung*, pp. 159-61.

44. Cf. Sabbe, who concludes that the Transfiguration Narrative is an apocalypse inspired by the Sinai theophany ('La redaction du récit de la transfiguration', 86).

45. Flusser, *Jesus*, pp. 96f.; Leaney, *The Christ of the Synoptic Gospels*, pp. 21, 25; cf. Liefeld, 'Theological Motifs', pp. 175-77; McCurley, '"And After Six Days"', 78f.

46. Cf. B.M. Nolan (*The Royal Son of God: The Christology of Matthew 1–2 in the Setting of the Gospel* [Göttingen: Vandenhoeck und Ruprecht, 1979], p. 170), who attempts to draw this Isaac typology into his royal Son christology by means of the identification of Mount Moriah with Mount Zion.

47. See above, pp. 55-57.

48. E.g. Tg. Ps.-J. Gen 22.4; Eccl R. 9.7 §1; Pesiḳ. R. Kah. 26.3.

49. Mt incorporates ἀγαπητός into his citation of Is 42.1 (Mt 12.8); for Mk, see 12.6f.; cf. Horstmann, *Studien zur markinischen Christologie*, pp. 93f.

50. *The Use of the Old Testament*, p. 30.

51. 'Die Verklärung Jesu', 191-93.

52. On the unlikelihood of the thesis of an annual enthronement festival, cf. above, pp. 40f.

53. Such as are present as early as Zech 14.16. See also Daniélou, 'La Fête des Tabernacles'.

54. See *Jésus transfiguré*, pp. 217-22.

55. 'La Fête des Tabernacles', 26.

56. A Zion connotation for σκηνή, though unconnected with the Feast of Booths, is also present in Tob 13.10, where the prayer 'that Thy tabernacle may be builded in thee [i.e. in Jerusalem] again with joy' is part of a lengthy description of Zion eschatology (vv. 7-18).

57. See Riesenfeld, *Jésus transfiguré*, pp. 276f.

58. Cf. Pedersen, 'Die Proklamation Jesu', 260.

59. *Studien zur markinischen Christologie*, pp. 90-96; also Riesenfeld, *Jésus transfiguré*. Although Riesenfeld's connection between enthronement and the Feast of Booths is doubtful, his discussion of enthronement can stand on its own.

60. See Gundry's discussion, *The Use of the Old Testament*, p. 30.

61. *Titles of Jesus*, p. 336.

62. And hence Fuller is not fully justified in his assertion on the basis of this citation that 'son of God *was just coming into use* as a Messianic title'; R.H. Fuller, *The Foundations of New Testament Christology* (London: Lutterworth, 1965), p. 32.

63. For the text, see J.A. Fitzmyer, 'The Aramaic Language and the Study of the New Testament', *JBL* 99 (1980), 14f.; cf. Hengel, *The Son of God*, pp. 44f.

64. On the whole question of the origin and significance of 'Son of God', see Hengel, *The Son of God*.

65. 'Die christologische Absicht', 185-87.

66. See O. Michel, 'Der Abschluss des Matthäusevangeliums', *EvTh* 10 (1950–51), 16-26; Jeremias, *Jesus' Promise to the Nations*, pp. 38f.; cf. Rengstorf, 'The Judean Royal Ritual'.

67. Above, pp. 37f.

68. Above, pp. 46f.

69. Above, p. 76.

70. Cf. Riesenfeld, *Jésus transfiguré*, pp. 217-22.

71. See above, pp. 35, 52.

72. 2 Pet 1.18 does not, as Coune suggests ('Radieuse Transfiguration', 46), throw any glances in the direction of Sinai.

73. Cf. Kee, 'The Transfiguration in Mark', 139; Horstmann, *Studien zur markinischen Christologie*, p. 90; Trémel, 'Baptême et Transfiguration', 74.

74. 'Die Proklamation Jesu', 241f.

75. Cf. Masson, 'La transfiguration de Jésus', 2.

76. A similar debate between Moses categories and Son-christology appears to lie behind Heb 1.1f., 3.1-6.

77. The most significant of these are: (1) the explicit mention of Jesus' face (v. 2); (2) the use of φῶς in the description of his garments (v. 2); (3) the order of the names Moses and Elijah (v. 3); (4) κύριε instead of ῥαββί (v. 4); (5) the addition of εἰ θέλεις and omission of Mk 9.6 (v. 4); (6) ἔτι αὐτοῦ λαλοῦντος (v. 5); (7) the description of the cloud as φωτεινή (v. 5); (8) the addition of ἐν ᾧ εὐδόκησα (v. 5); (9) the whole of vv. 6-7; (10) αὐτόν (v. 8); (11) τὸ ὅραμα for ἃ εἶδον (v. 9).

78. Cf. Coune, 'Radieuse Transfiguration', 56-60; Trémel, 'Baptême et Transfiguration', 75f.; Daniel, 'The Transfiguration', pp. 104-18; Lange, *Das Erscheinen des Auferstandenen*, pp. 427f.

79. Of the 40 LXX occurrences of ὅραμα, 24 are in Daniel.

80. Cf. Davies, *Setting*, pp. 51-56; Cope, *Matthew*, pp. 99-101; Gundry, *Matthew*, p. 342; P. Dabeck, '"Siehe, es erschienen Moses und Elias" (Mt 17.3)', *Bib* 23 (1942), 175-89.

81. Although the only verbal similarity is πρόσωπον αὐτοῦ/וינפ, the content of the descriptions is the same.

82. *Setting*, p. 50.

83. Cf. Sabbe, 'La redaction du récit de la transfiguration', 87; Argyle, *Matthew*, p. 132.

84. Cf. Davies, *Setting*, pp. 53f.

85. The replacement of ῥαββί by κύριε in v. 4, though typically Matthean, has no real bearing on the christology of the passage. While κύριος is an important christological title for Mt, it does not always carry full christological weight. It often has been added in situations where people approach Jesus for healing (8.2, 6; 9.28; 15.22, 25; 17.15; 20.31, 33); it is placed on the

lips of disciples in circumstances where their christological insight is evidently lacking (16.22; 26.22); and sinners as well as the righteous can use the term in the same way (25.37, 44). So it can appear in Mt as no more than a respectful term of address, used by people who do not have a full awareness of all that the term might mean. Because of Peter's evident lack of perception, and because Mt wanted to avoid the use of ῥαββί (which he reserves for Judas in 26.25, 49), the appearance of κύριε in v. 4 is not constitutive for the christology of the passage.

86. Kingsbury convincingly argues that 'Son of Man' in Mt has essentially the same content as 'Son of God', but that the two terms differ in that the former is a public term while the latter is a confessional one; see *Matthew*, pp. 113-22.

87. Cf. Coune, 'Radieuse Transfiguration', 57.

88. Cf. A. Feuillet, 'Les perspectives propres à chaque évangéliste dans les récits de la transfiguration', *Bib* 39 (1958), 298.

89. Pp. 99-104.

90. P. 100.

91. So Daniel, 'The Transfiguration', p. 115; Coune, 'Radieuse Transfiguration', 60. Baltensweiler's assertion that the term ὄρος ὑψηλόν by itself is sufficient to demonstrate that in the oral period the Transfiguration dealt with the same issues as appear in the third temptation (*Die Verklärung Jesu*, pp. 56-61), outruns the evidence.

92. Cf. Müller, 'Die christologische Absicht', 161f., 175.

93. So Thrall, 'Elijah and Moses', 314; Leaney, *The Christ of the Synoptic Gospels*, p. 21; E. Schweizer, *The Good News according to Mark*, trans. D.H. Madvig (Atlanta: John Knox Press, 1970), p. 182; cf. Carlston, 'Transfiguration and Resurrection', 240; Ziesler, 'The Transfiguration Story', 267; Nineham, *Mark*, p. 233—all of whom make the same observation about the function of the account in Mk, without reference to ἀκούετε αὐτοῦ.

94. Cf. Coune ('Radieuse Transfiguration', 57), who states that the two scenes of the Caesarea Confession and the Transfiguration form a 'diptyche archaïque'.

95. Cf. Boobyer, *St. Mark and the Transfiguration Story*, where such an attempt is made—viz. it points ahead only to the *parousia*. See also T.A. Burkill, *Mysterious Revelation* (Ithaca, N.Y.: Cornell University Press, 1963), p. 156; Daniel, 'The Transfiguration', p. 67. Cf. Thrall ('Elijah and Moses', 310f.), who argues that there are points of contact with Mk 16.1-8; A. Kenny ('The Transfiguration and the Agony in the Garden', *CBQ* 19 [1957], 444-52) and Feuillet ('Les perspectives propres à chaque évangéliste', 285), both of whom find links with Gethsemane; and Leaney (*The Christ of the Synoptic Gospels*, p. 19), who feels that Mk was written while the events of Mk 13 were being fulfilled, so that the Transfiguration is a foretaste of the bliss promised to the martyrs.

96. For a concise argument in favour of Mk 16.8 as the originally-intended

ending of Mk, together with relevant bibliography, see Alsup, *The Post-Resurrection Appearance Stories*, pp. 86-89.

97. For full documentation, see Boobyer, *St. Mark and the Transfiguration Story*.

98. As argued by Lightfoot (*Locality and Doctrine*) and others.

99. For links between these two passages, see Lange, *Das Erscheinen des Auferstandenen*, pp. 429-31; Hubbard, *The Matthean Redeaction*, pp. 77f.; Daniel, 'The Transfiguration', pp. 118, 148, 154-56; Sabbe, 'La redaction du récit de la transfiguration', 86; Coune, 'Radieuse Transfiguration', 62; Giblin, 'Doubt and Reassurance in Mt 28.16-20', 72f.; E. Lohmeyer, '"Mir ist gegeben alle Gewalte!" Eine Exegese von Mt 28,16-20', in *In Memoriam Ernst Lohmeyer*, ed. W. Schmauch (Stuttgart: Evangelisches Verlagswerk, 1951), p. 27; Schweizer, *Matthew*, pp. 349f.

100. Cf. Schweizer, *Matthew*, p. 349.

101. Cf. Coune, 'Radieuse Transfiguration', 62.

102. Cf. Schmauch, *Orte der Offenbarung*, p. 71; Lange, *Das Erscheinen des Auferstandenen*, p. 431.

103. The description is that of Lange (*ibid.*).

104. Above, pp. 101 f.

105. Cf. Rengstorf, 'The Judean Royal Ritual', 241f.

Notes to Chapter 10

1. For the eschatological role of the Mount of Olives, see above, p. 75 and below, p. 272 n. 16.

2. Cf. J. Blenkinsopp, 'The Oracle of Judah and the Messianic Entry', *JBL* 80 (1961), 55-64, esp. p. 55.

3. We suggested above (p. 97) the possibility of an underlying 'wilderness–Mount of Olives–temple' structure in Mk.

4. Lange excludes the Mount of Olives from his discussion of τὸ ὄρος in Matthew for this reason; see *Das Erscheinen des Auferstandenen*, 392.

5. Cf. Lk 19.29, 37; 22.39; also Schmauch, *Orte der Offenbarung*, pp. 64-67.

6. Evans (C.F. Evans, '"I Will Go before You into Galilee"', *JTS* 5 [1954], 3-18), following Hoskyns, argues that προάξω in Mk 14.28 has the spatial sense of 'leading the way', rather than a temporal one of 'arriving before'. While this may have been the intention of the original logion, Mk 16.7 excludes it as a possible meaning in Mk.

7. Mt 13.39, 40, 49; 24.3; 28.20; the only other NT occurrence of the term is in Heb 9.26.

8. See, e.g., p. 154 above.

9. The history of the discussion and its theological setting is perceptively surveyed by G.R. Beasley-Murray in his *Jesus and the Future* (London: Macmillan, 1954), esp. pp. 1-112. Pesch continues this history up to 1968 in

his *Naherwartungen*, pp. 19-47. Further bibliography can be found in R. Pesch, *Das Markusevangelium* (Freiburg, Basel, Wien: Herder, 1977), II, pp. 267f.

10. E.g. Bultmann, *History of the Synoptic Tradition*, p. 125; E. Klostermann, *Das Markusevangelium* (4th edn; Tübingen: J.C.B. Mohr [Paul Siebeck], 1950), pp. 131f.

11. As did T. Colani, who first suggested such a theory in 1864; cf. Beasley-Murray, *Jesus and the Future*, p. 17.

12. See *Jesus and the Future*, pp. 205-12.

13. E.g. Hartman, *Prophecy Interpreted*; Pesch, *Naherwartungen*; K. Grayston, 'The Study of Mark XIII', *BJRL* 56 (1974), 371-87; Weeden, *Mark—Traditions in Conflict*, pp. 72-96; W. Grundmann, *Das Evangelium nach Markus* (Berlin: Evangelische Verlaganstalt, 1971), p. 260; Green, *Matthew*, p. 196. Earlier proponents include Dibelius, T.W. Manson, Dodd, Bacon, Streeter, and M'Neile.

14. E.g. K.L. Schmidt, *Der Rahmen der Geschichte Jesu* (Darmstadt: Wissenschaftliche Buchgesellschaft, 1969 [1919]), pp. 290f.; W.G. Kümmel, *Promise and Fulfilment*, trans. D.M. Barton (3rd edn; London: SCM, 1957), p. 98; F.W. Beare, 'The Synoptic Apocalypse: Matthean Version', in *Understanding the Sacred Texts*, p. 121; J. Lambrecht, *Die Redaktion der Markus-Apokalypse: Literarische Analyse und Strukturuntersuchung* (Rome: Pontifical Biblical Institute Press, 1967); Haenchen, *Der Weg Jesu*, pp. 433-37; J. Schmid, *The Gospel according to Mark*, trans. K. Condon (Staten Island, N.Y.: Alba House, 1969), p. 232; Burkill, *Mysterious Revelation*, pp. 205-207; Albright, *Matthew*, p. 288.

15. E.g. Marxsen, *Mark the Evangelist*, pp. 161f.

16. The events of the last days are said to begin on the Mount of Olives (Zech 14.4); it played an important part in the aspirations of at least one messianic pretender (Jos. *Ant.* 20.169-172; *War* 2.261-263); and it was held to be the site of the resurrection (Pesiḳ. R. 31.10; Tg. Cant 8.5). For a discussion of these passages and the suggestion that the departure of the glory of Yahweh to heaven from the Mount of Olives (Ezek 11.23; cf. 43.1-5) had a part to play in the formation of some of these traditions, see above, pp. 75, 97. See also Schmauch, *Orte der Offenbarung*, p. 63.

17. The relevance of this eschatological background for the interpretation of the Olivet Discourse, particularly of Zech 14.4, is granted by G.A. Barrois, 'Olives, Mount of', *IDB*, III, p. 598; Grundmann, *Markus*, pp. 259f.; Lohmeyer, *Markus*, p. 268; Evans, '"I Will Go before You into Galilee"', 7; Fenton, *Matthew*, p. 382; Schweizer, *Matthew*, p. 453; Hill, *Matthew*, p. 319; Schniewind, *Matthäus*, p. 239; Green, *Matthew*, p. 198; Meier, *Matthew*, p. 278; Senior, *Invitation*, p. 228.

18. This may be the 'word of the Lord' to which Paul makes reference in 1 Thess 4.15.

19. See, e.g., H. Conzelmann, 'Geschichte und Eschaton nach Mc. 13',

ZNW 50 (1959), 212f.; Haenchen, *Der Weg Jesu*, pp. 436f.; Beare, *Earliest Records*, p. 215; Lambrecht, *Die Redaktion der Markus-Apokalypse*, p. 80; Nineham, *Mark*, pp. 343f.; Pesch, *Naherwartungen*, pp. 96f., though for his later position see below, pp. 160f.

20. See comments by Haenchen and Pesch in works cited in n. 19.

21. See Taylor, *Behind the Third Gospel*, pp. 101-25; Manson, *Sayings*, p. 325; cf. Hartman, *Prophecy Interpreted*, p. 222.

22. See pp. 72f., 82.

23. The combination of these two references perhaps suggests an origin before the final separation of Judaism and Samaritanism, i.e. before AD 70.

24. Grundmann (*Markus*, p. 261) calls the discourse an 'apocalyptic parenesis', and lists these missing features: description of the coming of the End; nationalistic messianism and Jewish *Herrschaft*; hatred and revenge; the final judgment; godlessness and the role of Satan. See also Beasley-Murray, *Jesus and the Future*, pp. 212-16; G. Neville, *The Advent Hope: A Study of the Content of Mark 13* (London: Darton, Longman and Todd, 1961), pp. 45-50; Hill, *Matthew*, p. 317.

25. Against L. Gaston (*No Stone on Another: Studies in the Significance of the Fall of Jerusalem in the Synoptic Gospels* [Leiden: Brill, 1970], pp. 47-52), the apocalyptic elements are more than just additions to a parenetic structure.

26. This aspect of Mk 13 is being increasingly recognized by redaction critics; see, e.g., Weeden, *Mark—Traditions in Conflict*, pp. 91-96; Pesch, *Naherwartungen*; and below, pp. 162f.

27. *Das Markusevangelium*, p. 274. For a list of these later mountain scenes, see above, p. 80. The Mount of Olives is featured in Acts of John 97-102; Apoc. Pet. 1; *PetPhil* (CG VIII,2) 133.13-16; 134.9-17; *SJC* (CG III,4) 90.14.

28. *No Stone on Another*, pp. 43-60. This position was anticipated to a degree by Schmidt, *Der Rahmen der Geschichte Jesu*, p. 290 n. 1. But in addition to the largely secondary nature of these mountain scenes, since nothing in Mk 13 points in the direction of a post-resurrection appearance, a Mount of Olives setting is evidence for such an interpretation of Mk 13 no more than it would be for Mk 11.1 or 14.26.

29. For various combinations of συντέλεια with αἰών, ἡμέρα and καιρός, see LXX Dan 9.27; 12.4, 13; T. Levi 10.2; T. Ben. 11.3.

30. Cf. Beare, 'The Synoptic Apocalypse', p. 124; J. Lambrecht, 'The Parousia Discourse: Composition and Content in Mt. XXIV–XXV', in *L'Évangile selon Matthieu*, ed. M. Didier (Gembloux: Duculot, 1972), p. 314; Schweizer, *Matthew*, p. 448; Bonnard, *Matthieu*, p. 345.

31. The important features of Mt's redaction can be summarized as follows. First, as far as the overall structure of the passage is concerned, with two exceptions Mt constructed his version of the discourse (up to 24.36) from blocks of Markan material. The first exception is 24.9-14, where Mt

found it necessary to compose a new paragraph (though based on features drawn from Mk 13.9-13; cf. Mt 24.9, 13, 14) since he already used this section of Mk in his mission discourse (10.17-22a). The second is in 24.26-28, where Mt expanded the warning of Mk 13.21-23 with sayings drawn from other sources. Mt's major deviation from Mk, however, comes at the end. In place of Mk's short ending of 13.33-37 with its repeated injunction to watchfulness, Mt has (1) a series of sayings drawn from Q (24.37-51; v. 42 echoes Mk 13.35), (2) two parables, one from Q (25.14-30) and one from another source (25.1-13), and (3) a description of the final judgment (25.31-46).

Looking at the smaller details of Mt's redaction, the following deviations from Mk are significant: (1) οἱ μαθηταί (24.1, 3); (2) the separation of the disciples' question into two parts (24.3); (3) παρουσίας, συντελείας τοῦ αἰῶνος (24.3); (4) θλῖψιν instead of συνέδρια (24.9); (5) a Gentile rather than a Jewish flavour in 24.9-14; (6) the new position of 24.14; (7) the more explicit relationship set out in 24.14 between the Gentile mission and the End; (8) μηδὲ σαββάτῳ (24.20); (9) εὐθέως (24.29); and (10) v. 30a.

32. So Allen, *Matthew*, p. 258; Plummer, *Matthew*, p. 335; Lagrange, *Matthieu*, pp. 466f.; Schniewind, *Matthäus*, p. 239; Gaechter, *Matthäus*, p. 765.

33. This is the central thesis of Pesch's *Naherwartungen*; so also Gaston, *No Stone on Another*, pp. 47-52; Grundmann, *Markus*, p. 261; Klostermann, *Das Markusevangelium*, pp. 131f.; Neville, *The Advent Hope*, pp. 45-49; Weeden, *Mark—Traditions in Conflict*, pp. 72ff., esp. 91-96; Beare, 'The Synoptic Apocalypse', p. 125.

34. 'Geschichte und Eschaton nach Mc. 13', 210-21.

35. See above, p. 16.

36. Neville (*The Advent Hope*, pp. 53f.) accuses him of doing just this.

37. So Lambrecht, 'The Parousia Discourse', p. 318; Schweizer, *Matthew*, pp. 448f.; Green, *Matthew*, p. 196; Meier, *Matthew*, pp. 278f.; Senior, *Invitation*, p. 232. For the less likely view that 24.3 emphasizes the close connection between the events of AD 70 and the End, see Beare, 'The Synoptic Apocalypse', pp. 124f.; Hill, *Matthew*, p. 319; Klostermann, *Das Matthäusevangelium*, p. 192.

38. Lambrecht is one of a number of commentators holding to a post-AD 70 date for Mt who argue that vv. 15-28 refer to the fall of Jerusalem and vv. 29-31 to the *parousia* without addressing at all the problems raised by εὐθέως for such an interpretation; 'The Parousia Discourse', pp. 318f.

39. So Beare, 'The Synoptic Apocalypse', p. 128; Strecker, *Der Weg der Gerechtigkeit*, pp. 240f.; Bonnard, *Matthieu*, p. 353; Trilling, *Matthew*, p. 185; Green, *Matthew*, pp. 197-201.

40. For such a suggestion, see Beare, 'The Synoptic Apocalypse', 128.

41. See Meier, *Matthew*, pp. 282f.

42. See Gaston, *No Stone on Another*, pp. 483-85; S. Brown, 'The

Matthean Apocalypse', *JSNT* 4 (1979), 2-27, esp. 12-14. Also, with different theological orientations, R.V.G. Tasker, *The Gospel according to St. Matthew* (Grand Rapids: Eerdmans, 1961), pp. 225-27; A. Feuillet, 'La synthèse eschatologique de Saint Matthieu (XXIV–XXV)', *RB* 56 (1949), 340-64; *ibid.*, 57 (1950), 62-91, 180-211.

43. *No Stone on Another*, p. 483.

44. Gaston argues that the 'sign of the Son of Man' is the heavenly manifestation reported in Jos. *War* 6.289 (*ibid.*, 484). But this is more likely an epexegetic genitive—i.e. the Son of Man is himself the sign; so Lambrecht, 'The Parousia Discourse', 324; R. Pesch, 'Eschatologie und Ethik: Auslegung von Mt. 24.1-36', *BibLeb* 11 (1970), 229; Bonnard, *Matthieu*, p. 352. The highly apocalyptic nature of these verses makes it unlikely that Mt intended them to be read historically.

45. Although a second τῆς is found in the majority text, in several Western witnesses (D W) and in f^{13}, its omission is both better attested (ℵ B C L Θ f^1 33 565 892 pc) and the variant reading which better explains the existence of the other.

46. Cf. above, n. 44.

47. For a similar interpretation of Mt's perspective, see Grundmann, *Matthäus*, p. 508.

48. E.g. 4 Ezra 6.22; 10.25, 26; 11.20, 26f., 33; 2 Bar 36.4; Ass Mos 7.1; cf. Lagrange, *Matthieu*, p. 467.

49. On Mt's distinctives, see Beare, 'The Synoptic Apocalypse'; Pesch, 'Eschatologie und Ethik', 223-38.

50. The classic study of eschatology in the Matthean discourses is Bornkamm, 'End Expectation and Church in Matthew', in *Tradition and Interpretation*, pp. 15-51, esp. 15-24.

51. Cf. Beare, 'The Synoptic Apocalypse', 131.

52. See 'Geschichte und Eschaton nach Mc. 13', 221.

Notes to Chapter 11

1. The first expression of this insight is often attributed to O. Michel ('Der Abschluss des Matthäusevangeliums', published in 1950). Lohmeyer, however, made a similar observation in the 1945 article '"Mir ist gegeben alle Gewalte!"'. Other literature treating the passage as a whole includes: Lange, *Das Erscheinen des Auferstandenen*; Hubbard, *The Matthean Redaction*; R.R. de Ridder, *The Dispersion of the People of God: The Covenant Basis of Mt. 28.18-20* (Kampen: Kok, and Grand Rapids: Baker, 1971); Strecker, *Der Weg der Gerechtigkeit*, pp. 208-14; Trilling, *Das wahre Israel*, pp. 6-36; Barth, 'Matthew's Understanding of the Law', in *Tradition and Interpretation*, pp. 131-37; Frankemölle, *Jahwebund*, pp. 42-72; Fuller, *The Resurrection Narratives*, pp. 79-93; F. Hahn, *Mission in the New Testament*, trans. F. Clarke (SBT, 47; London: SCM, 1965), pp. 63-68; N.

Perrin, *The Resurrection according to Matthew, Mark, and Luke* (Philadelphia: Fortress, 1977), pp. 46-54; Jeremias, *Jesus' Promise to the Nations*, pp. 38f.; Rigaux, *Dieu l'a ressuscité*, pp. 254-58; Ellis, *Matthew*, pp. 20-25; Bornkamm, 'Der Auferstandene und der Irdische'; Kingsbury, 'Composition and Christology'; J.P. Meier, 'Two Disputed Questions in Matt. 28.16-20', *JBL* 96 (1977), 407-24; Zumstein, 'Matthieu 28.16-20'; A. Vögtle, 'Das christologische und ekklesiologische Anliegen von Mt. 28.18-20', *StEv* 2 (1964), 266-94; J.B. Malina, 'The Literary Structure and Form of Matt. xxviii.16-20', *NTS* 17 (1970–71), 87-103; R.C. Tuck, 'The Lord Who Said Go: Some Reflections on Matthew 28.16-20', *ANQ* 7 (1966), 85-92; K. Smyth, 'Matthew 28: Resurrection as Theophany', *ITQ* 42 (1975), 259-71; G.R. Osborne, 'Redaction Criticism and the Great Commission: A Case Study Toward a Biblical Understanding of Inerrancy', *JETS* 19 (1976), 73-85; P.T. O'Brien, 'The Great Commission of Matthew 28.18-20: A Missionary Mandate or Not?', *RThR* 35 (1976), 66-78; U. Luck, 'Herrenwort und Geschichte in Matth. 28.16-20', *EvTh* 27 (1967), 494-508; H. Kosmala, 'The Conclusion of Matthew', *ASTI* 4 (1965), 132-47; O.S. Brooks, 'Matthew 28.16-20 and the Design of the First Gospel', *JSNT* 10 (1981), 2-18.

2. Although such formative early studies as those by Trilling and Strecker (cited in n. 1 above) dealt with 28.18-20 alone, most of the more recent work is in accordance with the insistence of Hubbard (*The Matthean Redaction*, p. 2 n. 2) and Meier ('Two Disputed Questions', 411f.) that the unit begins with v. 16.

3. The presence of Matthean vocabulary is frequently noted: e.g. Barth, 'Matthew's Understanding of the Law', 131; Kingsbury, 'Composition and Christology', 573-79. Even the most restrictive list would have to include: προσεκύνησαν, ἐδίστασαν, προσελθών, ἐξουσία, ἐν οὐρανῷ καὶ ἐπὶ τῆς γῆς, μαθητεύσατε, διδάσκοντες, τηρεῖν, συντελείας τοῦ αἰῶνος.

4. One of the most thoroughgoing studies of the passage—that of Lange (*Das Erscheinen des Auferstandenen*)—is predicated on the assumption that Mt's closing statement depends only on material found elsewhere in the First Gospel, especially 11.27; similar positions are taken by Kingsbury, 'Composition and Christology'; Kilpatrick, *Origins of Matthew*, pp. 48f. For a telling criticism of Lange's failure to take sufficient account of extra-Matthean parallels, however, see Meier, 'Two Disputed Questions', esp. 411-16.

5. So Bornkamm, 'Der Auferstandene und der Irdische', 173; Barth, 'Matthew's Understanding of the Law', 133; Strecker, *Der Weg der Gerechtigkeit*, pp. 209f.; Fuller, *The Resurrection Narratives*, p. 90; Hahn, *Mission in the New Testament*, p. 63; Meier, 'Two Disputed Questions', 411, 416; B. Steinseifer, 'Der Ort der Erscheinungen des Auferstandenen', *ZNW* 62 (1971), 247f.; Zumstein, 'Matthieu 28.16-20', 17f.

6. Michel cites these parallels: v. 18—Mt. 11.27 and Jn 3.35; v. 19—Mk 16.15; v. 20b—Mt 18.20; see 'Der Abschluss des Matthäusevangeliums', 20.

7. Including Bornkamm, Barth, Fuller, Hahn, Zumstein (cf. n. 5 above).

8. *Der Weg der Gerechtigkeit*, pp. 209-11.

9. See *The Matthean Redaction*, pp. 101-28.

10. The commissioning of Acts 1.6-11 contains each of the elements that Hubbard finds in the proto-commissioning—confrontation (v. 6a); reaction (v. 6b); commission (vv. 7f.); reassurance (vv. 10f.). The inclusion of this passage, therefore, would strengthen his thesis.

11. See 'Two Disputed Questions', 411f.

12. Cf. Meier, *ibid.*, p. 416.

13. So Strecker, *Der Weg der Gerechtigkeit*, p. 208; Hubbard, *The Matthean Redaction*, p. 73; Kingsbury, 'Composition and Christology', 575; Fuller, *The Resurrection Narratives*, p. 81; Zumstein, 'Matthieu 28.16-20', 16; Steinseifer, 'Der Ort der Erscheinungen des Auferstandenen', 249.

14. Schmithals adds to this list the account of the choosing of the disciples in Mk 3.13-19; see 'Der Markusschluss', 379-411.

15. Below, pp. 173f.

16. See above, pp. 138ff. To the advocates of such an approach listed there, add P. Seidensticker, *Die Auferstehung Jesu in der Botschaft der Evangelisten* (SBS, 26; Stuttgart: Verlag Katholisches Bibelwerk, 1967), pp. 43-58.

17. *Matthew*, pp. 302-305; cf. M'Neile, *Matthew*, p. 434. Allen's suggestion that Mk contained not only equivalents to Mt 28.9f. and 16-20, but also a now-lost middle scene in which Christ appeared to the Eleven 'repeating the command to go to Galilee and appointing a mountain as a place of meeting' (p. 303) is a striking example of the limitations of an approach that would attempt to solve all problems of the Gospels by resorting to source theories.

18. For E. Linnemann ('Der (widergefundene) Markusschluss', *ZTK* 66 [1969], 255-87), Mk 16.15-20 forms part of this lost ending; for A. Strobel ('Der Berg der Offenbarung (Mt 28.16; Apg 1.12): Erwägungen zu einem urchristlichen Erwartungstopos', in *Verborum Veritas*, ed. O. Böcher and K. Haacker [Wuppertal: Theologischer Verlag Rolf Brockhaus, 1970), 133-46] both Mt 28.16-20 and Acts 1.6-12 depend on this now lost conclusion of Mark.

19. The suddenness with which the mountain appears in 28.16 is used to argue both for its traditional nature (Meier, 'Two Disputed Questions', 408f.) and for its redactional nature (Steinseifer, 'Der Ort der Erscheinungen des Auferstandenen', 249). The arguments cancel each other out, which means that the issue cannot be decided on these grounds.

20. Cf. Meier, 'Two Disputed Questions', 408f.

21. τάσσω occurs in Luke–Acts (6 times) and in Paul (twice), but nowhere else in Mt (the variant reading ὑπὸ ἐξουσίαν τασσόμενος at 8.9 is dependent on Lk 7.8).

22. The exact meaning of οὗ ἐτάξατο αὐτοῖς is difficult to ascertain. Weiss's suggestion, that Mt is here referring to the mountain of the Sermon (i.e. 'where Jesus gave them commandments'; see Klostermann, *Das*

Matthäusevangelium, p. 231) is unlikely. Although τάσσω can mean 'to command' (e.g. Acts 18.2), one would expect the active voice and an accusative object (unless LXX Ex 29.43 is a counter-example). Equally unlikely is Chavasse's suggestion that the phrase refers to Mk 3.13 and should be translated 'the mountain where Jesus had appointed them' (C. Chavasse, 'Not "the Mountain Appointed"'. Studies in Texts: Mt 28.16', *Theol* 74 [1971], 478). Here, again, the dative αὐτοῖς is the stumbling block, for where the dative appears with τάσσω an accusative object is generally found as well (e.g. Acts 28.23). It is probable that we are dealing here with an elliptical expression with an infinitive such as ἐλθεῖν or ὑπαντᾶν (αὐτόν) being understood. Such a construction with τάσσω is found in Acts 22.10.

23. Cf. Meier, 'Two Disputed Questions', 411-16. For other considerations of the possibility of a link between 28.16 and Acts 1.12, see Hubbard, *The Matthean Redaction*, p. 73; Barth, 'Matthew's Understanding of the Law', 131f. Lange attempts to dissociate the two passages—and hence to deny a traditional origin of ὄρος—by arguing that the Mount of Olives location appears as a result of Lk's Jerusalem orientation (*Das Erscheinen des Auferstandenen*, pp. 437-40). While this may explain the *specific* location in Acts 1.12, it does not necessarily remove the general mountain setting from the discussion.

24. For lists of these, with discussion, see above, pp. 80f., 138ff.

25. τὸ ὄρος is also seen as traditional by Lohmeyer, '"Mir ist gegeben alle Gewalte!"', 24; Bonnard, *Matthieu*, p. 417; Schmid, *Matthäus*, p. 390; Schweizer, *Matthew*, p. 528.

26. See 'Der Berg der Offenbarung', 141-45. Similarly Seidensticker (*Die Auferstehung Jesu*, esp. p. 53), who draws 2 Pet 1.16-18 and the Transfiguration Narrative into the pattern as well.

27. So Seidensticker, *Die Auferstehung Jesu*, pp. 43-58; also H.-W. Bartsch, who sees a very early apocalyptic tradition lying behind 28.2-4, 9f., 16f. (for this reference, see Grundmann, *Matthäus*, p. 573).

28. See above, pp. 72f., 82.

29. While 28.16-20 is in a sense a revelation of the divine will and even of future events, the idea of commissioning finds no parallel in any of these apocalyptic mountain scenes.

30. Cf. Bonnard, *Matthieu*, p. 417; 'probablement une incohérence due à une tradition orale mal assimilée par Mat'. See also Lagrange, *Matthieu*, p. 543.

31. This form is characterized by a three-fold statement of exaltation, presentation and enthronement. Michel ('Der Abschluss des Matthäusevangeliums', 22f.), followed by Jeremias (*Jesus' Promise to the Nations*, pp. 38f.), and (with modifications) by Bornkamm ('Der Auferstandene und der Irdische', 174f.) see 28.16-20 as exhibiting such a form based on Dan 7.13f. Hahn (*Mission in the New Testament*, pp. 63-68) sees the pericope as

an enthronement statement based on Ps 110.1. For further discussion of enthronement ideas in 28.16-20, see below, pp. 180ff.

32. So Trilling, *Das wahre Israel*, pp. 33f. Troubling to this hypothesis is the fact that while Trilling is able to suggest OT parallels for the first two elements (the word of revelation and the command) and the last two (the command and the promise), he is not able to provide a parallel in which all three occur together.

33. So Malina, 'Literary Structure and Form'; followed by Nolan, *The Royal Son of God*, p. 199; D. Senior, 'The Ministry of Continuity: Matthew's Gospel and the Interpretation of History', *BibTod* 82 (1976), 672; Schweizer, *Matthew*, p. 531. While there are striking similarities between the two passages, it is doubtful whether a larger formal category can be found for 2 Chron 36.23 which is of any relevance to 28.16-20.

34. Frankemölle (*Jahwebund*, pp. 53-59) also sees 2 Chron 36.23 as lying behind 28.16-20, but argues in somewhat eccentric fashion that 2 Chron 36.23 is a *Bundeserneuerung*. De Ridder is no more successful in his attempt to see the passage against the background of the suzerainty treaty form of covenant; see *Dispersion*, pp. 175-79.

35. Smyth ('Resurrection as Theophany') argues that the whole of ch. 28 was modelled against this background. For a discussion of this position, see below, pp. 179f.

36. So Hubbard, *The Matthean Redaction*, pp. 25-72; followed by O'Brien, 'The Great Commission'; Ellis, *Matthew*, p. 22; cf. C.H. Giblin, 'A Note on Doubt and Reassurance in Mt. 28.16-20', *CBQ* 37 (1975), 74f.

37. Meier correctly notes that v. 18b fits into the pattern only awkwardly, and even then in a manner that fails to take due cognizance of the importance of this statement; see 'Two Disputed Questions', 423f.

38. So Meier, *ibid.*; Steinseifer, 'Der Ort der Erscheinungen des Auferstandenen', 247; Zumstein, 'Matthieu 28.16-20', 21.

39. See 'Der Abschluss des Matthäusevangeliums', 22f.

40. See Barth, 'Matthew's Understanding of the Law', p. 133; Meier, *Matthew*, p. 369; Ellis, *Matthew*, pp. 23f. The position is taken in less explicit form by Bonnard, *Matthieu*, p. 418; Lohmeyer, '"Mir ist gegeben alle Gewalte!"', 34f.; Frankemölle, *Jahwebund*, pp. 61-66.

41. See 'Das christologische und ekklesiologische Anliegen von Mt 28.18-20'.

42. See, e.g., Frankemölle, *Jahwebund*, p. 63.

43. See Rigaux, *Dieu l'a ressuscité*, p. 256; Zumstein, 'Matthieu 28.16-20', 18f.; O'Brien, 'The Great Commission', 71; Giblin, 'Doubt and Reassurance in Mt. 28.16-20', 73; Brown, 'The Two-fold Representation of the Mission', 23f.; Gaechter, *Matthäus*, p. 965; Grundmann, *Matthäus*, p. 577; Schweizer, *Matthew*, p. 531; Gundry, *Matthew*, p. 595; cf. Trilling, *Das wahre Israel*, pp. 6f.; Hahn, *Mission in the New Testament*, p. 66; G. Baumbach, 'Die Mission im Matthäus-Evangelium', *TLZ* 92 (1967), 890.

44. So Michel, 'Der Abschluss des Matthäusevangeliums', 22f.; Lohmeyer, '"Mir ist gegeben alle Gewalte!"', 47; Meier, *Matthew*, p. 369; Fuller, *The Resurrection Narratives*, p. 92; Ellis, *Matthew*, pp. 23f.; Bonnard, *Matthieu*, p. 418.

45. So Hahn, *Mission in the New Testament*, p. 66; Zumstein, 'Matthieu 28.16-20', 20.

46. See 'Composition and Christology'; *Matthew*, pp. 41-83.

47. 'Composition and Christology', 573.

48. On the basis of several passages in Eusebius which cite v. 19 as if it read μαθητεύσατε πάντα τὰ ἔθνη ἐν τῷ ὀνόματί μου, διδάσκοντες κ.τ.λ., a number of scholars argue that the command to baptize in the three-fold name was a later insertion and that Eusebius preserves the original text. See F.C. Conybeare, 'The Eusebian Form of the Text Matth. 28.19', *ZNW* 2 (1901), 275-88; Lohmeyer, '"Mir ist gegeben alle Gewalte!"', 29-33; Kosmala, 'The Conclusion of Matthew'; Green, *Matthew*, p. 230. The textual tradition is unanimously in favour of the longer reading, however, and one suspects that Conybeare and his followers have allowed dogmatic predispositions to overrule the usual canons of text criticism.

49. See *Das Erscheinen des Auferstandenen*; also Blair (*Jesus in the Gospel of Matthew*, pp. 66, 108), who sees 28.16-20 as a commentary on 11.25-30.

50. See 'The Son of God as the Torah Incarnate', 45.

51. Specifically, Jesus as a figure of power, together with the revelatory status of his words; see 'The Transfiguration', 148.

52. As for Mk 3.13-19, while there are some similarities between this passage and 28.16-20, they serve to explain why Mt omitted the pericope (i.e. he had plans to close his Gospel with a mountain commissioning of his own) rather than to demonstrate that he constructed his closing scene on the basis of this earlier Markan passage.

53. For example, the thought of Mt 11.27 is quite distinct from 28.16-20. What has been delivered (παρεδόθη, not ἐδόθη) to the Son in the former passage is not ἐξουσία, but knowledge of the Father.

54. Cf. Hubbard, *The Matthean Redaction*, p. 69, 73; Frankemölle, *Jahwebund*, p. 60.

55. E.g. Bornkamm, 'Der Auferstandene und der Irdische', 171; Osborne, 'Redaction Criticism and the Great Commission', 76f.

56. E.g. Lohmeyer, '"Mir ist gegeben alle Gewalte!"', 24f., 44; Davies, *Setting*, pp. 85f.; Hubbard, *The Matthean Redaction*, pp. 92-98; Perrin, *Resurrection*, pp. 51f.; Cox, *Matthew*, p. 188; Gundry, *Matthew*, pp. 593f.; but cf. Trilling, *Das wahre Israel*, p. 24.

57. The verb ἐντελλέσθαι is frequently found in LXX Dt, particularly in relative clauses of the form 'which I have commanded you'.

58. See Smyth, 'Resurrection as Theophany'. However, his attempt to establish Sinai typology on formal grounds, by arguing that all of Mt 28 is patterned after the Sinai theophany of Ex 19–20, cannot stand. The most

serious problem with such an attempt is the fact that the supposedly theophanic elements (earthquake, lightning; vv. 2f.) are associated not with the 'apparition' of Christ in vv. 16-20, but with the 'preparation for rendezvous' in vv. 1f.

59. That it is Christ himself who speaks sets this passage apart from typical enthronement hymns. Moreover, enthronement is not described, but only reported in v. 18b. In fact, the focus of the passage is not on v. 18b (i.e. on something done to Jesus) but on the commandment given to the disciples in vv. 19-20a. Cf. Hubbard, *The Matthean Redaction*, p. 9.

60. Cf. Bornkamm, 'Die Auferstandene und die Irdische', 174f.

61. See above, pp. 46f., 64.

62. For a discussion of this passage, see above, pp. 68f.

63. E.g. LXX Dan 3.97; Sir 17.2; 1 Macc 1.13; 10.6, 8, 32; 11.58; Mk 6.7; 11.28 par.; Mt 9.8; Lk 4.6; 10.19; Jn 5.27; 19.11; Rev 2.26.

64. ἐξουσία does not appear in the Pentateuch, and only rarely in the former and latter Prophets (2 Ki 20.13; Is 39.2; Jer 28(51).28 [A L]). It appears more frequently in the Writings, especially Daniel (23 times), and also in the apocryphal books.

65. See above, n. 64.

66. ἐξουσία generally renders the Aramaic שלטן in Daniel, and the Hebrew ממשלה elsewhere. But ממשלה is also translated as ἀρχή, βασιλεία, δεσποτεία, δυναστεία, κατάρχειν, οἰκονομία, and στρατιά. This suggests that ἐξουσία might have been used more frequently in the LXX if the translation had been done later.

67. The last line of which reads ὡς σκεῦος κεραμέως συντρίψεις αὐτούς.

68. See above, pp. 43f., 63f.

69. Above, pp. 44, 63f.

70. E.g. in the 'Servant Songs' of Is 42.4; 49.6; 51.4f.

71. Amos 9.11, where the salvation of πάντα τὰ ἔθνη is predicated on the restoration of ἡ σκηνὴ Δαυίδ, is the only possible exception.

72. Is 66.18-20; Jer 3.17; Zech 14.16; Tob 14.6.

73. E.g. Mic 4.1-4; Zech 2.10-12; 8.23; Tob 13.11; Sib Or 3.710-719, 772-775.

74. A heated discussion has developed concerning the meaning of πάντα τὰ ἔθνη in v. 19. Does it mean *Gentiles* (i.e. exclusive of Israel), as argued by D.R.A. Hare and D.J. Harrington, '"Make Disciples of All the Gentiles" (Matt. 28.19)', *CBQ* 37 (1975), 359-69; Walker, *Heilsgeschichte*, pp. 111f.; Lange, *Das Erscheinen des Auferstandenen*, pp. 302-305; and others? Or does it mean *nations* (i.e. inclusive of Israel), as argued by Trilling, *Das wahre Israel*, pp. 12-14; J.P. Meier, 'Nations or Gentiles in Matthew 28.19?', *CBQ* 39 (1977), 94-102; Hubbard, *The Matthean Redaction*, p. 84; Hahn, *Mission in the New Testament*, p. 125; Zumstein, 'Matthieu 28.16-20', 26; O'Brien, 'The Great Commission', 73-75; Brown, 'The Two-fold Representation of the Mission', 29; Schmid, *Matthäus*, p. 391? The heat arises not from the

meaning of the term itself, but from the interpretation placed on Mt's use of the term here by some in the former group—viz. that at the end of his Gospel, Mt abandons the Jews entirely and turns his face towards the Gentiles, who have now replaced Israel in *Heilsgeschichte*. We must comment on Matthean *Heilsgeschichte* at more length below. Suffice it to say here that the heat can be dissipated from the discussion by the observation that even if ἔθνη here means Gentiles, the command to preach to the Jews has already been given (ch. 10) and remains valid until the coming of the Son of Man (v. 23), i.e. until the *parousia*; cf. Hahn, *Mission in the New Testament*, p. 128. As for 28.19, while it is probable that Israel is not excluded (for parallels, cf. Mt 24.9; 25.32; Lk 24.47), since the extension of the mission to the Gentiles is the new thing here, this is where the emphasis has been placed.

75. Cf. Malina, 'Literary Structure and Form', 89f.; O'Brien, 'The Great Commission', 72. For other Matthean examples of this construction, see 2.8; 9.13; 10.7; 11.4.

76. Only in Mt do we find the terms 'the holy city' (4.5; 27.53) and 'the city of the great king' (5.35); cf. 23.16-22.

77. Brown has convincingly demonstrated that the allusions in Mt 2 to the eschatological pilgrimage of the Gentiles are due to Matthean redaction; see *The Birth of the Messiah*, pp. 165-201, esp. 187f.

78. E.g. LXX Is 35.10; 56.8; 60.4; 66.18; Jer 3.17; Mic 2.12; 4.6; Zech 2.6; 2 Macc 2.7; Tob 13.13; 1 Bar 4.37; *Life Jer.* 11-12; ἐπισυνάγω is used in the same way in 2 Macc 1.27; 2.18. Cf. Jeremias, *Jesus' Promise to the Nations*, p. 64.

79. Cf. de Ridder, *Dispersion*, pp. 51f.

80. While a full study of the Zion complex of ideas in Mt lies outside the scope of the present study, it is clear that Jerusalem and temple play a markedly different role in Mt than they do in Luke–Acts. For the third evangelist, Jerusalem and temple have independent theological significance: Jerusalem is of necessity the place where saving events occur (e.g. Lk 13.33), and it is the scene of significant events at which Jesus is not present (e.g. Lk 1.5-23; 24.49, 52f.; Acts 1.4; 2.1-4). In Mt, Jesus is the locus of eschatological fulfilment; any significance attached to Jerusalem and temple is derivative.

81. While both את and עם appear in this context in the MT, the LXX followed by the NT uses only μετά of the divine presence.

82. E.g. Abraham (Gen 21.22); Isaac (Gen 26.3, 24); Jacob (Gen 28.15; 31.3); Joseph (Gen 39.2, 21, 23; 48.21); Moses (Ex 33.14f.); Joshua (Dt 31.23); David (2 Sam 7.3, 9).

83. E.g. Dt 2.7; 20.4; 31.6, 8; 1 Ki 8.57; 2 Chron 36.23; Hag 1.13; Is 41.10; 43.2, 5; Jer 15.20; 42.11; 46.28.

84. *God and Temple*.

85. E.g. Dt 12.5, 11, 21; 14.23f.; 1 Ki 8.27-30; 2 Chron 6.18-21.

86. On both points, see Clements, *God and Temple*, pp. 79-99.

87. Reading the singular הר on the basis of the LXX and Targum readings; see above, p. 229 n.81.

88. See also the promise of God's presence in Sib Or 3.785-787 ('virgin' can only be a reference to Jerusalem).

89. Green (*Matthew*, 230) rightly recognizes that in v. 20 the restored temple has been replaced as the locus of God's presence, but he is wrong in suggesting that the new locus is to be found in the Gentile mission.

Notes to Chapter 12

1. Indeed, the most extensive study of Mt's mountain scenes to date (Lange, *Das Erscheinen des Auferstandenen*, pp. 392-445) has been carried out on the assumption that this is precisely the case (see esp. pp. 441-45). For our introduction of the distinction between the literary and theological aspects of the mountain motif, see above, p. 5.

2. As Brown has observed, it is not necessary to make theology and tradition sharply antithetical: 'It is perfectly logical to think that primitive Christian theology was built up on what was actually contained in the tradition, and that that is why the details fit the theology' (*John*, I, p. 245).

3. So Strecker, *Der Weg der Gerechtigkeit*, p. 98; Schmauch, *Orte der Offenbarung*, pp. 74-77.

4. Jn 6.3 is a passing reference which has not really engaged the attention of the evangelist.

5. Since in Mt 14.23 Jesus goes alone to the mountain to pray, this seventh occurrence of the mountain setting in Mt stands outside the pattern which has been outlined here. Some scholars have attempted to find in the more extended passage Mt 14.22-33 similarities with other Matthean mountain passages. Kingsbury notes, for example, that, in contrast to Mk, Mt brings Son of God christology into the conclusion of the account of the walking on the water (Mt 14.33; cf. Mk 6.51f.; 'Form and Message of Matthew', 21). Lange also suggests that in this whole account we see Jesus coming to his disciples from the mountain with the same type of aid which was promised on the Mountain of Commissioning (*Das Erscheinen des Auferstandenen*, pp. 404f.). Since the mountain is not the setting for the whole of 14.22-33, however, it is not at all certain that these themes have been deliberately brought into association with Mt's 'Jesus on the mountain' motif. It seems safer to conclude that Mt 14.23 is just a traditional reference that Mt has retained without incorporating it into his mountain motif. It was not inimical to his purposes, and hence—in contrast to the mountain setting of Jesus' encounter with demons and pigs (Mk 5.11)—did not need to be omitted. But because it was not the setting for an extended event in the ministry of Jesus, Mt was content to let it stand outside the pattern which he constructed with the other six extended passages. Gundry's argument that Mt's few redactional changes in 14.23 (ἀνέβη, κατ' ἰδίαν, μόνος) are the

result of an interest in Moses typology is not convincing; see *Matthew*, p. 297.

6. The expression is that of Michel, 'Der Abschluss des Matthäus-evangeliums', 21.

7. See Justin, *1 Apol.* 39; *Dial.* 109; Irenaeus, *Ag. Her.* 4.34.4; Tertullian, *Marc.* 3.21; 4.1; Origen, *Cels.* 5.33.

8. 2 Pet 1.18; Apoc. Pet. 15 (*NTApoc*, II, p. 680); Acts Pet. 20 (*NTApoc*, II, p. 302).

9. The Mountain of Transfiguration seen as the new covenant counterpart to Sinai: Tertullian, *Marc.* 4.22; the mountain of prayer (Lk 6.12) seen in the light of Is 40.9: Tertullian, *Marc.* 4.13; Jesus' spending the night on the Mount of Olives (Lk 21.37) seen as a fulfilment of Zech 14.4: Tertullian, *Marc.* 4.39.

10. Clement, *Prot.* 1; *Paed.* 1.10; *Str.* 6.14; 7.10; Tertullian, *Jud.* 3; *Marc.* 3.21; Origen, *Princ.* 4.1.22; *Cels.* 5.33; 7.29; *Comm. Jn.* 10.26; Cyprian, *Ep.* 74.1; *Test.* 2.16-18. Lactantius, *Inst.* 4.17.

11. See above, pp. 74, 77-79, 83.

12. W.D. Davies has come to a similar conclusion on the wider question of the NT interpretation of the concept of the 'holy land':

> The New Testament finds holy space wherever Christ is or has been: it personalizes 'holy space' in Christ who, as a figure of History, is rooted in the land... For the holiness of place, Christianity has fundamentally, though not consistently, substituted the holiness of the Person: it has Christified holy space (*The Gospel and the Land*, pp. 367f.; cf. Schmauch, *Orte der Offenbarung*, pp. 45, 67, 78).

It is in this perspective that the question of the significance of Galilee in Mt's mountain motif is to be seen. Mt's three unique mountain passages (4.23–5.1; 15.29-31; 28.16-20) are all located in Galilee, and there can be little doubt in light of Mt 4.12-16 that he attached special significance to Jesus' ministry there. But Mt does not see Galilee as a special 'land of salvation' in the absolute sense that Lohmeyer, Lightfoot and Marxsen have argued for the Markan situation. What significance Galilee possesses for Mt derives from Jesus' presence and ministry there. It is because of this fact that Mt is able to join mountain scenes from different geographical locations (Galilee, the wilderness of Judea, Caesarea Philippi (?), Mount of Olives) into a literary and theological unity. The common feature of the presence of Jesus on these mountains more than compensates for the differences in geographical location. For a discussion (with bibliography) of the place of Galilee in Mt which argues for a similar interpretation, see G. Stemberger, 'Galilee—Land of Salvation?', Appendix IV in Davies, *The Gospel and the Land*, pp. 409-38.

Notes to Chapter 13

1. For a concise summary of the discussion, see Kingsbury, *Matthew*, pp. 40-42.

2. Since we will be suggesting a different approach, it will be sufficient to direct the reader to Kingsbury for details. To his list of those who see κύριος as the most significant Matthean title, add Betz, 'Jesus as Divine Man', 125. On Son/Son of God, see further Albright, *Matthew*, p. clviii; Nolan, *The Royal Son of God*.

3. See *Jesus in the Gospel of Matthew*, esp. p. 46.

4. *Jahwebund*, pp. 169f.

5. Viz. 1.22f.; 2.15, 17f., 23; 4.14-16; 8.17; 12.17-21; 13.35; 21.4f.; 27.9f.

6. This general insight on which Redaction Criticism is based is especially true in the case of Mt; cf. Trilling, *Das wahre Israel*, pp. 3-5.

7. *Pace* Harnack; cf. Trilling, *ibid.*, p. 12.

8. On ecclesiology, in addition to Trilling, *ibid.*, and Frankemölle, *Jahwebund*, see Ellis, *Matthew*, pp. 113-25; Martin, 'The Church in Matthew'; K. Tagawa, 'People and Community in the Gospel of Matthew', *NTS* 16 (1969-70), 149-62. On salvation history, see Walker, *Heilsgeschichte*; Strecker, 'The Concept of History in Matthew'; Meier, 'Salvation History in Matthew'; Senior, 'The Ministry of Continuity'; Kingsbury, *Matthew*, pp. 25-36; Ingelaere, 'Structure de Matthieu et histoire du salut'.

9. See 'The Gentile Bias in Matthew', and above, pp. 14f. Cf. Gaston, 'The Messiah of Israel as Teacher of the Gentiles', in which all these passages come into discussion.

10. For a development of this position starting with 21.33-46 see Trilling, *Das wahre Israel*, pp. 37-47; for a similar development based on 22.1-14 see Walker, *Heilsgeschichte*, p. 9.

11. E.g. Trilling (*Das wahre Israel*, pp. 12-14) and Ellis (*Matthew*, pp. 119f.) still see a continuing mission to Israel.

12. Succinct summaries of this position can be found in Walker, *Heilsgeschichte*, pp. 9f.; Ellis, *Matthew*, pp. 114f. In addition to these writings and the works by Strecker, Gaston, Trilling and Clark cited in preceding footnotes, this approach is also taken by Nepper-Christensen, *Das Matthäusevangelium*; Rohde, *Rediscovering*, p. 87; Hare and Harrington, '"Make Disciples of All the Gentiles"'; Senior, 'The Ministry of Continuity', 675; van Tilborg, *Jewish Leaders*, p. 72.

13. Cf. the title of his Part I: 'Die Krisis Israels'.

14. Particularly 3.7-10; 8.5-12; 13.10-17; 15.13f.; 19.30–20.16; 21.18f., 28-32, 33-46; 22.1-14; 23.37-39; 27.25.

15. The term *massa perditionis* is used in this sense by Walker, *Heilsgeschichte*, p. 10.

16. For studies that treat at least some of these terms, see Minear, 'Disciples and Crowds'; van Tilborg, *Jewish Leaders*, pp. 142-65; Kingsbury, *Parables*, pp. 24-28; Walker, *Heilsgeschichte*, pp. 16-38.

17. See above, pp. 114f.

18. Note the redactional touches in 9.1-8, 32-34; 12.22-29; 21.46; 22.32f.

19. Note particularly 3.7 and 23.1f.

20. Van Tilborg (*Jewish Leaders*, p. 159) rightly recognizes that Mt does not treat the ὄχλοι in this way. But cf. Strecker ('The Concept of History in Matthew') who interprets the ὄχλοι data in a purely historicizing way. In his view, the positive response of the crowds, along with the Jewish mission itself, are present only to make the salvation-historical point; they have no significance at the level of the Matthean *Sitz im Leben*.

21. In addition to the statement—taken over from Mk (15.10)—that the leaders delivered up Jesus out of jealousy, Mt indicates some reluctance on the part of the crowds by stating that it was necessary for the leaders to *persuade* (ἔπεισαν) them (27.20; cf. Mk 15.11—ἀνέσεισαν, i.e. 'stirred them up').

22. Cf. J.A. Comber, 'The Verb *Therapeuō* in Matthew's Gospel', *JBL* 97 (1978), 433f.

23. Cf. Walker, *Heilsgeschichte*, pp. 16-38, where οἱ ὄχλοι are ignored completely in the discussion of 'Israel' in Matthew; cf. also van Tilborg, who recognizes the distinction between the leaders and the crowds even in the Passion Narrative (*Jewish Leaders*, p. 159), but assumes that all statements directed at the leaders are valid for the whole of 'Israel'.

24. We cannot attempt to demonstrate here how such an interpretation is borne out by a study of the Matthean data. Yet a word should be said about the important passage 21.43. When Trilling's point (*Das wahre Israel*, p. 43)—that if Mt wanted to speak of *Gentiles* here he would have used the plural ἔθνη; ἔθνος in the singular refers to the Church, in the sense of the 'holy nation' of 1 Pet 2.9—is observed, then this passage falls within the lines of interpretation laid out here: the reaction of the leaders and the crowds is sharply distinguished (v. 46); the parable of rejection is directed at the leaders (v. 45), whose place is to be taken by the Church (v. 43); the salvation-historical position of the crowds is left undefined.

25. Meier makes an important beginning in the redressing of the situation with his article: 'Salvation-History in Matthew: In Search of a Starting Point'.

26. Cf. Kingsbury, *Matthew*, pp. 35f.

27. Hence the ὄχλοι can remain an indeterminate quantity, for Mt has no need of a remnant doctrine.

28. Meier argues (in 'Salvation-History in Matthew') that the death-resurrection complex be seen in its totality as *die Wende der Zeit*. But while his defence of such a position contains many valuable insights, the fact that it obscures the absolute importance of 28.16-20 and fails to take into account the important place of fulfilment throughout Jesus' career, renders it unpersuasive; cf. Kingsbury, *Matthew*, pp. 34f.

29. A two-stage view of salvation history is also defended by Kingsbury (*Matthew*, pp. 25-27) and Ingelaere ('Structure de Matthieu et histoire de salut', 32).

30. Walker (*Heilsgeschichte*, p. 115) even uses the term '*die Mitte der Zeit*'.

For similar criticisms of such an approach, see Hummel, *Auseinandersetzung*, p. 168; Tagawa, 'People and Community', 152; Ingelaere, 'Structure de Matthieu et histoire de salut', 19f.

31. See S. Brown, 'The Matthean Community and the Gentile Mission', *NovT* 22 (1980), 193-221; 'The Two-fold Representation of the Mission in Matthew's Gospel'.

32. See, e.g., 'The Two-fold Representation of the Mission', 23-25.

33. For such a description of Jerusalem's approach to salvation history and mission, see J. Munck, *Paul and the Salvation of Mankind*, trans. F. Clarke (London: SCM, 1959), p. 272; K.F. Nickle, *The Collection: A Study in Paul's Strategy* (SBT, 48; London: SCM, 1966), pp. 130-32.

34. *Resurrection*, p. 56.

BIBLIOGRAPHY

1. Texts, Tools and Reference Works Cited

Bowker, J. *The Targums and Rabbinic Literature*. Cambridge: University Press, 1969.

Brown, S. 'A Critical Edition and Translation of the Ancient Samaritan Defter (i.e. Liturgy) and a Comparison of It with Early Jewish Liturgy'. Ph.D. Dissertation, University of Leeds, 1955.

Budge, E.A.W., trans. and ed. *The Cave of Treasures*. London: Religious Tract Society, 1927.

Charlesworth, J. *The Pseudepigrapha and Modern Research*. SBL Septuagint and Cognate Studies, 7. Missoula, Mont.: Scholars Press, 1976.

Dalman, G. *Aramäisch-Neuhebräisches Handwörterbuch*. 2 Aufl. Frankfurt: J. Kauffmann Verlag, 1922.

Diez Macho, A. *Neophyti 1*. Vol. 2. Madrid, Barcelona: Consejo Superior de investigaciones cientificas, 1970.

Etheridge, J.W. *The Targums of Onkelos and Jonathan ben Uzziel on the Pentateuch with Fragments of the Jerusalem Targum*. New York: Ktav, 1968 [1862-65].

Fitzmyer, J.A. *The Genesis Apocryphon of Qumran Cave 1*. 2nd edn. Rome: Biblical Institute Press, 1971.

Friedlander, G., trans. and ed. *Pirke de R. Eliezer*. New York: Hermon Press, 1965.

Jastrow, M. *Dictionary of the Targumim, the Talmud Babli and Yerushalmi, and the Midrashic Literature*. New York: Pardes, 1950 [1903].

Kraeling, C.H. *The Synagogue*. Part I of *The Excavations at Dura-Europos. Final Report VIII*. Edited by A.R. Bellinger *et al.* New Haven: Yale University Press, 1956.

Levy, J. *Wörterbuch über die Talmudim und Midraschim*. Edited by L. Goldschmidt. 2 Aufl. Berlin und Wien: Benjamin Harz Verlag, 1924.

Macdonald, J., trans. and ed. *Memar Marqah: The Teaching of Marqah*. 2 vols. BZAW, 84. Berlin: Töpelmann, 1963.

McNamara, M. *Targum and Testament*. Grand Rapids: Eerdmans, 1972.

Torrey, C.C. *The Lives of the Prophets*. SBL Monograph Series, 1. Philadelphia: Society of Biblical Literature, 1946.

Vermes, G. *The Dead Sea Scrolls in English*. Harmondsworth: Penguin Books, 1968.

Wernberg-Møller, P. *The Manual of Discipline: Translated and Annotated with an Introduction*. Leiden: Brill, 1957.

Yadin, Y. *The Temple Scroll*. 3 vols. Jerusalem: Israel Exploration Society, 1977.

2. Background

i. *Literature Dealing with Sacred Mountains and Related Themes*

Alfrink, B. 'Der Versammlungsberg in äussersten Norden (Isa. 14)', *Bib* 14 (1933), 41-67.

Anderson, B.W. 'The Place of Shechem in the Bible', *BA* 20 (1957), 10-19.

Barrois, G.A. 'Olives, Mount of', *IDB*, III, 596-99.

— 'Zion', *IDB*, IV, 959f.

Boehmer, J. 'Der Gottesberg Tabor', *BZ* 23 (1935–36), 333-41.

Bowman, J.W. 'Armageddon', *IDB*, I, 226f.

Burrows, E. 'Some Cosmological Patterns in Babylonian Religion'. In *The Labyrinth*, pp. 45-70. Edited by S.H. Hooke. London: SPCK, 1935.

Butterworth, E.A.S. *The Tree at the Navel of the Earth*. Berlin: W. de Gruyter, 1970.

Cadell, H. and R. Rémondon. 'Sens et emplois de τὸ ὄρος dans les documents papyrologiques', *Revue des Etudes Grecques* 80 (1967), 343–49.

Carlson, R.A. 'Elie à l'Horeb', *VT* 19 (1969), 416-39.

Causse, A. 'Le mythe de la nouvelle Jérusalem du Deutéro-Esaie à la IIIᵉ Sibylle', *RHPR* 18 (1938), 377-414.

Clements, R.E. *God and Temple*. Oxford: Blackwell, 1965.

Clifford, R.J. *The Cosmic Mountain in Canaan and the Old Testament*. Harvard Semitic Monograph Series, 4. Cambridge, Mass.: Harvard University Press, 1972.

Cohn, R.L. 'Mountains and Mount Zion', *Judaism* 26 (1977), 97-115.

— 'The Sacred Mountain in Ancient Israel'. Ph.D. Dissertation, Stanford University, 1974.

Daniélou, J. 'Le symbolisme cosmique du temple de Jérusalem chez Philon et Josèphe'. In *Le Symbolisme cosmique des monuments religieux*, pp. 83-90. Rome: Istituto Italiano per Il Medio ed Estremo, 1957.

Eliade, M. *Cosmos and History: The Myth of the Eternal Return*. Translated by W.R. Trask. New York: Harper, 1959.

Gärtner, B.E. *The Temple and the Community in Qumran and the New Testament*. SNTS Monograph Series, 1. Cambridge: University Press, 1965.

Hamerton-Kelly, R.G. 'The Temple and the Origins of Jewish Apocalyptic', *VT* 20 (1970), 1-15.

Hayes, J.H. 'The Tradition of Zion's Inviolability', *JBL* 82 (1963), 419-26.

Jeremias, Joachim. 'Golgotha und die heilige Felsen: Eine Untersuchung zur Symbolsprache des Neuen Testamentes', Αγγελος 2 (1926), 74-128.

Jeremias, Johannes. *Der Gottesberg*. Gütersloh: C. Bertelmann, 1919.

Kingsbury, E.C. 'The Theophany *TOPOS* and the Mountain of God', *JBL* 86 (1967), 205-10.

Levenson, J.D. *Theology of the Program of Restoration of Ezekiel 40-48*. Harvard Semitic Monograph Series, 10. Missoula, Mont.: Scholars Press, 1976.

Lewy, J. 'Tabor, Tibar, Atabyros', *HUCA* 23 (1950-51), 357-86.

MacCulloch, J.A. 'Mountains, Mountain Gods'. In *Encyclopaedia of Religion and Ethics*, VIII, 863-68. Edited by J. Hastings. New York: Scribners, 1916.

McKelvey, R.J. *The New Temple: The Church in the New Testament*. London: Oxford University Press, 1969.

McNicol, A.J. 'The Eschatological Temple in the Qumran Pesher 4QFlorilegium 1.1-7', *Ohio Journal of Religious Studies* 5 (1977), 133-41.

Margulis, B. 'Weltbaum und Weltberg in Ugaritic Literature: Notes and Observations on RŠ 24.245', *ZAW* 86 (1974), 1-23.

Metzger, M. 'Himmlische und irdische Wohnstatt Jahwes', *UF* 2 (1970), 139-58.

Müller, W. *Die Heilige Stadt: Roma quadrata, himmlisches Jerusalem und die Mythe vom Weltnabel*. Stuttgart: Kohlhammer Verlag, 1961.

Parke, H.W. *A History of the Delphic Oracle*. Oxford: Blackwell, 1939.

Patai, R. *Man and Temple in Ancient Jewish Myth and Ritual*. New York: Thomas Nelson and Sons, 1947.

Porteous, N.W. 'Jerusalem–Zion: The Growth of a Symbol'. In *Verbannung und Heimkehr*, pp. 235-52. Edited by A. Kuschke. Tübingen: J.C.B. Mohr (Paul Siebeck), 1961.

von Rad, G. 'The City on the Hill'. In his *The Problem of the Hexateuch and Other Essays*, pp. 232-42. Translated by E.W. Trueman Dicken. Edinburgh and London: Oliver and Boyd, 1966.

Roberts, J.J.M. 'The Davidic Origin of the Zion Tradition', *JBL* 92 (1973), 329-44.

Schäfer, P. 'Tempel und Schöpfung. Zur Interpretation einiger Heiligtumstraditionen in der rabbinischen Literatur', *Kairos* 16 (1974), 122-33.

Schmidt, H. *Der heilige Fels in Jerusalem*. Tübingen: J.C.B. Mohr (Paul Siebeck), 1933.

Schmidt, K.L. 'Jerusalem als Urbild und Abbild', *ErJb* 18 (1950), 207-48.

Schreiner, J. *Sion–Jerusalem: Jahwes Königssitz*. München: Kösel Verlag, 1963.

Siegman, E.F. 'The Stone Hewn from the Mountain (Daniel 2)', *CBQ* 18 (1956), 364-79.

Sperling, D. 'Mount, Mountain', *IDBSup*, 608f.

Strugnell, J. 'The Angelic Liturgy at Qumran–4Q serek šîrôt 'ôlat haššabāt', *VTSup* 7 (1960), 318-45.

Talmon, S. 'The Biblical Concept of Jerusalem', *JES* 8 (1971), 300-16.

— 'הר', *TDOT*, III, 427-47.

Terrien, S. 'The Omphalos Myth and Hebrew Religion', *VT* 20 (1970), 315-38.

de Vaux, R. 'Jerusalem and the Prophets'. In *Interpreting the Prophetic Tradition*, pp. 275-300. Edited by H.M. Orlinsky. New York: Ktav, 1969.

Wanke, G. *Die Zionstheologie der Korachiten*. BZAW, 97. Berlin: Töpelmann, 1966.

Warren, C. 'Golgotha'. *Dictionary of the Bible*, II, 226f. Edited by J. Hastings. New York: Scribners, 1903.

Wensinck, A.J. *The Ideas of the Western Semites concerning the Navel of the Earth*. Amsterdam: Johannes Müller, 1916.

Wildberger, H. 'Die Völkerwallfahrt zum Zion. Jes. ii 1-5', *VT* 7 (1957), 62-81.

Wright, G.R.H. 'The Mythology of pre-Israelite Shechem', *VT* 20 (1970), 75-82.

ii. *Other*

Anderson, A.A. *The Book of Psalms*. 2 vols. New Century Bible. London: Oliphants, 1972.

Baillet, M. 'Fragments araméens de Qumrân 2: Description de la Jérusalem nouvelle', *RB* 62 (1955), 222-45.

Beare, F.W. 'Greek Religion and Philosophy', *IDB*, II, 487-500.

Beyerlin, W. *Origins and History of the Oldest Sinaitic Traditions*. Translated by S. Rudman. Oxford: University Press, 1965.

Bowman, J. *The Samaritan Problem: Studies in the Relationship of Samaritanism, Judaism, and Early Christianity*. Translated by A.M. Johnson. Pittsburgh: Pickwick Press, 1975.

Braude, W.G. *Jewish Proselytizing in the First Five Centuries of the Common Era*. Providence, R.I.: Brown University Press, 1940.

Bright, J. *A History of Israel*. 2nd edn. London: SCM Press, 1972.

— *Jeremiah*. Anchor Bible. Garden City, N.Y.: Doubleday, 1965.

Büchler, A. 'Die Schauplätze des Bar-Kochbakrieges und die auf diesen bezogenen jüdischen Nachrichten', *JQR* o.s. 16 (1904), 143-205.

Charles, R.H. *The Book of Enoch*. London: SPCK, 1917.

— *The Book of Jubilees*. London: A. & C. Black, 1902.

Childs, B.S. *Exodus: A Commentary*. London: SCM Press, 1974.

— *Introduction to the Old Testament as Scripture*. Philadelphia: Fortress Press, 1979.

— *Myth and Reality in the Old Testament*. London: SCM Press, 1960.

Coggins, R.J. *Samaritans and Jews: The Origins of Samaritanism Reconsidered*. Oxford: B. Blackwell, 1975.

Collins, J.J. *The Sibylline Oracles of Egyptian Judaism.* SBL Dissertation Series, 13. Missoula, Mont.: Scholars Press, 1974.

Cross, F.M. *Canaanite Myth and Hebrew Epic.* Cambridge, Mass.: Harvard University Press, 1973.

Dahood, M. *Psalms I: 1–50.* Anchor Bible. Garden City, N.Y.: Doubleday, 1966.

— *Psalms II: 51–100.* Anchor Bible. Garden City, N.Y.: Doubleday, 1968.

Eichrodt, W. *Ezekiel: A Commentary.* Translated by C. Quin. London: SCM Press, 1970.

Finkelstein, L. 'The Development of the Amidah', *JQR* n.s. 16 (1925–26), 1-43.

Flusser, D. 'Two Notes on the Midrash on 2 Sam 7', *IEJ* 9 (1959), 99-109.

Gaster, M. *The Samaritans.* London: Oxford University Press, 1925.

Goldstein, J.A. *I Maccabees: Introduction and Commentary.* Anchor Bible. Garden City, N.Y.: Doubleday, 1976.

Helfgott, B.W. *The Doctrine of Election in Tannaitic Literature.* New York: King's Crown Press, 1954.

Hengel, M. *Judaism and Hellenism.* Translated by J. Bowden. 2 vols. London: SCM Press, 1974.

Jeremias, J. 'Μωϋσῆς', *TDNT*, IV, 848-73.

Johnson, A.R. *Sacral Kingship in Ancient Israel.* Cardiff: University of Wales Press, 1955.

Jonge, M. de. 'Christian Influence in the Testaments of the Twelve Patriarchs'. In *Studies in the Testaments of the Twelve Patriarchs*, pp. 191-246. Edited by M. de Jonge. Leiden: Brill, 1975.

— 'Once More: Christian Influence in the Testaments of the Twelve Patriarchs', *NovT* 5 (1962), 311-19.

— *The Testaments of the Twelve Patriarchs.* Assen: van Gorcum, 1953.

Kaiser, O. *Isaiah 1–12: A Commentary.* Translated by R.A. Wilson. London: SCM Press, 1972.

— *Isaiah 13–39: A Commentary.* Translated by R.A. Wilson. London: SCM Press, 1974.

Kramer, S.N. *Sumerian Mythology.* 2nd edn. New York: Harper & Row, 1961.

L'Heureux, C.E. 'The Biblical Sources of the "Apostrophe to Zion"', *CBQ* 29 (1967), 60-74.

Macdonald, J. *The Theology of the Samaritans.* London: SCM Press, 1964.

Martin-Achard, R.A. *A Light to the Nations.* Translated by J.P. Smith. Edinburgh & London: Oliver & Boyd, 1962.

Mendenhall, G.E. 'Covenant Forms in Israelite Tradition', *BA* 17 (1954), 50-76.

Milgrom, J. 'The Temple Scroll', *BA* 41 (1978), 105-20.

Montgomery, J.A. *The Samaritans.* New York: Ktav, 1968 [1907].

Mowinckel, S. *The Psalms in Israel's Worship.* Translated by D.R. Ap-Thomas. 2 vols. Oxford: B. Blackwell, 1962.

Mullen, R. *The Latter-Day Saints: The Mormons Yesterday and Today.* Garden City, N.Y.: Doubleday, 1966.

Neusner, J. 'Judaism in a Time of Crisis: Four Responses to the Destruction of the Second Temple', *Judaism* 21 (1972), 313-27.

Nicholson, E.W. *Exodus and Sinai in History and Tradition.* Richmond, Va.: John Knox Press, 1973.

Nilsson, M.P. *Greek Piety.* Translated by H.J. Rose. Oxford: Clarendon Press, 1948.

Noth, M. *The History of Israel.* Translated by P.R. Ackroyd. 2nd edn. New York: Harper & Row, 1960.

— 'Jerusalem and the Israelite Tradition'. In his *The Laws in the Pentateuch and Other Essays*, pp. 132-44. Translated by D.R. Ap-Thomas. Edinburgh: Oliver and Boyd, 1966.

Pardee, D. 'A Restudy of the Commentary on Psalm 37 from Qumran Cave 4', *RevQ* 8 (1973–75), 163-94.

Perkins, P. *The Gnostic Dialogue.* New York, Toronto: Paulist Press, 1980.

Philonenko, M. *Les interpolations chrétiennes des Testaments des Douze Patriarches et les manuscrits de Qumran.* Paris: Presses Universitaires de France, 1960.

Priest, J.F. 'The Messiah and the Meal in 1QSa', *JBL* 82 (1963), 95-100.

Purvis, J.D. *The Samaritan Pentateuch and the Origin of the Samaritan Sect.* Cambridge, Mass.: Harvard University Press, 1968.

von Rad, G. 'The Form-Critical Problem of the Hexateuch'. In his *The Problem of the Hexateuch and Other Essays*, pp. 20-26. Translated by E.W. Trueman Dicken. Edinburgh & London: Oliver & Boyd, 1966.

— *Old Testament Theology.* Translated by D.M.G. Stalker. 2 vols. Edinburgh & London: Oliver & Boyd, 1962.

Reitzenstein, R. *Hellenistic Mystery-Religions: Their Basic Ideas and Significance.* Translated by J.E. Steely. Pittsburgh: Pickwick Press, 1978.

Rowley, H.H. *The Missionary Message of the Old Testament.* London: Carey Press, 1944.

— 'The Samaritan Schism in Legend and History'. In *Israel's Prophetic Heritage*, pp. 208-22. Edited by B.W. Anderson and W. Harrelson. New York: Harper & Bros., 1962.

—'Zadok and Nehushtan', *JBL* 58 (1939), 113-41.

Russell, D.S. *The Method and Message of Jewish Apocalyptic.* Philadelphia: Westminster Press, 1964.

Snaith, N.H. *The Jewish New Year Festival: Its Origin and Development.* London: SPCK, 1947.

Stegemann, H. 'Der Pešer Psalm 37 aus Höhle von Qumran (4QpPs37)', *RevQ* 4 (1963–64), 235-70.

Stone, M.E. 'The Concept of the Messiah in IV Ezra'. In *Religions in Antiquity: Essays in Memory of E.R. Goodenough*, pp. 295-312. Edited by J. Neusner. Leiden: Brill, 1968.

Strugnell, J. 'Notes en marge du volume V des "Discoveries in the Judean Desert of Jordan"', *RevQ* 7 (1969–72), 163-276.

Teeple, H.M. *The Mosaic Eschatological Prophet.* JBL Monograph Series, 10. Philadelphia: Society of Biblical Literature, 1957.

Thiering, B.E. '*Mebaqqer* and *Episkopos* in the Light of the Temple Scroll', *JBL* 100 (1981), 59-74.

Vermes, G. *Scripture and Tradition in Judaism: Haggadic Studies.* Leiden: Brill, 1961.

Weiser, A. *Introduction to the Old Testament.* Translated by D.M. Barton. London: Darton, Longman, and Todd, 1961.

— *The Psalms: A Commentary.* Translated by H. Hartwell. 2 vols. Philadelphia: Westminster Press, 1962.

Yadin, Y. 'The Temple Scroll', *BA* 30 (1967), 135-39.

3. Matthew

i. *Commentaries*

Albright, W.F., and C.S. Mann. *Matthew.* Anchor Bible. Garden City, N.Y.: Doubleday, 1971.

Allen, W.C. *A Critical and Exegetical Commentary on the Gospel according to St. Matthew.* International Critical Commentary. New York: Scribners, 1907.

Argyle, A.W. *The Gospel according to Matthew: Commentary.* The Cambridge Bible Commentary: NEB. Cambridge: University Press, 1963.

Beare, F.W. *The Gospel according to Matthew.* New York: Harper and Row, 1981.

Bonnard, P. *L'Evangile selon Saint Matthieu.* 2nd edn. Neuchâtel: Delachaux et Niestlé, 1970.

Cox, G.E.P. *The Gospel according to St. Matthew.* Torch Bible Commentaries. London: SCM Press, 1952.

Fenton, J.C. *The Gospel of St. Matthew.* Pelican Gospel Commentaries. Baltimore: Penguin Books, 1963.

Filson, F.V. *A Commentary on the Gospel according to St. Matthew.* Black's NT Commentaries. London: A. & C. Black, 1960.

Gaechter, P. *Das Matthäus Evangelium.* Innsbruck, Wien, München: Tyrolia Verlag, 1963.

Green, H.B. *The Gospel according to Matthew.* New Clarendon Bible. Oxford: University Press, 1975.

Grundmann, W. *Das Evangelium nach Matthäus.* Theologischer Handkommentar zum NT. Berlin: Evangelische Verlaganstalt, 1968.

Gundry, R.H. *Matthew: A Commentary on His Literary and Theological Art.* Grand Rapids: Eerdmans, 1982.

Hill, D. *The Gospel of Matthew.* New Century Bible. London: Oliphants, 1972.

Johnson, S.E. 'The Gospel according to St. Matthew: Introduction and Exegesis'. In *The Interpreter's Bible*, VII, 229-625. New York, Nashville: Abingdon Press, 1951.

Klostermann, E. *Das Matthäusevangelium.* Handbuch zum NT, 4. Tübingen: J.C.B. Mohr (Paul Siebeck), 1971.

Lagrange, M.-J. *Evangile selon Saint Matthieu.* Paris: Gabalda, 1948.

Lohmeyer, E. *Das Evangelium des Matthäus.* 4th edn. Edited by W. Schmauch. Kritisch-exegetischer Kommentar über das NT. Göttingen: Vandenhoeck und Ruprecht, 1967.

M'Neile, A.H. *The Gospel according to St. Matthew.* London: Macmillan, 1938.

Meier, J.P. *Matthew.* NT Message, 3. Wilmington, Del.: Michael Glazier, 1980.

Plummer, A. *An Exegetical Commentary on the Gospel according to St. Matthew.* London: Robert Scott, 1909.

Rienecker, F. *Das Evangelium des Matthäus.* Wuppertal: Verlag R. Brockhaus, 1953.

Robinson, T.H. *The Gospel of Matthew.* Moffatt NT Commentary. London: Hodder & Stoughton, 1951.

Schmid, J. *Das Evangelium nach Matthäus.* 4 Aufl. Regensburger NT. Regensburg: Verlag Friedrich Pustet, 1959.

Schniewind, J. *Das Evangelium nach Matthäus.* 9 Aufl. Das NT Deutsch. Göttingen: Vandenhoeck und Ruprecht, 1960.

Schweizer, E. *The Good News according to Matthew.* Translated by D.E. Green. London: SPCK, 1976.

Senior, D. *Invitation to Matthew.* Garden City, N.Y.: Doubleday, 1977.

Tasker, R.V.G. *The Gospel according to St. Matthew.* Tyndale NT Commentaries. Grand Rapids: Eerdmans, 1961.

Trilling, W. *The Gospel according to St. Matthew.* Translated by K. Smyth. New York: Herder and Herder, 1969.

Wellhausen, J. *Das Evangelium nach Matthäus.* Berlin: G. Reimer, 1904.

Wilkens, J. *Der König Israels: Eine Einführung in das Evangelium nach Matthäus.* 2 vols. Berlin: Furche Verlag, 1934.

ii. *Literature Pertaining to Matthew's Mountain Passages*

(a) Mt 4.8

Bowden-Smith, A.G. 'A Suggestion towards a Closer Study of the Significance of the Imagery of the Temptation', *ExpT* 47 (1935–36), 408-12.

Bretscher, P.G. 'The Temptation of Jesus in Matthew'. Th.D. Dissertation, Concordia Seminary, 1966.

Comisky, J.P. '"Begone, Satan!"', *BibTod* 58 (1972), 620-26.

Doble, P. 'The Temptations', *ExpT* 72 (1960–61), 91-93.

Dupont, J. 'L'origine du récit des tentations de Jésus au désert', *RB* 73 (1966), 30-76.

— *Les tentations de Jésus au désert*. Bruges: Desclée de Brouwer, 1968.

Farrer, A.M. *The Triple Victory: Christ's Temptations according to Saint Matthew*. London: Faith Press, 1965.

Feuillet, A. 'L'épisode de la Tentation d'après l'Evangile selon Saint Marc (1.12-13)', *EstBib* 19 (1960), 49-73.

Freeman, G.S. 'The Temptation', *ExpT* 48 (1936-37), 45.

Gerhardsson, B. *The Testing of God's Son (Mt 4.1-11): An Analysis of an Early Christian Midrash*. Translated by J. Toy. Lund: Gleerup, 1966.

Graham, E. 'The Temptation in the Wilderness', *CQR* 162 (1961), 17-32.

Hoffmann, P. 'Die Versuchungsgeschichte in der Logienquelle. Zur Auseinandersetzung der Judenchristen mit dem politischen Messianismus', *BZ* 13 (1969), 207-23.

Holst, R. 'The Temptation of Jesus', *ExpT* 82 (1970-71), 343f.

Kelly, H.A. 'The Devil in the Desert', *CBQ* 26 (1964), 190-220.

Kirk, J.A. 'The Messianic Role of Jesus and the Temptation Narrative: A Contemporary Perspective', *EvQ* 44 (1972), 11-29, 91-102.

Mason, A. 'The Temptation in the Wilderness: A Possible Interpretation', *Theology* 4 (1922), 127-36.

Pokorný, P. 'The Temptation Stories and Their Intention', *NTS* 20 (1973-74), 115-27.

Powell, W. 'The Temptation', *ExpT* 72 (1960-61), 248.

Przybylski, B. 'The Role of Mt 3.13-4.11 in the Structure and Theology of the Gospel of Matthew', *BTB* 4 (1974), 222-35.

Riesenfeld, H. 'Le caractère messianique de la tentation au désert'. In *La venue du Messie: messianisme et eschatologie*, pp. 51-63. Edited by E. Massaux *et al.* Recherches Bibliques, 6. Bruges: Desclée de Brouwer, 1962.

Robinson, J.A.T. 'The Temptations'. In his *Twelve New Testament Studies*, pp. 53-60. London: SCM Press, 1962.

Smyth-Florentin, F. 'Jésus, le Fils du Père, vainqueur de Satan. Mt 4.1-11, Mc 1.12-13, Lc 4.1-13', *AssSeign* 14 (1973), 56-75.

Stegner, W.R. 'Wilderness and Testing in the Scrolls and in Matthew 4.1-11', *BR* 12 (1967), 18-27.

Taylor, A.B. 'Decision in the Desert: The Temptation of Jesus in the Light of Deuteronomy', *Int* 14 (1960), 300-309.

Thompson, G.H.P. 'Called-Proved-Obedient: A Study in the Baptism and Temptation Narratives of Matthew and Luke', *JTS* 11 (1960), 1-12.

Trémel, B. 'Des récits apocalyptiques: Baptême et Transfiguration', *LumVie* 23 (1974), 70-83.

(b) Mt 5.1 // 8.1

Bacon, B.W. *The Sermon on the Mount: Its Literary Structure and Didactic Purpose*. New York: Macmillan, 1902.

Bartsch, H.-W. 'Feldrede und Bergpredigt: Redaktionsarbeit in Luk. 6', *TZ* 16 (1960), 5-18.

Betz, H.D. 'The Sermon on the Mount: Its Literary Genre and Function', *JR* 59 (1979), 285-97.

Bowman, J.W., and R.W. Tapp. *The Gospel from the Mount.* Philadelphia: Westminster Press, 1957.

Campbell, K.M. 'The New Jerusalem in Matthew 5.14', *SJT* 31 (1978), 335-63.

Carré, H.B. 'Matthew 5.1 and Related Passages', *JBL* 42 (1923), 39-48.

Davies, W.D. *The Setting of the Sermon on the Mount.* Cambridge: University Press, 1964.

Dibelius, M. *The Sermon on the Mount.* New York: Scribners, 1940.

Dupont, J. *Les Béatitudes.* Vol. I: Louvain: E. Nauwelaerts, 1958. Vol. III: Paris: Gabalda, 1973.

Duprez, A. 'Le programme de Jésus selon Matthieu. Mt 4,12-23', *AssSeign* 34 (1973), 9-18.

Eichholz, G. *Auslegung der Bergpredigt.* 2 Aufl. Biblische Studien, 46. Neukirchen-Vluyn: Neukirchener Verlag, 1970.

Hoffmann, P. 'Die Stellung der Bergpredigt im Matthäusevangelium. Auslegung der Bergpredigt I', *BibLeb* 10 (1969), 57-65.

Kissinger, W.S. *The Sermon on the Mount: A History of Interpretation and Bibliography.* Metuchen, N.J.: Scarecrow Press, 1975.

Lachs, S.T. 'Some Textual Observations on the Sermon on the Mount', *JQR* 69 (1978), 98-111.

Mánek, J. 'On the Mount—On the Plain (Mt v. 1–Lk vi.17)', *NovT* 9 (1967), 124-31.

Marriott, H. *The Sermon on the Mount.* London: SPCK, 1925.

Neirynck, F. 'The Sermon on the Mount in the Gospel Synopsis', *EThL* 52 (1976), 350-57.

Perry, A.M. 'The Framework of the Sermon on the Mount', *JBL* 54 (1935), 103-15.

Riethmueller, O. 'The City on the Mount', *Student World* 30 (1937), 203-12.

Schnackenburg, R. '"Ihr seid das Salz der Erde, das Licht der Welt". Zu Mt 5,13-16'. In his *Schriften zum Neuen Testament*, pp. 177-200. München: Kösel-Verlag, 1971.

Skibbe, E.M. 'Pentateuchal Themes in the Sermon on the Mount', *LuthQ* 20 (1968), 44-51.

Souček, J.B. 'Salz der Erde und Licht der Welt: Zur Exegese von Matth. 5.13-16', *TZ* 19 (1963), 169-79.

Vaganay, L. 'L'absence du sermon sur la montagne chez Marc', *RB* 58 (1951), 5-46.

Windisch, H. *The Meaning of the Sermon on the Mount.* Translated by S. MacL. Gilmour. Philadelphia: Westminster Press, 1941.

Wrege, H.-T. *Die Überlieferungsgeschichte der Bergpredigt.* Tübingen: J.C.B. Mohr (Paul Siebeck), 1968.

(c) Mt 15.29

Boobyer, G.H. 'The Eucharistic Interpretation of the Miracles of the Loaves in St. Mark's Gospel', *JTS* 3 (1952), 161-71.

— 'The Miracles of the Loaves and the Gentiles in St. Mark's Gospel', *SJT* 6 (1953), 77-87.

Burkill, T.A. 'The Historical Development of the Story of the Syrophoenician Woman', *NovT* 9 (1967), 161-77.

— 'The Syrophoenician Woman: The Congruence of Mark 7.24-31', *ZNW* 57 (1966), 23-37.

Buse, I. 'The Gospel Accounts of the Feeding of the Multitudes', *ExpT* 74 (1963), 167-70.

Cerfaux, L. 'La section des pains (Mc 6.31–8.26; Mt 14.13–16.12)'. In *Synoptische Studien*, pp. 64-77. Edited by J. Schmid and A. Vögtle. München: Karl Zink Verlag, 1953.

Clavier, H. 'La multiplication des pains dans le ministère de Jésus', *StEv* 1 (1959), 441-57.

Farrer, A.M. 'Loaves and Thousands', *JTS* 4 (1953), 1-14.

Harrisville, R.A. 'The Woman of Canaan: A Chapter in the History of Exegesis', *Int* 20 (1966), 274-87.

Heising, A. 'Exegese und Theologie der alt- und neutestamentlichen Speiswunder', *ZKT* 86 (1964), 80-96.

— 'Das Kerygma der wunderbaren Fischvermehrung', *BibLeb* 10 (1969), 52-57.

Hiers, R.H. and C.A. Kennedy. 'The Bread and Fish Eucharist in the Gospels and Early Christian Art', *PRS* 3 (1976), 20-47.

Johnston, E.D. 'The Johannine Version of the Feeding of the Five Thousand— An Independent Tradition?' *NTS* 8 (1961–62), 151-54.

Knackstedt, J.K. 'Die beiden Brotvermehrungen im Evangelium', *NTS* 10 (1963–64), 309-35.

Légasse, S. 'L'épisode de la Cananéenne d'après Mt 15,21-28', *BLE* 73 (1972), 21-40.

Lohmeyer, E. 'Das Abendmahl in der Urgemeinde', *JBL* 56 (1937), 217-52.

Mánek, J. 'Mark viii.14-21', *NovT* 7 (1964), 10-14.

Montefiore, H.W. 'Revolt in the Desert? Mark vi.30ff.', *NTS* 8 (1961–62), 135-41.

Murphy-O'Connor, J. 'The Structure of Matthew XIV–XVII', *RB* 82 (1975), 360-84.

Negoiţă, A. and C. Daniel. 'L'énigme du levain. Ad Mc viii.15; Mt xvi.6; et Lc xii.1', *NovT* 9 (1967), 306-14.

Quiévreux, F. 'Le récit de la multiplication des pains dans le quatrième évangile', *RevSR* 41 (1967), 97-108.

Richardson, A. 'The Feeding of the Five Thousand; Mark 6.34-44', *Int* 9 (1955), 144-49.

Robinson, D.F. 'The Parable of the Loaves', *ATR* 39 (1957), 107-15.

Ryan, T.J. 'Matthew 15.29-31: An Overlooked Summary', *Horizons* 5 (1978), 31-42.

Shaw, A. 'The Marcan Feeding Narratives', *CQR* 162 (1961), 268-78.

Stauffer, E. 'Zum apokalyptischen Festmahl in Mk 6.34ff.', *ZNW* 46 (1955), 264-66.

Stegner, W.R. 'Lukan Priority in the Feeding of the Five Thousand', *BR* 21 (1976), 19-28.

Suriano, T. 'Eucharist Reveals Jesus: The Multiplication of the Loaves', *BibTod* 58 (1972), 642-51.

van Cangh, J.-M. 'Le thème des poissons dans les récits évangéliques de la multiplication des pains', *RB* 78 (1971), 71-83.

van Iersel, B. 'Die wunderbare Speisung und das Abendmahl in der synoptischen Tradition (Mk vi.35-44 par., viii.1-20 par)', *NovT* 7 (1964), 167-94.

Ziener, P.G. 'Die Brotwunder im Markusevangelium', *BZ* 4 (1960), 282-85.

(d) Mt 17.1 // 9

Baltensweiler, H. *Die Verklärung Jesu*. Zürich: Zwingli Verlag, 1959.

Boobyer, G.H. *St. Mark and the Transfiguration Story*. Edinburgh: T. & T. Clark, 1942.

Caird, G.B. 'The Transfiguration', *ExpT* 67 (1955–56), 291-94.

Carlston, C.E. 'Transfiguration and Resurrection', *JBL* 80 (1961), 233-40.

Coune, M. 'Radieuse Transfiguration. Mt 17,1-9; Mc 9,2-10; Lk 9,28-36', *AssSeign* 15 (1973), 44-84.

Dabeck, P. '"Siehe, es erschienen Moses und Elias" (Mt 17.3)', *Bib* 23 (1942), 175-89.

Daniel, F.H. 'The Transfiguration (Mk 9.2-13 and parallels). A Redaction Critical and Traditio-historical Study'. Ph.D. Dissertation, Vanderbilt University, 1976.

Daniélou, J. 'Le symbolisme eschatologique de la Fête des Tabernacles', *Irénikon* 31 (1958), 19-40.

Feuillet, A. 'Les perspectives propres à chaque évangéliste dans les récits de la transfiguration', *Bib* 39 (1958), 281-301.

Frieling, R. *Die Verklärung auf dem Berge: eine Studie zum Evangelienverständnis*. Stuttgart: Verlag Urachhaus, 1969.

Fuchs, A. 'Die Verklärungserzählung des Mk-Ev in der Sicht moderner Exegese', *TPQ* 125 (1977), 29-37.

Gerber, W. 'Die Metamorphose Jesu. Mk 9,2f par.', *TZ* 23 (1967), 385-95.

Kee, H.C. 'The Transfiguration in Mark: Epiphany or Apocalyptic Vision?' In *Understanding the Sacred Texts*, pp. 135-52. Edited by J. Reumann. Valley Forge, Pa.: Judson Press, 1972.

Kenny, A. 'The Transfiguration and the Agony in the Garden', *CBQ* 19 (1957), 444-52.

300   *Jesus on the Mountain*

Liefeld, W.L. 'Theological Motifs in the Transfiguration Narrative'. In *New Dimensions in New Testament Study*, pp. 162-79. Edited by R.N. Longenecker and M.C. Tenney. Grand Rapids: Zondervan, 1974.

Lohmeyer, E. 'Die Verklärung Jesu nach dem Markus-Evangelium', *ZNW* 21 (1922), 185-215.

McCurley, F.R. '"And After Six Days" (Mk 9.2): A Semitic Literary Device', *JBL* 93 (1974), 67-81.

Masson, C. 'La transfiguration de Jésus (Marc 9.2-13)', *RThPh* 97 (1964), 1-14.

Miquel, P. 'Le mystère de la Transfiguration', *QLP* 42 (1961), 194-223.

Müller, H.-P. 'Die Verklärung Jesu', *ZNW* 51 (1960), 56-64.

Müller, U.B. 'Die christologische Absicht des Markusevangeliums und die Verklärungsgeschichte', *ZNW* 64 (1973), 159-93.

Neyrey, J.H. 'The Apologetic Use of the Transfiguration in 2 Peter 1.16-21', *CBQ* 42 (1980), 504-19.

Nützel, J.M. *Die Verklärungserzählung im Markusevangelium*. Forschung zur Bibel, 6. Würzburg: Echter Verlag, 1973.

Pedersen, S. 'Die Proklamation Jesu als des eschatologischen Offenbarungsträgers (Mt. xvii.1-13)', *NovT* 17 (1975), 241-64.

Riesenfeld, H. *Jésus transfiguré. L'arrière-plan du récit évangélique de la transfiguration de Notre-Seigneur*. Copenhagen: Ejnar Munksgaard, 1947.

Roehrs, W.R. 'God's Tabernacles among Men: A Study of the Transfiguration', *CTM* 35 (1964), 18-25.

Sabbe, M. 'La rédaction du récit de la Transfiguration'. In *La Venue du Messie*, pp. 65-100. Edited by E. Massaux. Recherches Bibliques, 6. Bruges: Desclée de Brouwer, 1962.

Schmithals, W. 'Der Markusschluss, die Verklärungsgeschichte, und die Aussendung der Zwölf', *ZTK* 69 (1972), 379-411.

Stein, R. 'Is the Transfiguration (Mk 9.2-8) a Misplaced Resurrection-Account?', *JBL* 95 (1976), 79-96.

Thrall, M.E. 'Elijah and Moses in Mark's Account of the Transfiguration', *NTS* 16 (1969–70), 305-17.

Trites, A.A. 'The Transfiguration of Jesus: The Gospel in Microcosm', *EvQ* 51 (1979), 67-79.

Wagner, W.H. 'The Transfiguration and the Church', *LuthQ* 16 (1964), 343-48.

Ziesler, J.A. 'The Transfiguration Story and the Markan Soteriology', *ExpT* 81 (1969–70), 263-68.

(e) Mt 24.3

Beare, F.W. 'The Synoptic Apocalypse: Matthean Version'. In *Understanding the Sacred Texts*, pp. 115-33. Edited by J. Reumann. Valley Forge, Pa.: Judson Press, 1972.

Beasley-Murray, G.R. *A Commentary on Mark Thirteen*. London: Macmillan, 1957.

— *Jesus and the Future*. London: Macmillan, 1954.

Brown, S. 'The Matthean Apocalypse', *JSNT* 4 (1979), 2-27.

Conzelmann, H. 'Geschichte und Eschaton nach Mc 13', *ZNW* 50 (1959), 210-21.

Feuillet, A. 'La synthèse eschatologique de saint Matthieu (XXIV–XXV)', *RB* 56 (1949), 340-64; 57 (1950), 62-91, 180-211.

Grayston, K. 'The Study of Mark XIII', *BJRL* 56 (1974), 371-87.

Hartman, L. *Prophecy Interpreted: The Formulation of Some Jewish Apocalyptic Texts and of the Eschatological Discourse*. Translated by N. Tomkinson. Lund: Gleerup, 1966.

Lambrecht, J. 'The Parousia Discourse: Composition and Content in Mt. XXIV–XXV'. In *L'Evangile selon Matthieu*, pp. 309-42. Edited by M. Didier.

Gembloux: Duculot, 1972.

— *Die Redaktion der Markus-Apokalypse: Literatur Analyse und Strukturuntersuchung*. Rome: Päpstliches Bibelinstitut, 1967.

Neville, G. *The Advent Hope: A Study of the Context of Mark 13*. London: Darton, Longman and Todd, 1961.

Pesch, R. 'Eschatologie und Ethik: Auslegung von Mt 24.1-36', *BibLeb* 11 (1970), 223-38.

— *Naherwartungen: Tradition und Redaktion in Mark 13*. Düsseldorf: Patmos-Verlag, 1968.

(f) Mt 28.16

Alsup, J.E. *The Post-Resurrection Appearance Stories of the Gospel Tradition*. Stuttgart: Calwer Verlag, 1975.

Bornkamm, G. 'Der Auferstandene und der Irdische, Mt 28.16-20'. In *Zeit und Geschichte*, pp. 171-91. Edited by E. Dinkler. Tübingen: J.C.B. Mohr (Paul Siebeck), 1964.

Brooks, O.S. 'Matthew xxviii.16-20 and the Design of the First Gospel', *JSNT* 10 (1981), 2-18.

Chavasse, C. 'Not "the Mountain Appointed". Studies in Texts: Mt 28.16', *Theology* 74 (1971), 478.

Conybeare, F.C. 'The Eusebian Form of the Text Matth. 28,19', *ZNW* 2 (1901), 275-88.

Dodd, C.H. 'The Appearance of the Risen Christ: An Essay in Form-Criticism of the Gospels'. In *Studies in the Gospels*, pp. 9-35. Edited by D.E. Nineham. Oxford: B. Blackwell, 1955.

Ellis, I.P. '"But Some Doubted"', *NTS* 14 (1967–68), 574-80.

Evans, C.F. '"I Will Go Before You into Galilee"', *JTS* 5 (1954), 3-18.

Fuller, R.H. *The Formation of the Resurrection Narratives*. New York: Macmillan, 1971.

Giblin, C.H. 'A Note on Doubt and Reassurance in Mt. 28.16-20', *CBQ* 37 (1975), 68-75.

Hare, D.R.A. and D.J. Harrington, '"Make Disciples of All the Gentiles" (Mt. 28.19)', *CBQ* 37 (1975), 359-69.

Hubbard, B.J. *The Matthean Redaction of a Primitive Apostolic Commissioning: An Exegesis of Matthew 28.16-20*. SBL Dissertation Series, 19. Missoula, Mont.: Scholars Press, 1974.

Kingsbury, J.D. 'The Composition and Christology of Matt. 28.16-20', *JBL* 93 (1974), 573-84.

Kosmala, H. 'The Conclusion of Matthew', *ASTI* 4 (1965), 132-47.

Lange, J. *Das Erscheinen des Auferstandenen im Evangelium nach Matthäus*. Forschung zur Bibel, 11. Würzburg: Echter-Verlag, 1973.

Linnemann, E. 'Der (widergefundene) Markusschluss', *ZTK* 66 (1969), 255-87.

Lohmeyer, E. '"Mir ist gegeben alle Gewalt." Eine Exegese von Mt. 28,16-20'. In *In Memoriam Ernst Lohmeyer*, pp. 22-49. Edited by W. Schmauch. Stuttgart: Evangelisches Verlagswerk, 1951.

Luck, U. 'Herrenwort und Geschichte in Matth 28,16-20', *EvTh* 27 (1967), 494-508.

Malina, J.B. 'The Literary Structure and Form of Matt. xxviii.16-20', *NTS* 17 (1970–71), 87-103.

Meier, J.P. 'Nations or Gentiles in Matthew 28.19?', *CBQ* 39 (1977), 94-102.

— 'Salvation-History in Matthew: In Search of a Starting Point', *CBQ* 37 (1975), 203-15.

— 'Two Disputed Questions in Matt. 28.16-20', *JBL* 96 (1977), 407-24.

Michel, O. 'Der Abschluss des Matthäusevangeliums', *EvTh* 10 (1950–51), 16-26.

O'Brien, P.T. 'The Great Commission of Matthew 28.18-20: A Missionary Mandate or Not?' *RThR* 35 (1976), 66-78.

Osborne, G.R. 'Redaction Criticism and the Great Commission: A Case Study toward a Biblical Understanding of Inerrancy', *JETS* 19 (1976), 73-85.

Parkhurst, L.G. 'Matthew 28.16-20 Reconsidered', *ExpT* 90 (1979), 179f.

Perrin, N. *The Resurrection according to Matthew, Mark, and Luke*. Philadelphia: Fortress Press, 1977.

Ridder, R.R. de. *The Dispersion of the People of God: The Covenant Basis of Mt 28.18-20*. Kampen: Kok and Grand Rapids: Baker, 1971.

Rigaux, B. *Dieu l'a ressuscité. Exégèse et théologie biblique*. Gembloux: Duculot, 1973.

Seidensticker, P. *Die Auferstehung Jesu in der Botschaft der Evangelisten*. Stuttgarter Bibelstudien, 26. Stuttgart: Verlag Katholisches Bibelwerk, 1967.

Smyth, K. 'Matthew 28: Resurrection as Theophany', *ITQ* 42 (1975), 259-71.

Steinseifer, B. 'Der Ort der Erscheinungen des Auferstandenen', *ZNW* 62 (1971), 232-65.

Strobel, A. 'Der Berg der Offenbarung (Mt 28,16; Apg 1,12). Erwägungen zu einem urchristlichen Erwartungstopos'. In *Verborum Veritas*, pp. 133-46. Edited by O. Böcher and K. Haacker. Wuppertal: Theologischer Verlag Rolf Brockhaus, 1970.

Tuck, R.C. 'The Lord Who Said Go: Some Reflections on Matthew 28.16-20', *ANQ* 7 (1966), 85-92.

Vögtle, A. 'Das christologische und ekklesiologische Anliegen von Mt. 28,18-20', *StEv* 2 (1964), 266-94.

Zumstein, J. 'Matthieu 28:16-20', *RThPh* 22 (1972), 14-33.

iii. *Other*

Bacon, B.W. 'The "Five Books" of Matthew against the Jews', *Exp* 15, 8th series (1918), 56-66.

— *Studies in Matthew*. New York: Henry Holt, 1930.

Baumbach, G. 'Die Mission im Matthäus-Evangelium', *TLZ* 92 (1967), 889-93.

Blair, E.P. *Jesus in the Gospel of Matthew*. New York: Abingdon Press, 1960.

Bornkamm, G., G. Barth, and H.J. Held. *Tradition and Interpretation in Matthew*. Translated by P. Scott. Philadelphia: Westminster Press, 1963.

Bourke, M.M. 'The Literary Genus of Matthew 1-2', *CBQ* 12 (1960), 160-75.

Brown, S. 'The Matthean Community and the Gentile Mission', *NovT* 22 (1980), 193-221.

— 'The Two-Fold Representation of the Mission in Matthew's Gospel', *StTh* 31 (1977), 21-32.

Bussby, F. 'Did a Shepherd Leave Sheep upon the Mountains or in the Desert? A Note on Matthew 18.12 and Luke 15.4', *ATR* 45 (1963), 93f.

Butler, B.C. *The Originality of St. Matthew*. Cambridge: University Press, 1951.

Carlston, C.E. 'Interpreting the Gospel of Matthew', *Int* 29 (1975), 3-12.

Cave, C.H. 'St. Matthew's Infancy Narrative', *NTS* 9 (1962–63), 382-90.

Clark, K.W. 'The Gentile Bias in Matthew', *JBL* 66 (1947), 165-72.

Comber, J.A. 'The Verb *Therapeuō* in Matthew's Gospel', *JBL* 97 (1978), 431-34.

Cope, O.L. *Matthew: A Scribe Trained for the Kingdom of Heaven*. CBQ Monograph Series, 5. Washington, D.C.: Catholic Biblical Association, 1976.

Crossan, D.M. 'Structure and Theology of Mt 1.18-2.23', *CahJos* 16 (1968), 119-35.

von Dobschütz, E. 'Matthäus als Rabbi und Katechet', *ZNW* 27 (1928), 338-48.

Ellis, P.F. *Matthew: His Mind and His Message*. Collegeville: Liturgical Press, 1974.

Frankemölle, H. *Jahwebund und Kirche Christi*. Neutestamentliche Abhandlungen, 10. Münster: Verlag Aschendorff, 1974.

Gaston, L. 'The Messiah of Israel as Teacher of the Gentiles: The Setting of Matthew's Christology', *Int* 29 (1975), 24-40.

Gibbs, J.M. 'The Son of God as the Torah Incarnate in Matthew', *StEv* 4 (1968), 38-46.

Gundry, R.H. *The Use of the Old Testament in St. Matthew's Gospel*. Leiden: Brill, 1967.

Hummel, R. *Die Auseinandersetzung zwischen Kirche und Judentum in Matthäusevangelium*. München: Kaiser Verlag, 1963.

Ingelaere, J.-C. 'Structure de Matthieu et histoire du salut. Etat de la question', *Foi et Vie* 78 (1979), 10-33.

Kilpatrick, G.D. *The Origins of the Gospel according to St. Matthew*. Oxford: Clarendon Press, 1946.

Kingsbury, J.D. 'Form and Message of Matthew', *Int* 29 (1975), 13-23.

— *Matthew: Structure, Christology, Kingdom*. Philadelphia: Fortress Press, 1975.

— *The Parables of Jesus in Matthew 13*. Richmond, Va.: John Knox Press, 1969.

— 'The Verb *Akolouthein* as an Index of Matthew's View of His Community', *JBL* 97 (1978), 56-73.

Livio, J.-B. 'La signification théologique de la "montagne" dans le premier évangile', *Bulletin du Centre Protestant d'Etudes* 30 (1978), 13-20.

Martin, J.P. 'The Church in Matthew', *Int* 29 (1975), 41-56.

Martin, R.P. 'St. Matthew's Gospel in Recent Study', *ExpT* 80 (1968–69), 132-36.

Meier, J.P. *Law and History in Matthew's Gospel: A Redactional Study of Mt. 5:17-48*. Analecta Biblica, 71. Rome: Biblical Institute, 1976.

— *The Vision of Matthew: Christ, Church and Morality in the First Gospel*. New York, Toronto: Paulist Press, 1979.

Minear, P.S. 'The Disciples and the Crowds in the Gospel of Matthew', *ATRSup* 3 (1974), 28-44.

Neirynck, F. 'La rédaction matthéenne et la structure du premier évangile', *EThL* 43 (1967), 41-73.

Nepper-Christensen, P. *Das Matthäusevangelium—ein judenchristliches Evangelium?* Aarhus: Universitetsforlaget, 1958.

Nolan, B.M. *The Royal Son of God: The Christology of Matthew 1-2 in the Setting of the Gospel*. Göttingen: Vandenhoeck & Ruprecht, 1979.

Rigaux, B. *The Testimony of St. Matthew*. Translated by P.J. Oligny. Chicago: Franciscan Herald Press, 1968.

Senior, D. 'The Ministry of Continuity: Matthew's Gospel and the Interpretation of History', *BibTod* 82 (1976), 670-76.

— *The Passion Narrative according to Matthew: A Redactional Study.* Louvain: Leuven University Press, 1975.

Stendahl, K. *The School of St. Matthew and its Use of the Old Testament.* Philadelphia: Fortress Press, 1954.

Strecker, G. 'The Concept of History in Matthew', *JAAR* 35 (1967), 219-30.

— *Der Weg der Gerechtigkeit: Untersuchungen zur Theologie des Matthäus.* Forschungen zur Religion und Literatur des Alten und Neuen Testaments, 82. 2 Aufl. Göttingen: Vandenhoeck und Ruprecht, 1966.

Tagawa, K. 'People and Community in the Gospel of Matthew', *NTS* 16 (1969-70), 149-62.

Thompson, W.G. *Matthew's Advice to a Divided Community: Mt 17.22–18.35.* Analecta Biblica, 44. Rome: Biblical Institute Press, 1970.

— 'Reflections on the Composition of Mt. 8.1–9.34', *CBQ* 33 (1971), 365-88.

Trilling, W. *Das wahre Israel: Studien zur Theologie des Matthäusevangeliums.* Leipzig: St. Benno-Verlag, 1959.

van Tilborg, S. *The Jewish Leaders in Matthew.* Leiden: Brill, 1972.

Walker, R. *Die Heilsgeschichte im ersten Evangelium.* Forschungen zur Religion und Literatur des Alten und Neuen Testaments, 91. Göttingen: Vandenhoeck und Ruprecht, 1967.

4. *Other New Testament Studies*

i. *Dealing with the Mountains in the Ministry of Jesus*

Byington, S.T. 'Jesus' Mountain Sides', *ExpT* 65 (1953–54), 94.

Ewing, W. 'The Mount of Transfiguration', *ExpT* 18 (1906–07), 333f.

Farmer, L. 'Jesus' Mountain Tops', *ExpT* 65 (1953–54), 250f.

Foerster, W. ' Ὄρος', *TDNT*, V, 475-87.

Frieling, R. *Der Heilige Berg im Alten und Neuen Testament.* Stuttgart: R. Goebel, 1930.

Kopp, C. *The Holy Places of the Gospels.* Translated by R. Walls. New York: Herder and Herder, 1963.

MacMillan, H. 'The Mount of Transfiguration', *ExpT* 7 (1895–96), 139-41.

Schmauch, W. *Orte der Offenbarung und der Offenbarungsort im Neuen Testament.* Göttingen: Vandenhoeck und Ruprecht, 1956.

Schoenberg, M. 'The Location of the Mount of Beatitudes', *BibTod* 1 (1962–63), 232-39.

ii. *Other*

Albertz, M. *Die Synoptischen Streitgespräche.* Berlin: Trowitzsche & Sohn, 1921.

Barrett, C.K. *The Gospel according to St. John.* 2nd edn. London: SPCK, 1978.

— *The Holy Spirit and the Gospel Tradition.* London: SPCK, 1947.

— 'John and the Synoptic Gospels', *ExpT* 85 (1973–74), 228-33.

Beare, F.W. *The Earliest Records of Jesus*. New York, Nashville: Abingdon Press, 1962.

Bernard, J.H. *A Critical and Exegetical Commentary on the Gospel according to Saint John*. 2 vols. International Critical Commentary. Edinburgh: T. & T. Clark, 1928.

Bertram, G. 'Θαῦμα', *TDNT*, III, 27-42.

Betz, H.D. 'Jesus as Divine Man'. In *Jesus and the Historian*, pp. 114-33. Edited by F.T. Trotter. Philadelphia: Westminster Press, 1968.

Black, M. *An Aramaic Approach to the Gospels and Acts*. 2nd edn. Oxford: Clarendon Press, 1954.

Blenkinsopp, J. 'The Oracle of Judah and the Messianic Entry', *JBL* 80 (1961), 55-64.

Brown, R.E. *The Birth of the Messiah*. Garden City, N.Y.: Doubleday, 1977.

— *The Gospel according to John*. 2 vols. Anchor Bible. Garden City, N.Y.: Doubleday, 1966, 1970.

— 'Incidents that are Units in the Synoptic Gospels but Dispersed in St. John', *CBQ* 23 (1961), 143-60.

Bultmann, R. and K. Kundsin. *Form Criticism: Two Essays on New Testament Research*. Translated by F.C. Grant. New York: Harper and Bros., 1962.

Bultmann, R. *The Gospel of John: A Commentary*. Translated by G.R. Beasley-Murray. Oxford: B. Blackwell, 1971.

— *History of the Synoptic Tradition*. Translated by J. Marsh. New York: Harper & Row, 1963.

— *Theology of the New Testament*. Translated by K. Grobel. 2 vols. New York: Scribners, 1951.

Burkill, T.A. *Mysterious Revelation*. Ithaca, N.Y.: Cornell University Press, 1963.

Carrington, P. *The Primitive Christian Calendar*. Cambridge: University Press, 1952.

Charles, R.H. *A Critical and Exegetical Commentary on the Revelation of St. John*. 2 vols. International Critical Commentary. Edinburgh: T. & T. Clark, 1920.

Conzelmann, H. *The Theology of St. Luke*. Translated by G. Buswell. London: Faber and Faber, 1960.

Cullmann, O. *The Christology of the New Testament*. Translated by S.C. Guthrie and C.A.M. Hall. 2nd edn. Philadelphia: Westminster Press, 1964.

Dalman, G. *Sacred Sites and Ways*. Translated by P.P. Levertoff. London: SPCK, 1935.

Daube, D. *The New Testament and Rabbinic Judaism*. London: Athlone Press, 1956.

Davies, W.D. *The Gospel and the Land: Early Christianity and Jewish Territorial Doctrine*. Berkeley, Los Angeles, London: University of California Press, 1974.

Dibelius, M. *From Tradition to Gospel*. Translated by B.L. Woolf. New York: Scribners, 1935.

Dodd, C.H. *Historical Tradition in the Fourth Gospel*. Cambridge: University Press, 1963.

— *The Interpretation of the Fourth Gospel*. Cambridge: University Press, 1954.

Edwards, R.A. *A Theology of Q*. Philadelphia: Fortress Press, 1976.

Farmer, W.R. *The Synoptic Problem: A Critical Analysis*. New York: Macmillan, 1964.

— 'The Two-Document Hypothesis as a Methodological Criterion in Synoptic Research', *ATR* 48 (1966), 380-96.

Farrer, A.M. 'On Dispensing with Q'. In *Studies in the Gospels*, pp. 55-86. Edited by D.E. Nineham. Oxford: B. Blackwell, 1955.

— *St. Matthew and St. Mark*. 2nd edn. Westminster: Dacre Press, 1966.

Findlay, J.A. 'Luke'. In *The Abingdon Bible Commentary*, pp. 1022-59. Nashville, New York: Abingdon Press, 1929.

Fitzmyer, J.A. 'The Aramaic Language and the Study of the New Testament', *JBL* 99 (1980), 5-21.

Flusser, D. *Jesus*. Translated by R. Walls. New York: Herder and Herder, 1969.

Fuller, R.H. *The Foundations of New Testament Christology*. London: Lutterworth Press, 1965.

Gardner-Smith, P. *Saint John and the Synoptic Gospels*. Cambridge: University Press, 1938.

Gaston, L. *No Stone on Another: Studies in the Significance of the Fall of Jerusalem in the Synoptic Gospels*. Leiden: Brill, 1970.

Goodenough, E.R. 'John a Primitive Gospel', *JBL* 64 (1945), 145-82.

Grant, F.C. *An Introduction to New Testament Thought*. New York, Nashville: Abingdon, Cokesbury Press, 1950.

Grundmann, W. *Das Evangelium nach Markus*. Theologischer Handkommentar zum Neuen Testament. Berlin: Evangelische Verlaganstalt, 1971.

Haenchen, E. *Der Weg Jesu*. 2 Aufl. Berlin: de Gruyter, 1968.

Hahn, F. *Christologische Hoheitstitel: ihre Geschichte im frühen Christentum*. Göttingen: Vandenhoeck und Ruprecht, 1964. ET: *The Titles of Jesus in Christology*. Translated by H. Knight and G. Ogg. London: Lutterworth Press, 1969.

— *Mission in the New Testament*. Translated by F. Clarke. Studies in Biblical Theology, 47. London: SCM Press, 1965.

von Harnack, A. *The Sayings of Jesus*. Translated by J.R. Wilkinson. London: Williams and Norgate, 1908.

Hengel, M. *The Son of God*. Translated by J. Bowden. Philadelphia: Fortress Press, 1976.

Holladay, C.R. Theios Aner *in Hellenistic Judaism: A Critique of the Use of this Category in New Testament Christology*. SBL Dissertation Series, 40. Missoula, Mont.: Scholars Press, 1977.

Horstmann, M. *Studien zur markinischen Christologie*. Münster: Verlag Aschendorff, 1969.

Hoskyns, E.C. *The Fourth Gospel*. Edited by F.N. Davey. London: Faber and Faber, 1940.

Howard, W.F. *The Fourth Gospel in Recent Criticism and Interpretation*. Revised by C.K. Barrett. London: Epworth Press, 1955.

Jeremias, J. *Jesus' Promise to the Nations*. Translated by S.H. Hooke. Studies in Biblical Theology, 24. London: SCM Press, 1958.

Klostermann, E. *Das Markusevangelium*. 4 Aufl. Tübingen: J.C.B. Mohr (Paul Siebeck), 1950.

Knox, W.L. *The Sources of the Synoptic Gospels*, vol. 2: *St. Luke and St. Matthew*. Edited by H. Chadwick. Cambridge: University Press, 1957.

Koch, K. *Was ist Formgeschichte? Methoden der Bibelexegese*. 3 Aufl. Neukirchen-Vluyn: Neukirchener Verlag, 1974.

Kümmel, W.G. *Introduction to the New Testament*. Translated by H.C. Kee. London: SCM Press, 1975.

— *Promise and Fulfilment*. Translated by D.M. Barton. 3rd edn. London: SCM Press, 1957.

Kysar, R. 'The Source Analysis of the Fourth Gospel: A Growing Consensus?' *NovT* 15 (1973), 134-52.

Lagrange, M.-J. *Evangile selon Saint Jean*. Paris: Gabalda, 1925.

— *Evangile selon Saint Marc*. Paris: Gabalda, 1947.

Lane, W.L. 'Theios Aner Christology and the Gospel of Mark'. In *New Dimensions in New Testament Study*, pp. 144-61. Edited by R.N. Longenecker and M.C. Tenney. Grand Rapids: Zondervan, 1974.

Leaney, A.R.C. *The Christ of the Synoptic Gospels*. Supplement to the New Zealand Theological Review. Auckland: Pelorous Press, 1966.

— *A Commentary on the Gospel according to St. Luke*. London: A. & C. Black, 1958.

Lightfoot, R.H. *Locality and Doctrine in the Gospels*. London: Hodder & Stoughton, 1938.

— *St. John's Gospel: A Commentary*. Edited by C.F. Evans. Oxford: Clarendon Press, 1956.

Lindars, B. *The Gospel of John*. New Century Bible. London: Oliphants, 1972.

Lövestam, E. *Son and Saviour: A Study of Acts 13:32-37*. Lund: Gleerup, 1961.

Lohmeyer, E. *Das Evangelium des Markus*. Göttingen: Vandenhoeck und Ruprecht, 1967 [1937].

Manson, T.W. *The Sayings of Jesus*. London: SCM Press, 1949.

— *The Teaching of Jesus*. Cambridge: University Press, 1931.

Marshall, I.H. *The Gospel of Luke*. New International Greek Testament

Commentary. Grand Rapids: Eerdmans, 1978.

Marxsen, W. *Mark the Evangelist*. Translated by J. Boyce, D. Juel, and W. Poehlmann, with R.A. Harrisville. Nashville, New York: Abingdon Press, 1969.

Mauser, U. *Christ in the Wilderness*. Studies in Biblical Theology, 39. London: SCM Press, 1963.

Meeks, W.A. *The Prophet-King: Moses Traditions and the Johannine Christology*. Leiden: Brill, 1967.

Metzger, B.M. 'Methodology in the Study of the Mystery Religions and Early Christianity'. In his *Historical and Literary Studies: Pagan, Jewish, and Christian*, pp. 1-24. Grand Rapids: Eerdmans, 1968.

Meyer, B.F. *The Aims of Jesus*. London: SCM Press, 1979.

Morris, L. *Studies in the Fourth Gospel*. Grand Rapids: Eerdmans, 1969.

Munck, J. *Paul and the Salvation of Mankind*. Translated by F. Clarke. London: SCM Press, 1959.

Neirynck, F. 'The Argument from Order and St. Luke's Transpositions', *EThL* 49 (1973), 784-815.

Nickle, K.F. *The Collection: A Study in Paul's Strategy*. Studies in Biblical Theology, 48. London: SCM Press, 1966.

Nineham, D.E. *The Gospel of Mark*. Harmondsworth: Penguin Books, 1963.

Percy, E. *Die Botschaft Jesu*. Lund: Gleerup, 1953.

Perrin, N. *What is Redaction Criticism?* Philadelphia: Fortress Press, 1969.

Pesch, R. *Das Markusevangelium*. Freiburg, Basel, Wien: Herder, 1977.

Rengstorf, K.H. 'Old and New Testament Traces of a Formula of the Judean Royal Ritual', *NovT* 5 (1962), 229-44.

Robinson, J.M. 'On the *Gattung* of Mark (and John)'. In *Jesus and Man's Hope*, pp. 99-129. Edited by D.G. Buttrick. Pittsburgh: Pittsburgh Theological Seminary, 1970.

Rohde, J. *Rediscovering the Teaching of the Evangelists*. Translated by D.M. Barton. Philadelphia: Westminster Press, 1968.

Sanday, W., ed. *Oxford Studies in the Synoptic Problem*. Oxford: Clarendon Press, 1911.

Sandmel, S. 'Parallelomania', *JBL* 81 (1962), 1-13.

Schille, G. 'Der Mangel eines kritischen Geschichtbildes in der neutestamentlichen Formgeschichte', *TLZ* 88 (1963), 491-502.

Schmid, J. *The Gospel according to Mark*. Translated by K. Condon. Staten Island, N.Y.: Alba House, 1969.

Schmidt, K.L. *Der Rahmen der Geschichte Jesu*. Darmstadt: Wissenschaftliche Buchgesellschaft, 1969 [1919].

Schnackenburg, R. *The Gospel according to John. Vol. I*. Translated by K. Smith. New York: Herder and Herder, 1968.

— *Das Johannesevangelium. II*. Freiburg: Herder, 1971.

Schramm, T. *Der Markus-Stoff bei Lukas*. Cambridge: University Press, 1971.

Schreiber, J. *Theologie des Vertrauens. Eine redaktionsgeschichtliche Untersuchung des Markusevangeliums.* Hamburg: Furche-Verlag, 1967.

Schulz, S. *Q: Die Spruchquelle der Evangelisten.* Zürich: Theologischer Verlag, 1972.

Schürmann, H. *Das Lukasevangelium.* Herders theologischer Kommentar zum NT. Freiburg: Herder, 1969.

Schweitzer, A. *The Quest of the Historical Jesus.* Translated by W. Montgomery. 2nd edn. London: A. & C. Black, 1911.

Schweizer, E. *The Good News according to Mark.* Translated by D.H. Madvig. Atlanta: John Knox Press, 1970.

Smith, D.M. 'John 12.12ff. and the Question of John's Use of the Synoptics', *JBL* 82 (1963), 58-64.

Stein, R.H. 'What is Redaktionsgeschichte?', *JBL* 88 (1969), 45-56.

Stemberger, G. 'Galilee—Land of Salvation?', Appendix IV in *The Gospel and the Land*, pp. 409-38. By W.D. Davies. Berkeley, Los Angeles, London: University of California Press, 1974.

Streeter, B.H. *The Four Gospels.* London: Macmillan, 1924.

Sundkler, B. 'Jésus et les païens', *RHPR* 16 (1936), 462-99.

Taylor, V. *Behind the Third Gospel.* Oxford: Clarendon Press, 1926.

Weeden, T.J. *Mark—Traditions in Conflict.* Philadelphia: Fortress Press, 1971.

Wellhausen, J. *Das Evangelium Marci.* 2 Aufl. Berlin: G. Reimer, 1909.

Wilkens, W. 'Evangelist und Tradition im Johannesevangelium', *TZ* 16 (1960), 81-90.

INDEXES

INDEX OF BIBLICAL REFERENCES

318   *Jesus on the Mountain*

Mark (cont.)

Reference	Page
1.9-11	106
1.11	152
1.12f.	87, 97, 106
1.12	242
1.13	243
1.14f.	106
1.16-20	106
1.21-28	106
1.21f.	251
1.22	106
1.27	255
1.28	107
1.32-34	107
1.39	107, 251
3.1-6	108
3.7ff.	108
3.7f.	254
3.7	132
3.7-19	107-110
3.7-13a	251
3.10-13	123
3.10	257
3.11b	257
3.13-19	108, 179, 277, 280
3.13	214, 218, 251, 278
4.21	255
5.1-13	215
5.5	10
5.11	214, 215, 244, 283
6.6-13	122
6.6b	107
6.7-13	108
6.7	281
6.30f.	122
6.31-35	260
6.31	257
6.32-52	123
6.32-44	123, 257,
6.32f.	123
6.32	123
6.33-44	123
6.34	130, 257
6.35	215
6.37	257
6.38	257
6.39	258
6.40	260
6.41	257, 258
6.43	258
6.44	258
6.45-52	123
6.46	110, 123, 124, 214, 218, 257
	261
	123
	123
	123
	130, 257
	215
	257
	257
	258
	260
	257, 258
	258
	258
	123
	110, 123, 124, 214, 218, 257
6.51f.	283
7.2-4	14
7.25	263
7.27	132
7.31-37	122, 123, 127, 258
7.31	132, 258, 259, 261
7.36	260
8.1-10	123, 257
8.1	263
8.6	258
8.22-26	122, 260
8.27-38	153
8.29	99, 154
8.31-38	153, 264
8.33	100
9.1-11	264
9.1-9	136-49, 153
9.1	137, 150, 152, 153
9.2f.	265
9.2	10, 110, 214
9.6	150, 269
9.7	152, 153, 265
9.9f.	137, 154
9.9	11, 110, 151, 214
9.11-13	137
9.12	151
9.49f.	255
11.1	97, 157, 214, 273
11.11	97
11.23	219
11.28	281
12.6f.	268
13	158-61, 162, 163, 173, 273
13.1ff.	215
13.1-4	159, 160
13.2	159
13.3	110, 214, 219
13.4	161
13.5-27	158
13.5-23	163
13.5b-8	159
13.5f.	163
13.7f.	163
13.9-13	274
13.9	165
13.10	163, 167
13.12-16	159
13.14	10, 219
13.19-22	159
13.21-23	163, 274
13.24	163, 165
13.24-27	159, 162, 163
13.28-31	163
13.32-37	163
13.32	163
13.33-37	274
13.35	163, 274

INDEX OF AUTHORS

JOURNAL FOR THE STUDY OF THE NEW TESTAMENT
Supplement Series

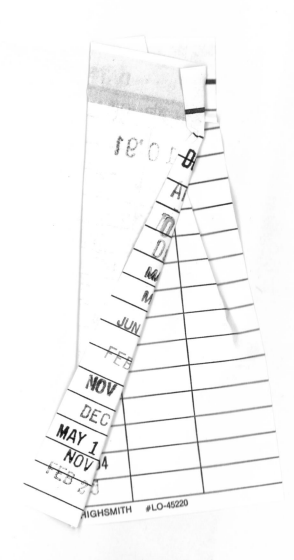